THE ESSENTIAL
Counselor

THE ESSENTIAL
Counselor

PROCESS, SKILLS, AND TECHNIQUES

David Hutchinson
JOHNSON STATE COLLEGE

Lahaska Press
Houghton Mifflin Company
Boston • New York

Publisher, Lahaska Press: Barry Fetterolf
Senior Editor, Lahaska Press: Mary Falcon
Editorial Assistant: Evangeline Bermas
Associate Project Editor: Eric Moore
Composition Buyer: Chuck Dutton
Associate Manufacturing Buyer: Brian Pieragostini
Senior Marketing Manager: Barbara LeBuhn

Cover image: © Bob Commander/images.com

For instructors who want more information
about Lahaska Press books and teaching aids,
contact the Houghton Mifflin Faculty Services Center at
Tel: 800-733-1717, x4034
Fax: 800-733-1810

Or visit us on the Web at
www.lahaskapress.com

Printed in the U.S.A.

Library of Congress Control Number: 2006921359

Instructor's examination copy

ISBN-10: 0-618-73183-0
ISBN-13: 978-0-618-73183-1

For orders, use student text ISBNs

ISBN-10: 0-618-42648-5
ISBN-13: 978-0-618-42648-5

123456789-QUF-10 09 08 07 06

Contents

CHAPTER **5**   **Assessment, Goal Setting, and Action Planning**   91

CHAPTER **11**   Advanced Action Skills: Moving Beyond Stability   252

CHAPTER **12**   Exceptional Counseling Challenges   274

CHAPTER 13   Skills for Ending   304

Preface

The Essential Counselor: Process, Skills, and Techniques is a foundational textbook for basic skills courses offered in graduate counseling programs. Having personally taught basic counseling skills courses for many years and having more recently supervised other instructors teaching this demanding course for the first time, I wanted The Essential Counselor to be useful to instructors at all levels of experience. For new instructors, the book provides a helpful framework and structure for approaching the teaching of these skills. Instructors new to the course may follow the text's lead quite literally for the 14- or 15-week time span of a typical course and feel confident that their students have been exposed to the critical foundation skills. The more experienced instructor will appreciate some of the unique features of the book, particularly the inclusion of certain skills and types of clients that are not routinely covered in other skills textbooks.

The Essential Counselor is practical and, I hope, inspirational. The book is intended to serve as a useful working tool for the instructor, but it is also meant to be reader friendly for the student. The tone is intentionally personal and conversational, and much of the book is written from a first-person perspective. The book reflects ideas about skills instruction I have found to be effective and have used repeatedly over twenty years of teaching in the classroom. The stories and case examples, most based on my own professional counseling experience and some based on experiences related to me by colleagues, illustrate and humanize many of the skills discussions.

My goal is to enable students to approach their work with greater confidence and competence. My basic premise is that good counseling practice can never be reduced to a set of formulaic, mechanical skills; however, I do provide a roadmap of sorts. I present a developmental model for linking the use of specific skills to specific client needs. If the varieties of counseling theories provide us with an array of approaches to working with people, a set of tools for intervention, this book shows students how those tools can be selected for best use. The counselor-in-training is asked to consider not only individual aspects of client functioning (e.g., intellectual or emotional factors) in assessing a client's needs but also the client's overall developmental level of functioning, primarily as it relates to the client's capacity to manage personal responsibility. This expanded approach to assessment provides a framework within which the student can then select appropriate intervention skills. The skills, which are taken from a variety of theoretical traditions, are matched with appropriate levels of client developmental function, thus providing counselors-in-training with some beginning ideas about how to link counseling theory to actual practice.

In writing *The Essential Counselor* I used the life span of the counseling relationship as a general guide for organization and layout. Chapters 1, 2, and 3 address tasks that need to be done before any clients are seen, describing the process of getting ready to begin a private, agency, or school counseling practice. Chapters 4 and 5 discuss skills needed to engage new clients and how to assess their specific needs. Chapters 6, 7, and 9 address the use of essential action skills to help clients move toward their chosen counseling goals. More advanced action skills for use with people who are more developmentally capable are addressed in Chapter 11.

Chapter 8 is devoted to helping new counselors develop ethical, culturally sensitive counseling practices, and Chapter 10 outlines how to work with clients in crisis situations. Chapter 12 focuses on some special clients—children, addicted clients, and the seriously and persistently mentally ill—and includes a section devoted to working with resistant, coerced clients. Chapter 13 addresses the effective ending of a counseling relationship, and Chapter 14 provides much needed information about counselor self-care and ways to avoid burnout.

The book is aimed at a wide array of counseling specializations and work settings. New counselors will find themselves in work situations that demand creative, specific skills for dealing with unique client situations, and a number of these needed skills (e.g., case management, uses of play and expressive arts therapies, skills for dealing with resistance) are addressed in a way that is rarely found in other books.

A central assumption is the importance of the counseling relationship, the *therapeutic alliance*. The use of foundation skills and the importance of counselor attitudes that help to form, develop, and manage the relationship are supported repeatedly throughout the book. Skills essential in helping clients move toward goals are dependent upon the successful implementation and use of those relationship skills.

Learning Aids and Demonstration Videos

To aid student mastery, I have included a number of personal reflection exercises and lab practice experiences based on the quadrad lab practice model that allow for considerable structured practice of skills. In addition, many of the skills described in *The Essential Counselor* are demonstrated in a set of videos developed to accompany the book. Again employing the quadrad lab practice model, four counselor educators take turns in the various roles: two supervisors and two role playing a client–counselor situation that depicts the use of specific skills. Each counseling session is followed by a short feedback and discussion session that focuses on alternative strategies that could have been tried and provides support for the counselor's work. The second important function of the discussion session is to provide models for how students can give one another supportive, constructive feedback. In an Instructor's Guide to the videos, the demonstration sessions are keyed specifically to the places in the text where those skills are discussed and lab practice exercises are suggested. Students will derive the most benefit from these counseling interviews and discussion sessions if they view the videos before practicing the skills themselves.

The Essential Counselor and its accompanying set of videos provide the instructor with ample material for conducting a pre-practicum, lab, or other skills course. It also gives the student the means for conceptualizing the developing counseling relationship and utilizing skills in a way that provides a solid foundation for his or her future counseling practice.

Acknowledgements

I'd like to thank a number of people for their help and support in bringing this book to its final form. Foremost, I extend grateful thanks to my family—to my wife, Katharine (Kaki), to my daughter, Kait, and to my son, Jon. Their encouragement, humor, and patience have helped to make this writing project a great experience for me. I am extremely grateful for their encouragement. A writer couldn't ask for a better family support group.

Heartfelt appreciation also goes out to my close friends and sports buddies who have provided guidance, balance, and fun in my life as this project has come to fruition. They have helped to keep me (mostly) sane. Special thanks to Don Schumacher, Annemie Curlin, Dan Higgins, Jane Kramer, and to Betsy Ferries and Peter Clavelle, Jon Frew, the Gourmet Club, and to the Gamers and the Gliders. To Jennifer Sweet, thanks for the fun, the fitness, and the good conversation. To Anne Geroski and Leslie Haws, thanks for your early encouragement. To the Daves, Michelle, Ellen, Jill, Joanne, Tony, and the Jeffersonville tennis crowd, thanks for the humbling lessons on the basketball and tennis courts. Special thanks to Sally Lonegren for wonderful friendship and for providing a great retreat space in which to lead groups.

My editor, Mary Falcon, deserves a huge vote of thanks for her guidance and expertise in this endeavor. I cannot imagine working with a better editor. She has been masterful in knowing when to shore me up and when to prod me into more productive action. Guiding me every step of the way, she helped me turn my notions about counseling skills from an incoherent scramble of ideas into a cohesive manuscript. A writer couldn't ask for a better editor, or friend. Thanks also to my skilled production supervisor, Merrill Peterson, to Kay Mikel for her expert copyediting, and to publisher Barry Fetterolf who has helped to make the experience of working with Lahaska Press a genuine pleasure.

I know how time consuming and demanding it is to read a textbook manuscript and make constructive criticisms, so I want to extend a special thank-you to the following reviewers whose astute and detailed evaluations of my first and second drafts enabled me to greatly improve the final product:

Craig S. Cashwell, University of North Carolina at Greensboro
Joyce A. DeVoss, Northern Arizona University
Kathy M. Evans, University of South Carolina
Douglas Guiffrida, University of Rochester
Ruth Harper, South Dakota State University
Brandon Hunt, Pennsylvania State University
Michael Laurent, California State University at Northridge
Carol Napierkowski, West Chester University of Pennsylvania
Yih-Jiun Shen, Texas Tech University
Shawn L. Spurgeon, Western Kentucky University
Sarah Toman, Cleveland State University
Rob Williams, San Francisco State University

Finally, I extend thanks and appreciation to my colleagues at Johnson State College in Vermont, David Fink, Ellie Webber, Gina Mireault, and Shellie Levine, who have helped to shape the thinking behind many of the ideas presented in this book, as well as to our able administrative assistants Cathy Higley and Annette Jalbert. It is a warm and supportive environment in which to work. And finally, I thank my students. Certainly one of the joys of this teaching work is to watch students grow and mature into professional counselors and to watch the good things they then do in the field. My work with them over the years is the inspiration behind this book.

David Hutchinson

CHAPTER 1

An Invitation to Counseling Work

If you don't know the kind of person I am
and I don't know the kind of person you are
a pattern that others made may prevail in the world
and following the wrong god home we may miss our star.
(from "A Ritual to Read to Each Other"
by William Stafford)

Y ou have your sights set on becoming a counselor. Your journey toward considering the counseling profession or some related work has undoubtedly been interesting and circuitous. If you are like many of the people drawn to the counseling profession, you look to this work both to better understand yourself and to learn how to work effectively with people.

Who Becomes a Counselor?

People do not gravitate to the counseling profession in the same way that people choose to become insurance agents, plumbers, or corporate executives. In interviews with new students in our graduate counseling program, my colleagues and I find that behind a vague desire to "help people" there is usually a person searching for a life of more meaningful connection, both with self and with others. Often the student's life had seemed filled with bad choices or ventures down blind alleys to dead ends, leaving the student looking for a better way to channel interpersonal energy. Sometimes individuals consider becoming counselors after overcoming some major life challenge such as addiction or a history of bad relationships. Perhaps an individual has encountered a particularly effective counselor or therapist and has a desire to follow in those footsteps. Others may have had a bad experience with counseling and concluded that it can be done better.

People do not think of this work so much as a job, or even as a career. More typically, a constellation of life experiences that demand explanation and a sense that others seek one out for assistance and emotional sustenance become driving forces leading one toward the counseling profession. Many people who come to this profession feel that they have been called to it in some fashion (Foster, 1996).

You may think of yourself as having some unique talents or gifts for understanding others. Maybe you have led a successful, outwardly exemplary work life—making lots of money and building a reputation—but have been left feeling unfulfilled and dissatisfied. You may be approaching the second half of life, where external trappings of success have become less meaningful than relationships with others and a solid sense of personal purpose. If this is the case, you, too, may be a good candidate for the counseling profession. There is ample opportunity to do work that is inherently, intrinsically rewarding—though perhaps without great financial reward.

Thus, you may come to this work from a history of personal pain or from a position of success and prominence or with a sense that you need to sharpen your intuitive interpersonal skills. All kinds of life experiences and a wide variety of motivations for wanting to become a counselor are legitimate. Any and all of these provide grist for the self-examination mill. You will want to examine your motivations because you will want to work cleanly with people, only minimally encumbered by your own unfinished business. This examination should involve both an intellectual review of your motivations and a review of the emotional issues related to your desire to do this work. Evidence (Goleman, 1995, 1998) suggests that your emotional connections to your desire for this work are at least as important as your intellectual ones.

Some people are, of course, drawn to this profession for the wrong reasons— to take advantage of others' vulnerabilities or to work out their own personal problems (Witmer & Young, 1996). While you should not be primarily involved with this profession to promote your own self-awareness and understanding, you can nevertheless take comfort in the fact that the profession can lead you toward a greater understanding of yourself. The best counselors commit themselves to lifelong growth and learning (Spurling & Dryden, 1989), much of which comes via the clients they serve.

REFLECTION EXERCISE 1.1   *Why Do You Want to Be a Counselor?*

Sit quietly. Think about some of the reasons, the events of your life, that steer you toward becoming a counselor. Which of those events bring warm, fond memories and feelings; which are more difficult and painful? What is it about you that will encourage others to talk about themselves personally, to look at some of the more troubling and difficult aspects of their lives? What kind of life wisdom do you bring to this professional calling?

How will all of your personal experiences help you make connections with other people? How will they help you to understand your clients' individual dilemmas? What might be some dangers in how your personal experience will affect your work with others?

Allow yourself to sit quietly for some minutes with these reflections. As your awareness returns to your everyday surroundings, take a few minutes to jot down some notes, perhaps in your journal, about your recollections and reflections. If you feel comfortable sharing some of these reflections with another, talk for a few minutes about your experience with one or two colleagues or friends. Share only that information that feels safe for you to reveal.

The Nature of the Work

You are being called to a noble profession. It is a profession with many rewards and with attendant responsibilities. It is a privilege and an honor to be invited to share in some of the intimate details of another's life, and you are obliged to respect the gift that that sharing implies. But what is it, exactly, that you may anticipate being called upon to do? The reasons people seek out counselors are many and varied. Many people come for counseling to resolve some kind of personal or life problem. Usually, these people come with a genuine, positive desire to be helped, but you will also encounter the occasional client who will manipulate and con you (Kierulff, 1988). Sometimes personal problems precipitate crises, periods of deep emotional pain. People can become extremely distraught, and you may be called upon to help them through these difficult times.

With desperate people who are trying to simply stay afloat in turbulent waters, your job is to provide an emotional life raft and maybe to help find the resources for them to move toward the safer shallows. Perhaps they have marital or financial problems, or problems dealing with a child. Sometimes problems are poorly defined—just a vague dissatisfaction or feeling of emptiness or depression. The problems may be multiple, overlapping, and complex or relatively simple and easily remedied. Some people may have emotional, mental, or physical problems that severely impair their ability to function well in the world.

Whatever problems clients may feel they have, they are looking to a counselor to help make things better. If someone is in critical straits, some kind of crisis intervention may be necessary. Similarly, you may work to help people reconcile and correct serious behavioral problems. Those problems may have gotten them in trouble, and other people may have directed them toward counseling. They may have problems with drugs or with the law. Your job may be to help monitor, supervise, and support positive behavioral change. In these roles, you may be called upon to enforce rules and use leverage to keep people in treatment. The work here is most certainly not always "warm and fuzzy," and it may run counter to what many people think of when they consider the nurturing, supportive role of the counselor. Tough enforcement of rules, however, might be the appropriate response.

People will also seek out a counselor to simply help make life better. A student wants help with course selections, or a man who wants a good job seeks out a career counselor. Much of your work here will be spent in assisting in personal growth for the people whom you serve. You may function in a kind of cheerleading or coaching role, providing suggestions and support for new courses of action. Much of this work will be in helping people to see their hidden talents and to recognize their own strengths that have gone unsupported.

Other clients of yours may function perfectly well but feel trapped within their functional lives, yearning for more but not knowing exactly what they want. A vast group of potential clients are those who are searching for personal growth and increased authenticity. They function well in their lives, may have solid jobs and intact families, and are successful by all traditional notions of the word "success." Yet they feel incomplete, unfulfilled, and have deep longings for something more, something just out of the grasp of awareness.

Years ago, one of the pioneers of the human potential movement, Abraham Maslow (1963), suggested that this desire for growth springs inevitably from a deep-rooted fear of standing alone in the world, from acting clearly on one's own behalf. It is a fear, he maintained, almost inherent in the human condition.

> We fear our highest possibility (as well as our lower ones). We are generally afraid to become that which we can glimpse in our most perfect moments . . . we enjoy and even thrill to the godlike possibilities we see in ourselves at such peak moments. And yet we simultaneously shiver with weakness, awe and fear before those very same possibilities. (p. 163)

Your job as a counselor may thus be to call your client to greatness, to become an ally in the search for nobility and for the heroic that resides within us all. You may need to help some of your clients acknowledge the ways they keep themselves from becoming truly free and self-directed, the ways they have created their own little prisons, their "mind-forged manacles," and some of the complex reasons for such retreat from real freedom. At its best, counseling is about assisting clients in responding to their particular calls to greatness. You will want your clients, to repeat the clichéd phrase, to be "the best that they can be."

We all search for the heroic within us. When we shrink from our desires to embrace our unique talents and the gifts we might bring to the world, we are eaten from within by our own dissatisfactions and stunted growth. It is this call to greatness that we assist many of our clients in answering and that we naturally seek to answer in our own lives. Here we are called on to play a philosopher-counselor role, and it stands to reason that the questions asked by our clients are similar to those with which we grapple ourselves.

The Analogy of Counseling as House Repair

People seek counseling for myriad reasons, and there are multiple ways you may respond. The true skill and sophistication of this work is finding an appropriate response to what is truly needed. This is the nature of our responsibility—or respond "ability"—to those with whom we work.

A rough analogy can be made between the counseling work we do and working on a house. You can think of helping your client as helping to make the house in which he lives a more fit place to live. In this analogy, the house has three levels (Figure 1.1). Your client resides predominantly on one of these levels, and typically seeks counseling to make that level more comfortable or to move up to the next level. All of the reasons people need to see counselors exist somewhere within the framework of this house. Children, or immature adults with immense problems in negotiating the basic demands of daily life, might be seen as residing at Level 1, the ground floor. Those for whom questions of life meaning and self-realization are paramount live at the top floor of the house, Level 3. Most adults living self-sustaining, self-supporting lives are in the middle, at Level 2 of the house.

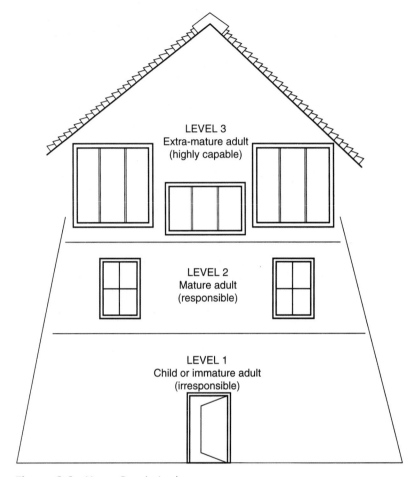

Figure 1.1 House Repair Analogy

The counselor is a building contractor who works with the client to improve the livability of the levels of the house where he is already residing and ultimately to build a staircase to higher levels of the house. The counselor's working tools are the essential relationship development and enhancement skills that we will examine in this book. These are the "facilitative conditions"—the empathic regard, the respect, and all of the other interpersonal tools that we use to support our clients. As the building and repair work proceeds in counseling, the counselor is simultaneously teaching skills to the client so that eventually the client will be capable of doing routine house maintenance and repair without the counselor's help.

This analogy of house repair is really a developmental approach to the use of counseling skills. As any student who has taken undergraduate psychology courses will probably recognize, this levels of a house analogy is similar to, and compatible with, Abraham Maslow's hierarchy of needs model, as well as other developmental models (Ivey, Ivey, Myers, & Sweeney, 2005), Piaget's model of cognitive development (1955/1923), and Kohlberg's model of values or moral development (1962, 1981). This way of conceptualizing client problems and goals in counseling work, which builds on Maslow's ideas about the hierarchy of needs (Bruce, 1984), has been developed schematically as a foundation for planning effective counseling interventions. This developmental model of counseling interventions and its implications for helping counselors to understand and respond to specific client concerns will be developed in later chapters.

You will need to choose approaches for working with your clients that fit their specific needs and capacities for responding to what you do. Thus, although you will naturally gravitate to using interventions that fit your theoretical orientation, you should also give serious consideration to the skills and deficits your clients bring to counseling. Assessment is the focus of much of Chapter 5, and the specific ways in which your clients' needs are represented in this "house" and the types of tools (that is, skills) you will choose to help your client deal with these needs are addressed in detail.

Some Fundamental Reasons for Seeking Counseling

The reasons many people who have at least made their way out of the "basement"—meaning that they are not in crisis and seem to manage life maturely—seek counseling can typically be reduced to two primary motivators. Assuming that basic physical and safety needs have been met, people want to reduce the level of fear they carry in their lives, and they want to increase the love they feel and their sense of belonging and connection with other people. They want to decrease the fear and increase the love. For many of the people we serve, responding to these two needs is what the counseling business is all about. When people cannot satisfy their basic needs for love and belonging, anxiety, stress, and sadness are often the result (Teyber, 2000). These basic unmet needs become layered with complicated feelings and behaviors.

The counseling and psychotherapy literature is not exactly overloaded with the language of love, and it cloaks the word "fear" in diagnostic garb. The words "love" and "fear" are global, imprecise, and loaded with potential for misinterpretation. Diagnostic language is more comfortable to the professional community, and it is also more descriptive. "Phobias," "dysfunctions," and "anxiety" describe the strange forms into which fear can constellate itself. The language of the diagnostic manuals is helpful because its description assists appropriate intervention.

Behind the diagnoses and the treatment planning, however, the fundamental problem is oftentimes some variant of that fear theme. As Deikman (1982) suggests, "It is hard to find a neurotic symptom or a human vice that cannot be traced to the desire to possess or the fear of loss" (p. 80). Greed and the fear of loss are simply two variants of the theme of fear. The antidote to fear that counselors supply is compassion and unconditional positive regard. Your job is to help to reduce the fear, thereby increasing the capacity to comfortably encounter self and others. This may sound simple, yet it takes great wisdom and experience to do this well, clearly and cleanly. There are many small steps, behavior changes, and insights to be made along the road to a life that is less fear-based.

You will want to be able to respond effectively to your clients, and this will require both thoughtful reflection about what is needed and compassion for them as people. It is a challenge to do this work with both heart and head. Developing this capacity to work on these multiple levels is a life's work. It is difficult to conceive of any work that is more relevant or important, whether our clientele be CEOs or grocery store clerks, young adults in college or children in public schools, imprisoned drug addicts or patients hospitalized with mental illness.

Counseling and the Promotion of Personal Responsibility

Just as the problems our clients bring to us can often be identified as some variation of fear, many of the best outcomes can be thought of as being our clients' increased ability to manage life more responsibly. We all are free to choose our own courses of action and paths in life, and it is easy to appreciate the essential counseling role of helping people recognize their freedom and their right to choose based on that freedom. However, our role in helping people assume responsibility for the choices they make in their lives is sometimes less clear. The famous existential psychoanalyst Viktor Frankl (1963) once suggested that we should have a Statue of Responsibility to complement the Statue of Liberty as a way of demonstrating our collective commitment to enhancing personal responsibility.

The avoidance of personal responsibility can take many forms, and may not be particularly obvious. Sometimes even the most conventional, apparently functional people may be avoiding taking real responsibility for themselves. Many, perhaps most, of the clients with whom I've worked begin with some variation of the notion, "I don't get enough _____." You can fill in the blank. Typically, it is "recognition" or "respect" or some variant of "affection." But the basic attitude is one of desire for the world to pay better attention to what the client wants and of blaming others when things do not go well. They have probably searched in all kinds of ways, often in all the wrong places, to find the love, the attention, or the recognition they are looking for, but have come up short. Sometimes they may have passed by another's love that begged for *their* attention, available but unacknowledged, and missed it. This search for love and attention can also be incredibly destructive, sometimes getting people into big trouble, particularly if it's expressed with minors or with violence. It is, nevertheless, important for the counselor to remember that it is the drive for love that fuels the fire.

A Personal Case Example

Maybe we remember our first clients most vividly. One of my first counseling clients has always been representative of the remarkable potential for joy and reward in this work, as well as for serving as an example of how a client's fear can be diminished if met with steadiness, understanding, and appropriate affection. Many years ago, I was a fresh and green doctoral intern at SUNY Buffalo's College Counseling Center. Claire was my first client, an attractive, bright student in the fine arts program. Her first question to me was, "Are you just a graduate student?" Right off the bat, here was a question about my competence, a challenge to see how I'd respond, and behind it a fear that I might not be up to the task.

Our beginning sessions were filled with more of her confrontational challenges to my age, to my competence, and with comments about my lack of experience. She danced around any attempts I made to get her to talk more personally about herself, or even to cogently talk about what she was looking for by coming for counseling. All of this was coming from a place of fear, the fear of judgment and rejection. Fear that I wouldn't be able to handle what she yearned to reveal.

Her critical comments, intelligent and sharply to the point, often reflected my own concerns about my competence. I was acutely aware of my inexperience. Her comments were cuttingly effective, sometimes hurtful. I recall not becoming overly defensive, at least with her, and saving my complaints about Claire and my lack of experience as a counselor for sessions with my clinical supervisor, Faith. I just rode through the sniping and bluffed not being hurt on more than one occasion. Not incidentally, I enjoyed Claire's wit.

My supervisor was terrific at helping me separate my doubts about my own competence from the defensive posturing that Claire was obviously using to keep me at a distance. Faith was supremely skillful in helping me see the ways in which Claire's attacks were thinly disguised attempts to test my ability to hang in with her: tests of my ability to be trusted, fear of letting someone get too close, too much under the slick veneer, and her great desire for contact and intimacy. Faith was also helpful in defining ways I could respond more effectively and truly become more competent. Letting off steam in supervision sessions, as well as sharing my fears about whether I could do a good job, allowed me the latitude to be present and nondefensive with Claire.

Eventually Claire began to drop her edginess, and she became more forthcoming about having some big "secrets" that were of critical concern to her. You will find that many of your clients have these kinds of "secrets," usually aspects of themselves about which they are ashamed or embarrassed (Kelly, 1998). She talked at length of her concerns about my not liking her if and when she chose to divulge the secrets. I assured her that I had no investment in her doing anything and that I had great respect for her intellect and ability to choose whether or when to share more personal material.

The paradox was that by not being pressured to talk of more personal material, she began to talk of more personal material. This was a great lesson I learned early on. By not pushing her, by not buying into her jibes and challenges, by simply being solidly present (which is actually not "simple" at all), I helped Claire allow herself to let down her guard. Eventually, when the secret concerns about her sexual identity and some stories of past physical abuses were aired, it was almost anticlimactic. Then began the considerable work of allowing her the time and space to negotiate her way through her ideas and feelings about those past and present difficult people and

(continued)

(Box 1, continued)

situations, but that work was all done on the foundation of respect and trust that now existed between us.

In this process of helping clients become more trusting, and more forthcoming, lies the beauty of this work. Much of the process exists within the evolution of the relation-ship between client and counselor. The "beauty of the work" is what this book is about. Behind their fear of trusting us, most of our clients have an abiding desire to be known. Part of your job lies in creating the context in which your clients can be released from fear.

Regardless of what clients want, successful counseling outcomes hinge on the development of more personal responsibility. It is about a shift from being a victim ("I don't get enough") to being an agent of action ("What can I do?"). It is a move away from blaming others to accepting responsibility for what one has and what one has to give. When a client has made the shift from "No one loves me" to "How may I be more loving?" the client has really grown. One of counseling's finest functions is to help people, in this safe and controlled setting, experiment with trying to reach out in different and more constructive ways (Casey, 1996). It is your job to help this growth, to help your client give birth to a new sense of personal responsibility. In a sense, you are the midwife to this kind of emotional development.

The Relationship: Counseling's Vital Ingredient

The counselor-client therapeutic alliance, this connection between people, is key to ensuring a successful counseling outcome. Some writers have suggested that the counselor's theoretical approach, as well as the techniques offered up during the process of counseling, are secondary to the relationship itself (Horvath & Symonds, 1991; Orlinsky, Grawe, & Parks, 1994). While most experts in the fields of counseling and psychotherapy may disagree with such an extreme position, they generally do agree that it would be difficult to overstate the importance or central role of the counseling relationship between client and counselor (Gelso & Carter, 1985).

In what was a revolutionary position of his time, Carl Rogers (1951) suggested that if counselors, or therapists, could supply their clients with a steady stream of certain basic human ingredients, the clients would solve their own dilemmas and feel better. In his writings and lectures, Rogers named three ingredients that counselors give to successful therapeutic relationships: congruence, unconditional positive regard, and empathic understanding. Other writers have maintained that while those ingredients might be necessary, they are probably of themselves insufficient to accomplish the broad goals and behavioral changes typically sought by our clients. Nevertheless, nearly all in the helping professions agree on the importance of those central factors to positive therapeutic outcomes. As counselors, it is essential that you learn how to be personally genuine (congruence), to give your clients total acceptance without judgment (unconditional positive regard), and to develop a great capacity to see the world as they see it (empathic understanding). This is the nature of the empathic relationship. It is in this nurturing context that your other activities with clients will work best.

Counseling, Psychotherapy, and Pride in Our Profession

Many of the beginning students in graduate counseling programs like to refer to themselves as "therapists" in training. Why do they shy away from being called "counselor," and prefer to be called "therapist"? This is a question my students and I take up at the beginning of our introductory counseling course. We talk about differences between professional helping roles, between social workers, psychiatrists, psychologists, psychiatric nurses, and the varieties of counselor roles in schools, mental health, and drug treatment settings. We talk about educational training requirements, credentialing, and licensure requirements. (If you have not yet had this discussion in your counselor training, you will. These are issues with which you will need to become familiar, particularly in regard to requirements in the state within which you live and plan to work.) In my counseling skills course, we continue to grapple with the similarities and distinctions between psychotherapy and counseling.

It appears that many of the distinctions between "counseling" and "psychotherapy" cited by my students have less to do with what actually happens in the work between client and professional and more to do with perceptions of power, prestige, and money. The counseling profession, springing from its earliest days of social activism and work with the disadvantaged in Boston (Bond, 2000), through the years of its work with veterans and its focus on vocational training (Sweeney, 2001), and into its further diversification to include broader issues of human growth and development (Gladstein & Apfel, 1987), has now emerged as a complex service field. The counselor must now respond to a range of complicated issues in a changing, diverse population. In its modern form, counseling has become a form of verbal interaction that deals with a wide spectrum of personal growth issues as well as helping people deal with an array of pathological problems (Smith, 2001). It is continually broadening its scope to include previously underappreciated problems—as with addiction issues, for example—and it has in recent years become much more sensitive to the multicultural, diverse world in which we operate (Ivey, D'Andrea, Ivey, & Simek-Morgan, 2002). As the newer professional "kid" on the block, the field of counseling has had to carve out its own identity and role definition. This business of making a separate, distinct identity has been difficult because of the significant overlap and similarity between counseling and psychotherapy activities. The public may not distinguish between these two activities, and even many professional texts make little, if any, distinction.

Some basic assumptions may differentiate psychotherapy activity from counseling activity, however. Central to the therapy model is the widely held belief that the "therapist" is in a helping role designed to "treat" some aspect of the "patient" that needs readjustment. The therapist is the technical expert, the patient the one who needs treatment. This is very much a psychological adaptation of the old doctor-patient medical model, a hand-me-down from the medical psychiatric tradition.

The counseling model is more generally egalitarian. The counselor is viewed as a client's fellow traveler on the road of life, not that different or removed from the person who has come for help. In this model the helper may be a bit farther along the road, but is a traveler nonetheless, and is one who also experiences many of the same problems in living. Clients are not so much to be treated as understood and assisted in finding their own solutions to those life problems. This is particularly true for school counselors or others who work with essentially "well" populations.

In practice, certainly, the distinctions blur. Counselors find themselves working with difficult, seriously disturbed people, and psychotherapists often explore those shared life problems with great humility and a sense of social awareness. One can have a difficult time, when looking from the outside, differentiating between "psychotherapy" activity and "counseling" activity, except in how the professionals define it. Those who call themselves "humanistic psychotherapists" take much the same egalitarian stance as counselors.

Professional counselor licensing, coupled with mandated insurance reimbursement for counseling services (in nearly all states), has helped to make counseling a publicly recognized, legitimate healing activity. If licensed (typically achieved by having obtained a master's degree in counseling plus meeting supervised practice and examination requirements), the community or agency counselor is usually able to access insurance reimbursement for services. School counselors, with their own licensing procedures, are certainly visible and prominent service providers in schools. These licensures, coupled with public acceptance of our profession, and with the added attraction that much of the counseling profession is still infused with its egalitarian ethos, make it the preferred mode of professional work for many of us.

The Joys of Counseling

Learning to be a counselor involves building a repertoire of assessment, responding, and helping skills. It involves, in other words, developing tools to help you help your client repair the mental and emotional "house" in which she lives. But it is much more than that. It is the development of wisdom; it is about learning how to connect effectively with people. It requires that you learn about yourself in the midst of assisting others. It is both science and art. You should find particular joy in a profession where learning about yourself is prerequisite to learning how to do the work with others. What other professions can make such a claim? Moreover, learning to do this work has the tremendous potential for reaching into the other realms of our lives and enriching them. There is distinct potential for improving the general quality of your relationships with others, particularly your most intimate relationships, as a side benefit of becoming an effective counselor. Again, what other profession can offer such rewards?

I cannot thank this profession enough, personally, for giving me the tools and wherewithal to deal more effectively with my own family, friends, and other close relationships. My wife and children still accuse me of having significant listening lapses, but I do at least know the difference between good and poor listening, the importance of solid emotional contact, and the need for give and take in a relationship. It is my fervent hope that this work benefits you in a similar fashion, for I am convinced it has that potential. As much as this work is about helping others, it is also about helping yourself. You will become involved in reciprocal learning relationships with your clients, and they may teach you significant things about life.

There is even more about this work that is compellingly important, however, and these aspects have global implications. If we are concerned about the fate of the world, about the enormous problems that confront the planet, what better arena in which to work than that which emphasizes improved interpersonal communication (Davis, 1996)? If we think of our own work as having the possible rippling effect of sending our clients, our students, and our colleagues out into the world with a greater appreciation of good communication and solid relationship skills, a greater sense of our shared humanity, we could consider ourselves pioneers for global connection. Toward the end of his life, the renowned psychologist Carl Rogers dedicated himself to the application of his principles of empathic, nondirective communication skills to international peace conferencing. There is no reason those of us who follow him should confine our own work to a smaller scale.

Building Multicultural and Ethical Competence

As you embark on the process of learning more about yourself and your motivations to be a counselor, as well as about the skills necessary to do this work, you will want to simultaneously heighten your appreciation of the multicultural, diverse nature of the world in which you work. It is part of your obligation to make sure that you work in ways that ethically protect the safety of both your clients and yourself. Chapter 6 is devoted solely to these issues of becoming an ethically adept and multiculturally aware counselor, but it is appropriate to emphasize the importance of ethical and multicultural awareness here as well. An awareness of issues related to dealing with people who might be different from you, and of the ethical principles that guide our profession, are as critical to doing solid counseling work as are self-understanding and a repertoire of skills. You want your clients to leave you feeling and doing better than when they started—or at the very least no worse. Your attention to the ethics of good practice, as well as to the worldview people bring to counseling, helps to ensure that no harm will be done.

Some of the basic assumptions held most sacred by European American theories about effective counseling fly directly in the face of many non-Western cultural traditions. Some of these assumptions are firmly entrenched in the Western cultural ways of thinking about people, and entrenched as well within the thinking of counselors who have been raised in that tradition. Such assumptions, if unchallenged by the unaware counselor, may result in an inability to connect with clients who have different worldviews. One obvious example of this kind of thinking has to do with the emphasis on the inherent value of the individual in most traditional counseling theories. A counselor who is grounded in such individualistic assumptions about people will have a hard time understanding the collectivist, more community-mindedness of non-Western clients (Greenfield, 1994; Schneider, Karcher, & Schlapkohl, 1999). Even worse, the counselor grounded in Western cultural values may ignore—or even help to perpetuate—some of the real abuses of power and oppression that some clients endure due to the political forces at play in the world that those clients inhabit (Hanna, Talley, & Guindon, 2000).

Adopting a multicultural worldview and learning about ideas related to counseling from such a multicultural perspective are essential for those who want to be effective counselors. You live in a rapidly changing, incredibly diverse world, and you will encounter clients who have experiences and perspectives that are very different from yours. Rather than seeing these differences as a block to understanding, you can embrace such differences as a great opportunity to stretch your own thinking. This is yet another opportunity to learn more about yourself in relation to others, to learn from the clients you serve.

The Organization of This Book

All counseling relationships have a beginning, a middle, and an end. They have a birth, where engaging the new client is the critical counseling task. That beginning quickly moves into a process of assessment, of finding out about this new person and his reasons for seeking counseling. Goals are articulated, and a plan for action is put into place. During the "action" phase, you work with your client toward those articulated goals. And, finally, the work you do together comes to an end. The entire process can be summed up as follows:

Engagement → Assessment → Action → Ending

Different skills and strategies are called for at each of these stages of the relationship.

The organization of this book roughly parallels the counseling process, focusing on the dynamics of the relationship and the skills necessary at different points of the relationship's life. I use the word "roughly" because the process is not neatly linear. Sometimes multiple steps are happening simultaneously. The process of engagement at the beginning stage, for example, is still ongoing as the assessment and goal planning activities of the middle stage kick into motion. Sometimes people regress, or backslide, and you will need to repeat things that have already happened. Counseling is a complex process. This book will highlight some of this complexity and help you to sort it out. Skills that foster the development and support of the counseling relationship run throughout.

Skills for Beginning, Engagement, and Assessment

In this chapter and the next (Chapters 1 and 2), I discuss the personal attributes of effective counselors and what it means to be a healthy counselor. Logistical and practical matters that need to be addressed in preparation for counseling clients in both community and school settings are reviewed in Chapter 3. Chapter 4 is concerned with the process of engaging and beginning to develop relationships with clients, and in Chapter 5 skills for assessment, goal setting, and action planning are articulated.

Skills for Relationship Building

To begin the section on building relationships, Chapter 6 focuses on ethical concerns and preparation for working with a diverse client population. Chapters 7 and 8 cover rudimentary and advanced relationship-building skills. Chapter 9 is devoted to the special relationship-building and counseling skills needed for crisis management situations.

Skills for Action

Chapters 10 and 11 detail the necessary skills and strategies that will prove useful for helping clients move toward the goals they have set for themselves. These skills are roughly divided into two broad categories: skills for working with people who function at Level 1 of our developmental house scheme, and those skills that can be helpful with people at Levels 2 and 3. The first action skills set is designed to help people organize their lives. The second, more advanced, action skills set helps people with already "organized" lives make life in their houses more satisfying and meaningful. Chapter 12 is devoted to special counseling situations related to populations of unique, challenging, and sometimes difficult clients. Skills for working specifically with children are also discussed here.

Skills for Ending

Chapter 13 reviews the dynamics and skills necessary for ending a counseling relationship. Some of the symbolic meanings of this ending are discussed, as are the means for reviewing and assessing client progress. Finally, Chapter 14 focuses on the importance of counselor health and renewal and how to avoid professional burnout.

Most chapters will have one or two reflection exercises, in which you are called upon to consider aspects of counseling in terms of your own life experiences. Suggested lab practice experiences provide ways for students to work together to practice the skills discussed. You are encouraged to keep a semester-long journal, using the journal as a place to write about these exercises. Each exercise, after time for personal reflection, may also serve as a vehicle for small group discussion or as vehicles for skills demonstrations within the classroom setting. Finally, each chapter ends with ideas for further research, reflection, and writing activities.

The Essence of This Book

I have assumed that readers of this book will most typically be enrolled in a first lab or skills course in a graduate counseling program or undergraduate upper level psychology or human services program. If you are such a reader, this book can give you some basic pointers about the fundamental skills of counseling. There are some things to learn about this work with people, and some skills can be efficiently taught and learned. The book provides a model for selecting skills to match client needs and presents a variety of advanced action skills that can be used effectively. While all existing counseling skills are not portrayed here, an array of those in current practice should provide a helpful foundation for work.

The developmental model for considering ways to match counseling skills to client needs provides something of a roadmap for the counselor. As you follow this rough roadmap, however, keep in mind that there is nothing automatic or formulaic about how counselors should do this work. Your growing experience, supported by trusted teachers and supervisors, will be your best guide to making effective interventions and decisions in your counseling work. This is not, in short, a cookbook. There is no easy recipe for becoming an effective, skilled counselor. Counseling is more than a collection of skills. Much of it is about who we are as people and how we choose to be with others. Thus, studying all the helpful information about counseling skills in this book and dutifully doing everything it says, contributes little to the essential "person" of the effective counselor.

This book talks about getting prepared to enter the private world of another human being, about having a set of engagement, observational, and management skills that provide a foundation for doing good work in this field. It cannot, however, call into play the humanity, the rich life experience, and the maturity that clients need from you to make this work truly effective. There is a clear bias in the book toward seeing the relationships we have with our clients as being central to the effectiveness of our work. Experiencing work in a diverse, multicultural world with openness and awareness, for example, will serve you far better in understanding those culturally different from you than will reading all of the written research about multicultural approaches to counseling. Your qualities as a mature human being with some wisdom in the world will serve you and your clients better than any set of mechanical skills. Your human qualities coupled with the skills and knowledge of the theory and research related to best counseling practice do make for a dynamite combination!

Integrating Skills and Theory

This book can give you a sense of what needs to be done to prepare to receive and hear the concerns of another. It can also help you to begin to make decisions about what to do once a relationship has been established, how to begin to think about the application of the theoretical approach to your clients' needs. It will lay the groundwork for effective counseling work. I encourage you to think of a range of theoretical approaches as having applicability to different client situations, but this book clearly also reflects a humanistic/existential bias. The relationship is viewed as primary. Different theoretical strategies are appropriate, however, when used at the right time, with the right client. You can integrate skills from different counseling theories to respond to diverse client needs. Building a house requires different tools for different jobs.

Just as I value the relationship that develops between you and your client, I also value the relationship that is being developed between you and me here. Many of the case examples are drawn from personal experience. I have certainly made mistakes in my own counseling work, and I shall do my best to talk about wrong turns taken with clients as well as some better moments. All client identities and stories have been altered to protect the real people they represent.

This book is aimed primarily at those who would be professional counselors in all kinds of settings: mental health, substance abuse, schools, vocational, rehabilitation, pastoral, and so forth. Case examples are drawn from a wide variety of areas. These essential skills are necessary and common to all counselors, regardless of the contexts within which they work. I refer to the people with whom we work as "clients," recognizing that they may actually be students if your work is being done in a school setting. Although imperfect, I personally prefer the term "client" to "patient" or "consumer." To deal with the gender imperfections of modern English, I have chosen to refer to counselors and clients sometimes as "he" and sometimes as "she," hopefully in equal proportions.

Concluding Thoughts: A Personal Perspective

As the poem at the beginning of this chapter suggests, we are all looking for our particular path in the world, looking for just the right star to follow. In my case, the counseling profession has certainly felt like the right star, but my entry into this profession was similar to that of many others. I came to it indirectly.

Teaching was the work I trained to do in college. I decided to go into counseling as a professional while teaching as a Peace Corps volunteer in Jamaica. At the time, I was working in four rural elementary schools on Jamaica's east coast (not the toughest of assignments), helping teachers in an in-service training program. I had spent my college career preparing to teach and was enamored with ideas of open education and experiential learning. I enjoyed my job and loved the people with whom I worked.

I hitched rides up into the bush to visit my schools, often on banana trucks or on donkey carts. The schools were simple, the materials primitive, and we did the best we could with what we had. Jamaica's beauty and the energy and passion of the people made up for what we lacked in school materials. It was a heady mix, that energy and beauty. It was certainly a wonderful work situation, a great coming of age and rite of passage for a young person on the brink of manhood, from the hills of Vermont.

I began to find, however, that what I most appreciated about this work was the more private one-on-one, or small group time that I was spending with people. I reveled in these more intimate conversations, sharing ideas, and being invited into people's lives. We talked about politics and about culture. My friends and colleagues began to share more personal issues. I thrived on these intimacies, these private conversations. I began to realize, however, that there were serious limitations in my ability to respond and that some of the problems my friends brought presented situations in which I was out of my depth.

Even more compelling, although certainly less acknowledged or understood, was my search for self-understanding and personal awareness. Having grown up in a home where there had been emotional difficulty, and having experienced a recent terrible loss, the death of a younger brother in a drowning accident, I was casting about for anchors and some ways of finding order in the universe. During my spare time, I began to read books in psychology and philosophy, and I was impressed by what I was reading in the humanistic psychology field, particularly that which related to the growing human potential "movement." The writings of

Rollo May, Victor Frankl, and the existentialists captured me, liked Sidney Jourard's emphasis on the need for authenticity a psychotherapists' work with people. I found the notion that be real people—something other than the rat observers I'd read about undergraduate days—fascinating.

As I finished my Peace Corps career, I applied to graduate counseling programs. Now, more than thirty years later, after many years of graduate training and of working as a counselor, supervisor, and administrator in public and private settings, I thrive in a work situation that affords a satisfying bridge between the counseling and teaching worlds. I am teaching again, this time about counseling, preparing people to work professionally in the field. It's been a great working life, and it is now a pleasure to be able to share with you some of the ideas that have been gleaned from these years working and teaching. I can only hope that your journey in this work is as satisfying for you.

For Further Thought

1. What do you think should be the fundamental goals of counseling? Compare and contrast your ideas about these goals with what other professionals in the field say. Either interview area professionals or review the literature to discover others' opinions.

2. What does the literature say about the role of love and fear in counseling?

3. Examine the literature regarding the reasons people want to become professional counselors. Which of these reasons do you think are legitimate? Which will necessitate personal examination and work? Why? How do these compare with your reasons for entering this profession?

4. Who are the seen and unseen mentors who have drawn you to this field? Have you read their written work? What is it about these people that you find compelling? If you haven't read their original writings, here's a suggestion that you do. Read biographies of their lives as well. Their theories are, after all, oftentimes extensions of their own lives.

References

Bond, T. (2000). *Standards and ethics for counseling in action.* London: Sage.

Bruce, P. (1984). Continuum of counseling goals: A framework for differentiating counseling strategies. *Personnel and Guidance Journal, 62*(5), 259–263.

Casey, J. (1996). Gail F. Farwell: A developmentalist who lives his ideas. *The School Counselor, 43,* 174–180.

Davis, K. (1996). Defining questions, charting possibilities. *Counseling Psychologist, 24*(1), 144–160.

Deikman, A. (1982). *The observing self*. Boston: Beacon Press.

Foster, S. (1996, December). Characteristics of an effective counselor. *Counseling Today, 21*.

Frankl, V. (1963). *Man's search for meaning*. New York: Simon & Schuster.

Gelso, C., & Carter, J. (1985). The relationship in counseling and psychotherapy: Components, consequences, and theoretical antecedents. *The Counseling Psychologist, 13*, 155–243.

Gladstein, G., & Apfel, F. (1987). A theoretically based adult career center. *Career Development Quarterly, 36*, 178–185.

Goleman, D. (1995). *Emotional intelligence: Why it can matter more than IQ*. New York: Bantam.

Goleman, D. (1998). *Working with emotional intelligence*. New York: Bantam.

Greenfield, P. (1994). Independence and interdependence as developmental scripts: Implications for theory, research, and practice. In P. Greenfield & R. Cocking (Eds.), *Cross cultural roots of minority child development* (pp. 1–37), Hillsdale, NJ: Erlbaum.

Hanna, F., Talley, W., & Guindon, M. (2000). The power of perception: Toward a model of cultural oppression and liberation. *Journal of Counseling and Development, 78*, 430–441.

Horvath, A., & Symonds, B. (1991). Relation between working alliance and outcome in psychotherapy: A meta-analysis. *Journal of Counseling Psychology, 38*, 138–149.

Ivey, A., D'Andrea, M., Ivey, M., & Simek-Morgan, L. (2002). *Theories of counseling and psychotherapy: A multicultural perspective* (4th ed.). Boston: Allyn & Bacon.

Ivey, A., Ivey, M., Myers, J., & Sweeney, T. (2005). *Developmental counseling and therapy*. Boston: Lahaska/Houghton Mifflin.

Kelly, A. (1998). Clients' secret keeping in outpatient therapy. *Journal of Counseling Psychology, 45*, 50–57.

Kohlberg, L. (1962). Moral development and identification. *National Society for the Study of Education Yearbook*, 277–332.

Kohlberg, L. (1981). *The philosophy of moral development*. San Francisco: Harper & Row.

Kierulff, S. (1988). Sheep in the midst of wolves: Person-responsibility therapy with criminals. *Professional Psychology: Research and Practice, 19*, 436–440.

Maslow, A. (1963). Neurosis as a failure of personal growth. *Humanitas, 3*, 153–169.

Orlinsky, D., Grawe, K., & Parks, B. (1994). Process and outcome in psychotherapy: Noch einmal. In A. E. Bergin & S. L. Garfield (Eds.), *Handbook of psychotherapy and behavior change* (4th ed., pp. 270–376). New York: Wiley.

Piaget, J. (1955). *The language and thought of the child*. New York: New American Library. (Original work published 1923)

Rogers, C. (1951). *Client centered therapy*. Boston: Houghton-Mifflin.

Scheinder, B., Karcher, M., & Schlapkohl, W. (1999). Relationship counseling across cultures. Cultural sensitivity and beyond. In P. Pederson (Ed.), *Multiculturalism as a fourth force* (pp. 167–190). Philadelphia: Taylor & Francis.

Smith, H. (2001). Professional identity for counselors. In D. C. Locke, J. E. Myers, & E. L. Herr (Eds.), *The handbook of counseling* (pp. 569–579). Thousand Oaks, CA: Sage.

Spurling, L., & Dryden, W. (1989). The self and the therapeutic domain. In W. Dryden & L. Spurling (Eds.), *On becoming a psychotherapist* (pp. 191–214). London: Tavistock/Routledge.

Sweeney, T. (1991). Counseling credentialing: Purpose and origin. In F. Bradley (Ed.), *Credentialing in counseling* (pp. 1–12). Alexandria, VA: Association for Counselor Education and Supervision.

Teyber, E. (2000). *Interpersonal process in psychotherapy: A relational approach* (4th ed.). Pacific Grove, CA: Brooks/Cole.

Witmer, J., & Young, M. (1996). Preventing counselor impairment: A wellness model. *Journal of Humanistic Education and Development, 34,* 141–155.

CHAPTER 2

The Effective Counselor

The man who would learn the human mind will gain almost nothing from experimental psychology. Far better for him to put away his academic gown, to say good-bye to the study, and to wander with human heart through the world. There, in the horrors of the prison, the asylum, and the hospital, in the drinking-shops, brothels, and gambling hells, in the salons of the elegant, in the exchanges, socialist meetings, churches, religious revivals, and sectarian ecstasies, through love and hate, through the experience of passion in every form of his own body, he would reap richer store of knowledge than textbooks a foot thick could give him. Then he would know how to doctor the sick with real knowledge of the human soul.
(Jung, 1961, p. 71)

Nobody said learning to become a counselor is easy. It is a rare profession indeed that requires academic preparation and training and also demands that you expand and examine yourself personally. Not only must you become an adept practitioner of a trade, you must also become wise in the ways of the world. You don't need to take Jung's advice literally because academic and intellectual training are critically important in learning to do counseling work, but his words remind us that we must attend to other responsibilities as well.

Who you are as a person will largely determine how effective you will be in working with others as a counselor. You are, in your individual person, your own single best tool for helping others. Your values, beliefs, and personal background—simply how you live your daily life—will influence the lives of your clients. All of your history, your personal conduct, and your attitudes about people and the world around you are at play in the counseling relationship. The degree to which you understand yourself will have a lot to do with how effective you will be with your clients (Kottler, 1993).

The Importance of Counselor Self-Awareness

Because self-awareness has such a major impact on a counselor's effectiveness, many programs in counseling, clinical psychology, and even social work require implicitly or explicitly that students engage in some kind of personal counseling or growth work as part of their training. Counselor self-awareness is also a primary ethical consideration because it ensures that we will, at the very least, do no harm to our clients by unconsciously working out our own emotional unfinished business through them. Counselors do not have to be perfect people, but the more we understand and have come to grips with our personal history, the less we will be controlled by that past or look to others to satisfy its deficits.

A counselor's unmet intimacy needs or desire to prove competency may actively interfere with delivering the best services possible. The effective counselor has learned how to use his particular personal difficulties as a way of relating to the specific emotional needs of his clients (Foster, 1996). Truly sound, effective, and ethical practice involves learning all you can about people and how they behave, as well as about yourself. Certainly, the degree of self-awareness that you are able to achieve is at least as important as the formal training you receive (Cavanagh, 1990). Self-awareness is a critical factor in developing the all-important empathy necessary for doing good counseling work (Brennan, 1987; Dixon, 1980), and learning about yourself is probably the best way to begin to learn about the development of empathy for others (Duan, Rose, & Kraatz, 2002). Although the connection between your personal history and your counseling effectiveness is not directly clear, a good case can be made for looking at your own background (Barta, 1999; Clemente-Crain, 1996; Softas-Nall, Baldo, & Williams,

2001). The best counselors are those who learn how to blend their formal knowledge and understanding of human relationships with a solid understanding of their own personal history (Cormier & Cormier, 1998).

Empathizing with Client Vulnerability

The requirement for counselor personal growth and self-examination may also provide a good firsthand introduction to how vulnerable it can feel to be a client. For anyone who has never experienced the joys, or the terrors, of being a client, it is an excellent empathy-enhancing experience. What better way to begin to understand how it feels to be a client than to sit in that other chair? It is a truism that seeking counseling is a courageous act. Seeking help or asking for assistance puts one in a position of vulnerability. The act can be doubly courageous for those who see asking for help as some kind of personal weakness (Shapiro, 1984). Many people who come to see you may have tried other ways of solving their problems, including using family, friends, and their own internal resources. This may be particularly true for people from some cultural backgrounds where seeking help outside the family is not valued and may be frowned upon (Pedersen & Ivey, 1993).

Ethical principles for counseling practice dictate closely guarded boundaries for the counselor-client relationship, proscribing interactions beyond those that occur within the actual time of professional contact. Protection of the vulnerable client from the more powerful counselor is a cornerstone of professional codes of conduct, which acknowledge that the counselor-client relationship has tremendous potential for harm as well as for help.

The Counselor-Client Relationship Matrix

The counselor-client relationship is further complicated by the vast array of past and present variables at play between the counselor and client, or what can be called the counselor-client relationship matrix. This matrix, or web, is a mix of both the counselor's and the client's present experience, ideas, thoughts and feelings, values, unique cultural background, and past experiences. Figure 2.1 illustrates this matrix. All of this material, these cumulative experiences and thoughts and feelings, swirl around and through these two people in an intricate dance when they meet together. It is this dance that makes for the excitement and drama of the unfolding counseling relationship, and it holds great potential for assisting client growth—if managed well.

To explain how this matrix of relationship variables will affect your work, consider this scenario. Teresa, a counselor-in-training, was raised by a perfectionistic, controlling mother and an emotionally distant and unavailable father. She emerged from childhood and adolescence into adulthood with a high degree of academic accomplishment and success but with unmet yearnings for closeness

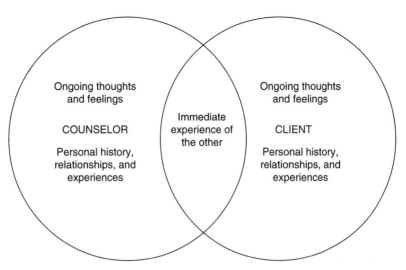

Figure 2.1   Counselor-Client Relationship Matrix

with others. Her attempts at forming close relationships have been hampered by her neediness and tendency to become too quickly dependent. Teresa believes that becoming a counselor will be a safe way for her to pursue intimacy with others without all of the risks attendant to the give and take of friendships and relationships with lovers.

In her work with clients, Teresa will interact with many people who also have had difficulties establishing sound interpersonal relationships, each of them carrying into counseling their histories of relationship, particularly their earliest ones with their families. Because of her own history, Teresa will have difficulty connecting with the pain her clients relate, and unless she comes to grips with some of her own issues, she runs the risk of becoming unhealthily enmeshed with her clients. Her desire for closeness may intersect with her clients' desires for closeness in ways that are distinctly not helpful, and may even be harmful. She may promote dependency, or serve to isolate her clients even further from the development of solid relationships with others because of her desire for them to see her as special. Her unacknowledged past could thus have a variety of harmful consequences for those who have sought her help. Without an awareness of her own neediness, what some have called her own "woundedness" (May, Remen, Young, & Berland, 1985), Teresa may harm more than help.

Self-Awareness and the Role of Unconscious Material

Beyond developing a high level of self-understanding, you should seek to understand your motivations for doing this kind of work and your hidden desires for what you plan to gain from it. If you are to learn both *what* you *want* and *why* you want it, you will need to bring as much personal material into your conscious awareness as possible. Plumbing your own depths will undoubtedly increase your appreciation for how much material is unconscious, or out of awareness, in all of us.

Sigmund Freud introduced the notion of the unconscious as a way of talking about material that exists in our minds, for each of us, out of our day-to-day awareness. He believed that all of the thoughts and feelings that exist in the unconscious are there because they are too painful to be remembered, that they have been "repressed" and pushed out of conscious awareness. He believed that these thoughts and feelings are related to early childhood psychosexual developmental issues and our fantasized notions of sexuality and power struggles with parents.

Many of Freud's original ideas have been challenged by other theorists both in and out of psychoanalytic schools of thought; however, the idea of the unconscious is broadly accepted by most major approaches to counseling and psychotherapy. Theorists may disagree about the specific nature and origins of material held in the unconscious, but they generally believe that we all function with elements of our past stored in our memories just beyond the grasp of our daily awareness. A function of most counseling is to help people access more of this material, to draw it into the realm of conscious awareness. This business of harvesting unconscious material is complicated. Your course work and clinical experiences will serve as an introduction to the reality and importance of this phenomenon, and a life's work in counseling will help you appreciate its complexity.

It is important for counselors to begin to recognize how their own unconscious material affects their work. To the degree that it is not understood, it can unwittingly influence the course of work with clients. There is, for example, a tendency for counselors to project their own unconscious material onto their clients (Hackney & Cormier, 2001). Counselors who have unresolved, unconscious needs for intimacy, power, or control can subtly work those needs out through work with their clients. This is why supervision is seen as a critical ethical responsibility for sound counseling practice.

A supervision story illustrates why this awareness of our own "unfinished business" is critical. A number of years ago I supervised a counselor named "Lisa." Lisa had been doing a lot of couples and family counseling. During one of our supervision sessions she commented on the number of people whom she'd seen who were getting divorced. We joked that maybe "something was in the water" or that some kind of divorce bug was going around. However, when Lisa began to look more seriously at the issue and this "coincidence," she could not escape the conclusion that perhaps she was acting with her clients in some ways—probably unconsciously—that encouraged separation and divorce. This inevitably led her to look at the subtle ways she had been encouraging this action in her communications with her clients, to consider her own motivations in such encouragement, and finally to examine her thoughts and feelings about her own marriage. Lisa's courage, her ability to truly take responsibility for her own material that had been seeping into the work with her clients, enabled her to step back and rethink her interventions with them.

This stepping back and taking responsibility for your own material allows for a clean working relationship with your clients. As an effective counselor, you will do what you can to leave the relationship, and the work your client needs to do, uncontaminated by your own unfinished, unexamined issues (Hayes, 2002). You will become as healthy and as uncontaminated by your past as possible and will recognize those areas where work remains to be done.

Self-Awareness and the Demands of This Work

I oftentimes suggest to my graduate counseling students that they interview counselors working in the field, either as part of a formally assigned experience or more informally for their own education. They sit down and talk with counselors working in schools, mental health agencies, and drug clinics and ask them about their joys and frustrations with the work. They come back with interesting reports of these interviews. Invariably, the graduate students talk of the delight many of these counselors take in watching their students, or their clients, grow and experience their lives. They talk of how these counselors themselves report that they grow and learn from their interactions with their clients. My students are inspired by these stories. It is confirmation of their own initial desires to enter the field.

But there are also the stories of overwhelming caseloads, of a parade of difficult clients, of unresponsive agency administrators, and of unending paperwork. Some school counselors talk of dramatically difficult student behavioral and emotional problems coupled with diminishing community support. Sometimes my students interview counselors who seem deadened by their work, not particularly fond of their clients or their colleagues, and ready to work elsewhere but unwilling to go out and look for another job. A general lassitude, lack of energy, almost a depression surrounds these counselors—and students cannot help but wonder about the toll counseling takes on those who work in this field. They correctly wonder about the degree of help these counselors can afford their clients and speculate about the motivations that will continue to keep them at work in a field where adequate interpersonal payback has ceased. Words like "burnout" come into play in these discussions.

Ongoing counselor self-understanding and personal examination is more than a casual, self-indulgent preoccupation with self, or ego gratification. It is an ethical, professional obligation that you manage your relationship matrix variables, your own history, and your current emotional life so that full attention can be paid to your client's relationship variables, history, and emotional life. You are also obliged to come to grips with counseling work itself should it ever become stale and unrewarding, for whatever reason, so that you can either quit and move on to something else or find ways to become revitalized and enthusiastic.

The Counselor's Professional Preparation

Life experience helps to shape the person of the counselor. The wider and more divergent the life experience, the greater the capacity of the counselor to do this work. Counseling is both science, represented by your professional course work and preparation, and art, represented by your personal evolution. In addition to developing your counseling skills, you need to develop your knowledge of contemporary thought about the forces that have shaped your clients' lives and the signs of normal and abnormal development. You need to have a working knowledge of basic diagnostic and assessment strategies, differential treatment approaches, and the ramifications of ethical and legal dilemmas you will confront in your work. All of this material is covered in the course work of most graduate counseling programs.

The course work recommended by the Council for Accreditation of Counseling and Related Education Programs (CACREP) encompasses a body of knowledge that counselors must acquire as a minimal foundation for doing this work. The CACREP standards for counseling competence dictate completion of a formal program of graduate study that includes course work and demonstrated competence in eight core areas, supervised clinical experiences, and supervised internships. CACREP also upholds standards for the number of graduate credit hours (ranging from 48 to 60), number of faculty in training programs, and the supervision of internships. CACREP-accredited programs must follow these standards (CACREP, 2001). Most of the programs that have chosen not to pursue CACREP accreditation still adhere, by and large, to the CACREP standards. This course work, as well as standards adopted by various licensing boards in the counseling field, provides some assurance of counselor competence.

Become familiar with the certification and licensure regulations regarding the practice of counseling in the area where you will work. Being professionally credentialed will give you visibility and will offer some assurance to the public of your competence. Some counseling jobs require licensure, and each counseling specialization (clinical mental health counseling, school counseling, and so forth) has its own licensure requirements. Credentialing may also afford you access to insurance reimbursement that would be inaccessible otherwise. Familiarize yourself with the legal requirements of the credentialing process that accompanies the kinds of counseling you wish to do (Anderson & Swanson, 1994).

Effective counseling involves both the science of the skills and the art of knowing how and when to use those skills (Wilcox-Mathew, Ottens, & Minor,

1997). Your journey in this profession necessarily involves both a drive toward personal wholeness and an accumulation of skills and knowledge about people and the best practices of counseling.

Characteristics of Effective Counselors

What is a healthy, or whole, counselor? What are those naturally occurring traits and features of personal awareness that contribute to wholeness, to health, and that result in effective counseling outcomes? There have been many attempts to isolate the specific characteristics of effective counselors, in no small part so that counselor education programs can become more adept at selecting candidates for training. The thinking here is that if we can select people who already have inherent personality characteristics that are suitable for this work, then training programs can focus on specific skills training to supplement those natural inclinations.

Many of these "laundry lists" of characteristics look like something out of the Girl or Boy Scouts Manual, using words like "trustworthy" and "loyal," and are not especially helpful in making discriminating decisions about whom to select for counselor training. Researchers have uncovered evidence that certain factors do tend to contribute to better work in this field. For example, counselors who are more personally confident and socially adept will have an easier time relating to their clients (Williams, 1999). The following ten favorable personality characteristics are also the least teachable to those who do not already possess them (Pope, 1996; Scheffler, 1984):

- Acceptance
- Confidence
- Emotional stability
- Empathy
- Fairness
- Flexibility
- Genuineness
- Interest in people
- Open-mindedness
- Sensitivity

Other lists of characteristics retain this range of personal characteristics and add specific qualities suggesting wisdom and maturity such as inner directedness, existentiality, feeling reactivity, spontaneity, self-regard, and capacity for intimate contact (Ritter, 1984), and spirituality and self-actualization (Smith, 2003).

The Counselor as a "Whole Person"

Counseling can be draining and difficult work, particularly when one's caseload is comprised largely of people who are consistently in serious difficulty. Chapter 14 considers some ways in which counselors can maintain themselves and stay fresh; this section examines the basis for wellness.

Wegscheider (1981) proposed looking at the counselor's state of wellness from the perspective of "wholeness." In this model different aspects, or "selves," comprise the whole counselor, each of which needs care and attention. I have found this model, with my own modification, to be extremely helpful, not only for thinking about counselor health but also as a way of considering client assessment. These "selves" of ours are comprised of the following elements:

- Physical self
- Emotional self
- Social and familial self
- Intellectual self
- Working self
- Aesthetic self
- Spiritual self

It should be readily apparent that counselors who wish to do good work with people need to function at relatively high levels in each of these areas. Effective counselors acknowledge that a balanced personal life is central to doing good counseling work (Reyak-Schelar & Feldman, 1984). A life that overemphasizes one or two of these areas, to the exclusion of others, is a life that runs a bit off balance and compromises the capacity to respond to those needs in others.

I once had the good fortune to take part in a workshop conducted by the noted existentialist Jim Bugental, who led participants in an unsettling, interesting experiment in which we explored that almost universally shared sense of yearning, a longing for some vague "more." We were divided into groups of three, and each of us was to alternately ask another person in the triad variations of only one question: "What is it that you really want?" We had 10 minutes to explore this question and, after the person answered, to ask it again using our own words but without varying from that central theme.

This may seem innocuous enough, contemplating what is "wanted," but my group of three found it difficult. Each time the question was asked and answered, we plunged more deeply into the truer, more basic elements of our desires. It was like peeling away the layers of an onion, each variant of the question, "So what is it you *really* want?" pushing us to go deeper into our essential wants. There was also a lot of pain associated with diving into these questions of yearning.

In the exercise that followed, we explored these questions: "How do you stop yourself from getting what you want?" and "What would you like to do to start acting on your own behalf?" Each of us, in turn, grappled with the complexities that such simple questions belie. Each of us had to think of the inhibiting factors, the personal histories and current realities of our lives that had blocked us from reaching for our dreams. For all of us in that little group, the clash between the call of daily duties and responsibilities and the inner rumblings of yearning soon became apparent. Those simple questions quickly called our most complex conflicts into the room. These are, of course, essential questions for us all: "What is it in life that you really want . . . and how do you plan to go after it?"

REFLECTION EXERCISE 2.1   *The Balance in Your Life*

As you contemplate becoming a professional counselor, periodically check in with yourself to make sure that you are certain about the work you want to do. This exercise is designed to help you consider this, and it can be repeated from time to time during your period of professional preparation. Take a few moments for some private, silent reflection. Contemplate your life, and ask yourself some focused questions about the state of who you are and where you are headed. You may have your own questions, or you may want to use these to stimulate your thinking:

- Am I happy with the professional path I have chosen, and do I feel like I'm going in the right direction?

- What are my unique talents and gifts, and have I found a way to bring those out into the world?

- As I survey my own personal "selves," is my life lived in balance? What could I do to make it more balanced?

- If I found out I had six months to live, what would I do with that time? Should I be doing some of those things now anyway?

- Is my chosen career path toward becoming a professional counselor congruent with what I see as my life tasks, and do I think this work will truly fulfill me?

There are no "right" answers to these questions. What works for one of us might not be right for another. You won't be able to fully answer some of the questions until you've tried certain things out. You won't know, for example, how fulfilling any work path is until you have traveled it for a while, but you may now have some intuitive glimpses of the correct fit of a certain kind of work and who you are as a person.

Finally, like all people, counselors change over time, so it is important that we ask ourselves these central questions periodically, throughout our careers, as a check on our own integrity and sense of purpose.

A Counselor's Levels of Awareness

You function on multiple levels of awareness regarding your thoughts and feelings, and your facility at managing and moving among those fluid levels is key to your success in work as a counselor. Figure 2.2 shows a three-tiered model you may use to think about these multiple levels of awareness.

In this model the foundation of counselor awareness is the *intrapersonal* level of awareness. It is how you are feeling and what you are thinking, and it is determined by the cumulative sum of your emotional and cognitive experience as it is acted upon by the current situation in which you find yourself. Descartes made famous the remark, "I think, therefore I am." You could also say, "I feel, therefore I am." Or, perhaps, "I think *and* feel, therefore I am." Some would argue that what we think determines what we feel. In any case, no one would deny that emotions are a large part of our total being or that caring for our emotional selves is a critical aspect of counselor self-care (Wilson, 1994). To be an effective counselor, you will need to regularly check in with yourself at this level, to look at your internal experience and reflect on what you are feeling and thinking.

At the second level is *interpersonal* awareness. This relates to the dynamics of your interactions with other individuals. It is about intimacy, contact, and conflict—all the relationship variables at play between you and one other person. Interpersonal awareness means that as you interact with a client, part of your mind is simultaneously standing back, looking on, and reflecting on the quality of the interaction. We shall talk in some depth about these important skills in later chapters. For now suffice it to say that throughout your practice as a counselor you will need to regularly check your awareness at both the intrapersonal and interpersonal levels.

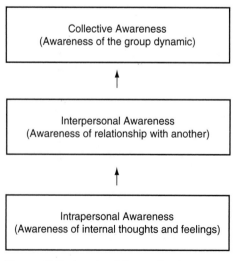

Figure 2.2 Levels of Counselor Awareness

REFLECTION EXERCISE 2.2   *Paying Attention to Your Internal World*

This is a brief exercise. You can complete it in 5 minutes or less. Close your eyes and let your attention move inward. Take note of the ideas and feelings passing through you. Pay particular attention to your feeling state; note it without judgment and without trying to attach it to any particular ideas or series of events. Open your eyes, bringing your awareness back into your current environment.

Repeat this each day, perhaps five to ten times a day, in various situations. With practice you will become much more adept at monitoring your ongoing feeling state and eventually linking that to the events and circumstances around you.

After a few days of repeating the exercise when alone, try doing this internal "check in" while with other people. While in conversation with someone, tune in to your internal thinking and feeling state. Make a conscious effort to note the feelings and thoughts that move within you. Think about which of those are related to this person with whom you are speaking and which seem extraneous. With practice you will be able to check in unobtrusively in any situation without closing your eyes or appearing to isolate yourself. Nurturing the ability to easily check in with your own internal world is invaluable for effective counseling.

Finally, there is the group or collective dimension of awareness. At this level, which is of particular relevance to those who do group counseling work, a complex set of dynamics and feelings fly between the members and leaders of a group. These dynamics are at play in all groups, not only counseling groups. These are the overt and covert emotional messages that exist among group members, the web of feeling and thought that makes for tremendous energy and excitement in much of group work.

It is, however, the first two dimensions that are of primary concern to us here. Your ability to keep a close eye on your shifting internal state (your intrapersonal awareness) coupled with your ability to monitor the feelings and dynamics of the relationship (your interpersonal awareness) are together fundamental to your ability to develop skill as a counselor.

A Counselor's Values, Beliefs, and Attitudes

In addition to your personality, your family and personal background, and your training, an important part of what makes up your "person" as a counselor is your worldview—what you believe to be true about people and the world. Your ideals and your fundamental beliefs about how things do and should work will intimately and profoundly affect your work with people. As a generation's poet laureate has said in song,

> Might like to wear cotton/Might like to wear silk
> Might like to drink whisky/Might like to drink milk
> Might like to eat caviar/Might like to eat bread
> You might be sleepin' on a floor/Or sleepin' in a king sized bed
> But you're gonna have to serve somebody
> Yes indeed/You're gonna have to serve somebody
> Well, it may be the Devil, or it may be the Lord
> But you're gonna have to serve somebody. (Dylan, 1979)

We all believe in something, and we serve those beliefs in all that we do. But in what do you believe? Do you believe in God, in many gods, in no god? Do you believe in the concept of Original Sin, or No Thing, or nothing? Are neuroses and psychoses the result of chemical imbalance, the result of conditioned responses to negative events, the product of inevitable psychosexual conflicts, profound philosophical statements about the human condition, or simply modern ways of saying our "sins"? The question here is not "What have your training and education taught you?" but "What do *you* believe?"

At some point each of us needs to take a stand, to articulate our beliefs about the world. If your beliefs are shifting and uncertain, then that uncertainty becomes your stance. A refusal to take any position becomes your position. A belief in no beliefs is a belief of sorts. Your core beliefs and assumptions form the bedrock on which you will develop theories of working with people. You need to take the time, not just once but repeatedly, to check in with yourself and examine your system of values. This, too, is part of your ethical responsibility to the people you serve.

There has been controversy in the counseling field regarding a counselor's use of values in work with clients. Some approaches to counseling advocate the counselor acting as value free as possible (Raths, Harmin, & Simon, 1978); others contend that counselors should actively use their own values in their work (Lickona, 1991) and plan for the utilization of values as a core part of the counseling process (Vachon & Agresti, 1992). Most agree that, one way or another, personal counselor values *do* influence work with clients, and they advocate clarity about what those values are (Patterson, 1989; Peterson, 1976; Rosik, 2003; Strupp, 1974).

Kinnier, Kernes, and Dautheribes (2000, p. 9) provide a "short list of universal moral values" that they maintain should serve as a guide for counseling work. Like the Golden Rule ("Do unto others as you would have them do unto you."), these values were designed to cut across all major religions and sectarian belief systems and to be relevant in any cultural context. Their list is as follows:

- Commit to something greater than oneself.
- Seek the Truth (or truths).
- Seek justice.
- Practice self-respect, but with humility, self-discipline, and acceptance of personal responsibility.
- Respect and care for oneself.
- Do not exalt oneself or overindulge; show humility and avoid gluttony, greed, or other forms of selfishness or self-centeredness.
- Act in accordance with one's conscience and accept responsibility for one's behavior.
- Show respect and caring for others (the Golden Rule).
- Recognize the connectedness between all people.
- Serve humankind and be helpful to individuals.
- Be caring, respectful, compassionate, tolerant, and forgiving of others.
- Do not hurt others (e.g., do not murder, abuse, steal from, cheat, or lie to others).
- Care for living things and the environment.

In my own counseling work, I have synthesized this list to create my own set of core values, which underlie my assumptions about people and deeply affect how I work with them. I would not expect my own list to be universally accepted, but I strongly recommend that each of you develop your own set of core values. Use the values presented here as a jumping off point to define your own core values, and do your counseling work with awareness of these values. Here are my five core values.

1. *A person's essential nature is pure and good.*

If you adopt this value as your own, you will operate from the belief that every individual was born with innate talents and gifts and that these have either been nurtured and supported or criticized and quashed. You will understand that

---

REFLECTION EXERCISE 2.3   Personal Counseling Challenges

Consider the following, individually and then in small groups. Are there people with whom you think it will be very difficult or impossible for you to work? Who are these people, and what is it about them that will make helping them in counseling so difficult? Perhaps more important, what is it about *you* that would make working with such people difficult? Do you see any possibility for reconciling these ideas and feelings in a way that will make counseling these kinds of clients possible for you?

---

much of the maladaptive behavior of children, adolescents, and adults is the result of learning in response to harmful environmental influences. Oftentimes negative behavior has been learned as a survival strategy in life-threatening situations. Your job as a counselor is to see the beauty of the person behind what has been learned and not be unduly put off by the negative behaviors.

2. *My primary role as a counselor is to support my clients' capacity to manage freedom and responsibility and to help them see the ways in which they influence and are influenced by greater social forces.*

Adopting this value means that one of your primary counseling functions will be to help people see and become aware of all the influences on their lives: psychological, sociological, and political. Too often the temptation for counselors is to think only of the psychological, to neglect the obvious impact of sociocultural forces that influence us all. Similarly, it should go without saying that your primary responsibility is to the individual you serve, not to external agents (including spouses and families) or to the state.

A longtime friend Jim Loewen (1995) has written extensively about race and history in this country. In a lecture at my college a few years ago, he asked for a show of hands of how many thought that their lives were shaped by forces beyond their control. About five hands in the audience of more than a hundred largely white, middle-class, young adult Vermonters went up. Jim went on to say that the proportion of hand-raising in a lecture he'd recently done at a predominantly black school in Mississippi was reversed—that in an audience of the same number, about 95 percent of the hands went up in answer to the same question. He maintains that people of color are far more intimately knowledgeable than are white people of the ways in which our lives are controlled by external political forces. Because of overt and covert racially motivated actions directed against them (e.g., police practices of racial profiling), people of color have no choice but to become knowledgeable about the people and agencies who do these things. Whites, he maintains, are also strongly influenced by outside forces, but because the effect is not directly visible in their everyday lives, they tend to personalize or "psychologize" it. A white factory worker forced into early retirement, for example, is likely to view his job loss as a personal failure rather than in political terms (e.g., as a tactic used by many U.S. employers today to lower the average wage of the work force).

Hillman and Ventura (1992) suggest that a studied ignorance of these larger forces by our profession has resulted in an entire generation of politically naïve and impotent counselors and therapists who are unable to mobilize energy sufficient to address compelling social issues. There are those who advocate that counselors and therapists become more politically active (Fox, 2003). Counselors should, at the least, become aware of their own tendencies to operate in unconsciously discriminating ways (Ridley, 1995) and recognize the ways in which their counseling may support the oppression of clients (Hanna, Talley, & Guindon, 2000).

A number of years ago I met for a single session with a woman who was distressed because her husband, complaining of depression and needing time alone, had left her. My distinct impression at the time was that he quite possibly could have been striking out for freedom, taking a stand on his own behalf, perhaps even in reaction to her desire to keep him firmly entrenched at home. I vaguely remember talking with her about taking his absence as an opportunity to learn more about herself, but I recall making no suggestions about ways to reel him back in.

She came back for one more session a few months later, mostly to thank me for my wonderful advice. My advice? What could be wonderful, I thought, about whatever nonadvice I'd given her? She thanked me profusely for helping to get her husband back. He was now on some terrific medications and was not talking about leaving any more. I was speechless. How had I played into this business of "getting him back"? What had I said? I still have no clue, and I am still distressed about the possibilities that I unwittingly assisted a process of coercing this man, a stranger to me, back into an environment that he may have found personally stifling.

Adopting this value means that you will have no interest in aiding your clients' attempts to control others. Furthermore, you will remain alert to the dangers of allowing your own counseling efforts to become a vehicle of control. Some awful abuses of power occur under the name of protecting people from themselves, or society from them. You need to be extraordinarily careful, in all counseling work situations, that you serve your client's best interests, meaning the pursuit of personal freedom and responsibility, not the interests of others. This is very difficult because sometimes people are truly out of control and need to be protected from themselves for a time until they can legitimately make good decisions for themselves.

3. *The fundamental driving forces that compel me to do this work are love and compassion.*

If you adopt this value, you will want to develop your ability see connections between yourself and other people, among all people, and indeed, among all living things. This relatedness, this sense of connection, will allow you to conduct yourself with your clients in a way that is truly caring. Think about a person you care deeply about, your child, for example, or your sister. When working with a "difficult" client, ask yourself this question: "How would I be approaching this person if she were my sister?" Obviously, there are many reasons to refrain from counseling your actual children or relatives (it would violate rules of both ethics and common sense), yet what a transformation it could make in your work if you were to treat all of your clients with this "as if" mentality. Your work would automatically be less about "treating" someone or some piece of behavior and more about "caring for" this client's well-being.

I recently attended an event honoring the "pioneers" of the hospice movement. One of the honorees at this event, Florence Wald, who helped found the first residential hospice program in America, suggested that it would be a good idea for all new medical students to spend six weeks doing service work in a hospice program before starting their medical training. What a concept! What an intriguing idea for anyone entering the helping professions—to sit with people where the only possible way of being with them is to be immediately present, without expectations of action or rehabilitation.

When you approach your work with love and compassion, you begin to see how people's lives are so often controlled by fear. So many human problems are the result of decisions or automatic reactions based on fear. When you can learn to deal with your own fears in a way that allows you to operate in a more empathic and loving fashion, this cannot but help your clients to act similarly.

4. *My rewards in this work are primarily intrinsic, as opposed to extrinsic.*

If you adopt this value, it means that you will be less interested in the external rewards that your work with people might yield, such as fees or professional status, and more interested in the less tangible satisfactions of the work, such as affection, connection, and personal learning. The noted analyst Erich Fromm (1989) called this a "being" orientation, as opposed to the "having" orientation, which is the more supported orientation in our culture today. Fromm and others (Wachtel, 1984) maintain that our culture, which is essentially capitalistic and materialistic, encourages the pursuit of money and things by playing on people's personal anxiety and sense of personal emptiness. They see people's attempts to accumulate material possessions, the "having" life, as a futile attempt to fill an internal void, a sense of personal emptiness. Far better, they suggest, to build a life around connections with people and attempts to promote personal self-awareness. This being orientation is not only far more personally rewarding and fulfilling, but it also serves a much better modeling function for our clients. Needless to say, adopting this value does not imply a vow of poverty or that we should not expect to make a decent living wage doing this work.

5. *I approach life with an attitude of gratitude and forgiveness.*

The fact of being alive is wondrous, each day a gift. You may choose the attitude you bring to this life and your work. Given this capacity to choose, why not embrace the positive? If you adopt this value, you will be making a conscious choice to always look at the brighter side. This does not imply denial of negative events, but why give those events more weight than the good things that happen? This also does not imply becoming a cavalier Pollyanna, for you can still maintain all of your critical faculties. You can hone your ability to see all sides of the events that pass by you and simply choose to emphasize the better aspects of those events.

One of the major benefits of having a positive attitudinal approach to life's fortunate and unfortunate happenings is the sense of control that it can give you over what transpires in your life. You are no longer simply at the mercy of life's "slings

---

REFLECTION EXERCISE 2.4   *Attitudes toward Others*

Think of a person or an existing situation in your life that causes you a moderate amount of difficulty (save the major pains for later once you're more practiced). Consider a list of all the negative and positive features of this person or situation, then focus your attention on the positive list, virtually discarding the negative. Think about what would happen if you were to approach this person or situation with this list, and only this list, in your awareness. This is not a list you would actually be sharing. It would simply permeate your thinking.

Should you wish to carry this exercise one step further, experiment carefully with carrying this attitude into actual contact with the person or situation. Note how your newly positive attitude affects the nature of your interaction with the person or situation and your feelings about it. The attitudes we carry very much affect how we actually feel. The cognitive-behavioral approaches to counseling have capitalized on this idea, much as did Norman Vincent Peale (1952) years ago with his book *The Power of Positive Thinking*.

---

and arrows," and you will not be as buffeted by difficulty. You have little control over many of life's events, but you have a great deal of control over how you respond to them. Here is another experiment for you to try.

Related to the concept of gratitude as a life attitude is that of forgiveness. By forgiveness I mean an attitude about life that is oriented toward letting go of the shame, resentment, and guilt you have directed toward yourself or others (Casarjian, 1992). This is a consciously engaged process, sometimes lengthy and difficult, in which a choice is made to no longer blame others for negative transgressions. It is, literally, letting people off the hook for real or imagined things that they have done to you and concurrently letting go of self-blame as well.

You may well ask why an attitude of forgiveness will help you be an effective counselor. Much of your work with clients will revolve around themes of shame, negativity, guilt, and blame. Before you can help them, you need to make peace with the negative themes of your own life. Terrible things may have happened to you personally, traumas and abuses that are excruciatingly painful to think about. Other abuses may have been subtle but perhaps even more insidious. Forgiveness does not imply not being angry about those events, but it requires engaging in a process of work and examination that can help to *detoxify* the hold those emotions have on you. It is actually more about letting yourself off the hook than it is about the other person.

As long as you are consumed by rage and blame over past abuses, you are controlled by them. If you are enraged, your rage ties you intimately to the objects of your resentment. Forgiveness is a process of working through the

---

REFLECTION EXERCISE 2.5   *Approaching Life with Gratitude*

Most of us experience an occasional morning when we wake up "blue," vaguely depressed, just a little off. We are a little more reluctant to leave our bed, and when we do there is a little less spring in our step. We're not clinically depressed, just off. Maybe something unpleasant happened last night, or maybe we're in a funk for no particular obvious reason.

On one of these mornings, try to simply assume a "chipper" attitude, choose to see all of the bright and wonderful things around you (or at least pretend they're lovely), and then bluff it. Simply act as if life is grand for a few hours. See what happens. Fake it, as they say, until you make it.

This may seem simplistic, even inane, but it often works in profound ways. Why? We each create much of our own reality, and people respond to our energy, negative or positive, and that serves to reinforce the attitude and feeling state that is already present. Your attitude and projected feeling state have a synergistic effect. When you are positive and enthusiastic, people are drawn to you, almost as if feeding on the energy. When you are negative, cynical, or depressed, people either avoid you or join in on your rancorous mood. We all surely know the experience of being buoyed by being with someone who is positive and enthusiastic, as well as the downward tug of being with someone who is consistently cynical and negative. Indeed, there is nothing so unpleasant as finding yourself in a room full of cynical, depressed people.

---

rage and blame so that those feelings no longer control you. This can be a major piece of work, which may call for personal counseling or engagement in some spiritual work. Learning the art of forgiveness is certainly a focal point for many spiritual disciplines. It is perhaps an interesting paradox that as you begin to be more forgiving of others, you also begin to forgive yourself. There is something about learning to be gentle with other people that allows you to be gentler with yourself.

Concluding Thoughts: Counselor, Heal Thyself

About midway through their program of study, counseling students often begin to doubt themselves, particularly their own relative mental health and emotional stability. They ask, "How can I help someone else, when I'm such a wreck myself?" This is a legitimate question (and unfortunately too rarely asked by those who need to ask it most). There is such a lot to think about and work through. Your own personal family history, your work life, your loves, your other relationships, your belief system—not to mention all of the course work you are trying to absorb—can all conspire to make you feel inadequate. At times it seems too complex, too cumbersome to sort through, yet there are glimpses of light and clarity that can give you hope and inspiration. You will find supervisors, mentors, and guides—or counselors of your own—to help you shoulder the burden.

It is important to remember that this profession does not require us to be perfect people. If it did, it would be a lonely, unpopulated field. Some of your greatest difficulties and struggles may, in fact, become your greatest assets in understanding the pains and difficulties of others. It is all about the awareness and understanding that you bring to your work, the capacity that you have for seeing yourself with all your strengths and blemishes, that will make it possible for you to work well with others.

You need to give yourself the time to learn about this profession and about yourself. Even the simple reflective exercises in this chapter could take a lifetime to fully appreciate. The process of increasing your self-understanding and the parallel process of learning to work effectively as a counselor is a lifelong, magnificent journey. The two processes feed upon and nurture each other. In this mutual nurturance lies much of the great satisfaction of this work.

For Further Thought

1. What does the literature say about the importance of counselors being relatively healthy people? What does it even mean to be a "healthy person," and what does the literature say about this? You may want to consider expanding your investigation beyond the confines of counseling and psychology literature.

2. Contact one counselor working in a school and one in an agency. Interview these counselors regarding their job responsibilities and the rewards gleaned from this work. To what degree do you see yourself doing this kind or work, and in which setting?

3. What does the research say about the importance of counselors investigating and understanding their own values?

4. Some people have suggested that the children of counselors/psychologists are probably more troubled and behaviorally disturbed than those of the general public. Discuss ways of investigating this question, as well as its relevance for your work. Why is this an important issue to examine?

References

Anderson, D., & Swanson, C. (1994). *Legal issues in licensure.* Alexandria, VA: American Counseling Association.

Barta, M. (1999). The effects of family of origin and personal counseling on self-perceived and supervisor rated counseling skills (Doctoral dissertation, University of Northern Colorado, 1999). *Dissertation Abstracts International, 60*(4-A), 1023.

Brennan, J. (1987). Effects of four training programs on three kinds of empathy. In G. A. Gladstein (Ed.), *Empathy and counseling: Explorations in theory and research* (pp. 135–153). New York: Springer.

Casarjian, R. (1992). *Forgiveness: A bold choice for a peaceful heart.* New York: Bantam Books.

Cavanagh, M. (1990). *The counseling experience.* Prospect Heights, IL: Waveland.

Clemente-Crain, V. (1996). Divorce and psychotherapy: The perceived impact of therapists' family of origin experience upon their practice of psychotherapy. *Dissertation Abstracts International, 56*(12-B), 7040.

Cormier, L., & Cormier, W. (1998). *Fundamental skills and cognitive behavioral interventions* (4th ed.). Pacific Grove, CA: Brooks/Cole.

Council for Accreditation of Counseling and Related Educational Programs (CACREP). (2001). *CACREP accreditation manual.* Alexandria, VA: Author.

Dixon, D. (1980). The caring curriculum. *School and Community, 67*(4), 13–15.

Duan, C., Rose, T., & Kraatz, R. (2002). Empathy. In G. Tryon (Ed.), *Counseling based on process research: Applying what we know* (pp.197–231). Boston: Allyn & Bacon.

Foster, S. (1996, December). Characteristics of an effective counselor. *Counseling Today,* 21.

Fox, D. (2003). Awareness is good, but action is better. *Counseling Psychologist. 31*(3), 299–304.

Fromm, E. (1989). *The art of being.* New York: Continuum Publishing.

Hackney, H., & Cormier, L. (2001). *The professional counselor: A process guide to helping* (4th ed.). Boston: Allyn & Bacon.

Hanna, F., Talley, W., & Guindon, M. (2000). The power of perception: Toward a model of cultural oppression and liberation. *Journal of Counseling and Development, 78,* 430–441.

Hayes, P. (2002). Playing with fire: Countertransference and clinical epistemology. *Journal of Contemporary Psychotherapy, 32*(1), 93–100.

Hillman, J., & Ventura, M. (1992). *We've had a hundred years of psychotherapy and the world's getting worse.* San Francisco: Harper Collins.

Jung, C. G. (1961). *Psychological reflections.* New York: Harper & Brothers.

Kinnier, R., Kernes, J., & Dautheribes, T. (2000). A short list of universal moral values. *Counseling and Values, 45*(1), 4–14.

Kottler, J. (1993). *On being a therapist.* San Francisco: Jossey-Bass.

Lickona, T. (1991). *Educating for character.* New York: Bantam.

Loewen, J. (1995). *Lies my teacher told me: Everything your American history textbook got wrong.* New York: Touchstone.

May, R., Remen, N., Young, D., & Berland, W. (1985). The wounded healer. *Saybrook Review, 5,* 84–93.

Patterson, C. (1989). Values in counseling and psychotherapy. *Counseling and Values, 33*(3), 164–176.

Peale, N. (1952). *The power of positive thinking.* New York: Prentice-Hall.

Pedersen, P., & Ivey, A. (1993). *Culture-centered counseling and interviewing skills: A practical guide.* Westport, CT: Praeger.

Peterson, J. (1976). *Counseling and values.* Cranston, RI: Carroll Press.

Pope, V. T. (1996). Stable personality characteristics of effective counselors: The Counselor Characteristic Inventory (Doctoral dissertation, Idaho State University, 1996). *Dissertation Abstracts International, 57,* 1503.

Raths, L., Harmin, M., & Simon, S. (1978). *Values and teaching: Working with values in the classroom.* Columbus, OH: Merrill.

Reyak-Schelar, R., & Feldman, R. (1984). Health behaviors of psychotherapists. *Journal of Clinical Psychology, 40*(3), 705–710.

Ridley, C. (1995). *Overcoming unintentional racism in counseling and therapy: A practitioner's guide to intentional intervention.* Thousand Oaks, CA: Sage.

Ritter, K.Y. (1984). Personality characteristics, training methods, and counseling effectiveness. *Journal for Specialists in Group Work, 9*(2), 77–84.

Rosik, C. (2003). When therapists do not acknowledge their moral values: Green's response as a case study. *Journal of Marital and Family Therapy, 29*(1), 39–45.

Scheffler, L. W. (1984). *Help thy neighbor.* New York: Grove Press.

Shapiro, E. (1984). Help-seeking: Why people don't. *Research in the Sociology of Organizations, 3,* 213–236.

Smith, M. R. (2003). The relationship between personality traits and trainee effectiveness in counseling sessions: Cognitive flexibility, spirituality, and self-actualization (Doctoral dissertation, University of Nevada, Reno, 2003). *Dissertation Abstracts International, 63,* 2469.

Softas-Nall, B., Baldo, T., & Williams, S. (2001). Family of origin, personality characteristics, and counselor trainees' effectiveness. *Psychological Reports, 88*(3), 854–856.

Strupp, H. (1974). Some observations on the fallacy of value-free psychotherapy and the empty organism: Comments on a case study. *Journal of Abnormal Psychology, 83*(2), 199–201.

Vachon, D., & Agresti, A. (1992). A training proposal to help mental health professionals clarify and manage implicit values in the counseling process. *Professional Psychology: Research and Practice, 23,* 509–514.

Wachtel, P. (1984) *The poverty of affluence: A psychological portrait of the American way of life.* New York: Free Press.

Wegscheider, S. (1981). *Another chance: Hope and health for the alcoholic family.* Palo Alto, CA: Science and Behavior Books.

Wilcox-Mathew, L., Ottens, A., & Minor, C. (1997). An analysis of significant events in counseling. *Journal of Counseling and Development, 75,* 282–291.

Williams, S. C. (1999). Counselor trainee effectiveness: An examination of the relationship between personality characteristics, family of origin functioning, and trainee effectiveness (Doctoral dissertation, University of Northern Colorado, 1999). *Dissertation Abstracts International, 59,* 4494.

Wilson, J. (1994). Is there a difference between professional and personal development for a practicing psychologist? *Educational and Child Psychology, 11*(3), 70–79.

Wittmer, J., Sword, R., & Loesch, L. (1973). Effectiveness of counselor trainees: A comparison of perceived parental behavior. *Journal of the Student Personnel Association for Teacher Education, 12,* 68–75.

Setting the Stage

Mary Rose O'Reilly, the educator and writer, relates a story told by a friend of hers about the preparation to "be present," about getting ready to receive and listen to the concerns of another. The friend had gone to a Buddhist retreat, primarily as a way of dealing with some personal troubles. She asked one of the monks to talk with her about the things that were worrying her.

"He told me to meet him in the garden, under the full moon. We sat down. He looked for a moment at the moon. Then he folded his robes under him and assumed the lotus position. He closed his eyes and said, 'Now I am ready to listen.' I talked for an hour and then he said, 'I understand what you are saying.'"
(O'Reilly, 1998, p. 31)

This monk is one who knows something about creating the space to be present, about "setting the stage." You don't need the robes, the moon, or the full lotus, but you do need to know how to prepare yourself to do this work. Good counseling practice begins with thoughtful consideration and planning of all the practical aspects of delivering your services. These are the "nuts and bolts" considerations that set the stage for effective counseling work with people. When approached with thoughtfulness and respect for how they will be received, these factors may greatly enhance your relationships with clients.

Exercising care with these practicalities is simply the first extension of the empathic consideration you try to build into your counseling relationships. These "details" convey much about you and about how you conduct your life. Your dress and your workspace say as much about you as does your explanation of your theoretical perspective and approach to the work. People can quickly begin to intuit your trustworthiness in the ways you explain the ground rules of your practice, or even in how you market your services. Far from incidental, these practical considerations form the bedrock of safety and security that are the hallmarks of all effective counseling.

In addition to your professional training and preparation, you will attend to four primary concerns before a client even walks in the door: (1) your personal appearance, (2) your workspace, (3) marketing your services, and (4) finding a good supervisor. Now you are ready to plan your first meeting.

Personal Appearance: The Power of First Impressions

I once worked in an agency where I supervised counselors who did presentations and prevention work related to substance abuse issues in local high schools. These two young men were popular with the kids, mostly because they were energetic and fun to be around. They believed strongly in the mission of their work, and their enthusiasm was contagious. The kids loved the way they dressed, which was much in the teen, young-adult fashion of the day. Despite their popularity with students, however, administrators had mixed feelings about these prevention workers. The administrators were convinced, simply by virtue of appearance, that these counselors used drugs themselves. On further questioning, they stated they were mostly concerned that the clothing was representative of an anti-authority, pro-drug attitude that they found troubling. They were primarily concerned—again, based solely on appearance—that the counselors were siding with students against the adult school authorities and its policies.

To resolve the issue, the administrators met with the counselors and shared their concerns. The counselors listened nondefensively, talked about their commitment to honor school policy and not undermine the administrators, and declared their disdain for drugs. The administrators, with their essential fears put to rest, let up on the dress issue. The counselors took away from this experience a heightened appreciation of the impact their appearance had had on these administrators. There is a lesson for us all here. The way we dress is representative of who we are, and it serves to provoke a response in the people with whom we work.

I certainly have recollections of the ways my own clothing and appearance have affected my clients. I vividly recall one such event with one of my first private clients. He had been referred to me by the local court diversion program, which offered him counseling treatment in lieu of jail time. (It's always flattering to be sought out as the more attractive alternative.) This man walked into my office, sat down, looked me in the eye and said, "I hate ties." Given that this was in the days before I decided to steer a more casual clothing course, I was wearing one of my finest regal-striped silk ties. I was actually quite proud of my tie and thought it made me look pretty sharp and professional. I was, however, able to put aside my pride, and I was quick enough to correctly surmise that his comment really had little to do with ties and much more to do with his historical relationship with authority, which was represented by all of those whom he'd encountered in the world of "ties." So we began a discussion about ties and all that they represented for him.

The tie was a provocative symbol for this new client of mine. In the absence of any real relationship, outward appearance was all he had to go on, and his suspicion was that I would probably be another authority figure who would try to tell him how to run his life. In the absence or lack of history of a relationship, appearance is all any of us have to go on. Whether your appearance is provocative,

---

REFLECTION EXERCISE 3.1 *Your Personal Appearance*

Briefly close your eyes and envision yourself in your mind's eye. See yourself standing, as if in front of a mirror. How do you appear? What is your general demeanor and appearance? How would you characterize your posture? Do you look comfortable? Do you like what you see? Take note of your hairstyle, your facial expression, and other obvious aspects of yourself. How are you dressed? What is your general impression of what you see in the mirror?

Consider how this view of yourself is the same or different from your picture of yourself five or ten years ago. Note how these changes in your appearance might reflect possible changes in your life.

Now consider the future. How do you think others will react to your appearance? What are your assumptions about their impressions? Will you change any aspect of your appearance when you meet with clients in the counseling workplace?

---

conservative, or gaudy, your clients will make snap judgments about your skill and professional abilities based on your "look."

Being thoughtful and consciously aware of your personal appearance is important. There's no getting around it—your attire and appearance will affect how your clients perceive your competence (Hubble & Gelso, 1978; Vargas & Borkowski, 1983). It is probably best to steer a moderate course when you dress for work (Heitmeyer & Goldsmith, 1990).

The Counseling Workspace

A primary consideration in getting started in any counseling practice—and this includes public, private, or a school setting—has to do with the place you choose to do your work, most likely some kind of counseling office. The best offices ensure privacy, are soundproofed, and feel comfortable to both you and your clients. The office is a sanctuary for your work, a place where the people you serve feel safe and protected. It must also be a place where you feel safe because some of your clients may be volatile. Physical safety issues (emergency exits, availability of other people for assistance, and so forth) should be a first item of concern when selecting your office space or evaluating the space provided to you. If you do not feel physically safe, you cannot provide any kind of emotional protection for your clients. Another important concern is sufficient parking and access for people with physical challenges.

The ideal workspace is a place where people can come to settle in and feel protected in this brief time-out from their regular lives. Your office should be neutral but not cold, the décor attractive and aesthetically pleasing. An office that is attractive and thoughtfully furnished is an asset to the counseling activities that happen there (Pressly & Heesacker, 2001). If you intend to work with children, you should also take into account the need to have toys and room for activities as well as furniture of an appropriate size (Erdman & Lampe, 1996).

If your office is in a school, you may encounter some unique challenges in creating a safe, inviting space for counseling work with students or parents. School counseling offices often do not provide much privacy, and they almost always have common waiting areas where anyone can see which students are coming for help. Typically, there is considerable activity in the area outside of offices, with all the energy that children and adolescents can generate. If you will be doing school counseling, you might want to visit some of the counselors in other area schools to get ideas about how people create good counseling workspaces in those environments. It is your job to do the best you can to make these offices as inviting and as private as possible while sensitizing school boards and administrators to the real physical space needs of school counseling services.

Ideal office spaces are adequately soundproofed so that people in a waiting area outside cannot hear conversation inside the office. Double doors, extra insulation, and soft music piped into waiting areas are all potential soundproofing aids. Good office planning also permits clients to come and go without being observed by others (particularly their neighbors and friends—a common complaint from many clients of community mental health services). A storefront next to a large supermarket is a poor choice for an office. This is typically more of an issue in small rural towns than it is in larger metropolitan areas. Ideally, you may consider separate waiting and exit areas, perhaps allowing for some time in an exit area for clients to put on a "street face" before going back out into the world. It will sometimes be difficult for your clients to reenter the everyday social whirl after talking about intensely personal issues, and it can be very helpful if you give them some private time and space to decompress.

Similarly, if you have control over scheduling appointments, stagger appointments so that your clients do not encounter each other coming and going. Allowing for some time between appointments can help to ensure that your clients will not run into each other, and it will also give you time to regroup between sessions. Just as your clients may engage in active fantasies about your life with your family, some will think about you with your other clients. That fantasizing is inevitable and may become part of the work the two of you do together, but it does not need to be made more intense by poorly designed spaces and tight appointment setting.

Over the thirty odd years that I've done this kind of work, I've had a wide variety of offices. One was in the back of a union hall in a rough neighborhood, another in an old farmhouse that was part of a residential drug treatment program, yet another in a downtown office building. For many years, my private counseling practice was held in a downstairs wing of my home, a place that was separate and distinct from the rest of the house, with its own bathroom and entrances. For personal convenience I certainly enjoyed this home office arrangement, but I eventually gave it up and would think long and hard before doing it again. I came to see problems associated with an office in the home, no matter how distinct and private the space seems. It's too easy, even with the best precautions, for the occasional confusions of family life to intrude on the privacy of the counseling work. There was, for example, the day that one of my clients had to pick his way over the fire hoses used by firefighters to put out a chimney fire, saying something like, "Maybe this isn't the best day to come." I'm sure my counseling office didn't seem like much of a sanctuary to him in the midst of all that. Then there were the occasional children's screams—no amount of soundproofing can block out all noise—and the confusion of cars coming and going in the driveway. I'm sure you get the picture. Your desire to establish a space for personal convenience has to be weighed against the implications for your counseling work.

Furnishing Your Office

Your office is your space, and it should be comfortable for you and reflect who you are. Personal mementos, photographs, and artwork are all appropriate but should be carefully thought about in regard to their potential impact on people who come there. Anything you have in your office may serve as either a comfort or a distraction. Photographs of your family may signal to your client that, in fact, you do "have a life," yet they may also provide opportunity for unhelpful fantasies and digressive conversations about the nature of your personal life. Your client may subtly engage in fantasized competitive struggles with your children or your partner—fantasies that are nurtured by your photos.

In one of my offices I once put up some framed political posters I had recently brought back from a trip to Cuba. After contemplating them, one of my clients spent the better part of a session talking about the Cuban revolution and his dislike for Castro. We were able, after some time, to turn this conversation in some more personally relevant directions, but I recognized that the posters were unnecessarily provocative. Shortly after that encounter, I took the posters down. Keep in mind that anything you have in your office may serve as an object onto which your clients may project thoughts and feelings.

Your furniture should be comfortable and inviting, but not overly intimate. Your office should communicate the message that this is a place for personal sharing, but not for seduction. Couches, for some clients, communicate too intimate a message, and two people (e.g., in group or couples counseling) may not want to sit so closely together. I favor comfortable chairs, a few feet apart, facing one another at an angle that allows for face-to-face contact but also affords the opportunity to look away. You want to maintain solid visual contact with your clients, yet sometimes they will need to visually get away from you, to go within themselves. Yalom (1985) refers to the best relationships we have with our clients as "interpersonal communion." In contrast, those relationships individuals have within themselves he calls "intrapersonal communion." Looking away allows for that different, inner, more internal introspection. Your chair placements subtly communicate your willingness to allow for both kinds of contemplation.

In arranging your furniture, give serious consideration to the possible need for flight in the event that a "difficult" client becomes threatening or loses control. It can happen. Positioning your chair closest to the door is one simple way to be prepared in the event that you are working with a potentially volatile person. With some clients you will want to leave your door open so that others can hear you if you need to call for help. And needless to say, you should schedule appointments with possibly volatile clients at times when outside help is available. Chapter 12 deals specifically with how to respond to difficult, hostile, or out-of-control clients.

You will most likely also have a desk and some peripheral equipment, such as computers, phones, filing cabinets, lights, and plants. Each of these requires thought and attention. The placement of your desk tells your client much about the power of the relationship between the two of you. If you sit behind it, the desk clearly states your desire to remain in the position of control and power. If you put it behind you, it suggests that the stage is set for communication between two equals. Computers and telephones have become an integral part of all of our lives and need to be managed so as not to intrude on real relationship encounters, particularly counseling relationships. Your phone should be silenced while you are working with someone, with no possibility that messages left on machines will be overheard. Computer information should be held as securely as possible, with no screens visible to someone entering your office. The amount of client information now traveling in cyberspace is staggering, particularly billing and diagnostic data, and the potential for privacy and confidentiality violations is great. Be wary about the information you contribute to this cyber glut.

Also, live and work with the awareness that even the best security may not be foolproof. My office was broken into once, most likely by someone looking for drugs. I am not a physician, so I don't prescribe medications and would never have had drugs on site, but an addict might not stop to consider the nuances of professional affiliation in the desperate search to get high. Fortunately for me, the burglar was not interested in examining records but did manage to find some billing forms and start a small fire in a back room. The fire did minimal damage, but the whole incident drove home with brilliant clarity the need for secure record storage. Bad things can happen.

Many schools and agencies have specific rules and regulations related to the storage of information about clients, in either electronic or actual hard copy format. You will certainly want to become informed about these procedures; in the absence of such directives, take steps to ensure the privacy of all your record keeping. You may also assume that at some point there will be a request to see your

---

REFLECTION EXERCISE 3.2   *Furnishing Your Office*

Sitting quietly, create a picture in your mind's eye of your ideal office space and its furnishings. What size is this space, what shape? Is it in a modern or an older building? Are there windows, and what kind of lighting do you have? What furniture and personal effects have you chosen to bring into this space?

As you imagine yourself alone in this office, consider the feelings that arise being there. Finally, if you have a real office now, how does your ideal space compare with the reality of what you now have?

---

records about some client. Develop clear protocols for detailing the situations and the information you will share and the process by which you will share that information.

Finally, it is helpful to have a clock with an appropriately sized display conveniently placed so that both you and your client can see it. This allows you both to know how much available time remains. The issue of time and time management is usually a major factor in a single counseling session, not only for its own value but also for the metaphoric value it serves.

Managing Distractions

A perfectly designed office is only as good as the way it is utilized. Answering the telephone while in the midst of some important career or college planning work with a student communicates a negative message about what you think of the relative importance of that student. Eating a sandwich while listening to a client's disturbing stories of difficulties with an abusive spouse is another variation of this kind of disrespect. It is your job, your primary obligation in this work, to be as fully present as possible with your clients during those times you have committed specifically to them. You do not owe them your life, but you do owe them your undivided attention.

Make sure that unwanted distractions from the outer world do not invade this space while you are at work with someone. Handle outside intrusions, such as visits or phone calls from colleagues and secretaries, in a way that ensures you won't be interrupted. Do not casually switch appointment times or take unannounced time away from scheduled time. Each appointment switch opens the door for clients' speculation about their relative worth in your scheme of things. Some of your clients will have ample speculation of this sort, even without your provocation. There is no need to add fuel to the fire.

More subtle, but no less important, is the frame of mind you bring to the counseling session. Just as important as managing the external distractions that potentially threaten your time with a client is the way you manage your internal world of distraction. You have all of the chatter of your life—the shopping to be done, the bills to be paid, appointments with your kids' teachers—with which to deal. Your real outer world problems, as well as your own inner world demons, may not only bedevil you but also serve to distract you from the work you need to do. Your job is to silence these distractions and demons in a way that allows you to be as present as possible for the person who sits across from you. This is the rationale for the traditional 50 minute hour, affording 10 minutes to purge yourself of the emotional grip of the last client with time to regroup to face the next client. Do whatever you need to do to maintain presence and focus, whether it is a quick walk around the block or a few minutes of meditation or simply sitting silently.

Home Visits

There may be job situations, or specific times, when you are not doing counseling work in any office. Your job may include outreach counseling, home visits, or allied counseling and case management work in a wide variety of settings. You might be a drug counselor working with addicts on the street or be part of a crisis intervention team being asked to interview a suicidal man at his home. Whether you are in someone's home or out on the streets, try to provide privacy and ensure confidentiality as best you can, perhaps finding the quietest and most protected place possible, and simply work with what you have. Never forget to do all you can, particularly in these situations, to ensure your own safety. This may mean doing home visits with a partner. Do what is necessary to protect both yourself and your clients.

I know counselors and social workers who go to clients' homes routinely as part of their work, and some enjoy and prefer home visits to work in an office. They say that particularly with people distrustful of formal settings they can establish the kind of relationship that would never happen in an office setting. They also especially like the firsthand look at family dynamics that these visits provide.

Home visits can become problematic, however, if not handled carefully. I was once consulting with a family at their home when they told me that their twelve-year-old son had recently stolen a car and run over and killed an elderly woman. They went on to tell me that he was hiding from the police in their back bedroom. This was in the early days of my counseling career, and I had made the mistake of promising blanket confidentiality with the family and what they shared with me, without discussing times when I would need to break confidence. In this case there was a clear need to notify the authorities, and I had placed myself in a difficult spot. The parents and I together eventually successfully negotiated bringing the boy into custody, yet after that event my relationship with the family fell apart. In addition to my error in initially promising total confidentiality, my supervisor and I both looked at the time I spent in the home as a negative factor. I became overinvolved in the family drama as an extension of the world of authority in ways that might have been avoided had I not met with them in their home.

In some work situations home visits are the expected norm (e.g., hospice counseling), or they may provide the best or only way of working. Sometimes a home visit or two is the best way to handle a new client's culturally based suspicions of professional office settings (Bean, Perry, & Bedell, 2002; Cole, Thomas, & Lee, 1988; Leventhal, 2002; Norton & Manson, 1997). But your goal should be to establish a trusting enough relationship to bring the client into the office for subsequent sessions. At some point in your counseling career, you may be expected to perform home visits, and you may even prefer to work in those settings. Simply enter each home with awareness, and pay attention to the dynamics as they unfold.

Launching Your Practice

Whether you work in an agency, a school, or have some kind of private practice, if you want to have clients come to see you, the community in which you work will need to know you're open for business. People need to know who you are, where you are, and what services you provide. It is your business to tell them.

Establishing Referral Networks

The first step in launching your practice is to begin establishing your referral networks. In a public community counseling setting, this primarily involves letting people with whom you work in the agency know that you're ready to accept clients and making sure that internal referral networks have you plugged into the system. These "networks" include secretaries, intake workers, and any colleagues who might be in a position to refer people to you. Similarly, in a school counseling system, make sure that people know where you are and take steps to make your availability an integral part of referral processes. Other school counselors, teachers, school-based clinicians, and special educators are all potential sources of student referrals. Regardless of the setting, knowing how the formal referral mechanisms work is as important as developing good relationships with your colleagues.

The Mandated Referral

In any of these settings, you may at times find yourself working with a client for whom counseling has been "recommended" (i.e., coerced or leveraged) by someone who thinks counseling for this individual would be helpful. When these clients enter counseling, they are more "pushed" by outside forces and less "pulled" by their own volition. If you prefer to work with clients who come to counseling of their own accord, you will need to develop strategies for defining what kinds of referrals you want and communicate those definitions to the world outside your office.

Some counselors love to work with mandated, coerced clients. They love the action of dealing with the resistant drug abuser, the potential school dropout, or the incarcerated offender. If you would love this work and want to serve these kinds of clients, contact lawyers, judges, and school officials, the people who would typically make such referrals. It may be possible to develop contracts or working service agreements with specific agents who might refer particular types of clients your way. Mechanisms of payment may also need to be negotiated, certainly if you are working privately.

As a member of the counseling profession, you should never agree to work under circumstances where people must see you with no personal volitional choice whatsoever. Being coerced is not the same as being forced into counseling. Coerced clients may face serious consequences for noncompliance with treatment recommendations, but they are nevertheless coming to you of their own accord. Sometimes the alternatives they face for not seeking counseling are ominous ("Would you rather see the counselor or stay in your jail cell?"), but the element of choice is still there. This is also an ethical issue, a reminder that you are always providing service to the individuals with whom you work, secondarily to the systems that oversee them.

Marketing Your Services and Creating Incentives

If you choose to see self-initiated clients only, you will need to develop strategies to attract clients. What will make your service attractive and preferable to other opportunities available to people? Whether practicing publicly or privately, you need to acknowledge that sales is an integral part of your work. Call it marketing, call it outreach, call it by whatever name seems most palatable to you, but somehow get the word out.

It helps if you have some kind of "niche," a counseling specialty for which you can become known in the school or community. Counselors who specialize in working with people with eating disorders or addictions, or with difficult adolescents, children with special needs, or non–college bound high school students provide a particular community with a clear and accessible form of assistance. As in any community, the availability of your services will be passed around by word of mouth. You will need to develop a track record of good work with these special issues and populations if you want the referrals to continue.

It is also helpful to think of incentives. In a school counseling setting, for example, what are the "carrots" that might entice students into your office? Perhaps not calling it "counseling" might be helpful. A number of school counseling programs promote certain of their services as "training" opportunities, in which students will learn techniques for working with others and receive lots of personal help in the process. The simple substitution of the word "training" for "treatment" suggests a far more positive activity, with far less possible stigmatization for participation. As shown in the boxed feature, this "training as treatment" model can be extremely effective in drawing in otherwise recalcitrant students.

Use of Media for Marketing

Billy Graham once remarked that his product, Jesus, was certainly a lot better than soap, so why shouldn't he try to sell Him at least as well as Proctor and Gamble sells soap? It's a crass analogy, perhaps, but you could say similar things about the product we "sell." In a consumer society, if we want people to avail themselves of what we do, we need to play the marketing game well. We can do this with proper perspective, however. Foremost in this perspective, we need to market ethically, meaning without detriment to our clients or our profession, but we do need to

Training as Treatment: Effective Marketing of School Counseling Services

A friend of mine, "Heidi," is a counselor working in a local high school who for many years has had outstanding success in drawing adolescents to her drug prevention programs. Early on in her work she recruited an area training program, a prevention institute, to assist her in getting a range of in-school programs off the ground.

In this institute's model, students are selected from around the state to participate in one-week training programs during the summer, and then they go back into their schools and work with their school counselors to create school-based, relevant prevention programs. The one-week summer program has a variety of informational sessions on family dynamics, substance abuse in families, and interpersonal communication skills. It is packed, in other words, with some great psychoeducational counseling material, tools for students to use both personally and with others. In Heidi's school, students who have been through the program are involved in selecting the next year's group of participants. Getting into these training programs and being selected as a "prevention trainer" has become very competitive. Students in this school are hungry for this training and are eager to be selected to do this group counseling work. Even though they are indirectly being helped in these trainings personally, the fact that they are receiving training to help others serves to elevate the status of the activity.

A simple renaming of "counseling" or "treatment" as "training" may destigmatize the way people perceive your services too. Some school counselors have had great success in attracting students to counseling via the creation of peer counseling programs. I know other school counselors who have become incredibly creative about the titles they invent for the groups they run. The "Banana Splits" certainly sounds a lot less stigmatizing and more inviting to a middle school child than does, say, "Children of Divorce Group."

Sometimes academic credit can be arranged for psychoeducational counseling activities in schools. More tangible rewards, such as food, are sometimes held out as incentives. Pizza or ice cream can be powerful incentives for omnivorous teenagers.

Naturally, if you work in another kind of counseling setting outside of a school, you will similarly strive to think of ways that will make your counseling services attractive to potential clients. Some community-based programs even pay people—with cold, hard cash—as incentives for participation (Reid, Bailey-Dempsey, Cain, Cook, & Burchard, 1994). Experiments in the use of cash incentives have also included attempts to assist in teen pregnancy prevention (Dolgan & Goodman, 1989) and to help clients lose weight (Jeffery, Gerber, Rosenthal, & Lindquist, 1983). Whatever kinds of appropriate incentives you use, they should make your counseling services attractive to those who might benefit from them.

learn how to let the community know about what we do and to help them see our work as an integral part of community well-being.

Counselors sometimes use media, particularly print media, to market their services. There are persuasive arguments on the side of effective marketing. Wittman (1988) argues that new counselors need to become conversant with a consumer-oriented model of counseling to effectively provide service to the

---

REFLECTION EXERCISE 3.3   *Marketing Your Counseling Services*

Create a mock-up of an advertisement that describes the counseling services you want to provide. Make sure that you include the name of the service, the location and the times you are available at that location, and some information about you and your qualifications. What kinds of graphics will you include with this? How would this be portrayed in a newspaper or a magazine? Now, how could you portray this same information in a television ad? How could you best convey your message in this medium? Would such advertising be appropriate?

As a variation, intentionally make some advertisements that are "tacky." Make them "sleazily effective." What is it about these new variations that make them tacky and unethical? Show your advertisements to your colleagues, both the sound and unsound versions, and discuss their relative merits as well as their potential problems.

---

community. Gilchrist and Stringer (1992) provide solid guidelines for counselors wanting to market their services professionally and ethically. They, as well as others (Fong-Beyette, 1988; Stadler, 1988), say that a marketing strategy should never demean the profession by way of gimmicky advertising, and that all strategies should be congruent with sound counseling practices and ethical considerations.

Community Service as Effective Marketing

Too many counselors simply wait in their offices for people to come to them. You need to be out in your community, serving on committees, providing assistance related to your specific skills, and participating in the world in which you live. All of these involvements will serve your community and will enrich your counseling work. Not all of these services will be financially reimbursed, but they may be seen as part of the professional community service role you play. Further, there is indirect benefit in that these involvements will alert people to your presence and the services you provide.

Naturally, the best insurance for steady referrals is doing good work. Whether you work in a school setting, in a jail, or in a community mental health clinic, the word will get around if you are a concerned and helpful ally and a worthy advocate. It will also get around if you are not. Learning to do this work well, with minimal distraction from your personal life, is the best way to guarantee continuing counseling business.

Finding a Good Supervisor

Central to any competent counseling practice is appropriate supervision. It sometimes comes as a surprise to new counselors-in-training that supervision is an expected, integral aspect of counseling work. They have typically thought of a supervisor as someone who passes the dictates of management down to the workers, the supervisees, makes evaluative judgments about work performance, and reports them to management. That is certainly the model of supervision used in many organizations.

The concept of supervision in counseling is different. In this profession, the clinical or school counseling supervisor is meant to serve the supervisee as a support person, as a mentor and a guide. This is a person to whom a counselor can turn when troubled, or when undecided about how to handle a difficult client. The supervisor is a confidant, a co-conspirator. If counseling were a NASCAR event, the counselor would be the driver and the supervisor would be part of the pit crew.

In some senses, a good supervisory relationship runs exactly parallel to the counseling relationship, with many of the same ingredients inherent in the effective counseling relationship (Beyer, 1995; White & Queener, 2003). If, as Rogers (1951) asserts, the counselor is to provide ample respect, genuineness, and positive regard to those she serves, then so does the supervisor provide those same things to the counselor under supervision. The capacity for empathy, the ability to understand and see the world from the other's perspective, is key to both successful counseling and supervision, and good supervisors have ample capacity to provide empathic presence. Counselors talk of the supervisor as someone to whom they can turn when in real difficulty, as well as for routine matters of consultation. In surveying the literature and professionals working in the field, Carifo and Hess (1987) and Smith (2000) identify a number of characteristics of ideal supervisors. Summarily, these include the following:

- Having empathy, respect, genuineness, and concern
- Being invested in the supervisee
- Having a working knowledge of human behavior and the counseling process
- Using appropriate teaching, goal-setting, and feedback mechanisms

A good supervisor may be hard to find. If your clients have multiple, co-occurring disorders, you may even need more than one supervisor with expertise in those areas of complaint. It is your job, an ethical expectation, to find a competent supervisor in the event that your school or agency doesn't automatically supply one. Unfortunately, our profession suffers from too few opportunities for learning how to do good supervision, a lack of clarity about legal implications for supervisors, and a dearth of the kinds of research evidence that might provide guidance for solid supervisory practice (Goodyear & Bernard, 1998; Herlihy, Gray, & McCollum, 2002; Osborn & Davis, 1996). All of these issues conspire to make the search for quality supervision sometimes a cumbersome process.

School counseling settings can be particularly difficult places to find consistent, ongoing supervision. Roberts and Borders (1994) suggest that school counselors are a little like cacti in that "both survive on a minimum of nutrients from the environment" (p. 103). They argue that school counseling supervision is often simply dressed-up administrative direction. Good supervision should certainly encompass much more than that. Despite the obstacles to finding a trained supervisor, you should be able to find a master counselor who, even though she may not have had formal supervisory training, is capable of providing supervisory support for less experienced colleagues. Also, there are models for developing peer support networks in places where supervision may not be readily available (Crutchfield & Borders, 1997).

When you are trying to choose a supervisor, look for a person who is empathic, respectful, and receptive to your ideas. You also want a supervisor whom you admire, a person who will be a kind of mentor, perhaps with a theoretical approach you would like to emulate. This is someone who will be as much teacher as counselor, and you want the lessons to be ones worth learning.

No matter what her theoretical orientation, level of personal warmth, and professional expertise may be, a supervisor also needs to have time for you. She needs to be available, not only for those emergency crises that may arise but also for the regularly scheduled times you are supposed to meet. Supervision should not be seen as expendable, as an add-on service, and this understanding should be clear from the outset. The time set aside for supervision should be inviolate for both counselor and supervisor. Undoubtedly, emergencies will arise that will necessitate canceling a specific supervision session, but if these emergencies become regular events, they signal difficulty, either with organizational functioning or with supervisor commitment.

Finally, in addition to personal characteristics and availability, the ideal supervisor is unconnected to organizational evaluation of the counselor's work. Your supervisor, in other words, should not be making recommendations to the administration about your job performance or relative worth to the school or agency. Your supervisor should be a person to whom you can turn at your most vulnerable times without fear that your job will be in jeopardy if you talk of your perceived personal inadequacies and your mistakes. This means that you may have two supervisors, one to whom you answer administratively, the other a trusted confidant and mentor. For your day-to-day work, an on-site administrative supervisor can provide adequate organizational and legal support. You may need to look outside your work setting for that other kind of supervisor, the one who lends emotional and clinical support.

Planning for Your First Meeting

Your first meeting with a new client is one of the most important times you'll spend with the client, for it is in this meeting that the client will make essential decisions about continuing. You might plan, if you have the latitude, on some extra time for this first session so that you can accomplish all that needs to be done. This extra time will be well spent if it pays off in fully engaging your new client (Tryon, 2002).

Broadly, you will be trying to accomplish three primary goals for this session: initial engagement (providing support and engaging the client in the process), education (giving the client information about counseling and about how you work), and assessment (beginning to ascertain this person's strengths and deficits).

To build rapport, a bond between you and your client, you will need to use all of your empathy-building skills to communicate your concern and understanding (Lyddon, Clay, & Sparks, 2001). For the client, engagement means not only feeling a rapport with the counselor but also believing that coming for counseling was the right decision. The client will be motivated to come back only if she leaves the first session with the hope that future sessions will be productive. The support you provide, as well as engaging and educating the new client about the process of counseling, will take up the bulk of this first session. The skills you'll use to build rapport while assessing your client's needs are discussed thoroughly in Chapters 4, 5, and 6. Before we go on, let us look at the practical matter of educating a new client about the counseling process in the first session.

Letting a client know what to expect from counseling, and what will be expected of him, has both practical and ethical value. You need to provide new clients with information, so plan for enough time in the first session to cover all the essentials. Here are some typical things you will need to cover in this first session:

- *Information about counseling and about how you work.* Some of your clients will have little or no experience with counseling and will want to know how this is going to work. A new client needs to understand what is to be expected of him. A new client might need to be told, for example, that it will be his responsibility to bring in material to talk about. As another example, this could be a good time to tell a client that you'll expect him to do homework assignments or other outside work.

- *Your qualifications.* A new client has a right to know about your professional background as it relates to your work with him. You can provide this information briefly for those clients who want to know.

- *Fees.* This is a time to talk about how your client will reimburse you for services, whether it's via insurance, direct payment, or some kind of sliding fee scale arrangement. School counselors, naturally, are exempt from this kind of information-giving.

- *Ground rules.* Clearly articulate the rules that will help to keep this counseling relationship secure. Times and length of meetings, confidentiality and its limits (e.g., with whom you'll share information, such as parents or insurance companies, and what kinds of information will be shared with them), including when you might need to report to outside authorities (in the event of abuse or risk of harm, for example) are all ground rule items that your client will need to understand.

- *Informed consent.* Your client needs to be fully informed about the counseling process and about how all information about him, including any standardized test results, will be used. If you think you'll recommend any testing, your client will need to understand something about those tests and what they mean. This may, of course, eventually be part of a longer conversation when the testing is done.

This is a lot of information. It is a lot for someone under the best of circumstances to remember. In this situation, however, you'll be giving this information to someone who feels vulnerable and is perhaps highly anxious (Moursund & Kenney, 2001). Because of this vulnerability and anxiety, the client may be only partially capable of retaining much of what you say. For this reason, many counselors I know hand new clients a fact sheet with much of this relevant information on it, so that clients can take it home and read it later. It has been my practice to do a brief overview of the most critical information with a new client in the office, and then to also send him home with a fact sheet.

Sandwich this information in and around the support you're providing, and make it an important part of the engagement. Try to make the information manageable and understandable, but don't let it dominate the session. Your client has come to you for help, and he wants to tell you his story. The information should help to support the hope you hold out for positive things happening between the two of you.

Concluding Thoughts: Putting It All Together

By now it should be obvious that the professional counselor's job is more complicated than simply sitting down and listening to someone. Advanced planning is important, not only to ensure that people will avail themselves of your services but also so that you will get off to the best start possible once you do sit down to talk with someone. Careful attention to the details of the context in which you work—your personal appearance, the setting in which you work, and your supervisory support system—will help to convey to your new client the notion that you are a safe and trustworthy person with whom she or he can work. That planning, coupled with your ideas about what needs to be done in the first meeting, will do much to communicate your competency to hear this person's concerns.

For Further Thought

1. Find advertisements in local newspapers, magazines, or in other sources that market counseling services. Discuss the relative merits of these. Also look at advertising for other professional fields and discuss its merits. Are there things the counseling field could learn and borrow from these other professions? Are there advertising strategies that other professions use that counselors should avoid?

2. Identify counselors in your area who work in different kinds of settings and have different professional affiliations. Visit them in their offices and ask about the positive aspects of their office settings and about the drawbacks of their offices. What is your personal impression of the spaces in which they work?

3. Call five counselors in your area and ask them how they are supervised. Interview them about the professional training, theoretical orientation, and personal style of their supervisors. Which of these supervisor descriptions most appeal to you?

4. Investigate the literature related to the impact of counselor attire on client outcomes. What implications do you see this having for your working attire?

References

Bean, R., Perry, B., & Bedell, T. (2002). Developing culturally competent marriage and family therapists: Treatment guidelines for non-African-American therapists working with African-American families. *Journal of Marital and Family Therapy, 28*(2), 153–164.

Beyer, G. (1995). Parallel process in psychotherapy supervision and its relationship to empathy. (Doctoral dissertation, Western Michigan University, 1995). *Dissertation Abstracts International, 56*(6-B), 3432.

Carifo, M., & Hess, A. (1987). Who is the ideal supervisor. *Professional Psychology: Research and Practice, 18*(2), 244–250.

Cole, S., Thomas, A., & Lee, C. (1988). School counselor and school psychologist: Partners in minority family outreach. *Journal of Multicultural Counseling and Development, 16*(3), 110–116.

Crutchfield, L., & Borders, L. (1997). Impact of two clinical peer supervision models on practicing school counselors. *Journal of Counseling and Development, 75*(3), 219–230.

Dolgan, J., & Goodman, S. (1989). *Dollar-a-day teenage pregnancy prevention program.* Denver: Planned Parenthood of the Rocky Mountains.

Erdman, P., & Lampe, R. (1996). Adapting basic skills to counsel children. *Journal of Counseling and Development, 74,* 374–377.

Fong-Beyette, M. (1988). Do counseling and marketing mix? *Counselor Education and Supervision, 27*(4), 315–319.

Gilchrist, L., & Stringer, M. (1992). Marketing counseling: Guidelines for training and practice. *Counselor Education and Supervision, 31*(3), 154–162.

Goodyear, R., & Bernard, J. (1998). Clinical supervision: Lessons from the literature. *Counselor Education and Supervision, 38*(1), 6–23.

Heitmeyer, J., & Goldsmith, E. (1990). Attire, an influence on perceptions of counselors' characteristics. *Perceptual and Motor Skills, 70*(3), 923–929.

Herlihy, B., Gray, N., & McCollum, V. (2002). Legal and ethical issues in school counselor supervision. *Professional School Counseling, 6*(1), 55–60.

Hubble, M., & Gelso, C. (1978). Effects of counselor attire in an initial interview. *Journal of Counseling Psychology, 25,* 581–584.

Jeffery, R., Gerber, W., Rosenthal, B., & Lindquist, R. (1983). Monetary contracts in weight control: Effectiveness of group and individual contracts of varying size. *Journal of Consulting and Clinical Psychology, 51*(2), 242–248.

Leventhal, J. (2002). Editorial: Preventing child abuse and neglect. We (you, your colleagues, and I) have to do more. *Clinical Child Psychology and Psychiatry, 7*(4), 501–504.

Lyddon, W., Clay, A., & Sparks, C. (2001). Metaphor and change in counseling. *Journal of Counseling and Development, 79*(3), 269–274.

Moursund, J., & Kenny, M. (2001). *The process of counseling and therapy* (4th ed.). Englewood Cliffs, NJ: Prentice-Hall.

Norton, I., & Manson, S. (1997). Domestic violence intervention in an urban Indian health center. *Community Mental Health Journal, 33*(4), 331–337.

O'Reilly, M. (1998). *Radical presence: Teaching as contemplative practice.* Portsmouth, NH: Boynton/Cook.

Osborn, C., & Davis, T. (1996). The supervision contract: Making it perfectly clear. *Clinical Supervisor, 14*(2), 121–134.

Pressly, P., & Heesacker, M. (2001). The physical environment and counseling: A review of theory and research. *Journal of Counseling and Development, 79,* 148–160.

Reid, W., Bailey-Dempsey, C., Cain, E., Cook, T., & Burchard, J. (1994). Cash incentives versus case management: Can money replace services in preventing school failure? *Social Work Research, 18*(4), 227–236.

Roberts, E., & Borders, L. (1994). Supervision of school counselors: Administrative, program, and counseling. *School Counselor, 41*(3), 149–157.

Rogers, C. (1951). *Client centered therapy.* Boston: Houghton Mifflin.

Smith, M. (2000). Supervision of fear in social work: A re-evaluation of reassurance. *Journal of Social Work Practice, 14*(1), 17–26.

Stadler, H. (1988). Marketing counseling: Caveat emptor. *Counselor Education and Supervision, 27*(4), 320–322.

Tryon, G. (2002). *Counseling based on process research: Applying what we know.* Boston: Allyn & Bacon.

Vargas, A., & Borkowski, J. (1983). Physical attractiveness: Interactive effects of counselor and client on counseling processes. *Journal of Counseling Psychology, 30*(2), 146–157.

White, V., & Queener, J. (2003). Supervisor and supervisee attachments and social provisions related to the supervisory working alliance. *Counselor Education and Supervision, 42*(3), 203–218.

Wittman, P. (1988). Marketing counseling: What counseling can learn from the other health care professions. *Counselor Education and Supervision, 27*(4), 308–314.

Yalom, I. (1985). *The theory and practice of group psychotherapy.* New York: Basic Books.

Skills for Engaging a New Client

When in doubt, make a fool of yourself. There is a microscopically thin line between being brilliantly creative and acting like the most gigantic idiot on the earth. So, what the hell, leap.

(Cynthia Heimel)

Starting a new counseling relationship demands that the counselor be able both to get the mechanics of the counseling relationship up and running and attend to the needs of the incipient relationship itself. Engage your new client in relationship with you, and find out who this new person is and why he has come to see you. This requires the ability to juggle some complexity and ambiguity. It is also helpful if you can tolerate a number of things going on at once, not necessarily in linear fashion. Experience will be helpful as you learn how to efficiently weave together engaging your new client, educating him about the process of counseling, and beginning the process of assessment.

All of these things you do with a new client should conspire together to create an empathic context within which the two of you can work. The working alliance between the two of you is nurtured by your ability to be present with genuineness, positive regard, and respect, all of which convey your empathic acceptance of this person. Each of the things you do and say, including your verbal and nonverbal behavior, is relevant to empathic communication. The importance of this empathic foundation is discussed more completely in Chapter 6.

This chapter examines some of the skills you can use to engage your client. Nonverbal behavior—both your own and your client's—is a good starting place. Much can be conveyed without saying a single word. In addition, questions, silence, and simple prompts can be used to draw your client into relationship with you and help you understand his reasons for seeking counseling.

The Importance of Nonverbal Behavior

I was once asked to take on as a new client someone with whom a counselor friend of mine had been working. She was having trouble working with him, she said, because she had gotten frustrated with the man's jailhouse mentality and his resistant behavior. She felt that they hadn't accomplished much together and that it clearly was time for someone else to try to work with him. I made an appointment to see him the next week.

When it was time for the appointment, he walked into the office, sat down next to my desk, and put his hands on the desk in front of me. He was smiling and seemed affable enough, but his hands were rolled up in fists. Crude tattooed letters, one per knuckle, stared up at me. The four letters on his left hand started with the letter "F," the three on his right, with "Y." Despite this display of limited vocabulary, the message was clear.

I didn't need many of my years of professional training and work experience to know that this was a young man with some "issues." I had watched him walk into the office with a gait that was controlled and filled with tension. His facial features, his posture, and his overall demeanor radiated defiance. And then there were the hands. I could simply look at this graphic message on his hands and begin to speculate about the abuses and trauma that he had perpetrated and to which he'd been subjected. I knew that he was probably similarly sizing me up. He probably looked at the way I dressed as representative of established authority and assumed that the fact that this meeting was taking place in my space meant that I had a lot of control about the way this counseling thing was going to go.

Volumes of information are available to you about your client, as well as to your client about you, in this time before any words are spoken. The way someone enters your workspace, the style with which he presents himself, his appearance and dress—all of this is important, observable material. Similarly, the way you nonverbally present yourself is an important opening clue to your client about what he can expect from you. If you have the opportunity to observe someone before your actual first interaction, capitalize on the opportunity to watch without being involved interactively. I am not advocating actually spying on new students or clients, but oftentimes it is possible to simply observe someone as he approaches your workplace.

The office I use for my counseling practice offers a good view of the parking lot and the outside grounds. I am able to watch a new client park her car and walk along the gardens and lawn to my office. All of this observed behavior becomes grist for the therapeutic mill. I watch how she carries herself, how preoccupied with herself she seems to be. Is there a skip in her gait, or is it heavy and ponderous? Can she take in and seem to appreciate the beauty of flowers and trees, or is she so wrapped up in herself that seeing outward is not an option?

Your ability to make mental notes of these styles and modes of behavior can be extremely helpful as you contemplate the ways of talking with someone. Similarly, your ability to respond to shifts in nonverbal behavior during your time with your client will play an important role in the outcomes of that work (Highlen & Hill, 1984). Practiced observation, particularly as part of skills training in nonverbal communication, can improve your effectiveness in this arena (Grace & Kivlighan, 1995).

Becoming a Student of Nonverbal Behavior

There is a wealth of information in how people carry themselves, if you can see it. The body tells you a great deal about a person's place in the world and about his attitude. Counseling theories that focus attention on the body as a vehicle for therapeutic work, such as Bioenergetics (Lowen, 1958), Gestalt therapy (Perls, Hefferline, & Goodman, 1951/1994), and Reichian therapy (Reich, 1949), contend that our bodies carry all of our emotional history and that we adopt characteristic body postures (e.g., tight shoulders, clenched jaws, frightened eyes) that betray our history. Although Reichian therapy and Bioenergetics are not widely practiced today, our everyday language still emphasizes this characteristic body posturing (Smith, 1985). "He carries the world on his shoulders" describes the toll responsibility can take on one. "She looks like she wants to bite somebody's head off" describes another's aggression. "He looks like a deer in the headlights" is an obvious reference to how fear can be reflected in our eyes. These common expressions speak to our collective understanding of the relationship between thought, feeling, and the body.

The more you can observe people and their bodies, in all kinds of settings, and the more you read what others have said about the relationship of the body and the emotional health of the person, the more adept you will be in taking stock of the nonverbal behavior of the clients who come to you. Reading about any of these body-oriented theories can provide further assistance in understanding the nonverbal behavior before you, as well as your own.

Although there is obvious danger in reading too much into client nonverbal behavior, it can provide wonderful clues as to who this person is. The number of clues that reveal themselves will depend on your ability to be observant. You certainly do not want to make assumptions about this new person or use your observations as a means for challenging her about incongruencies between what she says and how she behaves nonverbally (e.g., smiling while talking about emotionally difficult material), even though some evidence suggests that nonverbal behavior may more honestly portray someone's real thoughts and feelings than what the person tells you (Erickson, Rossi, & Rossi, 1976; Passons, 1975). Cautiously consider how to use your observations once a relationship has been developed and your working alliance is solidly established. The nonverbal behavior you observe at the beginning of the relationship can suggest avenues for future sensitive verbal exploration and assessment.

REFLECTION EXERCISE 4.1   *Observing Nonverbal Behavior*

Commit some time to observing others' nonverbal behavior. Pick a place where you can sit and watch people unobtrusively. A public gathering place such as a cafeteria or library can be a good place for this. Watch people as they move, sit, eat, and talk. Watch them when they are alone as well as when they are in interaction with others. Note differences in their behavior when they are alone or with others.

Focus your attention, again unobtrusively, on a single person's nonverbal behavior. Pay close attention to how this person carries himself in his body. What is his relative physical comfort level? If he has physical limitations, how do these seem to relate to his emotional well-being?

What assumptions might you make about this person's intellectual and emotional life based on your observations of his nonverbal behavior? Could you speculate about this person's interpersonal history based on this observed information?

Taking Stock of Your Own Nonverbal Behavior

The ability to observe a client's nonverbal behavior is important, but so is your awareness of your own nonverbal behavior. Significant evidence suggests that the counselor's nonverbal behavior plays an important role in interactions with clients (Tepper & Haase, 1978; Hill & Stephany, 1990; Kim, Liang, & Li, 2003; Smith-Hanen, 1977). The way you present yourself, your own nonverbal behavior, should be intentional and thoughtfully designed—in as natural a way as possible—to increase the potential for building a connection with this person who has come to see you (Barak, Patkin, & Dell, 1982; Norman, 1982). Use Reflection Exercise 4.2 to explore your own nonverbal behavior and that of a partner.

REFLECTION EXERCISE 4.2   *Communicating through Nonverbal Behavior*

Pick a partner to help you with this exercise, which should take about 10 minutes to complete. Sit facing one another. Tell her that you are going to sit there for about 5 minutes being aware of each other but saying nothing.

As you face this other person, simply sit quietly and observe her. Take in all you can, using all of your senses. Don't limit yourself to what is visually observable, but note even the smaller things like the particular smell of perfume or cologne. Note what happens when eye contact is made, and try to maintain silence throughout.

After a minute or so, focus on your own nonverbal behavior. Try to communicate your own receptiveness and openness to her. Make a mental list of the behaviors you are trying to use to communicate this openness.

Then change your focus to your partner. What kinds of silent cues emanating from this other person seem like invitations to talk? What do you see that increases your desire to talk with her? What behaviors seem less inviting? Make a mental list of all of these, still sitting there quietly.

Spend a minute or so making note of what thoughts and feelings you had while doing this exercise. How much were you influenced, particularly in how you felt, by this other person's presence? Were you distracted from clearly observing the other by thinking about your own presentation? To what degree?

Finally, share your observations with your partner. Focus on behavioral observations in your feedback and avoid any judgmental commentary. Also share, to the degree it feels appropriate, your own thoughts and feelings about your own behavior.

When I have asked students to do this exercise in my counseling classes, they are typically quite taken with how powerful it can be—all kinds of feelings and thoughts can be kicked into motion, simply by sitting silently with another. Take some time in class to reflect and talk about the experience before compiling a list of nonverbal behaviors that influence communication and could assist in developing counseling relationships.

Taking Control of Your Nonverbal Behavior

The lists of nonverbal behaviors my students have generated over the years bear remarkable similarity to the nonverbal behaviors researchers have identified that can influence interpersonal communication (Barak et al., 1982; Norman, 1982). Some influential nonverbal behaviors that seem to help, as well as some that hinder, our ability to connect with clients include the following:

- *Facial expression.* Is your face relaxed, smiling, or pinched up, holding tension and tight, unsmiling? How natural and spontaneous are your facial expressions? We communicate much of our internal world with our faces. Is what you communicate congruent with how you feel and what you want to communicate to your client?

- *Body language.* Are you sitting with reasonably good posture, in an open, straight-ahead fashion, or are your arms and legs crossed protectively? Are you reasonably still and comfortable, or nervous and jittery? Do you occasionally nod your head in understanding (I hope not so much as to look like a bobblehead doll)? Are you expressive with your hands and arms without being overly dramatic?

- *Eye contact.* Are you comfortable looking into the client's eyes, those "mirrors of the soul," or are you looking down or away? Are you able to afford your client some inner privacy by looking away occasionally so as not to become overly intimate or invasive?

- *Voice tone.* Beyond whatever you say, the way it is said can have a great impact on your client. A voice that is gentle and soft, yet clearly heard, communicates respect and a desire for engagement.

Simply becoming more aware of your own nonverbal behavior as you interact with others can be helpful in creating a receptive, engaging environment.

There is a danger, of course, in becoming overly sensitive and so concerned about all of this that you end up being more constricted and unnatural. Find a comfortable balance between the thought and attention paid to your own nonverbal behavior and simply assuming a natural, relaxed, personal way of being with people. As with so many of the counseling skills you are learning, your comfort level will improve with practice. Experience will enable you to let go of your judgments about how you should be behaving nonverbally.

Cultural Influences and Your Nonverbal Behavior

Cultural influences also affect an individual's use of the body as a communication tool (Watson, 1970). Take stock of your nonverbal behavior in terms of your own cultural background and learn to modify it to communicate effectively with clients with different cultural traditions. There are different cultural comfort zones regarding physical proximity and eye contact, for example. Latinos are much more comfortable with close physical proximity, as a case in point, than are Italian Americans or Irish Americans (Sue & Sue, 1990). In contrast to what we talk of here as establishing good eye contact with your client, some Asian Americans may consider too much intimate eye contact disrespectful. African Americans may maintain better eye contact while talking than while listening (Ivey, Ivey, & Simek-Morgan, 1993).

All of this implies that learning the nonverbal language of clients from different cultural backgrounds is part of the business of becoming an effective counselor. Engage all of your cultural empathy and observational skills to take note of your client's comfort zone regarding the varieties of nonverbal behavior, and learn which of your behaviors seem to elicit the most significant positive and negative reactions. You can also invite your client to become your teacher about some of these nonverbal reactions, perhaps even initiating discussion of these comfort zone concerns.

Finding Your Nonverbal Behavior Balance

You want to be able to manage your own nonverbal behaviors while taking stock of those of your client. Don't get so hung up in thinking about your own nonverbal behavior that it distracts you from the real business at hand—observing your client. This suggests a fundamental law of counseling: The more you are focused on yourself, particularly with communicating some kind of image, the less you are focused on the other.

Check in with yourself, with your ideas and feelings, mostly as a way of checking your responses to this other person for the purpose of understanding him. But never lose sight of that fundamental law because the degree to which you are concerned with your own performance, with presenting some image of yourself—even if it is the image of a competent counselor—is inversely related to your capacity to truly understand and respond to this other person as a competent counselor. As is true with so many aspects of this work, the goal is to achieve a balance, in this case a balance between self-awareness and non-preoccupation with self. This will become clearer as we talk more of the complexity of these developing counseling relationships.

Using Questions for Fact-Finding and Engagement

Questions are one of the primary tools at your disposal in the information-gathering process, but they should be used judiciously and only as needed. You will need to ask questions of this new person who has come to see you. For example, you will want to find out her reasons for coming, and there may be some general or specific information about her that you need to know. In most counseling

---

REFLECTION EXERCISE 4.3   *Observing the Effects of Questions in Interpersonal Communication*

Plan to attend some upcoming social event where you will be able to spend time observing interactions between people, perhaps at a party or a meeting. Your goal is to be a more or less nonparticipating observer, but to avoid drawing negative attention to yourself, participate in conversation as necessary.

During this event, watch and listen to interactions between people, and in particular observe what happens when questions are asked. Note the kinds of questions that seem to be genuinely helpful in furthering the dialogue and those that betray a lack of understanding or a lack of caring.

Expand this kind of observation to other social situations in which you find yourself. Observe interactions between colleagues, friends, and family members, and note the quality of these interactions. Much of the process of becoming an effective counselor has to do with the capacity to observe and learn from your observations. As you hone your observational skills and gain proficiency discerning how good listeners create effective questions, you will gain proficiency as a counselor.

Exercise Discussion

The purpose of this exercise is not to make you suspicious of the use of questions, for they serve a valuable purpose, particularly in these initial sessions. Questions are essential tools in helping you learn about your new client and about the reasons she is coming to see you. If your client is in a crisis situation, questions are your best tool for gauging the immediacy and seriousness of risk.

Questions are an invaluable resource for gathering information, but establishing a counseling relationship also requires that you build an emotional climate of trust, respect, and regard with this new client. Counseling is not a mining expedition; it is not about unearthing things in the life of your client. Rather, it is about providing an atmosphere in which your client can feel the freedom to reveal who she is. Counseling is not about doing things *to* people, which questions can imply, but about doing things *with* them. You want to find out things about your client and attend to the business of assessing her strengths and problem areas—for which questions are primarily beneficial—but you also want your client to feel understood and supported. Questions can sometimes interfere with communicating that understanding and support.

situations you will have a plan for gathering the kinds of information you need (Nash, 2003).

Much of our social conversation is based on questioning, oftentimes in detriment to the relationship and the well-being of the other person. Questions too often serve as a distraction rather than deepening our understanding of what has already been said. Questions are wonderful tools for information gathering, but they are generally less than effective for communicating genuine understanding. For example, a new client might say, "Sometimes I just feel like giving up on life and driving my car straight into a tree." If the counselor responds by asking, "Have you been having a lot of trouble with your car?" or "How long have you been driving?" the result is to send the conversation off on a different track rather than help to deepen understanding of the issue the client has raised. Truly inane or irrelevant questions like these insult your client's intelligence. More valuable questions such as "What kinds of thoughts are you having when you feel like this?" or "What do you suppose this is all about?" result in a deeper exploration of the issue.

Reflection Exercise 4.3 may help you understand the limitations of the use of questions.

The Appropriate Use of Questions

Having surveyed some of the problems with the use of questions, let's review possibilities for their effective use. There is definitely a place for the use of questions in the counselor's toolbox, and there is no better tool for quickly finding out the facts of a situation. Police detectives have always known this; questions are the staple of criminal investigations.

When used with skill, balance, and experience, questions can elicit information that might be inaccessible, or at least would take longer to clarify, with other skills. When used by a competent counselor, questions do not come off sounding like a crime drama interrogation, and they can be helpful in priming a new client to talk about herself. In addition, most of us have been conditioned to respond to questions, so your new client will most likely expect you to have a few to ask.

Two kinds of questions are reviewed here: those used for fact-finding (closed) and those used for engagement (open-ended). As the names imply, the former are utilized for speedy fact-finding, the latter for more leisurely elaboration and collaboration. Each of these deserves a place in the counselor's skills repertoire.

Using Fact-Finding (Closed) Questions

Your job may require you to gather certain kinds of information from new clients, or you may have some need to know certain things about them. For this kind of information gathering, fact-finding questions are appropriate. These closed questions are designed to elicit a short, typically factual response. "How old are you?" or "Where do you live?" are typical examples. Using closed questions, you can find out a fair amount of factual, perhaps demographic, information about someone in a relatively short period of time. Fact-finding questions do little to deepen a beginning relationship, however, and may put someone off if too many are strung together, sounding like a detective's interrogation. There is little evidence to suggest that fact-finding questions promote the therapeutic alliance (Barkham & Shapiro, 1986).

Using Engagement (Open-Ended) Questions

Open-ended questions, used to develop relationship and communicate real interest in the other, are designed to elicit a broader, more expansive response. These broader engagement questions often begin with words like "how," or "what," or phrases like "What was it like" (e.g., "to grow up in that kind of family?") or "What is it that's so terrible about that physics class?" These questions, particularly when followed by patient and attentive silence on your part, invite a longer answer. Research evidence suggests that open-ended questions can be helpful in assisting clients to explore feelings (Hill, Helms, Tichenor, Spiegel, O'Grady, & Perry, 1988), and they are generally more likely to yield longer, more in-depth client responses than closed, fact-finding questions (Sternberg, Lamb, Herskowitz, Yudelivitch, Orbach, Esplin, & Hovav, 1997).

Other Simple, Supportive Tools for Engagement

In later chapters we explore the counseling skills that are primarily designed to foster and develop relationship, the foundation of any counseling work. The most helpful of these skills, the reflection of content and feeling is the subject of Chapter 6. The use of silence and the simple prompt are introduced here as they are effective supplements when used with questions to begin the process of engaging a new client.

The Use of Silence

New counselors are sometimes reluctant to allow for silence (Gelso & Fretz, 1992). Anxiety can breed a desire to fill every silence, usually with some new question. Some silence is acceptable, even to be nurtured (Leira, 1995). Learn to avoid the temptation to fill the void that silence implies. Oftentimes there is a great deal happening for your client in that silence, and whatever it

CASE EXAMPLE 4.1   *Using Fact-Finding and Engagement Questions*

In this case, a middle school student has come to her school counselor because of a difficult classroom situation. The counselor has never met with the student but quickly ascertains that something is wrong. For the purpose of examining the use of questions, this counselor will respond only with questions in this interview.

COUNSELOR: So, what is it that brings you down here today? Can you tell me what's bothering you?

The counselor begins with an open-ended question, inviting an expansive response. The second question, although technically closed, is also invitational.

STUDENT: Sure. My Social Studies teacher's been a real jerk, and the other kids in that class are giving me a hard time. [The student has stopped talking but the counselor says nothing.]

The school counselor wisely decides to remain silent and wait for a longer response. Beginning counselors, oftentimes out of anxiety, may not allow for this kind of quiet time.

STUDENT: He always seems to know when I'm not prepared, and then he calls on me. I know the stuff, mostly, but I get all nervous, and then I stutter and stuff, and then the other kids make fun of me. I hate him, and them. I hate them! They're all a bunch of jerks.

The counselor takes in this information, trying to avoid the temptation to simply use the time the client is talking as an opportunity to come up with new questions. She listens intently and also observes the student's nonverbal behavior.

COUNSELOR: Can you tell me the specifics about this, maybe about the last time this happened?

This is technically a closed question, because the student could simply answer with a "yes" or a "no," but the invitation for a longer response is implied.

STUDENT: Well, like yesterday in class I was called on, and I didn't know the answer. We were supposed to have memorized all the capitals of Latin American countries, and I knew a lot of them, but not all of them. I mean, it's not like it's important or anything. I mean, nobody's going to go to any of those places. So, he calls on a couple of kids, and they get them right. But they were candy answers—Mexico, Mexico City. Nicaragua, Managua. Like, duh. Who wouldn't get those? Then he looks over at me, and he says, with this really sarcastic voice, "And what

The counselor is trying to picture this scene, and she begins to get a better sense of how emotionally loaded this situation has been for this student.

(continued)

(Case example 4.1, continued)

about Argentina, Christina? Do you know the capital?

So, of course I drew a blank. I didn't have a clue. I just sat there. I drew a complete blank. It seemed like it was for about 30 minutes, but it was probably only a couple of minutes. Then I tried to say something, but I couldn't get it out. *[She starts to cry.]*

Lots of new questions begin to occur to the counselor, but these are for internal inspection only. For example, "What of the teacher's role in this?" and "How accurate is this student's perception of the reality of the situation?" These are for her own assessment of the situation and not meant for discussion with the student.

COUNSELOR: What were the other kids like when this was going on?

Another open-ended, engagement question.

STUDENT: Oh, they were terrible. Really terrible. It was awful. This one girl behind me, Tammy—you know her, I think—she was the worst. She starts making this low mooing noise, like I'm a cow, or something. Then she goes, "Stooopid, stooopid, stooopid Christina. Cry for me Christina," you know, like that song, "Cry for me, Argentina." She thought she was so funny. And just because I stutter, and I'm big. You know, she really drags out that word "stupid." I hate her, I hate her. And all this time the other kids are cracking up, having a great time. I hate all of them, too. *[She's crying freely now, and getting red in the face.]*

The counselor is beginning to get a sense of how difficult this situation is for this girl. She pays attention to her own feelings as she hears this student begin to articulate hers. Maybe she can even identify with this kind of painful situation. She also notes the mention, again, of stuttering and of being "big."

COUNSELOR: What does the teacher do about all of this, especially about what Tammy's doing?

The counselor is widening the exploration of the situation, again using an engagement question.

STUDENT: Who knows. He wouldn't do anything even if he did know what Tammy was doing. He's such a creep. He's worse than they are. He'd probably jump in and start laughing right along with them.

COUNSELOR: Has this kind of thing been happening a lot?

Looking for specificity, this fact-finding question seems appropriately used here.

STUDENT: Yeah. At least once a week. It's getting so I have stomachaches before I come to school. I dread this class. And it's making me hate school. I mean, I never used to like it, but now I'm really growing

(continued)

(Case example 4.1, continued)

to hate it. I get sick in the morning, and
I can't even sleep.

COUNSELOR: How do you suppose I could
be helpful with all of this?

Engagement question.

STUDENT: I don't know. But last week my
mother told me that she'd heard that you'd be
a good person to talk to if anything went
wrong at school. She's worried about my
getting sick so much. And I guess you could
say things are sure wrong now. But I don't
want her to know about this. She'd get all
weird, come down here and yell at people.
I want to deal with this myself. I just thought
maybe you could help me. Listen to me,
maybe get me out of that class.

Case Discussion

As you see, these kinds of questions, coupled
with a judicious use of silence, can elicit significant material in a relatively short period of
time. They demonstrate the effectiveness of
building on what has already begun to be
talked about as opposed to going in a radically
new direction. This counselor also avoids the
problems associated with asking multiple
questions at one time, a beginner's mistake
that can cause confusion for the client.

Because it exemplifies much of the complexity confronting counselors, spend some time
considering the dynamics of this particular student and counselor interaction. Were the questions asked by the counselor effective? What
other questions could have been asked? If
given the latitude to respond with interventions
other than questions, what else could have
been said? What are the primary issues on the
table here, and how should the counselor begin
to think about responding to them? A swirl of
ideas about this student and her situation begin
to coalesce. The student has mentioned a
potentially caustic set of relationships with
other students and the teacher, perhaps even
harassment. Should the counselor simply provide support for the student taking action on
her own behalf, or will the counselor need to
advocate and act for her? The student has also
talked about not being prepared, and we can
begin to speculate about reasons for that. Her
size may be an issue. Might there be an eating
disorder?

Note that the counselor's questions, while
eliciting a great deal of information, did little
to provide support or empathy. We will consider other skills later that provide those critical and important ingredients. However, the
counselor's questioning has begun the process
of engaging this student in relationship by
demonstrating her grasp of the situation and
asking about it intelligently. The questioning
has also enabled the counselor to get a sense
of the scope of the issues at hand and to find
out a bit about who this girl is. Thus the
questioning has been a process of both
engagement and assessment. The counselor
will have some decisions to make about how
to proceed once more of a relationship has
been established.

is, it may become more apparent if the silence is left untrammeled. Of course, too many silences and exceedingly long silences can provoke great anxiety, for both your client and for you. The trick is in finding the right balance, in knowing when to jump in—and experience is the greatest teacher in perfecting your timing.

As a general guideline, allow for less silence with newer, less counseling-sophisticated clients. They will be the ones most likely to become overly anxious if there is too much silence. Clients whom you know better, particularly those who are experienced in the ways of counseling, can be allowed to sit with somewhat longer silences. And, again, careful observation of the client's nonverbal behavior in the silent interval can cue you as to its effect.

The Simple Prompt

An alternative to silence is the statement that asks for more information without stating the request as a question. There is little need to elaborate much about this particular mode of inquiry, for it truly is simple, yet it can be quite effective. "Tell me more about . . ." or "Let's explore more of . . ." are examples of such simple prompts, as is the succinct "Hmm. Go on." A head nod and a smile can be used as nonverbal simple prompts. Sometimes in the counseling literature simple prompts are referred to as "minimal encouragers" or "acknowledgments" (Stiles, 1978).

Such prompts are effective in that they nudge your client into more discussion of what's already being talked about. They do not tend to move the client away from the topic already in focus, and they make you sound more confident than the use of a question might.

Using the Lab Practice Activities in This Book

At the end of this chapter, a lab practice activity will provide you with the opportunity to use questions, simple prompts, and silence to begin to explore a new relationship with someone. It is the first in a series of lab practices presented throughout this book that provide opportunities to practice and to examine closely your own use of skills in counseling relationships. The lab practices are based on the Ivey (1971) Microcounseling Training Model (Figure 4.1, p. 82), which has been used for years to help new counselors learn and practice specific skills. The model provides ample opportunity for specific skills practice, feedback about the use of the skill, and the chance to experience the role of the client. This model may seem a bit complicated or cumbersome at first, but you will easily get the hang of it, and once mastered it will serve as a means for other skills practice

CASE EXAMPLE 4.2 *Integrating the Use of Questions, Simple Prompts, and Silence for Effective Engagement*

In this case example, a client has been referred to you by an Employee Assistance Program (a business-sponsored program that links troubled employees to counseling services) because his interpersonal problems with his supervisor and his clients are affecting his job performance. This is the first interview.

CLIENT: Ok, here I am. Nice to meet you.

COUNSELOR: Good to meet you too. Tell me a bit about what brings you here.

After the greeting, the counselor leads with a simple prompt. No reason not to get right down to business.

CLIENT: Well, my boss sent me to Employee Assistance, and they sent me here. They said I needed to see you to keep my job.

COUNSELOR: Hmm.

Another simple prompt. No need to ask any questions yet.

CLIENT: Well, yeah. Jim, my boss, says that I've been losing job time and my work performance is slipping because I can't get along with people [*says this sarcastically*]. What a joke. Like driving a limo means you have to be some kind of social whiz.

COUNSELOR: Tell me about the specifics of all this, about the difficulties, and then tell me about your work.

Instead of asking questions, the counselor adopts a more confident tone by utilizing these prompts and sets the stage for a potentially lengthy client description of his work.

CLIENT: Well, let's see, I work for Diplomat Limousine Service. Drive a limo, take lots of hot shots and visiting dignitaries around town. It's a great job, usually. I get to work on my own, take care of this great limo, and drive all over town. It's great except once in a while when a few clients complain, Jim gets on my back.

COUNSELOR: Yeah?

While technically phrased as a question, this is really just a simple prompt, an invitation for the client to elaborate.

CLIENT: You know how bosses can be. He thinks I'm drinking coffee or getting

(continued)

(Case example 4.2, continued)

doughnuts when I should be going to pick somebody up. No trust. He thinks I argue too much with clients. He's wrong. I got clients who love me. Like Mrs. Marsh. I been driving her to doctors, hairdresser, whatever, for years. And then last week when some of my clients complained about "my attitude," he hit the roof.

[The client stops talking, but the counselor says nothing, responding only with a head nod and an expectant look.]

Use of silence. With a less verbal client, such silence would probably not be as helpful.

CLIENT: Yeah, well, these people said they wanted to go to some address downtown. When we got there, they changed their mind. They gave me directions to this other place, and we got lost. When we finally found the place, they changed their mind again. It was snowing, I was late for my next pickup, and I had a bunch of idiots in my back seat. So I let them have it.

COUNSELOR: And how did you "let them have it," as you put it?

Engagement, open-ended question.

CLIENT: I blasted them. I told them what I thought of their screwy, lousy directions and their crummy planning. Didn't they think I had anything better to do than truck them all over town while they made up their minds about where they wanted to go? Felt great when I did it, but then they called Jim and filed a complaint.

Case Discussion

This case example shows how a counselor can integrate the use of questions, silence, and simple prompts to quickly engage the client and begin the process of exploration and assessment. Note how the use of the prompts makes the counselor sound more authoritative than if he'd relied solely on questions. The use of prompts instead of questions also implies that the counselor is not operating out of some fixed agenda of things he needs to know about and is open to the client describing his situation as he sees fit. The counselor, in fact, could probably have used no questions at all.

Even with the use of these prompts and silence, little in the way of reflective commentary has occurred that would let the client know he has been heard and understood. These prompts and silence, in other words, are like questions in that they do little to communicate respect and regard.

(continued)

(Case example 4.2, continued)

Using silence, particularly at the beginning of a counseling relationship, can be tricky. Counselor silence implies that the ball is in the client's court, but some clients, if new to the ways of counseling or if they have language or cognitive deficits, may not know what to do with the ball in their hands. Too much silence in the beginning can breed significant anxiety. Thus, while you do not want to jump in too quickly, neither do you want silence to drag on to the point where anxiety becomes a hindering factor. Again, experience will help you find this balance.

A fair amount of information has been elicited in this interview with the limo driver client, most of it by simply prompting the client to tell his story. The stage is being set for further exploration as the counselor begins to formulate some ideas about what needs to happen to help this man keep his job—assuming he wants to keep it and is willing to make the accommodations necessary to maintain it—and about what some goals might be for their work together. We could reasonably speculate, even this early in the development of this relationship, about some of the primary issues, as well as this client's strengths, and how those might lead to the creation of some mutually agreeable counseling goals.

---

training. Before you embark on this chapter's lab practice exercise, let's go over the general format of the lab practice model and some guidelines for participating in this learning process.

The lab practice model requires working in a group of three (triad) or four (quadrad) people. One of you will be the designated Client, one Counselor, and one Supervisor (in a "triad" group) or two Supervisors (in a "quadrad" group). Each person takes each of these roles for a fixed period of time, and then the roles shift, allowing each person to experience all roles during the time allotted for the lab practice session. An hour is probably an ideal amount of time for a lab practice, providing time for counseling practice sessions as well as for feedback sessions for each Counselor-Client interaction. Divide the time available equally among the members in the group. Because the quadrad format allows for two sources of feedback rather than one, I try to use it whenever possible in my classes.

The Client Role in the Lab Practice Model

To start, one of you will be the designated Client. The Client's job in this practice session is to think of a real or fictional issue that can safely be discussed with the group. This issue should be something that is not too emotionally loaded or threatening and does not have any implications for negative backlash if somehow others get wind of what you've talked about. It is important for the designated Client to have something to talk about when the practice interaction begins. It can

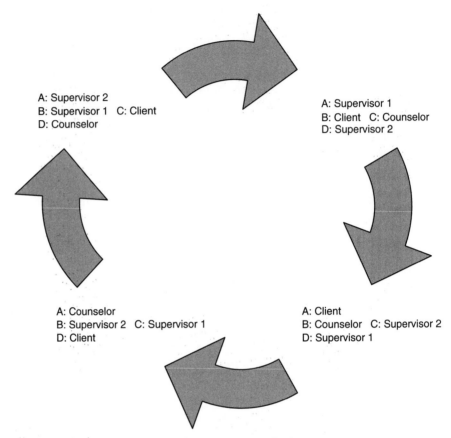

A: Supervisor 2
B: Supervisor 1   C: Client
D: Counselor

A: Supervisor 1
B: Client   C: Counselor
D: Supervisor 2

A: Counselor
B: Supervisor 2   C: Supervisor 1
D: Client

A: Client
B: Counselor   C: Supervisor 2
D: Supervisor 1

Figure 4.1 The Lab Practice Model with a Quadrad Group
Four individuals participate in the group (designated by A, B, C and D), with roles shifting four times in a session. When triad groups are used, there is only one Supervisor and three shifts.

be frustrating and anxiety provoking for a new counselor to have to deal with a client who is silent or in some other way not forthcoming with some kind of material to discuss. These interactions will probably be threatening enough without actively fostering that kind of difficult situation, so the Client should be prepared with something to talk about.

Examples of topic areas that might be helpful for these lab practice sessions include discussion of career goals, concerns about roommates, descriptions of current and family-of-origin members (but not significant problems with them), minor job issues, or significant accomplishments. These sessions do not need to be problem-oriented, so talking about positive events is certainly fair game for discussion. These practice sessions are meant for counselor training and skills development, not problem resolution, so Client problems are really not the focus of the interactions.

In the event that you, as Client, do not feel comfortable talking about any personal material at all, or if it would not be appropriate in the setting in which this is taking place, you might consider role playing some specific Client using fictitious material. Should this be your course of action, apprise the Counselor in the practice session of what role you are assuming, and then try to embellish the role as you play it during the session with realistic issues and their attendant feelings.

The Counselor Role in the Lab Practice Model

Another of you will serve as Counselor. Your job in this exercise is to use the skills at your disposal to find out about this person and the issue that's being brought to you and to make some kind of emotional connection with the Client. For example, in this first practice session, you will primarily use questions, simple prompts, and appropriate silence to elicit information from your Client. After the allotted time, the other person (in a triad) or two people (in a quadrad), called the Supervisor(s), will provide feedback about their perceptions of how this interview went.

The Supervisor Role in the Lab Practice Model

Supervisors should keep track of time and stop the session when the allotted time is over. They should be silent and as inconspicuous as possible during the interview. A Supervisor's primary job is to be an observer, keeping mental or written notes of what transpires during the session so that feedback can be given to the Counselor when the interview is over.

Timekeeping is important; if one session runs over, subsequent sessions will be shortchanged. Before beginning, the group might agree on a way of signaling the Counselor when the session is about a minute away from being over so that the Counselor can draw the session to a smooth conclusion.

The Role of Feedback in the Lab Practice Model

A brief period should be reserved after each interview as time for feedback and discussion of the interview. This is the opportunity for the Supervisors to provide the Counselor with information about what was seen and heard that seemed to be particularly helpful in eliciting Client information and in engaging this Client. It's also a time for the Counselor to talk about how he thought things went, and about whatever relevant thoughts and feelings accompanied the experience. It will be tempting to focus on Client issues in this feedback session, but the goal of lab practice is development of the participants' counseling skills. The primary purpose of the feedback is to provide information to the Counselors about their demonstration of skills.

Supervisor feedback should follow this set of guidelines for all lab practice sessions:

- Feedback should be designed to give the Counselor information about the relative effectiveness of specific skills used in the interaction, not to help the Counselor resolve the Client's issues.

- Feedback should be specific and behavioral, not judgmental. Focus on specific things the Counselor said, not generalizations or interpretations of the transaction. The best feedback observations are coupled with statements of how you, the Supervisor, might have felt if you'd been in the position of the Client. Thus it is better to say "When I heard you ask him about his mother, I started to get a little anxious," rather than "I thought that question about his mother was really strange."

- Feedback should be supportive, and most of it should focus on the positive aspects of the interaction. We all tend to be anxious and not particularly spontaneous when trying to practice this counseling work in front of other people. A little anxiety is not a bad thing, like a little stage fright. Too much anxiety, however, can be debilitating. The best way for us as Supervisors to help our classmates develop skills is to provide feedback within a positive and supportive environment—exactly the kind of environment we want to provide our clients. Remember, you want to give feedback in the same spirit in which you'd like to receive it.

Finally, all counseling relationships operate under a set of agreed-upon ground rules to ensure safety, primarily for the client, and these simulated counseling relationships (which may not actually seem simulated at all, once you get into them) deserve some rules for safety too. These ground rules, which should apply to any skills practice done in small groups, are as follows.

- In the role of Client, you may discuss personal issues that are not particularly sensitive, or, if no issue is apparent, you may create a fictional character and situation and role play that character. Which ever you choose to do, inform your group of your choice before you begin.

- Hold any personal information shared in these small groups in confidence. If you have concerns about anyone's safety, including your own, breaking confidentiality to seek help (as from an instructor) is appropriate.

- Respect privacy. As a Counselor, you might ask questions of your Client, but you should always respect her desire not to answer. When in the role of Client, you have the right not to answer questions, particularly those you find invasive.

The Lab Practice Model with Audio- and Videotaping

Audio- or videotaping lab practice sessions can be a valuable additional teaching and learning strategy. They allow for other avenues of feedback, which can be directly listened to and observed by someone practicing these skills. This kind of taping could be intrusively inappropriate in real counseling relationships, but it is a truly helpful adjunct in training exercises.

Graduate students in my counseling skills classes routinely audiotape all of their sessions when they are in the Counselor role in lab practice sessions. They take their tapes home and critique their skills and the dynamics between them and their Clients. They record their critiques on the tape, directly following the counseling session. I am not interested in listening to the feedback sessions, so I suggest that students not record that part of their work together. I then take the tapes, listen to the sessions and the critiques, and record my own feedback to them on the same tape. Such feedback from both student colleagues and from me usually amounts to more than enough feedback to digest.

These students maintain relationships within the same small groups for three or four weeks during a semester, so relationships are formed and developed. By the end of the semester, each student has an audio record of his or her own skill development and can track further progress over the course of the semester or year.

Periodically, sessions are also videotaped. Although students are not typically thrilled by the prospect of watching themselves work on videotape (an understatement), they nevertheless value the experience. They come to appreciate the fact that there is no better way to actually know how you are behaving interpersonally than to see it for yourself. When used routinely, as a matter of practice, the presence of audio- and videotaping equipment in the counseling room becomes less of a threatening presence. Familiarity breeds comfort.

I strongly suggest that you avail yourself of these technological aids as you practice in these lab sessions. If it is not a requirement of the course, students can create peer supervision networks in small groups where tapes can be swapped and critiqued. You can set up mechanisms for providing each other with supportive feedback and ongoing peer supervision using the tapes as a vehicle for discussion.

Concluding Thoughts: The Beginnings of an Alliance

Having an ability to ask some good, intelligent questions, the counselor is poised to begin to explore why someone has come for counseling as well as to

LAB PRACTICE 4.1   *Using Basic Nonverbal and Verbal Skills*

Armed with the guidelines and ground rules for these sessions, you will now practice the use of engagement and relationship building questions, simple prompts, and appropriate silences in a first interview. Begin the lab practice by determining who will be the first Client, who the first Counselor, who the first Supervisor(s). Decide on the total time you have for this exercise, perhaps an hour, and calculate how much time you'll have for each interaction, including feedback time. If equipment is available, tape-record your practice counseling sessions.

It is the job of each Client to come up with some issue to talk about. This may or may not be a real issue, but it should not be overly personal or emotionally loaded. It is the job of each Counselor to use questions and simple prompts to draw out and engage the Client.

Assume that this may feel mechanical and forced, particularly as you focus on using questions as a primary means of response. This is unlike usual discourse, and you will be hard-pressed to feel natural, particularly with onlookers watching the interaction. Do what you can to observe your own ability to ask about things that seem to resonate with your Client's desire to share more information. Let your natural curiosity about this other person and your genuine desire to find out more about her guide you.

After each counseling interaction, take time to discuss the Counselor's responses and the ways those served to engage the Client. In particular, note those responses that seemed to be really effective, and discuss your ideas about that. Give feedback that is nonjudgmental, in a way that it can be received and utilized. Try to manage the feedback that comes your way with openness to the ideas and input of the Supervisors in your small group. Try on their suggestions that seem to make sense, and discard the ones that don't seem to fit.

After everyone has had a chance to play all roles, discuss this exercise and your observations of it as a group. Can you make any generalizations about what happened in your small group? Did any particular themes emerge? Are there ideas about the use of questions or about responding to content and feeling?

If you are practicing this set of skills as part of a larger group (i.e., with a number of other small groups in a class), in the large group discuss how this went. Are there some general observations about the process and about the use of questions in interviewing? Care should be taken to ensure that personal information is not brought back into this larger group discussion. You will most likely see the tremendous potential that intelligent questions have in fact-finding and broad information gathering. Good questions cover lots of territory quickly. Questions and simple prompts are a great way to get things going. Your use of these skills, particularly your ability to ask concise, engaging questions, will improve with practice and feedback (Ivey, Gluckstern, & Ivey, 1993).

assess the client's general level of functioning. Your ability to respond intelligently to your client is clearly important to the success of this experience (Tryon, 1985, 2003). If you can discover your client's concerns and come to agreement with her about what needs to be done quickly and efficiently, you have a better chance for this first meeting or two to evolve into a successful counseling relationship (Busseri, 2004; Epperson, Bushway, & Warman, 1983; Magee, 1994).

Taken collectively, the use of nonverbal behavior, simple prompts, appropriate silence, and intelligent questions provides the counselor with a good set of tools to begin to work with and engage a new client. You will use these tools as you promote the development of the critical counselor-client relationship, the therapeutic alliance. The importance of this alliance to the overall effectiveness of the counseling experience is difficult to overstate (Havens, 2004; Horvath, 2001; Levy, 2003). Particularly when dealing with people in crisis, it is important to be able to develop this alliance quickly (Thurston, 2003). As a counselor working with a new client, you begin to explore the reasons for seeking counseling, start to form some initial impressions of who this person is, and communicate support and the hope for successful work together.

Starting a new counseling relationship can be scary, particularly for a beginning counselor. It can be even scarier if the new client is resistant and reluctant to be involved. The business of gathering information about this new person and giving out information about yourself and how the process of counseling works, while trying to lay down the foundation of a climate that is empathic and conducive to real communication, can feel overwhelming to someone just starting out. To prepare new counselors for all this, most counseling programs provide skills or pre-practicum, practicum, and internship courses in which you will practice with student colleagues and get started in actual work with a more or less willing clientele. Throughout your training, be patient with yourself, and remember that all of us had to start as beginners. With time, much of this process of initiating counseling relationships will come more easily, and you will feel more comfortable in the role.

For Further Thought

1. A lab practice model has been presented in this chapter that provides a framework to practice specific counseling skills. There are theorists and educators in our field who believe that such a skills-oriented approach misses the mark in that by focusing on specific skills the counselor may miss the more holistic view of the context of the counseling session. They would argue for looking at the entire interview, not at specific questions or other counselor interventions, and seeing whether the counselor responded adequately to the general themes of the client's issues in a way that seems helpful. What do you think about this? Can you find literature to support your argument? Is there a way to combine these perspectives that makes sense to you?

2. The study of nonverbal behavior in counseling relationships is a fascinating aspect of this work. There are some interesting readings about this area of counseling thought that you might consider as you contemplate closer examination of your client's nonverbal behavior, as well as your own. Included in these are the works of Alexander Lowen (1958), Wilhelm Reich (1949) (a controversial figure, a brilliant observer of nonverbal behavior), E. Smith (1985), and Milton Erickson (1989).

References

Barak, A., Patkin, J., & Dell, D. (1982). Effects of certain counselor behaviors on perceived expertness and attractiveness. *Journal of Counseling Psychology, 29*(3), 261–267.

Barkham, M., & Shapiro, D. (1986). Counselor verbal response modes and experienced empathy. *Journal of Counseling Psychology, 33,* 3–10.

Busseri, M. (2004). Client-therapist agreement on target problems, working alliance, and counseling outcome. *Psychotherapy Research, 14*(1), 77–88.

Epperson, D., Bushway, D., & Warman, R. (1983). Client self-terminations after one counseling session: Effects of problem recognition, counselor gender, and counselor experience. *Journal of Counseling Psychology, 30*(3), 307–315.

Erickson, M. (1989). *Healing in hypnosis: The seminars, workshops, and lectures of Milton H. Erickson.* New York: Irvington Press.

Erickson, M., Rossi, E., & Rossi, S. (1976). *Hypnotic realities.* New York: Irvington Press.

Gelso, C., & Fretz, B. (1992). *Counseling psychology.* New York: Harcourt.

Grace, M., & Kivlighan, D. (1995). The effect of nonverbal skills training on counselor trainee sensitivity and responsiveness on session impact and working alliance ratings. *Journal of Counseling and Development, 73*(5), 547–553.

Havens, L. (2004). The best kept secret: How to form an effective alliance. *Harvard Review of Psychiatry, 12*(1), 56–62.

Highlen, P., & Hill, C. (1984). Factors affecting client change in counseling. In S. Brown & R. Lent (Eds.), *Handbook of counseling psychology* (pp. 334–396). New York: Wiley.

Hill, C., & Stephany, A. (1990). Relation of nonverbal behavior to client reactions. *Journal of Counseling Psychology, 37*(1), 22–26.

Hill, C., Helms, J., Tichenor, V., Spiegel, S., O'Grady, K., & Perry, E. (1988). The effects of therapist response modes in brief psychotherapy. *Journal of Counseling Psychology, 35,* 222–233.

Horvath, A. (2001). The alliance. *Psychotherapy: Theory, Research, Practice, Training, 38*(4), 365–372.

Ivey, A. (1971). *Microcounseling: Innovations in interviewing training.* Springfield, IL: Charles C. Thomas.

Ivey, A., Gluckstern, N., & Ivey, M. (1993). *Basic attending skills.* North Amherst, MA: Microtraining Associates.

Ivey, A., Ivey, M., & Simek-Morgan, L. (1993). *Counseling and psychotherapy: A multicultural perspective.* Needham Heights, MA: Allyn & Bacon.

Kim, B., Liang, C., & Li, L. (2003). Counselor ethnicity, counselor nonverbal behavior, and session outcome with Asian American clients. *Journal of Counseling and Development, 81*(2), 202–208.

Leira, T. (1995). Silence and communication: Nonverbal dialogue and therapeutic action. *Scandinavian Psychoanalytic Review, 18,* 41–65.

Levy, S. (2003). The therapeutic alliance. *Journal of the American Psychoanalytic Association, 51*(1), 343–345.

Lowen, A. (1958). *The language of the body.* New York: Macmillan.

Magee, R. (1994). A marital therapy protocol. In L. VandeCreek, S. Knapp, & T. Jackson (Eds.), *Innovations in clinical practice: A source book* (pp. 359–368). Sarasota: Professional Resource Press/Professional Resource Exchange.

Nash, J. (2003). Beginnings: The art and science of planning psychotherapy. *Journal of Clinical Psychiatry, 64*(6), 736.

Norman, S. (1982). Nonverbal communication: Implications for and use by counselors. *Journal of Adlerian Therapy, Research, and Practice, 38*(4), 353–359.

Passons, W. (1975). *Gestalt approaches in counseling.* New York: Holt, Rinehart, & Winston.

Perls, F., Hefferline, R., & Goodman, P. (1994). *Gestalt therapy: Excitement and growth in the human personality.* Highland, NY: Gestalt Journal Press. [Original work published 1951]

Reich, W. (1949). *Character analysis.* New York: Orgone Institute Press.

Smith, E. (1985). *The body in psychotherapy.* Jefferson, NC: McFarland & Company.

Smith-Hanen, S. (1977). Effects of nonverbal behavior on judged levels of counselor warmth and empathy. *Journal of Counseling Psychology, 24*(2), 87–91.

Sternberg, K., Lamb, M., Hershkowitz, I., Yudilevitch, L., Orbach, Y., Esplin, P., & Hovav, M. (1997). Effects of introductory style on children's abilities to describe experiences of sexual abuse. *Child Abuse and Neglect, 21*(11), 1133–1146.

Stiles, W. (1978). Verbal response modes and dimensions of interpersonal roles: A method of discourse analysis. *Journal of Personality and Social Psychology, 36,* 693–703.

Sue, D., & Sue, D. (1990). *Counseling the culturally different: Theory and Practice* (2nd ed.). Oxford, England: Wiley.

Tepper, D., & Haase, R. (1978). Verbal and nonverbal communication of facilitative conditions. *Journal of Counseling Psychology, 25*(1), 35–40.

Thurston, I. (2003). Developing the therapeutic alliance in acute mental health care. *Psychoanalytic Psychotherapy, 17*(3), 190–205.

Tryon, G. (1985). The engagement quotient: One index of a basic counseling task. *Journal of College Student Personnel, 26*(4), 351–354.

Tryon, G. (2003). A therapist's view of verbal response categories in engagement and nonengagement interviews. *Counseling Psychology Quarterly, 16*(1), 29–36.

Watson, O. (1970). *Proxemic behavior: A cross-cultural study.* The Hague: Moulton.

CHAPTER 5

Assessment, Goal Setting, and Action Planning

> If you don't know where you're going,
> you might wind up somewhere else.
> *(Yogi Berra)*

The process of client assessment and goal planning helps to set a vision for where your relationship with this person is heading. This vision is important because you certainly don't want to wind up "somewhere else."

A classic situation, which is often discussed in addictions treatment workshops to introduce concerns about gender bias in treatment, relates the story of a woman who goes to the local mental health clinic in search of help for "feeling depressed." She's not been feeling well for some time and, in fact, has been secretly drinking herself into oblivion every evening. At the clinic she is referred to a physician, usually male in these stories, who asks her about many things, but never about drinking or drug use. He then makes an official diagnosis related to the depression and prescribes some kind of anti-anxiety or antidepressant medication. She leaves the clinic armed with a new batch of potentially addictive drugs. She is now a prime candidate not only for continued alcohol use but now also for prescription medication abuse. The point of the story is clear: You need to find out what your clients need, and sometimes that means asking about uncomfortable things. Your lack of understanding about what they really need can make things worse.

The Importance of Good Assessment

Assessment is an articulation of the problems, strengths, and complexities of the people with whom we work. Assessment reflects your ability to hear the complaints voiced by your client and to integrate that information with your deeper understanding of those things not talked about (Reid, 1997). Good assessment is the foundation of good counseling:

> Assessment is a systematic, continuous process which elucidates
> the initial clinical impression of the individual . . . problem, aids in
> the formulation of a treatment plan, helps match the client to an
> appropriate intervention, provides feedback on the course of treat-
> ment, and evaluates outcomes. (Yang & Skinner, 2001, p. 509)

Clearly, a lot rides on the ability to manage this process well. Beginning a new counseling relationship involves a complex set of tasks, and it can be daunting for the new counselor to consider all that needs to be done in these first sessions. A good assessment of your client's strengths and areas for concern is one of the central tasks. Who is this person sitting across from you? What unique issues and history have shaped this life? What has served to nurture and sustain him or hurt and harmed his chances of making his way successfully in the world? How capable is he of finding his own way and of creating the solutions to his own dilemmas? How severely impaired are some aspects of this person, and what untapped resilience can be mustered?

All of this falls under the purview of assessment. Assessment strategies in counseling are designed to elicit relevant information about your client. This information is used to help resolve the issues and conflicts that have brought this person to you. Sometimes this information is obvious, sometimes less so. Experience in handling this assessment process certainly helps you become more proficient, particularly in knowing what to look for (O'Byrne & Goodyear, 1997).

Some agencies or schools may have a designated intake specialist, whose job is solely to do front-end assessment interviewing with new clients. In other counseling worksites or schools, counselors may be expected to find out an array of specific information about clients, typically covering a range of problem areas. Psychological assessment questionnaires have been developed for use in this information gathering (Janik & Stout, 1993). The questionnaire can be a helpful tool in the intake interview (Hutchins & Cole Vaught, 1997). A written questionnaire might be given to a new client before a first meeting, but some counselors prefer to ask the questions during the first meeting. Some clients will come to you with a package of information already prepared by others. This might take the form of assessments from other agencies or school records regarding a student. A full array of assessment strategies in some places will also mandate, or provide as optional, testing as a means of gathering more information than may be readily available by interview.

Oftentimes these assessment tools are standardized tests. This means that your client's scores on these tests can be compared with others—regionally, nationally, or internationally—who have taken the same tests. These standardized tests may include assessment for mental status (Somers-Flanagan & Somers-Flanagan, 1999); achievement, aptitude, or intelligence; interests; or inventories of personality (Gibson & Mitchell, 2003). Any of these may be an appropriate tool in aiding the process of finding out more about your client. You will inevitably have course work during your program of study in counseling about assessment and evaluation tools. Those courses will help you make determinations about the appropriate uses and interpretation of these tests. You should have specific reasons for giving a test to any new client.

Sometimes, particularly when insurance companies or other third-party payers are reimbursing for service, counselors are expected to make an official diagnosis, a succinct problem definition, based on their assessment. Typically, these diagnoses are supported by use of a coding manual, usually the latest version of the *Diagnostic and Statistical Manual of Mental Disorders* (DSM), published by the American Psychiatric Association (2000). The current version is the DSM-IV-TR. Most graduate programs in counseling include course work on the use of the DSM and discuss the range of psychopathological problems one might encounter in this work.

Whatever process of information gathering is supported where you work, you will want to explore some essential issues with a new client. These essential issues are aspects of this client's life, aspects of her *whole person*. Good assessment is more than simple information gathering; it is an ongoing aspect of the developing counseling relationship. In addition to some early fact gathering, assessment is all about the ways someone becomes better known to us. In the best counseling relationships, we come to know our client's faults and foibles, her joys and frustrations, and this knowledge serves to support our work with the client. In sum, what you gather in the assessment process is more than just information, it is also impressions, reactions, and ideas about this person (Ruddell, 1997).

Assessment of the Whole Person

A number of theorists have talked about assessment as a process of examining the different aspects of a person's life and using the level of functioning in each of those aspects as a place to begin working therapeutically (Adler, 1954; Ivey, Ivey, Myers, & Sweeney, 2005; Satir, 1972; Witmer & Sweeney, 1992). Wegscheider-Cruse (1989) describes it as bringing a whole person perspective to the assessment process. This is a helpful and practical way to think about client assessment. Even though your worksite may have its own particular protocols and methods of conducting assessments, the whole person perspective is a fundamentally sound position from which to start. In this perspective you consider all of the different aspects of this person's life, your client's "selves." Even when it is not necessary or appropriate to conduct a thorough assessment with a new client (e.g., as with a high school student who is asking about college choices), you might still consider doing a condensed review of the whole person.

In Figure 5.1 I have modified Wegscheider-Cruse's model of this whole person to include seven critical selves: physical, intellectual, emotional, social-familial, spiritual, working, and aesthetic. These selves encompass the important domains of a person's life. Client assessment is a survey of the strengths and problem areas associated with each of those domains.

Assessing the Selves of the Whole Person

As you begin work with a new client, you review, either explicitly or implicitly, these multiple selves. You ask him, and yourself, how each of those selves seems to be doing and whether you need to pay special attention to specific areas. For a more formal assessment, in which you consider some of your client's selves in a more structured, organized fashion, you could utilize the Mental Status Examination, which assesses client functioning in the areas of appearance and behavior, cognitive ability, capacity for speech and language, thought processing, emotional functioning, and judgment (Erford, 2006; Gregory, 1999).

THE CLIENT'S PHYSICAL SELF

How is this client presenting himself? How is he dressed, and how does he appear physically? Is his facial expression animated and lively, or sad and depressed looking? Are there obvious physical problems? Are there medical problems? Are there

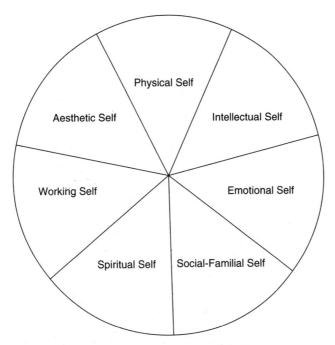

Figure 5.1 The Seven Selves of the Whole Person

physical issues that should be checked out soon? When did this person last have a physical examination?

Many clients have life difficulties that are directly or indirectly related to medical issues. You need to be fully aware of them, and you should be prepared to refer a client to a physician if there is any suggestion of something medical that should be checked out. A client who acts strangely, for example, may be more than psychologically disturbed. Neurological impairment may be the cause of strange behavior, and you will want outside medical help to ensure that this is not the case.

There are physical issues besides medical problems about which you need to be thinking. Is there a drug or alcohol problem? You might make it part of your routine to ask every new client questions about possible substance abuse. And what about physical violence? Is this someone who is or has been abused, or who abuses? This can be very sensitive, difficult terrain on which to tread with questions, but we need to ask if we sense that this may be someone in a volatile, explosive relationship, or if the individual is self-medicating with alcohol or other drugs.

THE CLIENT'S INTELLECTUAL SELF

How is this person's thinking? Does her thinking appear to be logical and ordered? Does she appear to be capable of higher order intellectual thought, or would she more likely be concrete and straightforward in her approach to intellectual tasks? Are there communication problems? Are there signs of any possible special learning disabilities or cognitive processing problems? Is she intellectually curious and thoughtful? Is she a reader, and does she have serious interests in the sciences, the arts, or mathematics? Does she find joy in intellectual pursuits? If this is a child, does her thinking and cognitive development seem to be on par with others of her age group?

Your assessment of your client's level of cognitive functioning will have important implications for your work with her. It will dictate the kind of language you use, and it will affect your thinking about her capabilities for understanding and the kinds of changes that can be realistically planned for this client.

THE CLIENT'S EMOTIONAL SELF

How is this person emotionally? Does he seem upbeat and optimistic about life, or depressed and negative? Are there issues with anger or sadness? Do those issues seem to be connected to life events or are they simply part of his persona? What kinds of problems, if any, do these emotional issues cause? Has he ever sought help for these problems in the past? Do any of these issues or problems seem potentially dangerous?

How is he with you? Do you feel energized in this person's presence or "on guard" and depleted? What are your own emotional reactions to this person's emotional state? Do you sense any potentially threatening conditions? If there are questions about a client's emotional safety or critical concerns about his emotional well-being, seek outside assistance. Actions you can take if you suspect that a client is dangerous, or is in danger, are discussed further in Chapter 10.

THE CLIENT'S SOCIAL-FAMILIAL SELF

What kinds of relationships does your client have with family and friends? Who are the members of her family? Did she have two involved parents, one, or none? What about grandparents? Are there brothers or sisters?

Would you say that this client, despite inevitable issues and problems with certain people, is generally well connected and nurtured/nurturing in relationships with others? Is this someone with many friends, a few friends, or no friends? What is the quality of these friendships?

Are there any legal problems? Has this person gotten into trouble with the law or with school administrators? Is help needed in resolving any of these difficulties, and do they point to some larger difficulties (e.g., impulse or anger management) that should be addressed?

What about love relationships? Is there a significant other or others? Children? What is the quality of these relationships? The Italian Jungian analyst Aldo Carotenuto (1989) asks himself whether a new client looks like he or she has ever been passionately embraced by anyone. This is a provocative, interesting way to consider your client's ability to form close relationships. Contemplate the meaning of this reflective question for a moment. If you are dealing with a child in your office, you could amend this question to whether she looks like she has been regularly hugged or read to. What interesting ways of thinking about a person these are! The obvious implication is that assessment does not need to be a dry and lifeless exploration of the purely factual.

Is this a person who is able to stand up for herself? Or does she have trouble with assertiveness and bend too easily to the desires of others? Are these assertiveness problems isolated, perhaps incidents in specific situations, or does this lack of assertiveness seem to have become part of an overall lifestyle of capitulation? Has this person perhaps even formed a way of being in the world that is centered around taking care of others to the extent that adequate care is not extended to her own self?

THE CLIENT'S SPIRITUAL SELF

What is this client's belief system? Is he involved with any kind of organized religion, and does that play an active role in his day-to-day life? Or is he without a sense of spiritual direction or apparent need of spirituality in his life? If that is the case, how does he seek meaning and purpose in his life?

Was this person raised in a particular religious or spiritual tradition? Is his spirituality now related to that background, or has he taken on new beliefs? Is there any conflict associated with family beliefs and practices and what he does for spiritual satisfaction now? Are his beliefs congruent with others in his currently configured family? If there is not congruence, is there conflict?

How would this client describe his mission in life, or what reasons would he give for why he was put on this earth? Or would he say, simply, that it's all one big accident and that there is no overall plan or planner? Does this seem to be someone who has an active "inner" life, or does he operate as if there is no such thing as an inner life? How much are his actions and behaviors a result of his belief system, and does he bring awareness to the connection between what he believes and what he does? Does he pray or meditate or spend time in contemplation?

THE CLIENT'S WORKING SELF

What is this person's work history? Does she have a job currently? Has there been a history of successful work? Are there difficulties with work aspects of her life, significant barriers to successful working experiences? If she is younger, a student, is she actively engaged in her education? Does she have long-range career goals and aspirations? Are her goals realistic? Has she been the primary architect of her own work life, or have the plans of parents, partners, or others been predominant?

Is she working toward realistic work or career goals? Is the level of education she has attained appropriate to these goals, and does she have educational aspirations as a part of, or distinct from, these goals? If she's working, does her work provide a sufficient living wage? Are there desires to make more money? What kinds of overall life skills does this person possess? Is this a person who can do a number of things well, has interests and hobbies, and takes a lively interest in the world around her?

THE CLIENT'S AESTHETIC SELF

Does this person have an appreciation for beautiful things? Does he make things, whether they be gardens, paintings, music, stone walls, or fine meals? Is he sensitive to his surroundings, including your office or workspace, and how they appear? Is there a general appreciation of things beautiful, and do you get a sense that concern for aesthetics is a priority in his life? Does this appreciation convey itself in how he talks about himself, how he presents himself, and how he appears? Does he articulate goals and hopes for the future that include making things and creating more beauty in his life and the world around him?

The Role of Consultation in Assessment

All areas of a person's life merit investigation. The agency or school context within which you work may have rigorous, specific ways to approach some or all of these areas. Alternatively, you may have the latitude to approach this "finding out" in a more informal and less rigorous fashion. Regardless of their approach to assessment, all counselors occasionally experience the need for more information than they can elicit themselves. Even the most experienced and self-confident counselor knows when it is time to consult with someone who has specific expertise. One of your students may be having difficulty concentrating in school and have a hard time with reading assignments. This student may need to be tested for learning

---

REFLECTION EXERCISE 5.1   Assessing the Whole Client

Either by yourself, or with another person or two, consider the questions and concerns associated with each aspect of those client selves. Which questions do you find to be particularly germane and important for consideration, and which less so? Which of these do you think are critical for counselors to have some knowledge of as work with a new client gets under way? What questions or concerns would you add to this list?

---

disabilities or perhaps have a medical examination to rule out any physical problems associated with these difficulties. One of your clients may tell you that he's been dealing drugs or that he's been involved with some other illegal activity. While you may be up to speed on agency policy and legal requirements related to reporting these activities, you'll still want to consult with colleagues and the school's legal advisor about appropriate actions to take.

This is one more reason to have a good working relationship with a supervisor, or at least colleagues with whom you may periodically consult, and access to experts in fields out of your expertise (medical, legal, special education, and so forth). One of a counselor's worst nightmares is to have failed to adequately consult with others related to some client problem that then results in some terrible event or outcome. Client suicides are perhaps the most obvious example of these awful outcomes. Undiagnosed medical complications, unreported sexual or physical abuse, or missed opportunities for medication are some of the other problems that can be avoided by seeking appropriate help. Most of us have access to a wealth of expert opinion in fields that are related to some of the difficulties our clients encounter. It would not only be foolish but arrogant to not avail ourselves of those services on our client's behalf.

Choosing Strategies for Action Based on Theoretical Orientation

In the initial sessions with a new client, you are beginning to determine the kinds of issues and strengths she is bringing into this relationship with you, and, at the same time, you are beginning to think about the strategies you will use to help her. As you foster the relationship with this client, your working alliance will form the critical foundation of your work together. All of the relationship-building skills you can muster in demonstrating your allegiance with your client will be invaluable in helping to set this foundation. This working alliance will go a long way in assisting movement toward successful outcomes, and the relationship itself can be used as a counseling action strategy.

You will most likely also use other tools in your work with this client. The other tools you choose will depend in part on your theoretical approach. As you have learned, or are learning, in your counseling theory course, different theoretical approaches advocate the use of different tools, and each has developed its own set of preferred techniques and skills. The theoretical orientation reflects your basic philosophy of the nature of humankind. If you view huma behavior as learned responses, for example, you have probably chosen a behavioral or cognitive-behavioral orientation. However, if you view human behavior as choices based on free will, you have likely chosen a humanistic or existential orientation.

Your philosophy and theoretical orientation also includes your views of normal versus maladaptive behavior, and the means you choose for making effective interventions will be, by and large, based on those beliefs.

The theoretical stance you adopt will largely determine how you approach clients, but you will select particular counseling actions based on what seems to be called for with any given client at any given point in time (Bruce, 1984; Nelson & Neufeldt, 1996; White, 2002). It is perfectly appropriate to use different theoretical positions to address the varieties of human complaint (Aspy & Aspy, 2000). Therefore, you need to be fluent in a number of theoretical positions and strategies, fitting what seems appropriate to the specific tasks at hand. There is nothing incompatible with having some core beliefs and ideas about human behavior and counseling theory yet acknowledging that no single theory or approach has the corner on the absolute truth. In dealing with different people in specific situations, a strategy from one theoretical position may work better than another in that specific situation. It certainly is more reasonable to fit theory to a particular human need as opposed to the reverse: fitting the person into a specific theoretical framework.

For example, you may be primarily nondirective and believe in people's ability to marshal their own resources, but when someone is about to jump off a bridge, it seems appropriate to grab him, or say, "Don't jump!" Saving life is the primary, immediate concern here. This would not be the time to ask him about his childhood or of his feelings about the bridge. Similarly, when you see that your client is engaged in other destructive behaviors, you are obliged to act, sometimes in very directive fashion to protect him and other people.

Assessing Overall Level of Functioning

In addition to your theoretical approach, the decision about how to best proceed with a new client is predicated upon your assumptions about her general level of functioning in the world. While you consider the person's level of functioning in each self area (physical, social-familial, intellectual, emotional, spiritual, working, and aesthetic), the aggregate—her whole person—presents a picture of your client's ability to handle responsibility and freedom and to act maturely in the world. Considering a person's level of functioning suggests a developmental approach to assessment, which has implications for strategies you'll bring to bear on your work with your client (Ivey et al., 2005).

When looked at together, how do these different aspects of your client reflect the overall level of responsibility and maturity your client displays? To what degree is this person able to rely on her own resources and skills to make good decisions in life? Put another way, to what degree does the person require attention and support from others to get through the day, the month, or life?

Assessing Levels of Maturity and Responsibility

Whatever the specific issues or problems a client brings to his work with us, part of our underlying goal is to assist him in recognizing and increasing his own personal responsibility for negotiating life. This goal may not be fully articulated between you and your client, but it will nevertheless be one of your most important goals in working together. Sometimes this need for more client responsibility will be obvious, as with someone who gets in trouble with the law or someone who drinks too much. It can be more complicated and is sometimes difficult to recognize, however, and we should discuss exactly what we mean by working to "increase" a sense of personal responsibility.

Your overall assessment of a client's level of maturity and responsibility enables you to decide on the kinds of intervention strategies that might be most appropriate. In Chapter 1 the client's level of functioning was compared to living at one of three levels in a house. Our job as counselors is to both ascertain the level in the house where he lives and to decide what tools to utilize to best serve this client at that level of functioning (Figure 5.2).

LEVEL 1 FUNCTIONING

Living at Level 1 are adults who may have some childlike characteristics, with behavioral control issues and relationships characterized by difficulty and confusion. Some of these immature adults have never had proper parenting or guidance, and some have given their lives over to substance abuse. Whatever the reason, they typically come to you in crisis. Their house is, metaphorically, falling down around their ears, and they are clearly in need of some lifesaving.

At Level 1, the immature, irresponsible characterization may be identified by any combination of the following:

- Lack of behavioral control
- Relationships characterized by excessive dependency, as well as chaos
- Undisciplined, fragmented thinking and work habits
- Drug, alcohol, or eating disorders
- Fear or anxiety when alone
- Little attachment to interest or subject areas
- Blames others for difficulties
- Little understanding of how personal actions affect consequences
- Potential cognitive deficits

This person is behaving in all sorts of ways that would be described as "childlike." He demands physical and emotional support (sometimes by way of social control) and will act out if that structure is not provided.

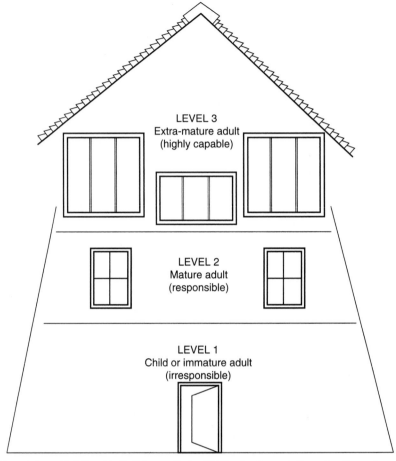

LEVEL 3
Extra-mature adult
(highly capable)

LEVEL 2
Mature adult
(responsible)

LEVEL 1
Child or immature adult
(irresponsible)

Foundation—Relationship-Building Skills for All Clients: Support, Empathy, Regard, and Respect

Skills for Level 3 Clients

- Advanced action skills, such as interpretation or dream analysis, to promote insight, understanding
- Least amount of counselor action or direction

Skills for Level 2 Clients

- Continued use of cognitive (action) restructuring skills
- Skills to help access feelings
- Skills to promote interpersonal effectiveness
- Beginning use of advanced action skills to promote personal understanding
- Counselor is less active, directive

Skills for Level 1 Clients

- Cognitive and behavioral (action) restructuring skills
- Support, direction, and action
- Reality-based interventions
- Crisis intervention
- Counselor is active and fairly directive

Figure 5.2 The House of Client Concerns and Counseling Skills

Keep in mind that some of the people living at Level 1 actually *are* children. Their need for help is age-appropriate, and the need is for direction, support, and guidance. You can provide this guidance and support, if it is called for developmentally, regardless of the actual age of your client.

LEVEL 2 FUNCTIONING

At the middle level of the house, Level 2, live those people who make up the mainstream of our adult culture. These are mature people who are self-supporting, who care for themselves and are able to maintain themselves without undue external support. They have people in their lives whom they love, and they are loved by others. They can live independently but are involved productively with others.

The responsible, mature, person at Level 2 is capable of emotional, physical, and intellectual self-support. This style includes the following:

- Relationships characterized by stability, give and take, and the absence of manipulation
- Capacity to be alone without undue anxiety
- Engagement in loving relationships
- Absence of major behavioral disorders
- Ability to maintain a task orientation that is focused and disciplined

This person has a life that, from the outside, appears purposeful and focused. She acts like an adult, one who has grown past the narcissism and demands of youth. She has replaced those demands with a capacity to give to herself. She is capable of being fully self-supporting, emotionally and physically. Her relationships with others are characterized by independence and an absence of neediness.

This person may seek counseling for help in becoming more interpersonally sensitive, becoming more in touch with feelings, or for assistance with any variety of life problems—career issues, relationship difficulties, or parenting concerns, to name only a few. Although this person is capable of handling responsibility for her own life, she nevertheless seeks help to make life more satisfying.

LEVEL 3 FUNCTIONING

In the upper reaches of the house, Level 3, are extra-mature people who have not only the wherewithal to responsibly manage their own lives but the additional capacity to respond and assist others. We might view this kind of "respond-ability" as an advanced form of responsibility. In this sense, responsibility means much more than doing what is "right" based on traditionally held notions of being duty-bound. It is about having the capacity to respond both to what is needed for oneself and to what is needed by others. It is about a person's ability to take care of himself well, in all of the aspects of the "selves" discussed previously, and also to acknowledge and respond appropriately to the needs of those around him.

The primary concerns these clients bring to the counseling table typically have to do with examining the meaning in life, looking for creative challenges, and reaching for higher levels of quality in relationships. Oftentimes these individuals have a desire to give back to others from what they have learned, and they yearn to reach out of and beyond the self. Jung suggests that this is a stance taken by many people in the second half of life. Using a sponge as an analogy, Jung said that, if the first half of life is comprised of soaking up, then the second half is spent in squeezing. Perhaps our increasing knowledge of the finiteness of our time left here leads us to strive to have our lives mean something beyond ourselves, and this fosters a desire to give back to others.

A Level 3 person has learned to function well in the world. This person's work life, interpersonal life, and emotional life maintain all those characteristics of the person at Level 2, but with additional characteristics. While outwardly functional, however, this person may nevertheless experience personal doubts, relationship difficulties, wrestle with concerns about work, or live with unnamed fears. This is not a perfect person, in other words, and he may seek counseling for help with these concerns.

The following characteristics reflect this Level 3, "extra-mature" person:

- A lifestyle characterized by outward simplicity and a rich internal life (to paraphrase the writer William Styron: "He simplifies the external in order to make the internal more complex.")

- When with this person, one is aware of being in the presence of someone who has some kind of gift or inner wisdom

- The capacity to listen intently, with an intensity of focus

- A primary focus on inward development and awareness, coupled with significant social involvement

- A heightened capacity for focused attention related to intellectual or aesthetic projects

- Values interdependence (attachments, bonds to others) even more than independence

- Problems for this person are often related to the assumption of too much responsibility

It is difficult to write of and describe this person concretely, but we have all known when we are in the presence of such a person. These are people who live with a certain grace, beset with the problems of living like any of us, but with the capacity to see them as learning opportunities. These are the world's true warriors, those who have learned that the crucial lessons of life have more to do with being loving than searching constantly for love from others. We find them in all walks of life, in and out of the helping professions, and all of us have been truly fortunate in our encounters with these people. They are surely not always from the helping professions, and they may wear their wisdom quietly. These are the *self-actualized* people Maslow (1954) wrote about. You may meet these people in the most unlikely places.

Some years ago, I met a man who I would characterize as at Level 3 near the Long Trail, Vermont's "footpath through the wilderness." The trail runs near the college where I work, and I have frequently given a lift to people coming off the trail who are looking to do laundry and to find a good meal in town. On one of these occasions, I picked up a grizzled old guy who told me that he was in his early seventies. He said he was a retired electrical engineer. He looked like he was built out of the mountain he'd just come off, tough and gnarled, and his pack seemed simply to be a contoured extension of his body. He said he'd walked north, starting on the Appalachian Trail, from Georgia. "My wife died a few years ago," he said, "and the good Lord gave me legs, so I walk." His plan was to walk back over to the Appalachian Trail, then into Canada, where he'd visit friends. Then, he said, his intention was to walk back to Georgia. This "walking" was taking him on a journey of many hundreds of miles over mountainous terrain. His walking, he said, was part of a quest to seek answers to some spiritual questions that concerned him deeply.

I spent less than 15 minutes with this man, yet he left me with a sense of having been in the presence of someone a bit larger than life. More than that, he left me with a sense that my life had been enlarged. He personified calm simplicity, yet emanated a sense of great depth. This meeting affected me deeply, and I still feel uplifted when I think about him these many years later. There is a sense in a person like this that there is a complex mix of joy, of gratitude about what life has given, and the capacity to endure great suffering. The joy and the capacity for suffering seem inexplicably interwoven, and without the suffering there would not have been the joy.

A developmental approach provides a way of thinking about your client's level of overall functioning and the skills to bring to work with her. Clearly, the strategies for working with a client who is acting irresponsibly and immaturely will be different from those for working with someone who is responsible and mature. However, in real life, these levels are rarely clear-cut. People may function at different levels in different aspects of their lives. In addition, people may shift between levels, growing or regressing, depending on personal and life circumstance. The model is just that, a model. It can be a helpful way of thinking about matching your perceptions of your client with the appropriate kinds of intervention skills, but it cannot be rigidly applied. And again, keep in mind that the developmental continuum should not be rigidly associated with chronological age. Each of us has known immature forty-year-olds as well as teenagers who are responsible beyond their years.

The Interplay of Intellect, Needs, Values, and the Capacity for Responsibility

This overall assessment of responsibility and the implications for counseling interventions is congruent and compatible with other developmental models related to overall functioning (Ivey, Ivey, Myers, & Sweeney, 2005), intellectual thought processing (Piaget, 1950), personal needs (Maslow, 1954), and values (Kohlberg, 1975). These are similar, parallel ways of thinking about human development and about how we might appropriately gauge our interventions and work with our clients. This model is also similar and roughly congruent with other developmental models that pair counseling approach to client development (Loevinger & Wessler, 1970).

In the whole person and developmental assessment process, we have a continuum related to a client's general level of functioning. It is appropriate to also consider how counseling intervention strategies could be related to responding to intellectual capacity and cognitive level of functioning, client needs (Bruce, 1984), or the ability to make sound values decisions. Table 5.1 displays all of these models side by side, and you can compare functioning levels on various dimensions.

It stands to reason that Maslow's "self-actualized" person would similarly most likely have the capacity to make higher order values decisions as well as to operate with high levels of responsibility in the world. It would also go without saying that the person would be capable of higher order thinking. At the lower levels, the person who has serious physical safety and love needs will also most likely make values decisions based on a fear of punishment and operate immaturely in questions related to management of responsibility.

The Assessment of Functioning and Implications for Counselor Action

The implications for counselors of a developmental approach to assessment are obvious. We need to structure our interventions, our activity and the things we say and do, with our clients in a way that reflects their ability to think, to manage responsibility, and to make moral decisions. We need to respond and work with them in ways that respect their capacity to understand and respond to us.

IMPLICATIONS FOR COUNSELOR ACTIVITY AND STRUCTURE

Activity refers to counselor action in counseling, including the things the counselor does and says. The higher the level of counselor activity, the more she is doing and saying. *Structure* refers to the kinds of things the counselor does.

A higher level of structure in a counseling session means that the counselor is more directive and provides more planned activities.

You will need to be most active, most structured, and most directive with clients operating at Level 1. You will ask more questions, stimulate discussion more actively, and perhaps even give instruction in ways that you wouldn't if you were less active. You will also construct more activities with people operating at lower levels on this continuum. This means that you will create more structure in your relationships with these clients. You will perhaps be making things, doing therapeutic art and play projects (with children), or constructing activities to engage client interest. You might be engaged in teaching activities with them. Similarly, the ground rules you adopt for work with them may be more structured and clearly defined. You will also be more active and provide more structure at the earliest stages of any counseling relationship as the details of how you will work together are negotiated.

The farther along the continuum you assess your clients to be, the less active, less directive, and less structured you will be. With Level 2 clients you will be relying much more heavily on client generation of material for the substance of what happens in the counseling session. These clients are capable of handling the responsibility for generating material themselves. Should you work with clients at Level 3, you will most likely adopt a thoughtful, much less active stance, letting the client take the lead in determining the direction of the interaction.

CHOOSING ACTION SKILLS BASED ON LEVEL OF FUNCTION

From the developmental perspective, it seems appropriate to choose counseling strategies, perhaps from a variety of theoretical orientations, that coincide most appropriately with what is needed by your client. Some theories seem naturally suited to people at one functional level, less so for those at others. Other theoretical techniques have greater flexibility and can be applied differentially, depending on what seems to be needed.

Directive and behaviorally oriented approaches (e.g., reality therapy and cognitive-behavioral approaches) might best be used for clients operating at Level 1, and perhaps for some of the problems associated with Level 2. These are clients for whom organizing thought as it influences feeling and behavior, and seeing how their behaviors clearly affect the consequences that follow, are typically critical learning tasks.

At Level 2, where clients demonstrate an ability to act more responsibly and can process information in a more sophisticated fashion, less counselor-active and more nondirective approaches (e.g., Gestalt or client-centered counseling) might help them find their own solutions to problems or access and express feelings.

For Level 3 clients, such as ourselves when we avail ourselves of counseling services, the insight-oriented therapies will most likely be solid choices for use.

Table 5.1 Comparison of Developmental Models

Level of Functioning	Cognitive Development (Described by Piaget and Post-Piagetian theorists)	Moral Development (Described by Kohlberg and Gilligan)	Motivational Development (Described by Maslow's hierarchy of needs)	Developmental Styles (Described by Ivey and Ivey)
Level 3 Extra-mature, responsible adult: operates at the upper reaches of responsible thought, action, and feeling; not problem free but has high levels of self-awareness, interpersonal skill, and capacities for acting with personal moral authority	Postformal operational thinking; capable of abstract reasoning, dialectical thought, able to view alternatives from multiple perspectives, synthesizing ambiguities and contradictions	Postconventional morality: emphasis on universal moral principles, ethics, social contract; integration of needs of self and others, ability to differentiate between laws and justice	Needs for self-actualization: needs for self-fulfillment, to live up to one's potential, to search out one's inner spirituality	Dialectic/systemic: capable of understanding problems from multiple perspectives; can step back and view self and others in global contexts and in the abstract
Level 2 Mature, responsible adult: functions independently and does not demand excessive external support, capable of stable, loving relationships; typically operates according to the social mores and conventions of the times	Formal operational thinking: capable of critical thinking, problem solving, and reasoning; able to choose among multiple alternatives	Conventional morality: conformity to social system; aware of needs of others but lacks distinction between laws and what is right for people	Need for belonging and self-esteem: to love and be loved; avoid loneliness and alienaton; to achieve, be competent; to be independent and respected by others	Formal/reflective: has discovered own identity; capable of differentiating self from others; can evaluate own behavior in terms of right and wrong

Level 1

Irresponsible, immature, child-like: demands support from others, even though he or she may vehemently deny that such support is necessary; concerns are typically immediate and crisis-oriented; moral decisions are based on fear of punishment	Concrete operational thinking: capable of thinking logically about concrete events; basic language skills; able to choose between simple alternatives	Preconventional morality: egocentric concern for self, unaware of others' needs; obeys rules to avoid punishment	Need for safety, stability, comfort need to feel that the world is organized and predictable; that basic physiological needs (hunger, thirst, warmth, etc.) are satisfied	Concrete/situational: incapable of taking perspectives other than own; incapable of generalizing; describes problems in terms of events, telling detailed linear stories

Table 5.2   Client Characteristics and Intervention Strategies

Client Level	Client Characteristics	Counselor Stance	Action Skills to Employ
3	Extra-mature, extra-responsible	Least active, least directive counseling stance	Interpretation; dream analysis; expressive arts; philosophical counseling; use of community service. Continued use of relationship skills.
2	Adult-like, mature, responsible	Less counselor activity and less direction	Restructure destructive thought patterns; assist with identification and expression of feelings; reframing; skills training; brainstorming; make activities appealing. Continued use of relationship skills.
1	Childlike, immature, irresponsible	High counselor activity, direction, and structure	Examine action-consequence behavioral sequences; help to reshape destructive behavioral patterns; restructure destructive thought patterns; provide direction, support, and guidance; brainstorming; skills training; appealing/cheerleading. Continued use of relationship skills.

Existential approaches, varieties of analytic approaches, or spiritually oriented theoretical stances may provide the help we need. Table 5.2 summarizes the action skills appropriate for each client level.

Armed with the assessment of your client's strengths and skills, a base of information about this new client and a sense of how capable he is of managing his own life, you are poised to put together an action plan for your work together. The problems and strengths identified in your new client, as well as the specific issues he has brought in to you, will create the basis of your goals to be formulated with him for future work. The assessed level of functioning will help you to select the strategies that you will bring to this emerging relationship.

Your selection of strategies will also be informed by your facility with different theoretical approaches and your experience in this work. Give yourself time to learn about the many strategies available and to avail yourself of the supervisors and teachers who can lend support and guidance in your search for the best strategies. Course work will be helpful in this, and good supervision in actual work in the field will be invaluable.

Goal Setting and Action Planning

During these first sessions, your new client becomes clearer about what she is looking for from you and from counseling. She begins to more distinctly articulate the forces that have driven her to come to see you. Simultaneously, your assessment of her strengths and problem areas, as well as her general level of functioning in the world, give you a clearer picture of how her desires for counseling help and her overall stance in the world hang together, or don't. Together, out of this combination of information, her desire for help, and your impressions, you begin to formulate counseling goals and an action plan for working together.

Sometimes this process of goal setting and planning is referred to as treatment planning (Beutler, Harwood & Holaway, 2002). I prefer the term *action planning* to remove implications that counseling exists within a medical model. This process of goal setting and action planning is not something we do *to* people, but rather *with* them. The assessment process, as well as the working agreements we strike with our clients, should reflect high degrees of counselor-client mutuality. It makes little difference how brilliant our observations or how succinct and clear our goals if the person we are working with is not fully complicit in the process of putting those together (Busseri, 2004; Tryon & Winograd, 2002). This conjoint process of articulating goals extends to our work with children as well as adults.

Strength-Based Goals

It can be tempting to focus on deficits, but the best client goal packages are those that actively build on strengths (White, 2002). Allowing a client's own substantial

---

REFLECTION EXERCISE 5.2   Goal Setting

Imagine that you are the counselor working with the young man in Case Example 5.1. He has agreed to work with you toward the general goal of landing after-school employment. The implications during this interview are that the counselor may want to address other issues with this student as employment is sought.

How could you articulate what some of those issues are (or might be, as you imagine them) in terms of some specific, strengths-based goals? Feel free to embellish the case example with imagined details. Be creative as you think of this student's "whole person" and general level of functioning, and furnish his character with the characteristics that create a more complete picture of this young man. As you formulate goals out of this picture, make sure to consider his desire and ability to work toward those goals. In other words, the goals must be based on mutuality.

When you have written out your goals for this work, compare your notes with those of another student.

CASE EXAMPLE 5.1 *Goal Setting and Action Planning*

This school counselor and student know each other well. The counselor has helped him out not only with course choices and some career planning but also with some interpersonal difficulties he's had with teachers and staff. This student is "rough around the edges." He has problems dealing with authority, hangs out with a negative peer group, is most likely involved with the school's drug subculture, and gets into occasional fights. He would probably be assessed at Level 1 on our functional continuum.

He respects and likes this school counselor, in part because she has helped him negotiate some difficult situations. We pick up this interaction at the point where he says that he is seeking her help to find an after-school job.

STUDENT: So, now that you've asked me all this stuff about myself, now can you tell me if you're going to help me get an after-school job?

COUNSELOR: You think an ally in this would be helpful?

This is a closed question. She wants to make sure she wants to answer his question, and this buys her a little time.

STUDENT: Yeah, I think you could help me a lot.

The implication here is that he thinks she can get him a job that he can walk into.

COUNSELOR: Sure, I'd love to lend a hand. I can help you track down some jobs. But my take on this is that it might be helpful to also look at why you've had so much trouble landing one. *[Pauses as she sees the student take this in.]* Maybe there are some things we can look at and do together to increase your chances of getting a good job.

The counselor decides to actively answer his question. She wants to help him in some broader ways than he's been seeking, however. She needs to be careful as he can easily get defensive and shut down. She wants to clarify her role as assistant, implying that actually getting the job is his responsibility. She is thinking about his negative, monosyllabic style of interacting and his reluctance to look her in the eye when he speaks. She is also speculating about the impact that his scruffy, unkempt appearance most likely has on potential employers.

STUDENT: What're you talking about? All I want is a job. I don't want to "look" at anything.

COUNSELOR: Yeah, I understand. I know a lot about how people get jobs, and I can talk with you about some of the ways you can put your

Here she needs to be careful. She wants to broaden the goals of their work together to include these other activities, but she doesn't want to make him

(continued)

(Case example 5.1, continued)

best foot forward. You know, we can practice interviewing skills, maybe role play some ways to interview well, look at the kind of job that would suit you best, stuff like that.

STUDENT: Um, OK. I guess I see what you mean.

COUNSELOR: Terrific. Let's get started by talking about what we'll do specifically.

Case Discussion

This business of goal expansion can be tricky, particularly when trying to include items that may seems provocative to your client (like this school counselor's perceptions of her student's negative attitudes and behaviors). There is a fine line between giving enough information to ensure that your client is aware of the fact that you think there is additional work to be done without showing all of your hand too soon. Timing is important, and too much information too soon is rarely helpful. You want to balance this giving of information with your desire to fully engage this new person. While you certainly don't want to be devious about your thought process, there is nothing wrong with not being totally forthcoming all at once.

overly defensive and resistant. She is being directive and suggests that a strong element of this counseling relationship will be an educational component. The process of working with him will allow opportunities to explore some of the attitudes and behaviors that might scare off potential employers.

As this school counselor–student interaction continues, the counselor specifically strikes an agreement with the student about how they can work together. The more specific and clearer these goals are, the more helpful they will be for both counselor and client (Rule, 1982). In continuing this discussion, the counselor will negotiate the details of their working relationship; that is, who will do what. In addition to the mechanical details of the relationship (times and length of meetings, projected numbers of meetings, and so forth), important ground rules also need to be negotiated. These will serve to help protect the safety of the relationship for both parties, particularly the client.

resources to serve as the foundation for your counseling relationship is not only empowering to your client but will also typically yield more positive outcomes.

This doesn't mean that you can't suggest to your new client something that you think might be a helpful part of the goal package. Your assessment of his various "selves" may lead you to believe that work on one or more of those areas may be especially productive in achieving his stated goals for coming to counseling. Some counselors also advocate adding their own values dimension to the goal-setting part of the process (Davis, 1996; Fisher, 1966; Romano & Hage, 2000), but caution should be taken to ensure that the client is fully complicit in whatever these might be.

Case Example 5.1 shows how a high school counselor beginning to put together a plan with a student might help the client broaden his goals.

Broad Goals for All Clients

Case Example 5.1 points to some goals we have for all of the people with whom we work. Our assessment discussion and the review of the whole person approach to thinking about the relationship between assessment and counselor activity should probably make these self-evident. Succinctly put, we want to help all of our clients heighten their capabilities in the following areas:

- Ability to manage personal responsibility (including the freedom to make healthy choices

- Personal awareness and self-respect

- Interpersonal awareness and sensitivity to the needs of others

The Need for Clear and Concise Goals

The counseling relationship is the vehicle in which you will drive with your client toward the goals the two of you have set for your work. What happens in the relationship is about the *process* of the counseling journey. The goals are about the destination or the *outcome* of the trip. To reach the goals, you need to pay attention to the journey. The outcomes are dependent on the process.

Generally, your overall goals will serve as a backdrop for all other specifically articulated goals. Regardless of the client's level of functioning, good counseling outcomes are dependent upon clarity and specificity of goals (Goodyear & Bradley, 1986). The goals are stated concretely and positively so that they are approached with enthusiasm and a sense of optimism. Goals should be easily understood by both you and your client. Finally, good counseling goals are couched in terms of behavioral change, affording the potential for actually measuring counseling outcomes.

Turning Your Client's Problems into a Prioritized Set of Goals

Your client will most likely come to you with a list of problems that are causing distress. If it's a coerced client, those problems may be causing other people distress as well. Once you have assessed the overall level of functioning, it is your job to help to articulate those problems and their resolution as workable, specific, clearly stated goals. The selected goals need to be prioritized so that the most critical issues are dealt with before those that are less important. "First things first," as they say in Alcoholics Anonymous. When there are life and death issues, for example, or severe behavioral issues that are out of control, as with drug abuse or physical abuse, those are preeminent. A woman who is being pushed around at home, whether literally or metaphorically, needs to attend to that before she can realistically consider career plans. Serious issues need to be brought under control before other concerns can be addressed.

| LAB PRACTICE 5.1 | *Whole Person Assessment* |

Following the lab practice procedures established in Chapter 4, take turns role playing a career Counselor and a Client who has chosen the counseling profession as his or her career. The task will be to conduct a brief "whole person" assessment of the Client. You will each play yourself when you are the Client, so before you begin your turn as the Client discuss with the Counselor the kinds of material that is safe and not safe to ask about and survey. The Counselor will respect those agreed-upon boundaries. When the Counselor has completed the brief assessment, he or she should then help the Client to articulate three or four concrete goals for the future year in continuing to move toward this career, as if you were going to continue to work together.

The Effective Counseling Action Plan: Clear Goals and Ground Rules

The action plan, the map of your journey, represents the culmination of the assessment process with your new client. The action plan is a written or more informally spoken agreement between you and your client that defines articulated goals and responsibilities. It defines what is to be expected of your client (e.g., coming for appointments on time, fees to be paid, finishing homework) as well as what is to be expected of you (e.g., being available when you say you will be, advance notification of time away, how you'll work). The best plans include goals that are definable and measurable; this enables you and your client to have a clear sense of outcomes at the end of the counseling experience (Blinder & Sanathara, 2003). The plan may also specify what kinds of client behaviors outside of the counseling relationship will be expected. Examples of these behaviors include specific expectations about what will happen in the event of physical violence or drug use, or agreements of no self-harm. Plans that specify these kinds of behavioral issues may also involve monitoring provisions, such as urinalysis or breathalyzers for drug and alcohol abusers.

The well-constructed plan gives the client as much responsibility as possible for managing his or her end of the process. It reflects the assessed level of functioning at which the client operates, and it is the foundation upon which you'll base many of your counseling activities (Bruce, 1984). Action plans for Level 1 clients, including children, will be tighter and more concrete than those for clients at Levels 2 or 3. It assumes that goals are mutually agreed-upon, and it supports the counselor-client alliance. The plan makes clear what information is to be shared with other parties (e.g., parents, school officials, insurance companies, police) and provides protection for the relationship between the two of you. Your client should always be clear about what information, and under what circumstances, you'll be giving to others. He then can make decisions, based on this knowledge, about what is safe information to share.

The plan tries to anticipate problem areas and plans for those. There may be backup plans, or contingencies, if one of you does not manage your end of the bargain. What happens, for example, if your client comes late or not at all? The contract assumes that these events will happen and plans accordingly. Oftentimes this contract is a verbal agreement between you and your client, but there will be times when you or your client will want it to be written. Some of your clients will be "forgetful," or resistant in other ways, and this will serve as a reminder of their responsibilities.

The process of putting this plan, or contract, together provides a good opportunity to talk about how this counseling relationship and work will proceed. Particularly for people who have never experienced counseling, it is a good way to introduce some of the basics of what you'll expect of them. Some people will need a little guidance with this, and they may not be particularly adept or experienced in talking about themselves. The planning process is as much about the opportunity for education about counseling as it is about putting an agreement together.

The adept counselor uses the plan as the glue that holds the therapeutic alliance together. The relationship is supported and reinforced by the well-constructed plan. You should do your level best to maintain your end of the bargain (e.g., not changing or canceling meeting times) as you are modeling the kind of responsibility you would like your client to emulate. You can also assume that your client will on occasion violate her end of the deal. If you work with children, you can assume that they will test the limits of the plan, and your patience.

Pushing the limits and boundaries of the action plan, of your contract for working together, is something many of your clients will do, so you should not be surprised when a client does not do what has been agreed upon. Pushing the limits of the plan, and your patience, is typical of many clients. It is part of the reason they come to see you. It is important to remember that there are no bad clients. Pushing the limits of a carefully formulated plan is your client's unspoken job. Part of why she's coming to see you is to learn how to become more responsible in the world. Sometimes violations of the action plan will be purely accidental, more often it will be a test of the relationship, a tweak to elicit counselor response. Some of the most skilled counselor work involves effective management of the boundaries of the plan.

The development of the action plan is a thoughtful, deliberative, collaborative process. Figure 5.3 illustrates the steps involved.

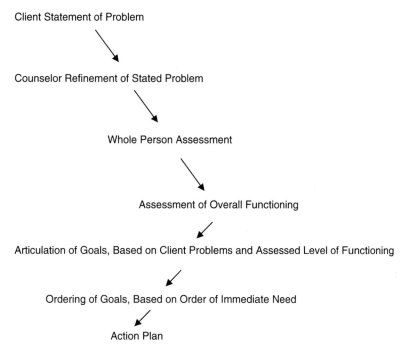

Figure 5.3   From Problem to Plan

Concluding Thoughts: Putting It All Together

Beginning work with a new client involves a complex set of tasks. You will want to communicate your availability and create an environment that conveys trust and safety. To create this environment of total communication, you must weave together your communication skills, the particular set of client problems and strengths you perceive, and the overall assessed level of functioning your client brings to counseling. The primary levels of functioning considered here include strengths and deficits in your survey of your client's "whole person," his capacity for moral/value decision-making, and the ability to handle personal responsibility.

This interplay of counselor communication, the work of engagement, and assessment of client functioning creates an interesting matrix of client-counselor interaction. If handled successfully, it provides a wonderful way of pairing need with theoretical technique. The complete assessment, which includes the client's perspective as to what is needed and desired, serves as the foundation on which the articulated goals and the action plan stands. All of this initial work, when done thoroughly and in the context of the developing alliance, lays the foundation for a productive counseling experience.

For Further Thought

1. Visit two or three agencies or schools in your area and ask about their assessment procedures. Collect and compare any forms they might use. What do you think of the relevance and usefulness of this information?

2. Think of a few kinds of problems that a client might bring into counseling. Turn each of these problems into a constructive goal or goals. How can you make each of these measurable?

3. As a follow-up to Lab Practice 5.1 in which you interviewed one of your classmates about how he or she has chosen the counseling profession as a career, configure the goals this "client" articulated into an action plan. Share this plan with the person you interviewed and see how closely your plan fits his or her plans for the future.

References

Adler, A. (1954). *Understanding human nature*. New York: Fawcett. (Original work published 1927)

American Psychiatric Association. (2000). *Diagnostic and statistical manual of mental disorders* (4th ed., text revision), *DSM-IV-TR*. Washington, DC: Author.

Aspy, D., & Aspy, C. (2000). Carkhuff's human technology: A verification and extension of Kelly's (1997) suggestion to integrate the humanistic and technical components of counseling. *Journal of Counseling and Development, 78*(1), 29–38.

Aveline, M. (1997). Assessing for optimal therapeutic intervention. In S. Palmer & G. McMahon (Eds.), *Client assessment* (pp. 93–114). Thousand Oaks, CA: Sage.

Beauchesne, D., & Belzile, G. (1995). The client action plan within employment counseling. *Journal of Employment Counseling, 32*(4), 181–196.

Beutler, L., Harwood, T., & Holaway, R. (2002). How to assess clients in pretreatment planning. In J. Butcher (Ed.), *Clinical personality assessment: Practical approaches* (pp. 76–95). London: Oxford University Press.

Blinder, B., & Sanathara, V. (2003). Outcomes and incomes: How to evaluate, improve and market your psychotherapy practice by measuring outcomes. *Bulletin of the Menninger Clinic, 67*(4), 367–368.

Bruce, P. (1984). Continuum of counseling goals: A framework for differentiating counseling strategies. *Personnel and Guidance Journal, 62*(5), 259–264.

Busseri, M. (2004). Client-therapist agreement on target problems, working alliance, and counseling outcome. *Psychotherapy Research, 14*(1), 77–88.

Carotenuto, A. (1989). *Eros and pathos: Shades of love and suffering*. Toronto: Inner City Books.

Curtis, R. (2000). Using goal-setting strategies to enrich the practicum and internship experiences of beginning counselors. *Journal of Humanistic Counseling, 38*(4), 194–206.

Davis, K. (1996). Defining questions, charting possibilities. *Counseling Psychologist, 24*(1), 144–160.

Erford, B. (2006). *Counselor's guide to clinical, personality, and behavioral assessment.* Boston: Houghton Mifflin/Lahaska.

Fisher, K. (1966). Ultimate goals in therapy. *Journal of Existentialism, 7*(26), 215–232.

Gibson, R., & Mitchell, M. (2003). *Introduction to counseling and guidance* (6th ed.). Upper Saddle River, NJ: Prentice-Hall.

Gilligan, C. (1982). In a different voice: Psychological theory and women's development. Cambridge, MA: Harvard University.

Goodyear, R., & Bradley, F. (1986). The helping process as contractual. In W. P. Anderson (Ed.), *Innovative counseling: A handbook of readings* (pp. 59–62). Alexandria, VA: American Association for Counseling and Development.

Gregory, R. (1999). *Foundations of intellectual assessment.* Boston: Allyn & Bacon.

Humes, C. (1986). From learner to earner. *Academic Therapy, 21*(4), 483–489.

Hutchins, D., & Cole Vaught, C. (1997). *Helping relationships and strategies* (3rd ed.). Pacific Grove, CA: Brooks/Cole.

Imber, S. (1992). Then and now: Forty years in psychotherapy research. *Clinical Psychology Review, 12*(2), 199–204.

Ivey, A., Ivey, M., Myers, J., & Sweeny, T. (2005). *Development counseling and therapy: Promoting wellness over the lifespan.* Boston: Houghton Mifflin/Lahaska.

Janik, J., & Stout, C. (1993). Forms for rapid client assessment. In L. VandeCreek, S. Knapp, & T. Jackson (Eds.), *Innovations in clinical practice: A source book* (pp. 313–328). Sarasota: Resource Press/Professional Resource Exchange.

Kohlberg, L. (1975). The cognitive-developmental approach to moral development. *Phi Delta Kappan, 56*, 671–675.

Loevinger, J., & Wessler, R. (1970). *Measuring ego development* (Vols. 1–2). San Francisco: Jossey-Bass.

Maslow, A. (1954). *Motivation and personality.* New York: Harper & Row.

Nelson, M., & Neufeldt, S. (1996). Building on an empirical foundation. *Journal of Counseling and Development, 74*(6), 609–616.

Obyrne, K., & Goodyear, R. (1997). Client assessment by novice and expert psychologists: A comparison of strategies. *Educational Psychology Review, 9*(3), 267–278.

Piaget, J. (1950). *The psychology of intelligence.* New York: Harcourt, Brace.

Reid, C. (1997). Rehabilitation client assessment. *Rehabilitation Education, 11*(3), 211–219.

Romano, J., & Hage, S. (2000). Prevention and counseling psychology: Revitalizing commitments for the 21st century. *Counseling Psychologist, 28*(6), 733–763.

Ruddell, P. (1997). In S. Palmer & G. McMahon, (Eds.), *Client assessment* (pp. 6–28). Thousand Oaks, CA: Sage.

Rule, W. (1982). Pursuing the horizon: Striving for elusive goals. *Personnel and Guidance Journal, 61*, 195–197.

Satir, V. (1972). *Peoplemaking*. Palo Alto, CA: Science and Behavior Books.

Somers-Flanagan, R., & Somers-Flanagan, J. (1999). *Clinical interviewing* (2nd ed.). New York: Wiley.

Tryon, G., & Winograd, G. (2002). Goal consensus and collaboration. In J. Norcross (Ed.), *Psychotherapy relationships that work: Therapist contributions and responsiveness to patients.* (pp. 109–125). London: Oxford University Press.

Wegscheider-Cruse, S. (1989). *Another chance: Hope and health for the alcoholic family* (2nd ed.). Palo Alto, CA: Science and Behavior Books.

White, V. (2002). Developing counseling objectives and empowering clients: A strength-based intervention. *Journal of Mental Health Counseling, 24*(3), 270–280.

Witmer, J., & Sweeney, T. (1992). A holistic approach for wellness and prevention over the lifespan. *Journal of Counseling and Development, 71,* 140–148.

Yang, M., & Skinner, H. (2001). Assessment for brief intervention and treatment. In N. Heather, T. Peters, & T. Stokwell (Eds.), *International handbook of alcohol dependence and problems* (pp. 509–522). New York: Wiley.

Skills for Developing the Relationship

> Very early in my work as a therapist, I discovered that simply listening to my client, very attentively, was an important way of being helpful. So when I was in doubt as to what to do in some active way, I listened. It seemed surprising that such a passive kind of interaction could be so useful.
> *(Rogers, 1980, p. 137)*

Carl Rogers, a prominent voice in the development of the counseling profession, was also the primary champion of a relationship-based approach to counseling. He believed that successful counseling is dependent upon the counselor's ability to provide an empathic set of conditions in which the relationship between client and counselor can flourish (Rogers, 1951). These "empathic (or facilitative) conditions," he said, also include genuineness, unconditional positive regard, concreteness, and respect. If supplied in a fashion that could be consistently experienced by the client, Rogers maintained that these conditions were both necessary and sufficient for client growth and for successful counseling outcomes.

The Empathic Foundation

Many current-day theorists agree with Rogers's contention that empathy is a necessary ingredient in counseling relationships (Bohart & Greenberg, 1997), and virtually all researchers, theorists, and clinicians agree that empathy plays a central role in successful counseling relationships and outcomes (Tryon, 2002). Some may not agree about its sufficiency for facilitating change, but they would agree about its necessity. Empathy enables you to see the world through your client's eyes; it is metaphorically about walking in your client's shoes for a while. This requires the ability both to intellectually understand the world from the other's perspective and to know how that world feels to the other (Duan & Hill, 1996).

Allport (1961) called empathy the "imaginative transposing of oneself into the thinking, feeling, and acting of another" (p. 136). I've also heard empathy described as the "ultimate leap of imagination." Honing your ability to be empathic with your clients is a central task in learning how to be an effective counselor. This includes learning how to suspend your own opinions, judgments, and values when you are with a client so that you can effectively identify with and experience her world. This is particularly true when your client's cultural worldview is very different from your own (Ivey, Ivey, & Simek-Morgan, 1997). Life experience, as well as counseling training programs which help to foster this empathic capacity, will serve you well in this kind of empathy education.

Empathy, of course, is not sympathy. It is not feeling sorry for your client or simply being sad about his circumstances. Sympathy can immobilize effective responding, whereas empathy prepares you for constructive action. Sometimes empathy provides the context for direct, difficult, tough challenges; it is not a soft or "mushy" approach to working with people.

Some counselors and theorists view Rogers's nondirective, client-centered theoretical approach to counseling as limited. They say that although these empathic conditions are necessary for good counseling practice they are not always sufficient to facilitate changes in client behavior. Other things, they suggest, may need to happen, such as providing direct guidance or working to help reshape destructive behavior and thought patterns. The central role and importance of empathy in developing solid relationships with our clients, however, is not disputed. You may not want to adopt Rogers's overall person-centered approach. You are, nevertheless, urged to consider empathic relationship development as the foundation of the critical therapeutic alliance and to couple it with whichever theoretical stance fits your client best.

Effectively Listening to Your Client

The key to your communication of empathic regard is your ability to listen effectively to clients. Your clients deserve not only your physical presence but also your undivided attention. If you can't be there emotionally and psychically, you shouldn't be there. You can only supply empathy and positive regard in an atmosphere of attention, when you are fully present and listening.

Listening with Full Attention

To respond accurately, you need to hear what your client says. This is not as simple as it sounds because most of us are used to listening with only partial attention. We live in an age of multitasking where giving undivided full attention to any one thing is rare. Your relationship with a new client begins growing and developing as you undertake the business of finding out what has brought her to you, and what some of her strength and problem areas are. You begin to establish how you will work together, and toward what goals, and you do all of this with an eye toward establishing trust and a working therapeutic alliance. This is a large package of responsibility, a lot to manage, and you will find that you need more than an ability to ask intelligent questions to bear the weight of all this.

Good listening is firmly rooted in undivided attention. Much of your ability to listen well will hinge upon your conscious decision to bring your attention squarely to bear on this person across from you. The more you practice this, the more focused your attention will become. To listen to another effectively, you must do your best to quiet your own internal chatter. The little voices at play inside you as you sit down to listen to your client will distract you. Ask them to subsist for a while and make a conscious effort to ignore them. Shift your attention, as completely as possible, to your client.

This is not always easy. I once went from visiting one of my very sick parents in the hospital directly into a counseling session. I remember how hard it was to push my thoughts and concerns about illness and hospitals into the background and let my client's concerns become paramount. I remember how hard it was to focus on the seemingly endless stream of demands of a particularly needy client when one of my own children was having a difficult time at school. And I remember the day I tried to focus on the stories my chronically mentally ill client was telling me as I sat squirming from the discomfort of a recent bike accident.

Good listening may actually be a kind of meditation, an interpersonal variety of contemplative practice. There is, for example, this story about Elizabeth Kubler-Ross, psychiatrist and author of the famous book *On Death and Dying*. Dr. Kubler-Ross once told a well-known guru, a teacher of meditation, that she had never had her own formal meditation practice. He told her that of course she had—what else would she call listening so carefully and concisely to all of those dying patients?

Listening to Both the Obvious and the Hidden Content

Giving conscious attention to your clients will make it more possible for you to understand the concerns they share with you. Your ability to listen and respond accurately to your clients' concerns will have a great deal to do with your ability to understand the material your clients present. You will need to focus and really listen to what they say, to both the spoken and not-yet spoken material.

To be an effective counselor, you will become a bit of a suspicious person in the positive sense; that is, you won't believe that what your client presents is all that exists. Listening for the unspoken is an intuitive process, and experience will help you to learn more of this language. The psychoanalyst Theodor Reik (1951) called this kind of listening "listening with the third ear." The writer D. H. Lawrence referred to this kind of "suspicious listening" as "looking behind the eyes," suggesting this same kind of intelligent attention. Pay attention to both the obvious and the more hidden content of what your client tells you—both the blatant and the latent content.

Things may lie below the surface and not be spoken of for many reasons. Some things might be frightening or embarrassing or filled with feeling, and some things just need more time to surface. Many clients, perhaps most people, harbor aspects of themselves of which they are ashamed deep inside. These may be things they have done, or things that have happened to them, that they feel shame about. One of counseling's best moments is when a client chooses to reveal one of these aspects of herself. It becomes a truly great moment, a potentially healing moment, when the counselor can hear this fact of a client's life and respond with understanding and without judgment or reproach.

A client may be reluctant to share material for many reasons, and it is not your job to go on a mining expedition to look for it. You can be subtly aware of the secrets through listening with your "third ear" and your intuition, and you can allow the material to come to the surface of its own accord. Safety and empathic listening set the stage for such emergence. Try to suspend your desire to be brilliant, and give free rein to your natural curiosity about this other person. Good responses to the content and the feeling of what is said will drive your client more deeply into the material that's being discussed; do not shift away from the topic at hand. Accurate listening, coupled with the empathic responding we'll discuss in a moment, will serve you well in general social interactions as well. Others will experience your listening skills as a real gift.

As we begin to talk about how to respond to what you've heard from a client, remember that there is no one correct way to respond. Indeed, you may miss the mark entirely with one or more of your responses and not do significant damage to the developing relationship. You can gauge the success of a given response of yours by following what happens next. Does your client go more deeply into the material and visibly appear to feel understood—or does he look confused and seem unsure where to go next? If you are generally on target, and if your client thinks you are getting the general drift of his thinking, he will usually hang in there with you through the occasional mistake. A counselor's desire to understand and to articulate a client's concerns will usually be intuited and sensed by the client, and the counselor's "good will," will compensate for the occasional blunder and inaccuracy.

Effectively Responding to Your Client

How do you communicate genuine regard and respect or emit an aura of empathy? How can you demonstrate a real interest and desire to know another? What can indicate your capacity to understand? What does empathic communication look like? What do you do with all that material you've listened to with such focused attention?

There really may be intuitive, or even spiritual, aspects of such communication of positive regard and empathy, but there are also some very specific skills you can use to begin to establish a solid relationship with your clients (Williams, 2002). When you are able to be with your clients with minimal distractions of your own, and when you are able to hear what they say well enough to respond cogently to the content and feelings of what they've expressed, you will have gone a long way toward demonstrating your respect and regard.

Try to respond to your client in a way that allows her to know she's been heard accurately and that also paves the way for her to begin to think more deeply about the issues that she's brought up. Your use of intelligent questions can prime the interpersonal communication pump, it can get things going, but effective reflection of content and feeling indicates true listening. These are the skills that will help to make your clients feel truly heard and understood.

Other reflection skills refer to the ways you can respond by not asking questions yet responding to the material your client has presented in a way that shows your understanding of that material. This involves listening attentively to what your client says, observing the nonverbal behavior that accompanies what is being said, and then responding to the content of what you've heard (and seen) in a way that not only indicates your understanding but also leads your client to consider the material in some new ways.

The Range of Responses

The ways we respond to our clients' statements can be characterized along a continuum from the simplest response styles to the more complex (see Figure 6.1). The simplest way to reflect what you've heard is to restate it. You simply say back, perhaps in somewhat altered fashion, exactly what's just been said. This is not a particularly effective way to communicate your understanding, however. Responding intelligently to the content of what your client has said requires more than a simple restatement, or parroting, of what your client has said. A better way to demonstrate your understanding of the essence of what your client has said is called "reflection of content," or "paraphrasing." This reflection, when done really well, captures and reflects not only the obvious spoken material but also some of what is implied that lies under the surface.

Reflections that include responding to the emotional content, called responding with "reflection of content *and* feeling," are even better. These ways of responding are certainly a cut above simple restatement. Research shows that all of these varieties of reflection are used frequently by experienced counselors and that they are positively related to all aspects of the counseling process (Williams, 2002). Evidence also suggests that this kind of reflection can help clients become more active as engaged partners in the relationship (Allen, Coyne, Colson, & Horwitz, 1996).

One other kind of reflection, called interpretation, which is discussed in Chapter 11, is a truly sophisticated reflection of content. It draws together different aspects or themes of your client's thoughts and may also involve some of your own perspective. Interpretation is the mainstay of pyschoanalytic work.

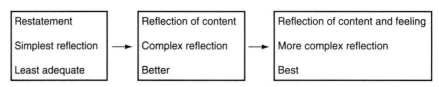

Figure 6.1   The Continuum of Response Complexity

Increasing Levels of Counselor Response

Consider this brief client statement and the counselor responses demonstrating different modes of reflecting the client's statement. As you will see, these responses become increasingly more sophisticated.

CLIENT: I had a terrible day. My dog got hit by a car, but I think he's going to be OK. I saw it happen, and it was really awful. You know how much I love him. It's like he's my best friend. I never should have let him off the leash. And then getting help for him . . . it just made a mess of the rest of my day.

Responding with Restatement

Restatement is simply giving back, in perhaps somewhat altered form, exactly what your client has said. This is not a distortion of what the client has said, but it certainly doesn't lead the client to any deeper thinking about the situation.

COUNSELOR: You had a bad day. Your dog got hit, and it really made your day a mess.

Responding with Reflection of Content

Responding to content, or paraphrasing, implies that you understand the material. Your response can help the client go into more depth with it. The best reflections of content are brief, to the point, summary statements of what has been said. These reflections are truly outstanding when they respond not only to the obvious content but also to the latent, or hidden, content. More about this shortly.

COUNSELOR: Today was lousy for you. There was the trauma of your dog getting hit, and then the confusion it caused for you in trying to deal with everything else.

Responding with Reflection of Content and Feeling

Intelligent reflections of content and feeling not only capture the essence of what the client has said but also the feeling associated with the content. These responses can help the client explore further and also communicate the counselor's emotional understanding and connection with the client. This conveyed understanding typically results in increasing your client's ability to explore and express feelings (Highlen & Baccus, 1977). The best reflections of content and feeling express both the thoughts and the emotions that have been presented. They accurately reflect what has been said, with minimal distortion.

COUNSELOR: That's awful. You love this dog so much, and you had to go through the trauma of watching it get hit. No wonder your day got scrambled.

Discussion

Reading these different responses, you can get a sense of the different levels of counselor understanding and ability to relate to the client's troubles. The responses are increasingly sophisticated. Your client will respond best to you when your reflections are not only accurate in meaning but also capture the feelings that have been conveyed. The counselor's ability to identify with the client's situation and fully comprehend the client's perspective is key. It is like being inside your client's world and giving him the language to understand it (Kohut, 1984). This is truly empathic responding.

Responding accurately to content and feeling is usually a more effective way to deepen the relationship than asking questions. Reflecting content and feeling will help more of the story unfold in a way that allows the client to feel understood.

When your client feels that you are really with him, with both the content and feeling of what is being talked about, he may allow himself to go more deeply into his feelings. He may

(continued)

(Increasing levels of counselor response, continued)

allow himself the luxury of expressing these feelings freely, and this can be a peak experience in the counseling relationship. This expression of emotion serves a cleansing function. Its healing effect is referred to as "catharsis" in the analytic literature.

REFLECTION EXERCISE 6.1   *Creating Accurate Reflections*

You may do this exercise alone, or in conversation with a partner or two. Think about Case Example 6.1 and about the responding style of the counselor. How might you say things differently, or the same, with the intent of accurately summarizing and reflecting the content of what the client has presented? How could this be done differently or better?

Write out three or four alternative reflections of content and feeling for each of the client statements in this interaction. Which of these seem best, and how might any of them alter the direction of the interaction? As you consider how this conversation might continue to unfold, what do you guess will happen next? What primary issues and themes will be of interest? How might you focus on, or selectively attend to, those issues? What issues might be saved as secondary?

Discussion

The best responses are elegantly succinct, capturing the essence of what's been said, and perhaps adding a little extra thought, in as concise a fashion as possible. They are brief and to the point. One or two short sentences are best. Lengthy responses tend to distract clients from their own thinking process and redirect the focus more toward the counselor. If you find that your response is longer than the client's preceding statements, you've talked too much.

Responding to the feelings of your client requires more than simply using words to label the feelings, although even simply labeling is a start. It is best when you are able to actually be in an "as if" experience, meaning that you understand the feeling "as if" you were your client.

Accuracy of language is also helpful. The response that starts with, "You feel . . ." should be completed with some kind of feeling word, not an idea or thought. Beginning counselors sometimes find it difficult to break the habit of using "I think" and "I feel" as interchangeable versions of "I think." Get in the practice of accurately identifying feelings with "I feel . . ." statements.

CASE EXAMPLE 6.1 *Using Accurate Reflections*

In the following dialogue, the counselor focuses on reflections of content and feeling, demonstrating how dialogue can unfold without using any questions.

CLIENT: I don't understand it. My mother is such a drag. She told me that as long as I kept my grades up, stayed out of trouble at school, and didn't smoke any more pot, that she'd let me use the car. *[Tears up.]* I did all that, and still "no car." Parents! You can't trust anybody to do what they say.

This is a complicated situation about which we don't know much. We know that some kind of agreement has been struck, perhaps not honored, between our client and his mother. We don't know how accurately he's portrayed the situation, but he certainly feels upset.

COUNSELOR: You believe that you kept your end of the bargain and feel cheated. What a pain. It just doesn't seem fair.

The counselor wants to support how the client feels without taking sides about the situation. This reflection is aimed at doing just that.

CLIENT: Yeah, you bet. She's unbelievable, a real pain in the ass. Sometimes I think I should just split. *[A period of silence follows.]* You know, one small slipup, and she changes the rules. Here we had this deal, and things . . . well, you know . . . they change at the drop of a hat.

OK. This is getting clearer. Some kind of "slipup" has occurred to tighten Mom's grip on the car.

COUNSELOR: Hmm. Something happened. And the rug got pulled out.

This reflection simply sets the stage, more effectively than would a question, for the student to talk about the incident.

CLIENT: *[Gets quiet. A few silent moments pass.]* She went ballistic. I wasn't even going to actually smoke it. She found the joint in my pants pocket when she was going to do laundry. I got busted, grounded, and I didn't even do anything wrong.

COUNSELOR: There doesn't seem to be, for you, anything about this that has to do with that contract you made with her.

This reflection is not meant to be evaluative or judgmental. The counselor is simply trying to get a sense of the student's thinking—he may actually see no connection between what he's done and his mother's reaction.

CLIENT: Sure. How could she know if I was or wasn't going to smoke it? I actually had forgotten that it was there, and I might've thrown it away, or given it to somebody, if I'd

(continued)

(Case example 6.1, continued)

remembered. *[More silence.]* This is such a drag. I finally got Erin to agree to go out with me, and now look at this, no car. I can't believe it.

COUNSELOR: This is really upsetting. You're stuck. Misunderstood at home, and now . . . with Erin, all dressed up and no way to go. Tell me more about the specifics of this.

The counselor's response, said with genuine feeling, is meant to relay her full understanding of the situation. The "all dressed up" comment is meant to be part of this reflection, and is not meant to be flippant or dismissive.

Case Discussion

Let's take a look at this brief interaction. First, note that the counselor's responses are all reflections of content or of feeling. There are no questions. Each of these responses is designed to convey understanding of what this client has said as well as reflect it back in a way that invites new thinking and discussion. There is an implied allegiance with the client in the counselor's responses, yet no side has been taken in the dispute related to the mother's decision to withhold the car. The counselor's last response is a simple prompt for more information, still not posed as a question.

This distinction, between support for the client but not necessarily for the issues under discussion, is important. The counselor really doesn't know about this client's history of drug use, about his motivations in leaving a joint to be found, about the dynamics at play within this family, or any other specifics of the situation. The counselor does want to convey a sincere desire to more fully understand this complexity, and she wants to support the client's desire to talk about and deal with all of this.

The counselor here knows that the problems of adolescence can seem melodramatic and overblown, with an adolescent careening wildly about in a swirl of emotional ups and downs, but she has done a nice job of taking this client's concerns seriously. Problems of adolescence may seem fleeting and insignificant from an adult perspective, but they are intensely real and immediate for the adolescent himself. This counselor respects that fact.

Rating Your Reflections

In the late 1960s, Robert Carkhuff (1967) designed a 1 to 4 point rating scale to judge the accuracy and helpfulness of various reflections. The top levels of responses (4 and 5) were seen as significantly adding, in an accurate and positive way, to the client's thoughts and feelings of the material under discussion. Responses rated as level 3 accurately convey understanding but are neither significantly additive nor detracting. Level 1 and 2 responses were seen as significantly detracting and disrespectful. Carkhuff and his colleagues (Carkhuff, 1969; Carkhuff & Berenson, 1967; Truax & Carkhuff, 1967) conducted a number of studies in which they utilized judges who had been trained to rate counselor responses, looking at the ways these reflections affected the development of counseling relationships.

We can simplify Carkuff's system to measure our own responses. Instead of a 1 to 5 point scale, let's use −1, 0, and +1. In this scheme, a score of minus one (−1) is given to responses that detract from what the client has said; responses that miss the mark, or, as one of my students suggested, "It's like the boat left the wharf and you weren't on it." A zero (0) score is given to reflections you make that are neutral, safe, and accurate without being particularly additive. A score of plus one (+1) is given to reflections that really seem to capture the essence of your client's thoughts and feelings and may even accurately add something to the content.

Level +1 Reflection → accurate and additive

Level 0 Reflection → neutral: does not distort, does not add

Level −1 Reflection → distorts and detracts

If you audiotape your interviews, particularly your lab practice sessions as suggested in this book, rate each of your responses as detracting, neutral, or additive (−1, 0, or +1). You can then look at the overall context and flavor of the interview and see how your ratings compare with your general impressions of how things went. This, essentially, is a test of your ability to be empathically responsive. If most of your self-ratings are positive, your client (or others) is most likely seeing you as being truly responsive.

To test this rating scale, rate the reflections you wrote out for Reflection Exercise 6.1. Alternatively, you could swap your responses with someone else's, and rate each other's responses.

Using Reflection Skills to Deepen the Relationship

Arnold Lazarus (1971) poses a model for thinking about the information people share about themselves that consists of a series of concentric circles. The outer circles are the safe, socially polite pieces of information we share about ourselves, and the inner circles represent the increasingly more personal, risky things we share. Others (Feder, 1982; Schooler, 1999) have likened this material that clients present to us as being like the layers of an onion. When counseling relationships are safe and trusting, clients peel back the layers, moving closer to the core as they choose to become more personal and trusting.

Figure 6.2 shows these layers, with the core being the real, authentic self. The more trusting and intimate the relationship, whether it is a counseling relationship, a love relationship, or a friendship, the safer people feel about peeling the layers away to reveal the inner aspects of who they are. Different levels of intimacy

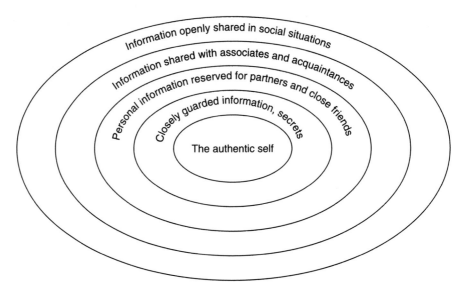

Figure 6.2   The Onion Model of Client Self-Disclosure

yield varying levels of self-disclosure, with only the most intimate relationships cutting to the core of this onion.

Good counseling relationships aim to deepen the level of client self-disclosure. To deepen your relationship with a client, you must provide an environment where it's safe for her to peel the layers back. This can be a difficult and scary process for your client, particularly when there has been abuse or trauma in her life. The layers have been added for protection, and there may be shame or fears of your judgment in showing what lies beneath. It is truly important to remember and respect the fact that these layers of your client's "onion" may have been adopted as protection, or as survival strategies for coping with unpredictable, unsafe environments. Your client may choose to not peel away some of these layers and may choose to keep some aspects of her inner self secret. We should always trust and respect this desire for privacy.

The best way to provide the safety and security necessary for increasing levels of client self-disclosure—and provide that critical empathy—is to listen intently and then to accurately reflect the content and feeling of what's being disclosed. A primary function of counseling, a goal that may or may not be consciously articulated in your action plan with your client, is to help your client become more authentic. As he gains authenticity, his inner world, the inner layers of his "onion," will become available to him in a way that gives your client more choice about what aspects he shows the world. Learning to become more self-disclosing with you may enable your client to become more self-disclosing and open with others.

| LAB PRACTICE 6.1 | *Responding to Content and Feeling—and Rating Your Responses* |

For this exercise you will utilize the quadrad (or triad) lab practice model that you learned in Chapter 4. Working with three (or two) other people, first designate roles. Determine which of you will be the first Client, the first Counselor, and the first Supervisor(s). Decide on the total time you have for this exercise, perhaps a little more than an hour, and calculate how much time you'll have for each interaction, including feedback time. With this exercise, try to factor in a little more time for reflection and feedback than you did in Lab Practice 4.1. If equipment is available, tape-record your practice counseling sessions. As before, it is the job of each Client to come up with some issue to talk about. This may or may not be a real issue, but again, it should not be overly personal or emotionally loaded. Remember that in these lab practices, the emphasis is on skill development, not problem resolution.

In this interaction it is the Counselor's job primarily to respond to content and feeling, only minimally using questions. You might even try to make a point of asking no questions at all. The Supervisor(s) will watch and listen to these interactions, paying particular attention to responses that elicit the most thought and reflection from the Client. Try to capture the essence of what your Client says in your reflections, giving back to the Client the meaning of what's been said to you in concise, clear statements. Avoid saying too much; as long as you're generally on target, your reflections will be received well. When you can identify feelings associated with the content of what's being said, reflect them as well.

Supervisors in this practice session should take notes on specific reflections you make and rate their relative effectiveness. After each counseling interaction, take time to discuss the Counselor's responses and the ways they served (or did not serve) to deepen the conversation and the Client's thinking. In particular, note responses that seemed to be really effective, and discuss your ideas about that. Which reflections served to draw the Client deeper into the material and exploration of the issues at hand, and which served to distract? Again, focus your feedback on the Counselor's responses, not on the Client's problem. Be supportive of each other in this exercise, focusing on Counselor strengths. Give feedback that is nonjudgmental in a way that it can be embraced and utilized by the recipient.

After everyone has had a chance to play all roles, discuss this exercise and your observations of it as a group. Can you make any generalizations about what happened in your small group? Did any particular themes emerge? What are your ideas about the use of questions and about responding to content and feeling?

This exercise can be repeated periodically and practiced until you feel fluent in this mode of response. It may initially feel like an unnatural way of interacting, particularly if this has not been a part of your interpersonal skills repertoire. You will feel more comfortable and confident with this skill as you practice it more.

Finally, if you have audio- or videotaped these practice sessions, go back and rate the reflections you made as a Counselor. Using the −1, 0, and +1 rating scale discussed earlier, see how you would rate each response you made. Note how these rated reflections affected the flow of the interview, particularly the impact each reflection had on subsequent Client thought and reaction.

CASE EXAMPLE 6.2   *Using Reflection to Deepen Client Self-Disclosure*

This case example reinforces the use of reflections of content and feeling. It demonstrates how these reflections can deepen conversation and foster depth, again without the use of questions.

CLIENT: I'm at my wit's end. I'm sure my husband's having an affair, but I don't want to talk with him about it. If he is, if he is fooling around with that little tramp, I don't want to even think about it. If he's not, then I don't know what's wrong with us. I tell you, I'm so worried about this, I can't sleep or do anything.

COUNSELOR: This is tough stuff. You're caught between the rock of wanting to know and the hard place of what that would mean if you knew for sure. I can see how upsetting this is.

This is reflecting the content, ending with reflection of feeling. Note that the counselor has used her own language to capture the essence of the dilemma.

CLIENT: Exactly. Eighteen years of marriage. You think everything's sailing along just great, good kids, good jobs, vacations, everything's great . . . and then this. What a bum! Men. You can't trust any of them.

COUNSELOR: The marriage seemed so wonderful, and yet . . .

Again, reflection of content, leaving it open-ended for the client to continue. The counselor has chosen to respond to the personal aspects of this material, laying the sociopolitical issues of gender aside. If this counselor were a man, with the implied issues about trustworthiness, that too would be filed away for later consideration.

CLIENT: Yeah. We got married when we were young. He was 23, in college, and I'd just

(continued)

(Case example 6.2, continued)

finished high school. I was 18. We thought
I was pregnant, so we got married. Turned out
I wasn't. But we loved each other, and then
we had two kids right off. They're teenagers
now, terrific kids. He got a job at the plant in
town, started there while he was still in school,
and he's making big bucks there. It's a great job.
I mean, he grumbles about being bored and all
that, but I know that's just talk.

COUNSELOR: Everything seemed so great.
No clues of trouble or anything. And then . . .

CLIENT: Boom. It hits the fan. I started to get
ideas about him and Alice a couple of months
ago. We've known her for years. From high
school. She's a teacher in the local elementary
school, and one of our kids had her. I can't
believe they'd let someone like that work with
little kids. There ought to be a law. You should
see her. Little short skirts, bleached hair, the
works. I can't believe he'd see anything in her.

COUNSELOR: It seems incredible. You think you
know someone really well, and then it turns out
there's all this stuff going on behind the scenes.
Scary and sad . . . and enough to make you
really angry.

*These reflections of content, and of the feelings,
are an attempt to capture the realm of this woman's
experience of this situation. The feeling words,
"scary, sad, angry," are general and inclusive at
this point. As time goes on, the counselor will
become more specific and focused about which of
these feelings and associated thoughts are most
relevant.*

Case Discussion

Here, again, the counselor has used no questions,
yet significant information has been disclosed in a
relatively short period of time. Undoubtedly, this
counselor is pondering many questions internally:
Why doesn't she want to talk directly to her husband about this? What about the "false" pregnancy that initiated the marriage? What has this
marriage really been like? Does she work or have
a life outside of the home?

These questions, which remain unasked,
have to do with the hidden content of a

client's inner life. As you consider how to
respond to your client, you will also be forming ideas about the material that has been
presented, about its meaning, and about what
has not been said. Unless you need to collect
a lot of information quickly, you don't need
to ask many questions. If you can be present,
pay attention, and respond with respect
and caring, your client will tell you his story.
All that you need to know will unfold in
due time.

Working with Your Client's Feelings

Dealing with clients' feelings can be a tricky business. Helping your clients learn to identify, manage, and appropriately express feelings is one of the best things you can do with them. The more facility you have in the language of feelings, the better you will be at helping your clients articulate and deal with their feelings (Hill & O'Brien, 1999). This takes practice, skill, and experience, for it is truly a complicated aspect of this work. Some people seem to be awash in feelings, a veritable stew of everything from anger and sadness to anxiety and depression. They are volatile and sometimes unpredictable in how they experience and express their feelings, and they may seem under the control of the emotions that swirl within them. It can be exciting and sometimes a bit frightening to be in the presence of someone who is operating with such powerful emotional material.

Other clients may show no noticeable affect at all. You may sit there wondering if this person ever experiences any emotion, let alone the volatility of the person awash in feeling just described. He may appear to be flat, expressionless, and talk about even difficult material with a distinct absence of feeling. You may find yourself speculating about what kind of socialization process has rendered such flatness, such control. Some of your clients, portraying yet another emotional style, may seem to be perpetually angry, perpetually sad, or in the grip of some other single emotion. Their entire being seems overrun by this emotion, and they seem defined by it.

You will see a range of styles and skills among your clients in their abilities to identify, experience, and manage their feelings. Part of your job is to help them to improve their skill level in this arena, to help them increase their ability to be emotionally fluent and able to maintain a healthy relationship with their emotional "self." Your ability to recognize and deal with your client's feelings may, in fact, be one of the most important things you can do to demonstrate your trustworthiness and promote the working alliance between the two of you (Murphy, Cramer, & Lillie, 1984).

Helping Your Client Understand the Language of Feeling

You can assist your clients with the language and expression of feelings by helping them to identify and name their feelings. Some people, and children are certainly in this group, experience a lot of feeling but have no language to describe what is going on inside. You can help them learn to describe these feeling states. Many elementary school counselors—and other counselors who work with children—have charts of "feelings words" tacked up on the walls to help their clients with this identification. You can help your clients learn this language of feeling by using feelings words in your reflections of content and feeling about the material they give you, much as was done in Case Example 6.2, where the counselor used the words "scary" and "sad" and "angry" to help the client recognize the range of feelings she was experiencing.

Part of building your counseling skills is developing your repertory of feelings words and incorporating them in your reflections of the content and feelings that you imagine your clients are experiencing in situations they describe. Most feelings words are variations of the basic feelings quadrad: mad, glad, sad, or scared. Thus, when your client tells you about a particularly bad day at work, you can suggest, "And when your boss told you that you'd done a lousy job, you could feel your self getting angry, frustrated." By supplying words to describe the emotional experience, you begin to give your client some tools for making order out of the confusion within. The more accurate you can be about the feelings you imagine to be transpiring, the better, but your client will usually tell you if you're off the mark. "I don't know if I felt angry, but yes, I definitely felt frustrated. No matter how hard I try, I just can't please my boss." Your ability to accurately identify and reflect feelings will go a long way toward demonstrating your capacity to relate with empathy to your client (Egan, 2002).

There may be some interesting gender issues at play in this business of identifying and expressing feelings. Some are undoubtedly due to cultural conditioning. Men are generally conditioned to be less comfortable with identifying and expressing feelings than are women (Scher & Stevens, 1987), and my experience suggests that they are typically least comfortable expressing sadness and fear. A woman's emotional expressiveness may be closely tied to her conditioning as well. You may misinterpret a female client's emotions if you do not understand and appreciate some of the political realities with which she deals (Foster & May, 2003). You will miss the boat, for example, if you assume that a woman's tears are always about sadness. In fact, they may signal anger or even rage about some unfair personal or political situation.

Your job, with both women and men, is to assist them in a process of destigmatizing their gender "inappropriate" feelings, usually through your own demonstrated comfort with those feelings. Your work with both men and women is to help them become more able to identify and verbally express the range of feelings they experience, including those with which they feel less comfortable. Naturally, this process begins with your becoming fluent in the different ways men and women approach and share their emotional experiences (Lee & Robbins, 2000).

Similarly, there may be cultural differences in how people experience and express emotional states (Channabasavanna & Bhatti, 1982; Palmer & Laungani, 1999). Different cultures are variously rigid in their gender-specific expression of emotions, for example. This can result in an interesting, complex mix of cultural and gender factors influencing how your client may approach the business of sharing feelings with you. Your job is to respect and try to understand these differences, while still helping your client to be as expressively free as possible within his or her own cultural context. You also need to take great care not to generalize and stereotype individuals based on cultural heritage; there is great individual variation within cultural groups.

Your client may talk about her "bad" feelings. She may have stigmatized her own feeling state and labeled how she feels as inappropriate. Your job with her, in addition to helping her to expand her emotional language, will be to assure her that there is no such thing as a bad feeling. People do sometimes do bad things springing from how they feel, but that does not make the feeling bad. Feeling enraged, and then striking out, is not usually a great thing to do. It's the striking that could be labeled as "bad," however, not the rage. All feelings are what they are, and our choices about what we do with those are something else. There may be bad behaviors, but there are no bad feelings.

Finally, as we talk about this language of feeling, our clients sometimes make a simple mistake that makes for messy emotional communication. Someone may use the words "I feel" when what is actually meant is "I think." For example, "I feel that war is wrong" is not a statement about feelings at all; rather, it is an idea about war. You can help your client by gently and consistently reinforcing the use of "I feel" to actually precede a statement about an internal feeling state. This may take some repeated work with your client, but it can be very effective.

Helping Your Client Manage Unruly Emotions

Each of us experiences our emotions differently. Some of us experience and express our emotions freely and with abandon, some are much more controlled (Ivey, 2003). Some of your clients will have fallen victim to their own emotions. They ride a sea of tumultuous feeling that threatens to swamp them or to harmfully affect others. They may seem to be perpetually angry, thinking that the world is a horrible, unsafe place in which to live (and some of their experiences may have supported this), or terrified and traumatized by terrible life events. And this perpetual rush of feeling may prompt them to do rash, unwise things, either to themselves or to other people.

With a client who seems to be behaviorally running amok, you need to begin by helping him bring the behavioral acting out under control. Clients who are in the throes of emotional crisis, or who are severely disturbed, should also be treated carefully with regard to emotional expression (Brammer & MacDonald, 1996). Anger management programs, stress reduction training, anxiety containment programs, or behavior-shaping strategies can be helpful tools in managing emotions that run out of control. Later chapters in this book, particularly those that talk about action skills and crisis management, describe ways to assist the process of emotional management.

Once the negative behaviors have been addressed, or as they are being addressed, work with your client to find appropriate ways to express those feelings. The use of play (particularly, though not exclusively, with children) or programs of expressive arts can be helpful tools. More usually, however, continued talk, with language clarification and support for direct expression, is the best vehicle. The same reflective stances, helping your client to identify and clarify her feelings, are most effective.

With a client who seems to present the same emotional state consistently, whether it be anger, sadness, or anxiety, it can be very helpful to consider what else might be going on. Oftentimes, when a client has created a lifestyle around a particular feeling state, it is as a defense against more primitive, frightening feelings underneath. The client may, for example, feel pretty comfortable in her consistent expression of anger, but you may consider and wonder about the feelings under that anger—the sadness about inevitable past losses or her fears about the future. You can encourage her to consider the wider range of feelings by responding to those with your reflections when you suspect that they are present.

The Expression of Feelings: A Word of Caution

At this point I must pause for a caveat about this expression-of-feelings arena. For some of our clients, particularly those in dangerous situations, honest expression of feeling may, literally, not be safe. You need to be aware of and respect this fact and avoid putting clients at risk. For an incarcerated client, anger may be a safe emotion to express; sadness and vulnerability, although they may be present internally, may not be safely expressed. For children or women in abusive home situations, honest expressions of feeling may not be safe. In such situations, your job is twofold: do what you can to ensure safety (e.g., reporting physical abuse); and talk with your client about where it is safe to express feeling (e.g., in your office), and where it is not (e.g., in jail). Helping our clients to stay physically safe is the first priority—expressing feelings is secondary.

Other situations may also be unsafe, but not physically. A student in your school counseling office may be reluctant to fully experience the grief of the recent loss of a pet when she has to return to class soon. A woman may be hesitant to share her feelings of anger with an unfair boss, and some of that hesitancy may be based on the real threat to her job. You need to respect these concerns as well. The woman in this example can be helped to identify and own her feelings while sorting out the optional outcomes associated with expressing herself with her boss. For some in this situation, blowing off steam with you in your office may be enough. For others, that emotional release with you may simply be a prelude to doing it with others. Your job is to help people identify the feelings, as well as the risks attendant with direct expression of feelings.

Helping Emotionally Reluctant Clients to Express Themselves

At the other end of the emotional continuum are clients who have an iron hold on their emotions. They keep their feelings under wraps and let little out in the way of expressed emotion. They may talk fluently about their feelings (graduate counseling students can be masters at this) without actually seeming to experience those feelings much. The talking, in fact, may be yet one more defense against actually allowing the experiencing of feeling.

We can speculate that these are people for whom rationality and control are paramount, that perhaps they have been trained to hold themselves in check. For whatever reason, there may be negative connotations associated with the spontaneous release of feeling, so they hold themselves closely in check to avoid letting any feeling leach to the surface. Perhaps they have experienced some trauma, the memories of which have been long buried and ignored along with all of the feelings associated with them. Someone may be terrified of loosening the grip on all of those inner feelings for fear that they will overtake and consume him. Some of my clients have told me that they are afraid to start crying, because if they do, they will never stop.

People pay a price for denying themselves the experience of their own feelings. A rigidity and hardness develops, which serves to isolate one from oneself as well as from a genuine experiencing of others. Shutting off access to one kind of feeling has the effect of shutting off access to most other feelings as well. When a client denies herself the experience of acknowledging her so-called bad feelings, she also denies herself the full range of capacity to experience joy. This frozen feeling is what lends itself to the appearance of rigidity.

Provide a safe, secure, welcoming environment for the expression of feeling, and make accurate feelings reflections to assist the process of learning the language of feelings. You serve a *containing* function for the feelings your client expresses. That is, by accurately understanding and responding to a client's internal world, you help the client to safely manage, to contain, his thoughts and feelings so that he doesn't have to fear being overwhelmed by them (Levy, 2004; Spurling, 2004). This safety you provide makes it possible for more feelings to be shared by the client. While you may try specific experiments or techniques to help people access feelings (e.g., expressive arts or Gestalt techniques), it is primarily through the trusting relationship with you, and particularly in your receptivity to feelings expression, that most of the action really occurs.

Some people have catastrophic fears about what will happen if and when they let themselves publicly share their feelings. They fear ridicule and judgment. What usually happens, should they choose to let feelings out with trusted others, is the opposite. It's paradoxical. Other people usually experience such sharing as a gift and are drawn to those who choose to share difficult emotions. Not only that, the person who has shared usually cares less about what others think after an emotionally cathartic experience, for there is personal power experienced in letting the feelings flow. People, in fact, do not cry forever, and they almost universally feel better after a good bawl.

It is a privilege to be in the presence of a client who chooses to let her feelings thaw and flow after a long period of deep freeze. You are like a midwife to the birth of these feelings, and you can express your support, respect, and gratitude when your client shares such an experience with you. Your comfort with your own feelings is key to your receptivity and openness to the feelings of others.

REFLECTION EXERCISE 6.2   *Dealing with Your Own Emotions*

Given that you will be expected to deal with your client's emotions, it stands to reason that your relationship with your own emotional world is important. The more familiarity you have with your emotional life, the better prepared you will be to deal with that of your client.

Take stock of your emotions and of your usual style of dealing with them. Do you have a characteristic emotional style, and are you comfortable with that style? Do you expresses emotions freely, or do you hold them closely inside yourself? What is the general emotional demeanor that you present to the world?

Create an emotional rating scale for yourself. Imagine a 1 to 5 scale, with 1 representing "not expressive" and 5 "very expressive," and rate your expressiveness on basic emotions (e.g., sad, mad, glad, scared). With minimal judgment, survey your ratings. What are the positive benefits or negative consequences of how you express yourself?

Are you comfortable with how you deal with your own emotions? How do you think your responses to your own emotional world might affect your work with clients? Are your ways of dealing with your emotions a good model for your clients? To the degree that you feel comfortable, discuss your personal reflections with a small group of colleagues.

Concluding Thoughts: Listening with Head and Heart

Good counseling involves the ability to respond to both your client's thoughts and feelings. In a sense, it is about using both your head and your heart as you build a relationship with this person. Many of us are naturally inclined to respond more easily and readily in one of those domains, so it is incumbent upon each of us to develop that side with which we are less familiar. If you are familiar and feel comfortable with your client's ideas but less so with his (and maybe your own) feelings, you will need to stretch yourself to become more at home with the world of emotions. Conversely, if you are a feeling-oriented person, you may need to nurture your thought-oriented side.

Supervision and honest contact with your colleagues and friends can help with this. Ask for feedback about how others perceive your response style, and experiment with new ways of listening and responding. Exercises, like the ones in this book, can help you develop your listening and responding facility. Your natural curiosity about yourself and other people, coupled with your desire to hone your abilities to be an effective listener and responder, will be your biggest assets in this search.

For Further Thought

1. Examine the literature regarding the concept of empathy. Investigate the ways different theoretical schools consider and deal with the concept. Look at research that has been done on the subject. How does all of this fit together for you, particularly as it relates to your emerging thoughts about your own counseling work?

2. Talk with elementary, middle, and high school counselors in your area about their ability to form relationships with students. What kinds of pressures are there, whether because of time or for other reasons, that might hurt their ability to form solid counseling relationships with students? Do their schools value the formation of counseling relationships, or are counselors so burdened with other activities that counseling is seen as a peripheral activity?

3. Talk with counselors in local mental health agencies about the size and composition of their caseloads. How do these factors affect their ability to pursue counseling relationships with clients? What about the number of sessions or length of time they are allowed to keep a client on their caseload; how does that affect their relationships with clients?

4. Consider how counselors or psychotherapists are depicted in popular films. The films *Good Will Hunting*, *The Prince of Tides*, *Ordinary People*, and the television series *The Sopranos* portray working counselors. View one or more of these and critique the role of the therapist. Can you identify with any of the counselors in these films? Do you have any problems with these portrayals?

References

Allen, J., Coyne, L., Colson, D., & Horwitz, L. (1996). Pattern of therapist interventions associated with patient collaboration. *Psychotherapy, 33,* 254–261.

Allport, G. (1961). *Pattern and growth in personality.* New York: Holt, Rinehart, & Winston.

Bohart, A., & Greenberg, L. (Eds.). (1997). *Empathy reconsidered: New directions in psychotherapy.* Washington, DC: American Psychological Association.

Brammer, L., & MacDonald, G. (1996). *The helping relationship: Process and skills* (6th ed.). Boston: Allyn & Bacon.

Carkhuff, R. (1967). Toward a comprehensive model of facilitative interpersonal processes. *Journal of Counseling Psychology, 14,* 67–72.

Carkhuff, R. (1969). *Helping and human relations.* New York: Holt, Rinehart, & Winston.

Carkhuff, R., & Berenson, B. (1967). *Beyond counseling and therapy.* New York: Holt, Rinehart, & Winston.

Channabasavanna, S., & Bhatti, R. (1982). A study on interactional patterns and family typologies in families of mental patients. In A. Kiev & A. Rao (Eds.), *Readings in transcultural psychiatry* (pp. 149–161). Madras: Higgenbothams.

Duan, C., & Hill, C. (1996). The current state of empathy research. *Journal of Counseling Psychology, 43,* 343–350.

Egan, G. (2002). *The skilled helper* (7th ed.). Monterey, CA: Brooks/Cole.

Feder, B. (1982). *Peeling the onion: A Gestalt therapy manual for clients.* Montclair, NJ: Author.

Foster, V., & May, K. (2003). Counseling women from feminist perspectives. In N. Vacc, S. DeVaney, & J. Brendel (Eds.), *Counseling multicultural and diverse populations* (pp. 163–187). New York: Brunner-Routledge.

Highlen, P., & Baccus, G. (1977). Effect of reflection of feeling and probe on client self-referenced affect. *Journal of Counseling Psychology, 24,* 440–443.

Hill, C., & O'Brien, K. (1999). *Helping skills: Facilitating exploration, insight, and action.* Washington, DC: American Psychological Association.

Ivey, A. (2003). *Intentional interviewing and counseling: Facilitating client development in a multicultural world.* Pacific Grove, CA: Brooks/Cole.

Ivey, A., Ivey, M., & Simek-Morgan, L. (1997). *Counseling and psychotherapy: A multicultural perspective.* Boston: Allyn & Bacon.

Kohut, H. (1984). *How does analysis cure?* Chicago: University of Chicago Press.

Lazarus, A. (1971). *Behavior therapy and beyond.* New York: McGraw-Hill.

Lee, R., & Robbins, S. (2000). Understanding social connectedness in college women and men. *Journal of Counseling and Development, 78,* 484–491.

Levy, S. (2004). Containment and validation: Working with survivors of trauma. In S. Levy & A. Lemma (Eds.), *Perversion of loss: Psychoanalytic perspectives on trauma* (pp. 50–70). Philadelphia: Whurr.

Murphy, P., Cramer, D., & Lillie, F. (1984). The relationship between curative factors perceived by patients in their psychotherapy and treatment outcome: An exploratory study. *British Journal of Medical Psychology, 57,* 187–192.

Palmer, S., & Laungani, P. (Eds.). (1999). *Counselling in a multicultural society.* London: Sage.

Reik, T. (1951). *Listening with the third ear.* New York: Pyramid Press.

Rogers, C. (1951). *Client-centered therapy: Its current practice, implications, and theory.* Boston: Houghton Mifflin.

Rogers, C. (1980). *A way of being.* Boston: Houghton Mifflin.

Scher, M., & Stevens, M. (1987). Men and violence. *Journal of Counseling and Development, 65,* 351–355.

Schooler, J. (1999). Seeking the core: The issues and evidence surrounding recovered accounts of sexual trauma. In L. Williams & V. Banyard (Eds.), *Trauma and memory* (pp. 203–216). Thousand Oaks, CA: Sage.

Spurling, R. (2004). *An introduction to psychodynamic counselling.* Basingstoke and New York: Palgrave Macmillan.

Truax, C., & Carkhuff, R. (1967). *Toward effective counseling and psychotherapy.* Chicago: Aldine.

Tryon, G. (2002). Empathy. In G. Tryon (Ed.), *Counseling based on process research: Applying what we know* (pp. 97–231). Boston: Allyn & Bacon.

Williams, E. (2002). Therapist techniques. In G. Tryon (Ed.), *Counseling based on process research: Applying what we know* (pp. 232–264). Boston: Allyn & Bacon.

CHAPTER 7

Skills for Furthering Relationship Development

This work is about transformation—from the person who we are to the person we really are. In the end, we can't be anyone else.
(Marion Rosen)

In the previous chapter we looked at some fundamental ways in which you can respond thoughtfully, and with feeling, to your clients. In this chapter we focus on other specific skills and uses of language that can add depth and substance to the growing relationship and the therapeutic alliance you strive to solidify. These skills may serve as a bridge to further communication and will supplement your effective use of questions and reflection of content and feeling.

Focusing

As you engage your client, you will continually make choices about how to respond to the things your client talks about. Selectively attending to one part of the material over another is referred to as *focusing*. In Case Example 6.2, the counselor dealt with a woman who suspected that her husband was having an affair. The woman talked of her suspicions, and she also started to talk about her questions about how trustworthy men are in general. The counselor chose to respond to the part of this material that related directly to the woman and her relationship with her husband, not to the material about the trustworthiness of men. The counselor tried to keep the client focused on the personal nature of the relationship with her husband and away from a political discussion about men in general. The more you can keep your client on track, focused on what you perceive as most important in the moment, the more effective this experience will be for your client (Brammer, 1973; Carkhuff, 1967; Carkhuff & Berenson, 1967).

The place where you work and your theoretical orientation will also play a role in how you selectively attend to material and focus your client. If you work in a drug clinic, you will attend particularly to issues related to drug use. A family counselor might attend more to the interplay between family members and be less concerned with issues involving non–family members. A counselor with a psychoanalytic orientation would probably focus more on the client's family of origin than would a counselor with a cognitive-behavioral orientation, and so on. You have considerable freedom of choice, power in fact, in choosing what to reflect to guide the discussion.

Generally, focusing helps to create order in the material your client presents. Particularly for clients whose thinking and presentation are scattered, focusing can help them begin to create some structure in how they contemplate the array of issues in their lives. Focusing can help prioritize problems, for example, and this can help both you and your client think more constructively about how to actively approach them in an organized fashion.

You may choose to have your client be a full participant in this process of focusing. You can use a reflective comment to summarize the array of concerns he has enumerated, and then ask him to select which is most important. You might say, "Well, you've talked about your concerns about work, about your family, and about your relationship with your friend. Which of these is most important right now?" This sets the stage for a more focused discussion, but instead of your choosing, the client takes command of the choice process.

Personalizing to Promote Responsibility

Many clients have a great deal of trouble talking about the events of their lives in a way that seems connected to them. For example, a client may use the word *it* to describe feelings, as in "It feels good when there's a lot going on." By reflecting this material in a personalized way, by simply substituting *you* for *it* ("You feel good when there's a lot going on"), you can help the client make the connection of personal responsibility for her own material. Another client may talk abstractly about life events in a manner that seems to lack personal connection. For example, in Case Example 6.2 the client remarked that "You just can't trust men. They're all untrustworthy." You can help this client make a personal connection to those abstract ideas by saying in reply, "You don't trust men" rather than "Men aren't trustworthy." This may seem like only a slight variation in language, but it serves the purpose of making a much stronger personal connection to the material.

Your goal is to help clients incorporate personalized language into the way they speak about themselves and their experiences. The client who learns to say, "I feel that people will like me more if I make them laugh" instead of "You have to be funny to be popular" is learning to take responsibility for his own material. This is one small but significant step along the client's road to the realization that being responsible for his own behavior means that he has the power to change his behavior.

Immediacy

Many of the ways a client behaves in the world come into play in the counseling office. Your direct experience of your client, in the here and now of the counseling session, gives you a sense of how she operates in that greater world. Your client is not totally different in her relations with others than she is with you. It is also true that your client's direct experience of you in the here and now of the counseling session gives her a sense of how other people operate in the greater world. Your direct experience of her and her direct experience of you can translate into learning opportunities for your client, if used productively. Focusing on the material as it relates to you and the relationship between the two of you is called *immediacy*.

There are two ways of making a client's material more immediate: (1) relate material to the relationship between the two of you, and (2) reveal your personal reactions to your client and what she talks about—also known as *self-disclosure* (Cormier & Cormier, 1991).

Increasing Immediacy in the Relationship

When you respond to your client about some aspect of how he is dealing with you, either obviously or in a more hidden fashion, you make the engagement between you more immediate. I find this skill to be one of the most potent sources of learning because it is gleaned directly from the counseling relationship itself. When the two of you sit and talk together, all of the client's relationship skills and difficulties are at play. As counselors it is here that we have our most direct, observable evidence of how clients most likely behave with other people. The defenses, the charm, or whatever other ways of relating that have served clients well or poorly in other relationships eventually find their way into the counseling office. It is for exactly this reason that the counseling relationship is often defined as a microcosm of your client's interpersonal world.

A short example of making the relationship more immediate may help illustrate this. In Case Example 6.2, if the counselor happens to be male, the trustworthiness of men is no longer simply a theoretical, "out there" concern. A male counselor can make the material more immediate by commenting on the obvious fact of his being male and the implications for her being able to trust him: "You say that men aren't trustworthy, so you must have some concerns about my capacity to be trustworthy as well." This personalizes the abstract statement and makes it more immediate regarding the current situation between client and counselor. This is akin to experiential learning in the classroom, wherein the material under review is made more relevant by virtue of direct experience of what it means.

Sometimes, particularly in group counseling, this reflection for immediacy is referred to as *process commentary*. The *content* of a discussion is the material, or subject, under review. It might be work or families or career goals or some other topic of concern. It is the *what* of the discussion. *Process,* on the other hand, is about the *how*. In individual counseling, process is about the interaction between the counselor and the client; that is, it is about the counseling relationship itself.

In the previous example, the male counselor personalized the female client's abstract statement by focusing it on himself. But what do you do when the client chooses to make you, or the relationship between you, the subject of the discussion? The true skill and art of making good solid responses to immediate relationship issues is in being able to personalize the material without taking it personally. In other words, you want to be able to use yourself and the counseling relationship as vehicles for teaching, but not in a way that you become emotionally hooked, or defensive, about whatever the issues are. If you do find yourself becoming unduly hooked, some unfinished business of your own, some reminder of past people or situations, is probably infringing on the current situation.

There is a brilliant scene in the popular film *Good Will Hunting* in which the bright, articulate, and troubled college-aged client, played by Matt Damon, hooks his counselor (Robin Williams) by making barbed references to the counselor's wife. Unbeknownst to the client, the counselor's wife is dead, and his life has been turned upside-down by his unresolved grief surrounding her loss. In the painful silence that ensues, the counselor struggles to contain his powerful feelings. It is an explosive moment in the film, as it is in any therapeutic relationship where similar dynamics unfold. It is a moment that has become immediate and personal. In the film the counselor is able to recoup with some remarkably adept teaching responses, some reflections related to the interactions between the two of them, and this marks a positive turning point in the counseling relationship. The theme of this film is the simultaneous redemption of the counselor and the client. In real life, however, this kind of vulnerability should be more skillfully avoided by the counselor.

An effective counselor chooses when to respond to relationship issues as part of the overall selective attention process. Counselors time interventions about process variables just as they would any other intervention, always keeping in mind the goal, which is to best serve the client's efforts to resolve his issues. Discussion of the dynamics of the process between client and counselor is appropriate when it does not distract from other more pertinent and compelling things being discussed and when it sheds light on the issues the client has and does not detract from actively pursuing his stated goals. In Case Example 6.2, for example, the counselor would probably wait until later to talk about the client's "untrustworthy men" comment and its implications for the relationship with a male counselor, focusing first on the specifics of her marriage and the unfolding current events that affect it.

One of the things you will be able to do as you gain experience as a counselor is to monitor the events of your external world and those of your internal world with greater ease and fluidity. You will become adept at checking in with your intrapsychic experience—your thoughts and feelings—as you take in the unfolding story and events of your client's life. This fluidity and ability to rapidly check in with yourself makes it possible for you to promote immediacy in the relationship based on your own internal experience of your client and the things that transpire between you.

This ability, shifting from the intrapersonal level of awareness to the interpersonal level of awareness and back again, sets the stage for making reflections about your relationship, or about your own reactions to your client, in a way that would not be possible otherwise. The more you are in touch with your own internal world of experience, the easier it will be for you to make reflections that foster immediacy.

Self-Disclosure to Promote Immediacy

It can be extremely helpful for our clients to know that we have experienced life, losses, and personal difficulty (Nyman & Daugherty, 2001). The use of self-disclosure can promote immediacy in your relationship with your client, this time by sharing something about yourself as it relates to the material being talked about. This sharing may be about some experience or about some internal thought or feeling state of yours that relates to your client's material or to what is going on in the relationship.

Case Example 7.1 *Using Immediacy to Promote Client Responsibility*

In this case example, a school counselor and a high school student have had a few meetings together, during which the counselor has asked lots of informational background questions. A primary stated goal for this student is to learn how to get more "respect" from adults, to have them treat him more as an equal. Toward that end, the counselor wants the student to begin to take more responsibility for deciding the direction in which the counseling goes. She wants to assume a less directive stance while he assumes more responsibility (a shift from Level 1 to Level 2 in our developmental model) in their relationship. The counselor uses a simple type of reflection—silence—to foster immediacy and focus the client's attention on the process.

STUDENT: You know, it's been a lot of the same old stuff. Hassles with teachers, hassles with parents, they just never leave me alone. It's crummy. They never let me make any decisions for myself.

COUNSELOR: So, there's a lot going on. I wonder, of these, if there are any specific interactions that were really bad.

This vague reflection is followed by the wondering comment, which is designed to promote focusing. She wants him to zero in on something specific they can work on.

STUDENT: Oh, I don't know. It's all pretty confusing, there's so much going on. I don't know which is most important, the stuff with my teachers, or the stuff with my parents. *[Long silence.]*

COUNSELOR: It can be really hard to come up with one compelling issue. *[Another long silence.]* You'd really prefer it if I'd choose. *[Silence, again.]*

This first reflection, followed by silence, focuses on the process of what is transpiring. It is designed to promote immediacy. The counselor has avoided the temptation to pick a topic and instead comments on the "spaces," both in the student's internal processing and what passes between them. This is followed by another reflection about the counselor's assumption of what the student wants.

STUDENT: Well, yeah, I mean it's rough. I don't know who's worse, my parents or my teachers.

The student's remarks betray his lack of comfort in making the choice, which may be indicative of the

(continued)

(Case example 7.1, continued)

And you're the expert. Can't you give me a clue about which way to go here?

struggle he has with adults. He may not be aware of how he sets things up to wind up feeling personally powerless. This is a classic adolescent struggle, with lots of potential learning about functioning as an adult. His "you're the expert" comment is tinged with hostility and is a potential trap. "You choose, and then I'll resent the choice."

COUNSELOR: Sure, I can pick, if that's what you really want. I'll point out that might be exactly like what happens between you and your teachers and your parents. It's a bit of a setup.

The counselor avoids the student's barbed request to choose, but says she will, if that's what he really wants. She wants to avoid a power struggle. Her reflective comment about "exactly what happens" is interpretive (drawing inferences to his issues with adults via the direct relationship between them) and promotes immediacy in the relationship.

STUDENT: OK, I think I get the drift of this. You're saying that I let other people choose for me, and then I get mad when things don't work out.

And then, bingo, the student gets it. He draws the connection the counselor has pointed out. If only it were usually this easy.

Case Discussion

The counselor here is interested in using the relationship, and the communication patterns between her and this student, as a direct source of learning about the things he deals with in his greater world. The business of transferring learning from the counseling relationship back to the client's outside life is a primary goal of counseling. Responses to process, promoting immediacy, are usually a great way to initiate this. There are an infinite number of ways to do this, with no single set of responses being absolutely correct.

In this example, the counselor is making many assumptions about the student, his relationship with authority, and the implications for their own relationship together. Each of these is a mini-hypothesis, which merits pursuit and checking out. Our clients will eventually provide the verification of our ideas and assumptions about their lives, or not, if we listen well.

In the film *Good Will Hunting*, the counselor eventually decides to tell the client about his love for his wife, her death, and his struggle with grief. A parent who has lost a child may think that no one could know anything about that experience except one who has experienced a similar loss. The same is true of a survivor of abuse or violence or addiction. People who are in the throes of withdrawal from drugs or in the newly immediate pain of having lost a loved one seem to draw special solace and support from those who know, firsthand, how truly difficult this really is. If you have such a significant experience in common with your client, and you feel safe in sharing it, you can consider letting your client know about

---

REFLECTION EXERCISE 7.1   *Paying Attention to Your Feelings*

Pick someone with whom to do this exercise. Sit across from this person and casually look at him or her. Take in the way this person is dressed, the way he or she sits, and other details about this person. Spend two or three minutes, certainly not longer than feels comfortable, to fully experience this other person's presence.

When you have completed this observation experience, turn your attention inward. Close your eyes, look away, you might even turn your chair around if that will help you focus more intently on your own internal experience. Take note of your feelings, particularly in regard to this other person and your experience of doing this exercise.

Any number of feelings may surface—anxiety, attraction, whatever. These are all natural and acceptable. What thoughts run through your mind as you note your feelings and your experience of doing this? Are your thoughts related directly to this experience and this other person, or do other thoughts intrude? What are they about? You might write about this experience, or talk about it with your partner in the exercise, to the extent that feels safe. In what ways do you imagine this is just like, or unlike, what transpires in a counseling session with a client?

---

this. In making this decision, ask yourself if you have sufficiently worked through your own feelings and thoughts about the material you are about to disclose. If not, better to let this lie fallow.

Self-disclosure of personal experiences can be a powerful tool in the development of appropriate intimacy in a counseling relationship (Nyman & Daugherty, 2001), but don't let self-disclosure get in the way, or diminish, your client's ability to relay his own experience. Most of the time, the bonds of understanding can be communicated subtly, often with few words. Saying something simply and with feeling, such as "Yes, I really understand" or "I get it, I've been there" can convey the depth of your understanding and experience. Once again, there are no absolutes, and each of us needs to find our own way with this. There are many arguments in favor of counselor self-disclosure (e.g., modeling, rapport-building, giving encouragement) and many against (e.g., boundary blurring, merging, concern about counselor welfare). Weigh the pros and cons carefully in each situation (Simone, McCarthy, & Skay, 1998).

There are two kinds of self-disclosure. One variety is related to the information and the details of our life experience, the things that have happened in our lives. The other has to do with our internal experience, our thoughts and feelings.

Self-Disclosure—Some Pitfalls and Provisos

Counselors sometimes grapple with the problem of inappropriate self-disclosure. That is, giving the client too much information about his own experience or feelings or thoughts. In *Love's Executioner* (Yalom, 1989), a valuable collection of counseling stories and vignettes, Irvin Yalom describes a situation that captures this potential danger perfectly. In one story, a woman counselor is coleading a group, and she describes her experience of being raped. One of the members, a provocative and fairly offensive man, presses her for details of the rape, and she eventually correctly surmises that he is not only goading her but also getting off on the details. She is devastated and leaves the group crying. This self-disclosure was inappropriate for two reasons: there was no legitimate helpful reason to talk with the group about her own rape (it served no useful, thoughtful purpose), and she also still had a lot of unresolved feelings about the experience.

There is a common societal belief that goes like this: "When I tell you about experiences I have had that are somewhat like yours, it will suggest to you that I really understand your experience and that I can be trusted. If I have experienced losses somewhat like yours or trauma like yours or an addiction like yours, I can share my experience with you, and you'll feel more understood and accepted." Unfortunately, my experience suggests that the opposite usually occurs. When I, as a counselor, begin to relate my experience that I think is so similar yours, I commit two errors in reasoning. The first mistake is in assuming that our experiences are anything alike. Even though I am also a recovering addict or a survivor of abuse or have experienced terrible losses in my life, nothing ensures that my experiences were anything like yours. To the degree that we are each unique, so are our experiences.

Second, whenever I begin to talk of myself, it takes the focus away from whatever it was that you were talking about. My desire to make you more comfortable by sharing an experience of mine has the paradoxical effect of telling you that your experience, at least right now, is not worth pursuing. Better that I sit and truly listen and take in the experiences that you feel comfortable sharing with me. In addition, cultural differences for some clients may make self-disclosures inappropriate or counterproductive. Typically, these differences relate to a desire to see the counselor as an expert, in which case, self-disclosure makes the counselor appear to be untrained, even incompetent (Cherbosque, 1987).

While it is usually safer and more appropriate to share feelings from our internal world with our client—as opposed to our experiences—in that this is directly related to our work with them, it is not always helpful to do so (Hendrick, 1988). Your desire to promote immediacy in the relationship by way of sharing your internal experience of what your client is saying or doing may be harmful for your client, and it may also be harmful for you. Some people may try to use information about you in destructive ways. Should you choose, for example, to tell your adolescent client of your past drug-using days, he may use that information in ways that could harm you. He could share it with people who you might not want to know about it. Sharing any information about yourself, particularly about your past transgressions, could come back to haunt you.

More typically, however, the primary concern has to do with the impact self-disclosure has on your client. I once supervised a new counselor whose job in the agency was to do intake interviews with new clients. He strongly believed in being transparent (not holding back what is felt,

(continued)

(continued)

letting clients know about ongoing feeling states) and readily shared his experience of feeling anxious with new, highly anxious clients. Sharing his feelings of anxiety with me, his supervisor, was appropriate. Sharing those anxious feelings with new clients, however, only served to heighten their already skyrocketing anxiety and drove some of them away. Someone who is highly anxious and agitated usually does much better with a support person who is grounded, steady, and solid in demeanor. We'll talk more about this in Chapter 10.

This kind of counselor self-disclosure is sometimes referred to as *transparency* (Jourard, 1971). Decisions need to be made about the wisdom of sharing either kind of experience, and these decisions should be made on the basis of our assessment of the help that it might be, as well as the timing of the sharing (Bishop & Lane, 2001).

Before any self-disclosure is made is, ask yourself this question: "What real purpose will my telling about this serve?" Will this really be in the service of my client, or is it more about my needs, for example, my need to convey what a good, trustworthy person I am? Once a disclosure is made, evaluate what happened as a result. Did the relationship deepen, with the client becoming more self-disclosing about herself, or did the conversation fizzle and go nowhere? If it went nowhere, the self-disclosure was not helpful. The proof of the intervention, in whatever it is we say to our client, is in what comes afterward. Unsuccessful interventions translate into dead space, switched topics, and superficial conversation. Successful interventions, including our self-disclosures, translate into deeper communication.

Transference and Countertransference in Relationship Immediacy

When material that is directly evident in our relationship with a client is used to highlight issues that exist in the client's outside life, it is a powerful vehicle for learning. *Transference* often plays a central role in this learning. The transference phenomenon has to do with the ways in which our clients bring old unfinished business, usually involving significant figures in their past, particularly parents, into the current relationship with us. In Case Example 7.1, for example, the client's relationship with the counselor is entangled with his relationships with other adults, especially his parents, but also with teachers and others in authority. The counselor articulates this entanglement by pointing out the ways the client is trying to force the counselor to make choices for him. The client has *transferred* his feelings about his parents and other adults and his reactions to what they do to this situation with the counselor. By refusing to go along with the client's transference, the counselor provides an opportunity for the client to deal with her in a new, more adult fashion.

The counselor has her own unique reactions to her client as well, some of which are based on the reality of who he is and some based on her own unfinished business. The counselor's unfinished business is the stuff of *countertransference,* the mirror image of the client's transference. Counselors as well as clients have active inner lives filled with fantasies and conscious and unconscious material from the past, and all of that affects current work with a client. Client behavior triggers and sets that material in motion, and it can be a helpful or hindering aspect of the work. It is helpful to the degree that you as a counselor are able to become conscious of it and are not controlled by it. This is one more reason to have good supervision.

It has been my experience that two typical countertransference reactions give counselors the most trouble. One of these has to do with those times when a counselor is unusually frustrated by some kind of client action or inaction; the other is when the counselor is unusually attracted to a particular client. The first of these is perhaps more easily understood. A counselor wants to be helpful and can become exasperated by a client who refuses to follow through with agreed-upon courses of action or who, for whatever reason, simply stays stuck in old, self-destructive patterns of behavior. Fremont and Anderson (1986) cite that kind of counselor frustration, in addition to counselors sometimes feeling personally attacked by clients or, at the other end of the spectrum, relied on too heavily by clients, as particularly burdensome. All of those client behaviors can be frustrating for a counselor. Although feelings of frustration may be understandable, it is problematic when a counselor then acts out of anger with the client. The counselor's desire to be helpful, and to see that help translated into client action, is largely based on countertransference thinking that probably goes something like this: "My worth is wrapped up in how well I do (perhaps an old parental message), so clients had better do well or I'll be a failure." This counselor's worth should not be tied to client performance. This is perfect material for supervision discussion.

The other frequent countertransference hang-up, being attracted to a client, can be even more difficult because counselors can easily deceive themselves about their true motivations and feelings. Haule (1996) talks about the inevitability of this happening some time in every counselor's career because of the intimacy and closeness of contact that therapeutic relationships intentionally foster. It is a given that erotic feelings will arise from some of these encounters, and counselors with the most significant unmet love needs and yearnings for closeness will be most vulnerable to "falling in love" with their clients. The picture is even more muddled and confused when the counselor's countertransference colludes with the client' transference, evolving into an erotically charged dance between the two of them. Counselors can get into all kinds of hot water if they get blind-sided by this variety of countertransference, and once again, all of this should be material for the supervision office.

It has often struck me as unfortunate that professionals in related occupations—teaching, primarily—don't receive some information and training about countertransference because it surely exists in these other kinds of helping relationships as well. Think of how much misery could be avoided if teachers were a bit more savvy about countertransference, and could step back and look more critically and objectively at their relationships with students.

It is likely that you will "fall in love" with at least some of your clients during the course of your career. Wonderful. These are great feelings to be savored. What you do with those feelings, however, is something else again. Your question, to be aided by discussions in supervision, is "How can these feelings be put to work in service of my client—not to meet my own needs?"

Using Hunches

As a relationship with your client develops, more skills can be introduced. You may begin to have some ideas about the material being presented to you and want to voice those ideas out loud. A way to do that without making pronouncements or sounding too heavy-handed is to wonder with your client about the issues of concern. One way of doing this is with the use of interpretation, which is discussed in Chapter 11. Another, more tentative means is by employing *hunches*. You can make your client a co-conspirator with you in trying to work through issues by tossing out hunches, ideas that are tentatively stated. You might, for example, wonder aloud, giving voice to your idea that there may be something going on below the surface.

In Case Example 6.1 the counselor might say, "I wonder what it is about your ideas about your husband's affair that keeps you from talking directly with him about it?" With this kind of speculation you give voice to your concern about the issue in a way that implies allegiance with your client. While it is a question, it is not a direct question, which might sound accusatory (e.g., "Why don't you just talk with your husband about this?"). It is an invitation to the client to wonder as well.

Alternatively, you might phrase your hunch as a simple declarative statement such as "It's curious that you don't talk with your husband about this." This is another way of saying essentially the same thing, and again, though not in question form, it invites the client to speculate as to the reasons for her behavior.

The hunch invites the client to speculate with you about the meaning of what she does and says. Using a hunch with your client is a little like tossing out a hypothesis, your "take" on some aspect of the material, for testing: "Perhaps asking your husband about his relationship with this other woman would yield more information than you could handle." This hunch is really simply a tentative interpretation. The client can take the bait and dive more deeply into speculation about what such a conversation with her husband might mean, or not. You are suggesting that talking with her husband about his affair is a very high-stakes discussion, and that it is potentially terrifying. Your "hunching" with her—again, this is a tentative interpretation—about this acknowledges the scariness and invites her to talk more about it without your being overly certain or authoritative. The hunch is usually preferable to some statement that begins with "I think that . . ." The hunch leaves *you* (as in "I think") out of it, with the focus still squarely on the client.

Using Challenges

There will be times when you will want to *challenge* your client; that is, give the client a little push in some direction that seems relevant and important. You may want your client to get a clearer grasp of the reality of a situation; for example, help an abusive drinker acknowledge the severity of his drinking problem. Pointing out the discrepancies between the way your client sees a particular situation and the ways other people see it could be an extremely helpful form of challenge.

A challenge is always designed to instruct. It is for the client's benefit, and it is not done out of anger. This is a critical distinction. At times a client may read you well and find ways to get under your skin and antagonize or test you. When you react out of anger, countertransference has once again raised its ugly head. Counselor responses to these obnoxious behaviors should be instructive, not self-defensive. If you find yourself becoming overly defensive, some kind of countertransference (again, the counselor's unfinished business) is probably being triggered by this client action, meaning that it is more about you than about your client. This is why we have supervision, to help sort out whose business is really in action.

Challenges cover a lot of ground, from the gentle push in the form of a suggestion to *confrontation*, a more severe form of challenge. Early in my working career, some of which was in residential addictions treatment facilities, confrontation was one of the favored techniques. The idea was that someone's denial about the severity of his drug abuse could best be cracked by confrontation. Counselors were encouraged to use confrontation freely and severely, and in some group sessions an entire group would be encouraged to strongly and vigorously confront one of the members about his drug use or some other behavior. "Oh sure, you can stop anytime you want. That's bullshit, man! You're an addict, a full-of-shit addict, just like the rest of us, and it's about time you faced up to it!" The person being

Case Example 7.2   *Combining the Use of Challenges and Immediacy*

Consider this scenario. The same student and school counselor from Case Example 7.1 have been meeting for some number of weeks together. The sessions are brief, primarily supportive in nature, and the young man is now concerned about his relationship with his girlfriend. He tells lots of stories, which are becoming repetitive, about their times together and about her always wanting to break up with him. The student is funny and charming, and his stories are usually entertaining. While the relationship between this counselor and student has been a bit rocky at times, both are aware of the other's liking and respect.

STUDENT: Last Friday night it was the same old story. We got some pizza, then we went to the dance. *[He then continues, taking considerable time, to talk about the details of what they had to eat, the car they drove in, and the people they ran into at the dance. The long monologue is typical of these sessions. And then . . .]* I thought we were having a great time, and then out of the blue she says she wants to go home.

COUNSELOR: Something happened.

STUDENT: Naw. She just said she was bored. She said she was sick of talking, or of just listening to me talk, and that she wanted to go home. So I got all mad and frustrated and took her home. We haven't talked since.

COUNSELOR: But you still really like her.

STUDENT: You bet. I love her. I'd do anything for her, and I just don't get it.

COUNSELOR: Maybe something happens that leaves her feeling dissatisfied. In the talking, I mean. I'm wondering . . . and this is just speculation . . . if what goes on for her is like what happens for me, in here. When you tell me the stories of what you do, I sometimes want to know what it is you're looking for from me. Maybe that happens for her too.

STUDENT: You don't like what I tell you?

The attempt here is to draw a parallel, based on the counselor's immediate experience, to the situation with the girlfriend. This is followed with a gently challenging comment, which is about the counselor's immediate experience. It is moderated with enough support to suggest a desire for greater connection. It also has an element of self-disclosure, which is clearly in service of some student learning.

He's getting defensive.

(continued)

(Case example 7.2, continued)

COUNSELOR: No, that's not it. You're very enter-taining, and your stories are funny and descrip-tive. I simply wonder where I fit in, what you want me to do—and that's maybe the same thing your girlfriend feels.

Again, an attempt to be supportive and to defuse the student's defensiveness. The counselor reiterates the attempt for more immediacy as well.

STUDENT: My friends tell me I'm funny. They like my stories.

Still defensive.

COUNSELOR: You are funny, entertaining. And I understand that it may be hard to take in what I've told you.

This reflection of content and feeling is speculative. The counselor knows there are feelings the student holds closely under the surface. She assumes some of those might involve some hurt, but she doesn't want to be too specific.

STUDENT: She tells me all the time. "Why don't you listen to me," she says? She's always telling me that I don't care enough to hear about her. Now you're telling me I talk too much. *[Long silence.]* I don't get it. How could I get her back? I don't want to bore people.

COUNSELOR: You just made a shift. You just got more personal. You asked me for help. I sure feel involved now.

This is a reflection about his shift in direction, and it also involves counselor self-disclosure. It is meant to reinforce his talking more personally and directly.

Case Discussion

This short interaction is quite complex, and we can speculate about many of the underlying dynamics of the relationship as well as about the history these two have together. We can speculate that this student has gotten a lot of mileage out of telling stories as a way of making connections with people. He's now entering interpersonal situations, as with the girlfriend, that demand new, more personal ways of relating. The counselor is attempting to use her relationship with the student to graphically display his style of relating to others. By simultaneously challenging the student and changing the focus of the discussion to their relationship, the counselor is taking a risk. One hopes that this risk is based on the history of a positive relation-ship. The risk is calculated, and the timing is important.

A counselor needs to know that a client has the ability to go where we're nudging him. Some people do not seem to have the intellectual tools to engage on this more personal level, or perhaps it simply scares them too much. It would be wrong to try to push them there. One gets the sense that perhaps something has hit home with the student in this interaction. It is a tricky moment. If he feels attacked in this, he will most likely back off and go into retreat mode. If he is able to truly experience the counselor's desire to improve communication, both in the counseling relationship and in the student's relationships with others, he will likely hang in to find out what a different kind of communication might look like.

Assuming the student does hang in, the next step is to begin the educational process, still using this counseling relationship as the

(continued)

(Case example 7.2, continued)

teaching context, of learning about more intimate communication. With some work, he will be able to make the transition from using communication as entertainment to using communication for real engagement with others.

---

confronted would eventually fold under this kind of pressure, and the group would feel validated by forcing this compliance.

I came to really dislike this kind of behavior, in group counseling as well as in individual counseling. It reminded me a lot of the fraternity hazing I'd seen in college, and it seemed downright abusive. What possible gain could be made through this kind of destructive assault on a client? Even if someone changed his behavior, stopped his drug use, was it justified? For addicted clients we saw who were survivors of abuse and neglect, wasn't this simply inflicting further trauma, another kind of abuse?

Some counseling theories suggest guidelines for the effective use of confrontation. They believe confrontation can be a way to move a client out of an entrenched way of thinking or behaving. Fritz Perls, one of the founders of Gestalt therapy, used confrontation and provocation as primary techniques to help people deal more honestly with their natural aggressive impulses and their emotions (Lobb & Salonia, 1996). It has been pointed out, however, that others in the Gestalt community have not been so enamored of Perls's methods (Melnick, 2002). I would urge you to think long and carefully about how you use anything like confrontation.

The best challenges are gentle and positive, meaning that they highlight client strengths and attributes that may be hidden from their awareness. Some of these challenges take the form of asking a client to look at self-destructive thought patterns, which we'll examine more closely in Chapter 9.

Case Example 7.3 illustrates one of these positive challenges, an interaction between a college student client and a counselor in the college counseling center.

A cautionary word about these gentle challenges is worth mentioning. There is, in this kind of response, always the potential for embarrassment or even humiliation. Be particularly careful about gauging the potential for such a reaction. If there is any reasonable doubt about your client's ability to handle your challenge without embarrassment, you should rethink using it. Your notion of "gentle" may sound very different to your client. Never underestimate the amount of power your client perceives you as having. You are not in the business of embarrassment, no matter how clearly you think you see the issues. Part of your ongoing assessment of your client is being able to judge her capacity to hear and handle the kinds of comments you have to make.

CASE EXAMPLE 7.3 *Using Gentle Positive Challenges*

CLIENT: You won't believe what a week this has been. I've never had so much work. The semester has really caught up with me. My professors all seem to think that their course is the only course I have. The workload is unbelievable. It's all good stuff, especially the theater production, but I'm swamped.

COUNSELOR: You really do a lot. It's amazing how much you can manage on your plate at one time.

Reflection of content.

CLIENT: Nuts, huh? Who else would be dumb enough to take all of this on? Sports, a play, a full, tough course load—and a boyfriend. Really dumb.

Here the client seems to be sincere, not just fishing for contradiction, in her appraisal of taking on so many things.

COUNSELOR: What an interesting assessment. That this is all "dumb."

Reflection of content, focusing in what the thinking behind this is all about.

CLIENT: How many students do you know who do all this? I look around, I see people hanging out, fooling around, getting drunk sometimes, and I just don't enjoy that. I get off on doing all this other stuff. How dumb is that?

The student enjoys what she does but feels abnormal. Her peers are clearly not as focused or involved with such a range of activities.

COUNSELOR: Somehow you think there's something wrong with having lots of interests and investing the time and energy in those to make them work. That does seem a little strange. It'd be one thing if you felt compelled to work, couldn't relax, but that's not how you describe your life. You just enjoy doing these things, then feel weird about it all. That's what seems strange.

This is a challenge to the client's thinking. The counselor is supporting the young woman's engaged college activities, her energy and enthusiasm. It is a challenge to help the client see her energy and involvement as a positive attribute, not a negative abnormality.

Case Discussion

One senses that there is a strong, positive relationship between this counselor and client. This client seems to be denying the strength of her own ability to manage a range of activities, not to mention the breadth of her interests. The fact that she has a boyfriend also suggests that these interests have not laid waste to her interpersonal connections with people. The counselor is simply acknowledging that her ability to manage is a real strength, positively atypical of those around her. It is a sad fact that many students, even in elementary school years, will "dumb down" to not appear different, to fit in. Counselors can be strong allies in supporting the strength that being bright, articulate, and accomplished truly exemplifies.

LAB PRACTICE 7.1   *Use of Reflections, Hunches, and Challenges*

This experience has you working again with classmates in a small group, a triad or quadrad. As in the previous exercises, you will take turns in the Counselor role. Use the same format utilized to practice skills in previous chapters. Divide the time equally among you in the group, allowing for adequate feedback time after each counseling session.

This lab session involves a counseling session with any type of Level 1 or Level 2 Client that each participant chooses to role play. The Client could, for example, be an overwhelmed single mother of three. Her widowed father came to live with her when he was still healthy enough to mind the children after school, but now that he has developed Alzheimer's disease, he can't help with the children and needs care himself. Or the Client could be a high school student who has been referred because of slipping grades, a few behavioral incidents, and some suspected pot smoking. There might be some family difficulty, perhaps a separation or divorce in the works.

When it's your turn to role play the Client, try to imagine the thoughts, and especially the feelings, that might be yours in this kind of situation. Feel free to embellish your role with whatever details you think will make this more interesting and realistic. Try to make it possible for your Counselor to interact with you relatively easily and to engage you in the process. For example, while you might be reluctant to be there, you are not impossibly difficult.

When you are the Counselor, you will be trying to engage the Client while finding out a bit about what's been going on. This is a first meeting. Supervisors should manage time and watch these interactions carefully. Which reflections, challenges, hunches, and other skills seem to yield the most Client reaction and engagement? Which seem less effective? When giving feedback to the Counselors, remember to be supportive, positive, and specific regarding skills usage.

Tracking the Themes of Your Client's Material

Good counseling is more than the cumulative set of specific responding skills. In addition to understanding and using the set of responding and reflection skills set out in these chapters, you will need to grasp the larger context in which those skills are used. Just as a person's life is more than a set of isolated incidents, so too is counseling more than responding to the isolated, specific things that are told to you by your client.

Try to get a holistic view, a broader picture, of your client, and respond to that as well as to the individual events. A primary way you can do this is by tracking the themes, or connections, between the different things your client tells you. Carkhuff (1987) refers to this as making *thematic summaries*. These summaries—or you could call them interpretations—are reflections on how many of the different things your client has told you, including the feelings, relate to one another. A woman may tell you a number of stories about troubling or failed relationships, and perhaps all of those relate back to a troubled childhood. Your thematic summary, or reflection, talks about the connections and parallels in these various life situations. These thematic reflections can be made about the material that is discussed in a single session, and they can also reflect work in multiple sessions in which the same themes recur.

Your ability to make cogent, accurate thematic reflections is a hallmark of your developing maturity as a counselor. It is a sophisticated skill that demands your full attention and a capacity to look below the concrete surface of what is being spoken to the underlying ways this specific material connects to the other events of this person's life. When you begin to see these connections and are able to point them out to people in a way that they can understand and integrate them internally, you will know that you have developed some real ability for this work.

Danger Areas in Responding to New Clients

There are some dangers in this process of responding to a new client about which any counselor needs to be watchful. These traps are easy, naturally seductive ways in which counselors can unwittingly undermine the very growth they are trying to foster.

Giving Advice

Particularly at the beginning of your relationship with your client, you may want to give advice about some course of action. Especially with a child or a Level 1 adult client, this may be appropriate if the person is incapable or temporarily in a position where he is not able to make healthy, informed choices. "Don't run in front of that car," or "Don't beat your kids," or "Go for help," are all examples of directive advice that can be timely and appropriate.

Advice giving can be problematic, however. When you tell others what to do, it presupposes that they do not have the ability to make the choice themselves. It is demeaning to your clients for you to make suggestions about things they are capable of deciding for themselves. Discussing options and making sure that all sides of an argument are fleshed out are perfectly appropriate and oftentimes helpful counseling strategies, but when the line is crossed and the counselor lands heavily on the side of one of the options, there is inherent danger.

You can comfortably give advice and advocate for those clients who may not be able to advocate for themselves, but you are in swampy territory when you do it for those not needing the wisdom of your choice making. You should always give your clients as much responsibility for their own decision making as they can handle. When I have fallen into one of these advice-giving or advocacy traps myself, I have invariably paid the price for my error. The advice given has usually not been what was really wanted, and it has rarely worked out well. On at least some of these occasions, by not following my advice, I think that my client may have been telling me that I was out of line in giving it in the first place. The evolving evidence of the fact of my bad advice, in other words, has usually been my client's subtle statement that he knows better about what is good for him.

It can be very frustrating for a counselor to watch a client make stupid, self-destructive choices, even repeatedly, but we need to constantly remind ourselves that all of us have the right to our own bad choices. Someone who continually makes the same mistake, such as gravitating to the same kind of inappropriate partners and spouses, certainly has some things to learn—but not by way of our making other choices for her. Again, this staying away from advice giving is for those of our clients who have the capacity to choose. It is perfectly appropriate, and would in fact be wrong not to tell your client to stop using drugs, or to go into treatment, or to get out of an abusive situation. The question always is, "Does this person have the skills and the wherewithal to make his or her own choices in this situation?" If the answer is "yes," we let the client make the choice.

One of the greatest of the dangers in advice giving can lie in assuming too much responsibility for a client, and typically this comes under the guise of advocacy. Advocacy refers to the ways in which a counselor may act on a client's behalf, usually with other people. It might be in helping a student resolve a dispute with a teacher or negotiating certain special social services for a client. Much of the work we do with some clients involves case management services, meaning that we help to orchestrate the range of special services that someone may need. No matter how appealing the outcome appears to be, any time this is done in a way that suggests the person does not have the capacity to do the same for him- or herself, it is potentially demeaning. Any time a client has the capacity to act on his or her own behalf, it is potentially belittling to have someone else act instead. We'll talk more about the helpful role of client advocacy in Chapter 12.

Responding to Direct Questions

Another problem area in the developing counseling relationship that sometimes gives new counselors particular difficulty is handling direct client questions. Sometimes a client will ask a direct informational question: "What time is it?" or "How much do you charge?" These can easily be answered under the assumption

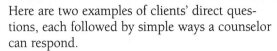

CASE EXAMPLE 7.4 *Responding to Direct Questions*

Here are two examples of clients' direct questions, each followed by simple ways a counselor can respond.

CLIENT: Look, I told you I was going to talk to my wife about this. I will, I will. I'm just not exactly ready to do it yet. She's going to bust a gut. But I told you I'd tell her. Don't you trust me?

COUNSELOR: Still, it's interesting that three weeks have gone by since you said you'd bring this up with her. This is really tough stuff.

This use of the word "interesting" prefaces a bit of a gentle challenge. Note that the counselor, using selective attention, has not responded to the "trust" question. Refusing to get caught in the defensive ploy, the counselor has avoided the parrying trap implied by the question (because this issue has nothing to do with counselor trust) by simply not answering it and has kept the focus on the issue at hand.

CLIENT: This looks like a great new job opportunity, but it means I'll have to move my family. I'd make a lot more money, and we could sure use it to help with the kids' college bills, but I'd hate to leave all my friends here. Man, oh man. . . .What do you think I should do?

COUNSELOR: This is a really tough decision to make, with a lot riding on it. It'd be a lot easier if someone else would make it for you.

Both statements by the counselor are reflective comments on content, with the second one subtly answering the question "What should I do" by reflecting on the client's desire to not have to take responsibility for choosing. Implied in this response is refusal to answer the question directly.

Case Discussion

We can assume that this client does not really need, or expect, the counselor to come up with a solution to his dilemma. On some level he probably would love it if there were some magic response that would make everything clear, some mystical power that the counselor could use to convey hidden truth. Our clients would both love and hate it if we could really supply magical solutions. They would love the ease of the solution but resent having been robbed of the freedom to choose. It is in this recognition and facilitation of our clients' capacity to choose—and their right to choose—and the responsibility of personal choice wherein much of the beauty of our work lies.

that there is no hidden meaning or hook attached to the question. Often, however, the questions are little tests of us, perhaps either a subtle challenge to our expertise or a desire to draw us unwittingly into giving advice. Case Example 7.4 addresses this issue.

Concluding Thoughts: Deepening the Relationship

Developing a relationship with a new client depends a great deal on your ability to listen clearly and to accurately respond to the concerns the client brings to you. You will need to continually nurture your ability to listen and respond intelligently, both to your client's concerns and to your own internal world. You will need to help him delve more deeply into the issues at hand, and you'll begin to assist the process of his bringing his own resources to bear in service of the counseling goals that will soon be articulated.

The process of finding out about this new person is assisted both by the ways you fashion your questions and by the way you reflect upon and respond to what he tells you. You use these listening and responding tools to find out what he looks for from counseling, what his goals and aspirations are, and to identify the strengths and problems that will help or hinder a successful outcome.

The process of your client's talking about himself and your active responses to his concerns serves to develop and deepen the relationship between you. It is in this deepening, particularly via your focusing skills and the promotion of immediacy in the relationship, that you build the working alliance that binds you and facilitates the working toward goals. It is in this newly developing relationship, where your client begins to more clearly show himself as he really is, that you begin to experience the honor and privilege associated with doing this work. Through these encounters you are slowly let into this person's life and entrusted with the information and details of his life experience. It is in this "being let in" that you begin to experience the joy and real reward of being a counselor. Watching what people can do with the strength of this kind of relationship backing them, and watching them take their new learning out into the world, really makes the work worthwhile.

For Further Thought

1. Some suggest that all of our relationships are based on some kind of transference, particularly that originating from our relationships with our parents. As you contemplate the significant relationships of your past and current life, what do you think about the possibility of their containing elements of transference?

2. What role has confrontation played in your life? Are you comfortable with that mode of interaction? When you have been confronted, how have you responded? What role will challenging, or confrontation, play in your counseling work?

3. Has anyone ever given you advice that you've considered and taken? Was it good advice? If you have received particularly effective advice, how was it given, and what was the context?

4. Significant life events may have shaped your life and may have led you to the counseling profession. Which of those, if any, might you consider sharing with clients who have experienced similar events? What might be the reasons for this disclosure, and are there any conditions you'd place on this sharing?

References

Bishop, J., & Lane, R. (2001). Self-disclosure and the therapeutic frame: Concerns for novice practitioners. *Journal of Contemporary Psychotherapy, 31*(4), 245–256.

Brammer, L. (1973). *The helping relationship: Process and skills.* Upper Saddle River, NJ: Prentice-Hall.

Carkhuff, R. (1967). Toward a comprehensive model of facilitative interpersonal processes. *Journal of Counseling Psychology, 14,* 67–72.

Carkhuff, R. (1987). *The art of helping.* Amherst, MA: Human Resource Development Press.

Carkhuff, R., & Berenson, B. (1967). *Beyond counseling and therapy.* New York: Holt, Rinehart, & Winston.

Cherbosque, J. (1987). Differential aspects of counselor self-disclosure statements on perception of the counselor and willingness to disclose: A cross-cultural study. *Psychotherapy: Theory, Research, Practice, Training, 24*(3), 434–437.

Cormier, W., & Cormier, L. (1991). *Interviewing strategies for helpers: Fundamental skills and cognitive behavioral interventions* (3rd ed.). Belmont, CA: Brooks, Cole.

Fremont, S., & Anderson, W. (1986). What makes counselors angry? An exploratory study. *Journal of Counseling and Development, 65*(2), 67–70.

Haule, J. (1996). *The love cure: Therapy erotic and sexual.* Woodstock, CT: Spring Publications.

Hendrick, S. (1988). Counselor self-disclosure. *Journal of Counseling and Development, 66*(9), 419–425.

Jourard, S. (1971). *The transparent self.* New York: Van Nostrand Reinhold.

Lobb, M., & Salonia, G. (1996). From the "discomfort of civilisation" to creative adjustment: The relationship between individual and community in psychotherapy in the third millennium. *International Journal of Psychotherapy, 1*(1), 45–54.

Melnick, J. (2002). Why do we knock heroes off their pedestals? *Gestalt Review, 6*(3), 181–183.

Nyman, S., & Daugherty, T. (2001). Congruence of counselor self-disclosure and perceived effectiveness. *Journal of Psychology, 135*(3), 269–278.

Simone, D., McCarthy, P., & Skay, C. (1998). An investigation of client and counselor variables that influence likelihood of counselor self-disclosure. *Journal of Counseling and Development, 76*(2), 174–183.

Yalom, I. (1989). *Loves executioner*. New York: Basic Books.

CHAPTER 8

Developing Ethical and Cultural Competency

> You cannot help but learn more as you take the world
> into your hands. Take it up reverently, for it is an old piece
> of clay, with millions of thumbprints on it.
> *(John Updike)*

You want to engage your new clients in a way that gives them some reason for hope and makes them want to come back to see you. While you are engaged in this process, make sure you follow the well-worn proviso, "First, do no harm."

Providing help without harm is, in part, a function of your professional training and your level of skill in being able to respond appropriately to what your client needs. This chapter provides an overview of some of the issues concerning sound ethical practice and the role of cultural diversity as they affect the work you do in your counseling practice or in your school. Becoming familiar with the guidelines of ethical counseling practice will help to ensure safety for both your client and yourself. Becoming more sensitive to cultural and other differences will contribute to creating a respectful, empathic environment and to achieving your goal of helping without harming. Becoming a culturally sensitive counselor is an essential aspect of creating the ethical context in which you work.

Establishing the Ethical Foundation for Good Practice

Effective counseling practice serves a *containment* function; that is, it provides a safe and secure space in which people can deal with difficult personal material. Good ground rules, a working knowledge of the principles of ethical practice, and a trusted supervisor will all assist you in providing this safety function.

In addition to the practical ground rules discussed in Chapter 3 (e.g., frequency and length of meetings), good ground rules also include ethical guidelines that are immediately shared and discussed with any new client (e.g., confidentiality and informed consent). They are a subset of the greater ethical context in which you work and serve as part of the explicit working contract between you and your client. You will typically establish and discuss these ground rules of the client-counselor alliance during the opening session(s) of working together.

A range of ethical principles serve as an overall guide to practice. It is a safe assumption that a good heart, as well as a sincere interest to serve the best interests of your client, provides a solid underpinning to your work with people, but it is also clear that many situations will emerge in your work that defy simple ethical solutions. It is an unfortunate fact that bad things do happen to clients at the hands of unscrupulous, uneducated, or misguided counselors. Some errors are perpetrated by counselors who show bad judgment, either intentionally or by miscalculation. Others errors are due to lack of thought or to misinformation, perhaps fed by inexperience and maybe even inaccurate advice. Sometimes counselors simply take advantage of people in vulnerable circumstances.

Bad things also happen to good counselors. We live in a litigious society. Sometimes errors in judgment, even simple mistakes, can come back to haunt an unsuspecting counselor by way of a lawsuit from a disgruntled—or delusional—client. Because of this possibility of bad things happening to even the most proficient among us, every practicing counselor needs to consider the advisability of maintaining professional liability insurance. Unless explicitly protected by an agency or a school, most counselors should purchase this insurance. Some counselors decide against this coverage, sometimes for political reasons, sometimes under the assumption that such coverage simply invites lawsuits. This is a good topic for discussion with a supervisor.

Your knowledge of the ethics of good counseling practice serves to protect you, your clients, and the profession (Meara, Schmidt, & Day, 1996). With the encouragement of state licensing boards and national accreditation bodies, such as the Council for Counseling and Related Education Programs (CACREP), graduate programs of study for counselors now include specific course work focusing on legal and ethical issues in counseling.

In recent years, CACREP has encouraged counselor training programs to become much more sensitive to the need for counselor awareness of cultural differences, particularly as these differences are affected by and affect counseling work. Increasing your knowledge of cultural difference is integral to creating a sound, ethical practice (Roach, 1999), and some have even argued for a clearer articulation of multicultural issues in existing professional codes of ethics (Ibrahim & Arredondo, 1986). Expanding your multicultural awareness as a primary ethical consideration is discussed later in this chapter.

For now, let us look briefly at some relevant ethical guidelines that serve to highlight the potential problems counselors might encounter. Our focus is on those ethical principles that have the most direct impact on counseling relationships. This brief coverage is not meant to serve as a substitute for course work and thorough examination of the legal and ethical standards—and the dilemmas—that influence your work, but it does provide an introduction to the principles that should guide your relationships with clients.

In addition to studying the general ethics codes provided by the umbrella organizations of our profession, such as the ACA (American Counseling Association) and the APA (American Psychological Association), counselors need to develop a solid working understanding of the ethical principles that guide their specific professional work—for example, the ethics codes of the ASCA (American School Counselor Association), AAMFT (American Association for Marriage and Family Therapists), and ASGW (Association for Specialists in Group Work)—and find good supervisory and consultative support (Kitchener, 1994). It's also not a bad idea to have legal counsel handy for particularly tricky incidents; most schools and agencies have this kind of contracted assistance.

The discussion here is based on the *ACA Code of Ethics* (2005), which is divided into eight sections: the counseling relationship; confidentiality, privileged communication, and privacy; professional responsibility; relationships with other professionals; evaluation, assessment, and interpretation; supervision, training, and teaching; research and publication; and resolving ethical issues. We are primarily concerned with the ethical guidelines that best protect and safeguard the counseling relationship. It is in the counseling encounter, in face-to-face situations, that the counselor's ethics will be most severely tested.

Ethical Dilemmas and Corresponding Ethical Principles

The best way to think about ethical principles is to imagine how you would apply them in real life situations, especially when the right thing to do is not all that clear-cut; that is, when the situation poses an ethical dilemma. Therefore, I have posed a series of ethical dilemmas for your consideration. As you read each one, think about what you would do if you were the counselor in the situation; then, if you have access to colleagues or classmates, discuss your solution with one or two of them. Jot down some notes about your ideas, including your concerns about the situation.

To grasp the meaning and intent of how ethical decision making plays a role in protecting our clients and ourselves, consider the following hypothetical situations wherein a knowledge of ethical principles is required. Each of these dilemmas is a typical situation that any counselor might encounter. Following each dilemma is a restatement of the relevant ACA ethical standard and discussion of the dilemma in terms of the relevant ethical principle.

ETHICAL DILEMMA 1

You are working as a school counselor in the local high school. A lawyer calls you asking for information about one of the students on your caseload. She says that the information is important and that the family says it's OK for you to talk with her. What do you do?

Ethical Principle: Keep your information about clients, including records, confidential. This includes information about their identity.

Clients have a right to privacy in their relationships with you. You are bound by your professional code of ethics to hold confident everything a client tells you. This right ensures safety in the relationship and may prevent harm in clients' encounters in the outside world. The right to privacy also includes anonymity—you are bound not to reveal the identities of your clients. You are bound to protect this privacy—including anonymity and confidentiality—in all of your discussions with others. You are also ethically required to maintain confidentiality in the ways you maintain records and computer information about clients. Do not divulge information about any of your clients without written permission (Mitchell, 2001). This may really be a lawyer on the phone, or it may not be a lawyer. It doesn't matter. You do not even reveal that you know the child in question.

There are some notable exceptions when you are required to break the confidential bond. Usually these are to ensure a client's (or someone else's) safety or to comply with a court order for release of information. These special situations are undertaken with strong supervisory, and perhaps legal, guidance. Depending on where you practice, there may be specific state, agency, or school directives that govern the release of such information. In any case, confidential information would only be shared after obtaining written client consent (parental or guardian consent in the case of a minor).

ETHICAL DILEMMA 2

A young woman comes to your office in the local mental health agency. She says she's in counseling with a male counselor in another agency but that she'd really like to work with a woman, and she's heard some very nice things about the way you work. She asks you to take her on as a client. What do you do?

Ethical Principle: *If a person is already in a counseling relationship, do not engage that person in counseling without consent from the other counselor.*

It makes common sense not to infringe on the professional relationship one of our colleagues may have with any given client (Welfel, 2002). There may be times when it is appropriate for two counselors to work with a given person—for instance, if they are working with distinctly separate issues—but each should be aware of the other's work and should occasionally consult with each other if the client gives permission. Sometimes a client will intentionally keep secret the fact that he is seeing multiple counselors. This inevitably makes for an interesting set of dynamics when the truth finally comes out— and it usually does. As long as the counselors remain unaware of the client's ruse, no ethical standards are being broken. But once they find out, they are ethically bound to deal with the situation, most likely by having one counselor exit the scene.

ETHICAL DILEMMA 3

You run a group in your school for young parents. One of the participants, a teen mom, says that she's been having trouble with anger and that she has shaken her baby a few times recently to stop it from crying. What do you do?

Ethical Principle: *Inform authorities if there is a possibility of imminent danger to the client or others.*

You are ethically bound to protect the physical safety of your client and those who might be harmed by your client, and you must report suspected abuse to the proper authorities (Henderson, 2003). When you have a client who is out of control and is a danger to herself or someone else, you need to be prepared to step in and take action. It is not your job to become a detective, sleuthing out the truth of reported abuse. That is the job of those to whom you report the abuse. Counselors need to familiarize themselves with their school or agency protocols for reporting suspected abuse and threats of violence.

This is, yet again, a time when supervision is indicated. It is always a good idea to consult with a supervisor regarding these kinds of questions. This serves two purposes: to help make a truly informed best decision about the matter at hand and to protect yourself in the case of a bad event happening. Should one of your clients attempt to hurt himself or someone else, you will be less likely to be blamed for something not done if you have consulted with others about the situation beforehand. When decisions are shared with superiors, there is always less individual culpability. The supervisor or director of an agency may even be held legally responsible for the agency counselors' work.

ETHICAL DILEMMA 4

One of your clients, an attractive person about your age, suggests going out for coffee some afternoon next week. What do you do?

Ethical Principle: *Avoid all other kinds of relationships with clients, particularly those of an intimate, sexual nature.*

This seems to be an obvious and easily followed sanction on its face, yet it is too often violated. Unwary or manipulative counselors can become entangled unnecessarily in complicated dual relationships with clients. These "entanglements" may have financial, sexual, or simple friendship qualities that seriously jeopardize the primary professional counseling relationship. Whenever a dual relationship is allowed to develop, conflict of interest issues inevitably emerge (St. Germaine, 1993). When you become involved with someone as a client, this is the only kind of relationship you should maintain with the client.

You should also, for similar reasons, not engage in a counseling relationship with your family members, friends, or people with whom you have other kinds of previous relationships—those, too, would have qualities of the dual relationship. Neukrug, Milliken, and Walden (2001) suggest that this business of nonsexual dual relationships is the most difficult ethical arena for counselors to manage without problems. It is most likely trickiest in small town or rural areas, where everyone eventually interacts with everyone else. Do the best you can in those circumstances to avoid duality, and try to establish clear guidelines with your clients about how you will interact with them when you unavoidably meet in other social situations.

Discussion continues in the field about the appropriateness of pursuing other kinds of relationships with clients, or with students who have terminated or graduated. The ACA ethical guidelines suggest that a minimum two-year period after termination should pass before entering into any other kind of relationship, and only then when there is clearly no possibility for exploitation. The APA is hesitant to attach a time frame to its discussion of this kind of relationship expansion, but it is clear in its sanctions against entering blithely into them.

You will, perhaps even routinely, have strong affectionate, even erotic, feelings for some of your clients. That is a wonderful aspect of this work, having to do with the deep emotional bond that forms between us and the people with whom we work. These feelings have a tremendous potential for help or harm. If used in the best service of your client, or student's, growth, it can have great reparative powers. If used for your own gain, no matter how cleverly you rationalize otherwise, it is only destructive. The feelings of love, even the erotic ones, are tender indicators of your respect and affection for the person in your care. Some of these feelings may have to do directly with your client; others may be related more to your own past relationships or unmet love needs. This is the business of countertransference. How you manage those feelings, as well as how you choose to act with them, makes all the difference. This business of managing your own feelings, coming to grips with the countertransference, is a primary reason to have a good supervisor.

Finally, be aware that we are protectors of the profession when it comes to the question of unethical dual relationships. When you hear from clients or colleagues of unethical behavior on the part of some colleague, you are duty bound to assume responsibility for dealing with that misbehavior. This will involve your own application of ACA ethical principles to the offending behavior and consultation with objective colleagues and the appropriate licensing board, assuming the individual is licensed (Herlihy, 1996). Failing to do so might jeopardize not only that professional's current and future clients but also your professional standing. You are liable, like it or not, for your colleagues' misbehavior.

ETHICAL DILEMMA 5

You think that one of your clients in the residential counseling program in which you work is ready to go home. You talk this over with your supervisor, the director of the clinic, who advises you to keep this client around for another few weeks. Because this client is fully covered by a good insurance policy, keeping the individual in the program helps to defray the costs of other clients who are not adequately covered. This is the reason the director wants you to continue to keep this client in the program. What do you do?

Ethical Principle: *Your primary obligation is to provide adequate service to your client; financial considerations are secondary. When you and the client agree that the counseling goals have been met and that it is time to end, it is unethical to keep the client in counseling for other reasons.*

Counseling should not continue any longer than is necessary. You and your client will generally be able to arrive at agreement that it's time for counseling to end, either when goals have been met or when sufficient progress toward them has been stalled. It may sometimes be difficult to assess exactly when the best time to end is, but this decision is always based on what is in the client's best interest. Other matters, such as personal financial gain or agency benefit, should not play a role in that decision.

Although the agency's desire to serve clients who cannot afford full payment is admirable, its manipulation of other clients' participation in programming to make up the financial difference is not. Counselors who are asked to participate in questionable, unethical activities by agency administrators need to seriously consider whether they want to continue working for agencies that put them in these kinds of unethical binds.

ETHICAL DILEMMA 6

You have a private counseling practice in a racially mixed community. Your clientele, however, are nearly all European Americans. When you examine the referrals you've received in the past months, you note that all of them are European Americans as well. What do you do?

Ethical Principle: *Ensure equal access to treatment and allied services for all clients, regardless of race, religion, physical ability, and socioeconomic status.*

It should go without saying that you do your utmost to avoid discrimination in your counseling practice. This can be challenging, however, in that all of us have biases and misunderstandings that operate outside the realm of our awareness. You may have little knowledge about the cultural context within which your clients or students operate, and they may see you as alien, and even threatening. The whole concept of counseling may be foreign to some of the people in your community. It is important to acknowledge that it is an ethical responsibility to provide equal service to all and to find appropriate ways to provide help. It is unethical to reject possible clients who are racially different from you, but you are also ethically obliged to make special efforts to reach out to members of all the diverse groups in your community, and to make your counseling office accessible to members of the community who have disabilities. Some of this effort will involve examining your own attitudes about race and ethnicity. We'll talk of ways to increase your own cultural awareness later in the chapter.

Your counseling service should also include help for people of limited economic means. There are certainly some clear economic disparities in how we currently provide counseling services in this culture. It is your job to provide the best possible service—or to find low-cost reasonable alternatives—in the face of those difficulties. You owe this to all clients, regardless of their ability to pay.

Some Additional Ethical Principles

Finally, here are some additional principles that apply to the best ethical management of counseling relationships.

1. *Form appropriate consultative relationships with colleagues, assuring that there is no conflict of interest in these relationships.*

One of the greatest reasons for suggesting that a new, inexperienced counselor work in a public setting has to do with the opportunity for collegial contact and support that those settings provide. There are typically people available for help when it is needed, and supervisory contacts are routinely established. Counselors in these settings also have an opportunity to make connections with colleagues in other work settings, which provides a network of assistance that can be called on when needed. This includes negotiating to find a good supervisor.

2. *Respect the integrity of your clients and promote their welfare.*

Our primary reason for working with people is to help them to live more fulfilling, productive lives. To do this we must respect their integrity and general welfare. Inherent in this respect is a belief in the credo, "Do no harm." Do not impose

---

REFLECTION EXERCISE 8.1   Responding to Moral Dilemmas

Imagine that you are standing in line at the supermarket, waiting to pay for your groceries. Ahead of you in line is a man with a child in his cart. The little boy appears to be about two years old. The child is grabbing for candy on the racks next to their cart, and the man starts to yell, really loudly, at him. What would you do?

This is a hypothetical situation I have frequently posed with my graduate counseling students as a way of beginning discussion about the relationship between our professional conduct and our personal responsiveness to the dilemmas of everyday life. Professional ethics codes don't address this kind of situation; it is more a personal moral dilemma than a professional ethical or legal issue. Each of us has our own style and some ideas about how a situation like this should be approached. Some of us would try to confront the father, others would try to distract or help with the child, still others would simply head down another aisle.

Considering how you would respond to these kinds of everyday situations is good preparation for considering how you will deal with ethical situations involving your clients. So, back to the grocery store. What would you do? Discuss the situation with your classmates and compare what you would do with any decisions for action they might choose to make. Brainstorm other everyday moral dilemmas. In what ways are they comparable situations you might come across as a counseling professional?

---

your own values on your clients (Gladding & Hood, 1974), and try not to leave them feeling or behaving more poorly than when they first came to see you.

3. *Inform clients, at the outset of counseling, of all the goals, purposes, techniques, and procedures to be used in counseling.*

As discussed in Chapter 3, clients have a right to know certain things about the way counseling will happen when they begin to work with us. They should know about our qualifications (and limitations) to do this work, the broad parameters of how we'll work with them, what they can expect to get out of this counseling work, and who else might be involved (e.g., supervisors or referral agents). This information is best presented in a way that is a helpful adjunct to beginning a relationship with the client, and not as an informational avalanche that can overwhelm the client or scare her away.

4. *Advise clients about the limitations of computer technology in safe record keeping, and advise them as to their use for counseling purposes.*

You will most likely use computers in some aspect of client or student record keeping. You may also send and receive information about clients to other parties (e.g., other schools, agencies, or insurance companies). Clients need to know about this and know that information is sometimes loosely guarded in cyber-space. Sometimes client information shared via computer is even inaccurate (Sampson, Kolodinsky, & Greeno, 1997). This is a new frontier and has hidden dangers related to privacy violations. Despite your best efforts to maintain client confidentiality, problems could still emerge. Your clients have a right to know of these risks.

Expanding Cultural Competency

In addition to doing all you can to protect the privacy, confidentiality, and integrity of the counseling relationship, your position as a counselor, and the profession as a whole, you also have the responsibility of becoming fluent in the cultural differences that your clients bring to their work with you. This means becoming educated in the ways that your clients look at the world that are different from yours. Only with an appreciation of differing cultural perspectives will you be able to understand the strengths, problems, and dilemmas they bring to your counseling office.

Reminders of this need for multicultural understanding have consistently popped up during my career as a counselor. Sometimes these lessons in cultural differences have reflected subtle, less obvious attitudes that affect our work and have served to remind me of the complex role that cultural differences play in our approach to people. One of my first supervisory jobs was as an administrator of a small outpatient alcoholism clinic in Burlington, Vermont (this was in the days before comprehensive alcohol and drug services). I observed and supervised the work of five counselors and did what I could to nurture meager funding supports from the state and local charities.

One of the counselors I inherited to supervise when I became agency director (although he always balked at the term "supervised") was a short, Irish, bulldoggish-looking guy named Eddie. Eddie had been working at the clinic for a number of years, and I had great respect for Eddie and for the ways in which he challenged my notions of what "good" counseling is all about. Eddie was arrogant, a bit pompous, very funny, and the consummate showman. He was terrible with paperwork, bridled at any kind of administrative oversight, and was suspicious of people with multiple degrees. Formal credentialing for counseling professionals had not yet been established, and Eddie's only training had been via state-sponsored workshops. Our clients loved him.

I spent considerable time working with Eddie trying to help him hone his counseling skills, and to his credit he was open to reasonable suggestions for improving his work. I also spent considerable time trying to fathom why he was so apparently successful with the people with whom he worked. He ran a "rap group," for example, on Wednesday evenings that would draw crowds of 80 to 100 people, where there would be a mix of inspirational speeches and personal testimonies, a lot of laughter, and a lot of shared miseries. Something wonderful was obviously happening in these gatherings. More than that, he had a remarkable facility for bringing people into the agency, engaging them in counseling, and helping them to get sober.

It was finally one of our board members, an Episcopal priest, who began to clue me in. This neighborhood, she explained, was comprised largely of first generation French and Irish Catholic immigrants. Eddie operated much as a surrogate parish priest, with people responding to his charisma and charm much as they might have to the priests in their own background. I knew that my wise colleague on the board was onto something. Moreover, I noticed that Eddie spoke the language of the streets and put the terminology of addictions into language people could understand. "Loss of inhibition," he would say to one client, for example, "was what happens when you get drunk and piss on the wall behind the bar. You get drunk, the judge in your head goes on vacation, and you do wacky things." Sweetly succinct and accurate. He never patronized with these examples, and he didn't try to absorb the language of the streets to fit in or be accepted; rather, he strictly used the lingo as a communication tool.

As a program administrator, I learned a great lesson about good matches and fits between counselors and clients. I used Eddie as a model for matching counselor strength with new clients. Eddie could easily engage many of the people who were referred to him, yet he was not always proficient, for example, with women clients. Some of the traits that made him so effective with our male clients were lost on some women. His skills as a counselor in tapping into the religious and cultural roots of our clients were not necessarily matched by his skills in working with emerging sensitivities related to gender differences. Thus, as an administrator, I tried to steer female clients toward other counselors on the staff whenever possible.

I began to have renewed appreciation for the fact that each of us has such strengths and such "blind sides." We create easier alliances and relationships with people whose background, worldview, and ways of operating we understand, that are familiar to us. If we wish to expand the range of clients with whom we feel comfortable, we need to expand our own worldview and to minimize our ignorance about cultural differences. If you want to work with a diverse range of clientele and be effective with them, you need to diversify your own cultural sensitivity. This means becoming familiar with the differences that people carry into your office. Some of these differences might be seemingly apparent, such as racial differences, others less immediately apparent, such as class differences, and others more hidden and less obvious, such as the attitudes shaped in part by those racial and class differences. This is all about expanding your own cultural awareness and sensitivity to diversity.

The counseling profession is increasingly sensitive to the need for heightened awareness of multiculturalism, calling this the "fourth force" in counseling; the first three being psychodynamism, behaviorism, and humanism (Pedersen, Draguns, Lonner, & Trimble, 2002). Most graduate programs in counseling now incorporate course work on multicultural approaches to counseling, and students are encouraged to think broadly about the cultural contexts in which they'll work. Given the dramatically changing cultural face of this country, this makes sense. The neighborhood that Eddie and I worked in, the city's "old north end," was comprised back then of families of Irish and French immigrants, but it is now also home to immigrants from Eastern Europe, Africa, Asia, and South America. Many of these people are refugees who have endured long and heroic journeys to escape desperate poverty or war.

Some of the people from these other cultural contexts have little familiarity with counseling. Their heritage may cherish values that are contrary to some of the basic tenets of counseling. Consider, for example, that our profession is based on a bedrock of traditional North American and European values that include the following:

- People are self-contained, and their behavior is shaped by internal psychological forces.
- Pathology is divided into problems of the body and problems of the head.
- There is a split between thinking of behavior as being shaped primarily by culture or by biology. (Lewis-Fernandez & Kleinman, 1994)

Basic to Western culture is a shared belief in the primacy of the individual. Self-interest, competition, and personal freedom are Western cultural ideals, whereas in Eastern cultures people think much more collectively about centrally important values. They might emphasize the importance of sharing, communal activity, and submission to authority (Beery, Poortinga, & Segall, 1992). These very different world perspectives can make for some profoundly interesting values clashes when a client comes from one cultural background and the counselor from another. The very lack of research on counseling outcomes with non–European American clients is proof that the prevailing treatment paradigm has until recently ignored the fact of real cultural difference (Jackson, 2003).

You will want to add your voice and understanding to this fourth force in counseling and to become adept in your cultural awareness and sensitivity about the differences that abound in the world in which you live and work. One of the most pertinent tasks of a counselor in this new millennium is to add multicultural competence to your set of skills (Arthur & Stewart, 2001).

The following sections address some of the most obvious areas in which you might experience these cultural differences.

Racial and Ethnic Differences

This is one of the first areas of difference that many consider when they think of developing multicultural awareness, and it is certainly important. Many of the ways you perceive your clients, as well as the ways you are perceived by them, are influenced by racial and ethnic similarities and differences. Being racially different from your client often presents a visible, obvious difference that cannot be ignored. Being racially similar to your client may provide you with a certain amount of automatic credibility that would otherwise have to be earned (Sue & Zane, 1987). Sometimes attitudes based on racial differences can even lead counselors to have mistaken ideas about the capacities of their racially different clients. They may severely underestimate the abilities of those clients (Mishne, 2002). Subtle discriminations and treatment differences can be even more profound for more severely disturbed or physically challenged clientele who are racially different (Geraghty & Warren, 2003).

Specific ways clients think of their racially dissimilar counselors are receiving increasing research attention. Native Americans may be distrustful of and suspicious about the motives of non-Native counselors (Johnson & Lashley, 1989). European Americans may be unaware of the ways culture and society influence their lives and may be suspicious of counselors who suggest they are controlled by those larger forces. This may be related to the fact, as some have suggested, that those in power are less aware of those larger forces than are those who are oppressed by power (Hanna, Talley, & Guindon, 2000). Asian Americans may stay in counseling only briefly (Ho, 1990) and only work toward therapeutic goals highly correlated with family needs (Marsella, 1993). Counselors who do not acknowledge these differences may not do well with these clients (Kim, 2003). African American, Arab American, and other ethic groups also have definite expectations and potential wariness with counselors who are not of those ethnic groups (Gondolf & Williams, 2001; Nassar-McMillan & Hakim-Larson, 2003). This may hold true for Latino clients as well.

I have experienced some disconnects myself, as a teacher, when dealing with students of different ethnic backgrounds. Typically a number of students attending the summer institute courses I teach are from other countries., During one of those course experiences, I called a young exchange student from China aside after the first session or two and asked why he had been so reticent to ask any questions in class when he was so clearly engaged with the material, with other students, and with me outside of class. He told me that he would never ask me, the professor, a question publicly in class, for it would run the risk of embarrassing me if I didn't know the answer. His desire to be polite and respectful of authority superseded his intellectual curiosity. This led to a lengthy discussion of the role of culture in education.

In that same class were students from India who were amazed when some students in the class characterized their childhoods as "unhappy." These Indian students could not conceive of such a thing, they said, and described their own childhoods as idyllic. This led many students of North American heritage in the class to suggest that these Indian students were simply living in a state of denial about the real circumstances of their upbringing. Another clash of cultures, with its own really interesting ensuing discussion.

The picture gets even more clouded with the addition of other complicating factors. People of different races are marrying with far greater frequency and bearing children with multiracial characteristics. This can present special challenges for school counselors (Looby, 2001) and for counselors who work with families (Leslie & Morton, 2001). People of one race adopt children of other races with similarly increasing frequency. On top of all this, many of the newer immigrant populations of this country who are of varying racial or ethnic backgrounds are refugees, fleeing economic oppression and war. They bring a multitude of new, intriguing situations to the school and mental health counselors' offices. When people with such negative life experiences seek counseling, imagine the complex client-counselor interactions that must transpire.

We used to talk of the United States as the great melting pot, a veritable stew of differing races and cultural traditions. The idea was that all of these people would blend together to form a new, homogeneous cultural whole. The current picture appears to be more complex than that characterized by this melting pot analogy. Maybe we are learning to do something different from "melting" together. It does stand to reason, however, that people of different cultures want an equal opportunity to survive and thrive here, as well as to maintain their own cultural identity. As counselors, we should be able to support those desires. We can become students of the cultural heritages, histories, and philosophical backgrounds of the clients we serve to more fully understand the issues they bring to us (James & Prilliltensky, 2002).

We are beginning to look more rigorously at the ways counselors view their racially or ethnically different clientele. Counselors may serve to perpetuate stereotypical biases or may provide opportunities for new connections and understanding by virtue of their abilities to challenge their own assumptions and latent prejudices (Daniel, Roysircar, Abeles, & Boyd, 2004). For each of us, the challenge is to bring our own prejudices to the surface, into the light of day, so that they might be examined more closely.

Differences Based on Socioeconomic Class

You will work with some people who are richer than you, others who are poorer than you. If you work in a publicly funded program, many of your clients will be

REFLECTION EXERCISE 8.2   *Racial Bias*

Spend a few minutes writing down all of the ethnic/racial groups, including your own, that attend your college or live within a hundred miles of the college. After you have assembled this list, write down the defining characteristics, issues, and values of each group that might affect your relationship with a member of that group should that individual seek you out as a counselor. Then contemplate and write about the ways you might respond to those issues.

Now, read what you have written and evaluate it as impartially as you can. What aspects of your list, as you examine it honestly, are made up of valid appraisals of ethnic or racial realities, and what aspects may well reflect stereotyping and possible prejudice? Upon what are the prejudices, stereotypes, and inaccuracies based? Where did those come from?

Next, consider this question, but beware—you will have to dig deep to answer it: What items for each of those groups didn't you write down, either because you didn't want other people to see them or didn't want to even admit them to yourself? We live in a time when political correctness is enforced in a way that sometimes minimizes opportunities for honest dialogue, even the conversations we hold within ourselves. For at least a few minutes, try to suspend "correct" thinking and reflect honestly about your ideas.

When you are finished, sit with classmates who have also done the first part of this exercise and compare your responses. What differences and similarities do you see in your lists?

---

people who find themselves in difficult economic circumstances. Many people, usually by virtue of a multitude of problems, live at the margins of our society. Multiple problems—mental illness, addiction, joblessness, even homelessness—may constellate around an adult individual, making an agency counselor's job truly difficult. The multiple problems of children who are experiencing learning difficulties at school, family problems at home, and violence in the streets challenge the determination and fortitude of inner-city school counselors. Multiple issues, usually exacerbated by financial problems, typically call for more case management strategizing than traditional counseling, and they call into play skills that are often not taught in graduate counseling programs.

Clients with multiple problems, often marginalized by society, call into question a counselor's primary values about individual self-worth, social class, and the role of the counselor as an agent of change. You will have to make decisions about where you stand on these issues, as well. At some point, you will be confronted by people who are challenged by multiple problems and who seem to have little in the way of resources to support them. What will you do?

I remember the evening I sat with a homeless man who had just wandered into my office off the street. Somehow he'd bypassed the clinic's secretaries and outer office personnel. He hadn't eaten, he had no place to stay that night, and he was hearing voices that told him to stay away from the local shelter. It was six o'clock, I was already late leaving to go home, and the next day was Thanksgiving. Most of my colleagues had left the building. Relatives were arriving from out of town, and I wanted to be at home when they arrived.

This was one of my moments of personal challenge that pitted my notions of personal comfort against my commitment of service to people in more difficult circumstances. I did not want to be dealing with this man that night. I had places to go. I had relatives to meet. After an hour or so of phone calls, I managed to find a friend who was able to help. This woman, a nun with a local church, had a reputation for helping out with situations like this, and she gladly welcomed the opportunity to step in and assist. She offered to find him shelter and to follow up with finding other needed services in the morning.

During this evening I had to confront my own limitations as one of those agents of service. I saw that I was no saint; I was not prepared to go that extra distance offered by my friend. I also, however, did not ignore this man who had come to me, and I recognized my competing obligations, so there wasn't undue guilt. It was simply a personal, internal confrontation about the limits of my own ethical reach; how far I was willing to go to care for someone who could not care for himself.

I have no doubt that you will have similar personal, internal confrontations of this sort. You will encounter people who are in difficult circumstances, stigmatized by many in our society. You will work with people who have been marginalized by society, people who are economically and politically oppressed. It behooves you to become a student of the ways counseling can empower people in those oppressed circumstances as well as of the ways counseling can serve to support the forces of oppression (Totton, 2005).

You, too, I imagine, will find yourself somewhere on the continuum between sainthood and callous indifference, but at least you will have awareness of the issue and will have grappled with the level of personal responsibility with which you feel you should respond. I hope that you will take it upon yourself to accept the challenge of feeling a responsibility to be involved, to help, without undue guilt about not being able to do more.

Differences Based on Gender

Men and women are different. Many of those differences are based on the ways girls and boys are raised and how they are treated in the prevailing culture. Broad

REFLECTION EXERCISE 8.3   *Socioeconomic Class*

Another personal experience of mine serves as a prompt for this exercise. I invite you to try this as an examination of your own attitudes about social class. I have a vivid memory of walking one winter's evening down a fashionable street in Manhattan. It was in mid-December, holiday season, and the street was ablaze with all of its dazzling lights and alluring shop windows. I was thoroughly enjoying my evening in the city amidst all of its festive decorations when my attention was suddenly caught by two people sitting on the opposite ends of a sidewalk bench. What caught my attention were the remarkable differences between them and their obvious indifference to each other. One of the people on the bench was a man garbed in ragged clothes, with a trash bag as an overcoat, and the other was a woman in expensive clothes and a full-length mink coat. Each seemed absolutely oblivious to the other. They may have been sharing a bench, but they were on different planets.

Picture these people yourself. Imagine what their days are like and what their nights will be like. What will they do; who will they see? What conceivable thing might happen that would engage them in conversation with each other? Is that the kind of thing that you could, or would, initiate if you were on the scene?

What would your attitude toward each of these people be if each were sitting in the chair opposite you in your counseling office? Would you speak to them differently? What assumptions would you make about them? What would you assume about their educational background? Their ethnic background?

This kind of self-examination can be uncomfortable. It can also be uncomfortable to confront these realities in the world. As the renowned social activist and educator Jonathan Kozol once said, "The last thing people want to see outside the marquee of *Les Miserables,* after they leave their $250 seats, is the real *miserables,* the children on the sidewalk."

After you've had a chance to think about this yourself, talk it over with some classmates. How might they think of this differently, or the same? What are those different opinions about, and what values do they represent? What of the backgrounds of the people who hold those values, and what of your own background?

---

stereotypical Western cultural assumptions include ideas about women as being primarily suited to nurturing roles and as being less competent than men in other kinds of roles. These cultural assumptions portray men as being overly competitive and driven by external notions of success. Women and men both pay a price for these assumptions, particularly when they internalize them and believe the implicit limitations imposed by these assumptions.

The literature suggests that because of these assumptions women may suffer job discrimination and be offered jobs that emphasize their nurturing ability and underplay their other competencies (Basow, 1992). They may even feel devalued because of their nurturing capabilities, particularly in their ability to connect with others in relationship (Gilligan, 1982, 2002; Miller & Stiver, 1997). Any number of pathological symptoms, such as depression (Jack, 1991), agoraphobia, or eating disorders (Miller & Stiver, 1997; Sue, Sue, & Sue, 2000), can result from this combination of being undervalued and seeing oneself as inferior. An ugly cycle of political oppression and self-blame perpetuates itself.

Men, on the other hand, may drive themselves so much to fulfill their own and the prevailing culture's notions of success that they miss out on the intimacies afforded by close relationships with others, and they may develop symptoms of their own that are driven by cultural expectations and assumptions. They can literally work themselves sick. Disorders that are typically associated with male gender issues include problems of addiction, violence, workaholism, and general feelings of inadequacy (Real, 1997, 2002).

You can increase your own awareness of some of these political issues by being aware of the ways your male and female clients have been shaped by and have internalized these cultural messages. You can become a student of feminist theory (Enns & Hackett, 1993; Gilligan, 1982, 2002), examining the particular ways culture affects a woman's self-image, and you can also look at the literature about the relationship of culture and male development (Kelly & Hall, 1994; Real, 2002). This increased awareness of the politics of gender will help to alert you to its problems and related symptoms when you see them in your clients. This awareness is also important so that you don't reinforce the prevailing cultural norms and stereotypical assumptions about gender roles in your own counseling practice. This would serve to oppress your clients even further.

Learning how counseling practice is affected by and affects attitudes about gender roles is a critical part of any counselor's training (Stevens-Smith, 1995). Counseling that helps a woman to experience her own power, including her strengths of association with others, may serve a wonderfully liberating function. Helping a man to experience the joys of close relationship with others and the simple pleasures of life itself can be similarly rewarding. Helping any of your clients to learn about the complex interplay of culture and gender can be a great counseling service. For both women and men, learning to live with more awareness about how gender roles are shaped by culture is freeing.

You, too, have been somehow affected by these prevailing norms and assumptions, and your attitudes about how you have been affected intimately affects your work with others. Your ability to help your clients examine the bonds imposed by gender role stereotyping will only be as proficient as the degree to which you have become aware of your own.

Differences Based on Sexual Orientation

Unless you live in one of the rare communities where deviations from prevailing notions about "appropriate" sexual orientations (e.g., "straight," heterosexual) are openly tolerated, your clients with other kinds of sexual orientations undoubtedly face public stigma and discrimination. How you respond to clients with sexual orientations that are different from yours will have a tremendous impact on how they feel about themselves and their sexuality (Adams, Jaques, & May, 2004; Lasser & Gottlieb, 2004; Pachankis & Goldfried, 2004; Robertson, 2004).

To the degree that you are comfortable with your own sexuality, your role as a counselor in helping a client understand and come to grips with his or her sexuality, whether it's similar or different from your own orientation, can serve as a tremendous source of support. In this role you may help clients to consider how open they want to be about their sexuality, whether they want to "come out" in the community in which they live. You may also work with clients who have become infected with AIDS, or who have lost loved ones to AIDS. Your ability to accept the person with the disease can also serve as a great support (Springer & Lease, 2000).

Differences Based on Religion

Religious difference may challenge you. You may have profound differences of opinion, outstanding philosophical and values differences, with the people whom you are asked to counsel. You may not have had any training in how to deal with these differences (Levitt & Balkin, 2003; Schulte, Skinner, & Claiborn, 2002).

You may find yourself stuck between your desire to be empathic and your disagreement with your client's belief system. Assume, for example, that you are a school counselor who is dealing with an avowed Christian parent who wants his child pulled from the Biology course because it is teaching about evolution, not about creationism. Or, assume the opposite—that you are a Christian counselor who is counseling a parent who wants evolution taught in that Biology class. These kinds of dilemmas can be challenging, particularly when you are confronted by an unusually dogmatic client.

The struggle for you, the counselor, is to find the common ground on which you and your client can stand together, even in the midst of the largest chasms of disagreement. This will probably be easiest if you are able to see the other's worldview. Counselors who adopt a pluralistic attitude about religion and spirituality are probably most able to relate empathically to the religious views of others. There may be one journey (spirituality) but many roads (religions) to get there (Zinnbauer & Pargament, 2000). Counselors who have fixed religious views that would come into harsh conflict with those who believe differently would probably work best in settings that support those views. When all efforts to find common ground fail, referral to another counselor is the most appropriate action to take.

Working with a client around issues of spirituality and religion can be richly rewarding. I have found that most clients, from young children to older adults, have serious questions and convictions about life's meaning that can provide fascinating material for the discussions surrounding how they live their lives. These questions and your clients' answers to them will affect all aspects of their lives— their career choices, their intimate relationships, and their attitudes about themselves. You will be prepared to field their questions and concerns to the degree that you have asked some of those same questions of yourself. Building your spiritual empathy, as well as your tolerance of others' views about spirituality and religion, involves immersion in your own personal search for solutions to your questions about life's meaning and design.

A World of Difference: Building Cultural Competency

The list of the ways in which you might be different from your clients is endless. We could talk about difference based on geography or food preferences or virtually any personal characteristic. Some of that discussion might merit serious consideration, some might serve only to demean some of the really pertinent questions of difference that profoundly influence your work. What is of real value in any of this discussion is the degree to which it leads you to question and consider your own relationship to issues of difference, particularly the ways in which you are different from your clients. Much of the value in this discussion is about increasing self-awareness. What are your personal attitudes, biases, even prejudices that affect your ability to build relationship? How do your own values and beliefs reflect real differences? How much are they simply old messages from your past? How much interest do you have in learning about people who are different?

Bringing attitudes that lie darkly under the surface into the light of awareness is a major piece of work that you can do to increase your cultural competency as a counselor. You can choose to put yourself into situations that will challenge your comfort level, and this will bring your own biases into sharper perspective. You can also choose to expand your cultural awareness and desire for greater understanding to the world outside your counseling office and make promotion of multicultural perspectives in counseling part of your broader professional activism (Bingham, 2003).

Self-awareness is part of the means of increasing cultural competence, and you can also become more competent by increasing your knowledge base of cultural and diversity issues. Read the research about multicultural counseling, and read what the emerging research suggests is best practice. You can read about cultural groups other than your own, and you can sample the literature of those other cultures. (I am using the word *culture* in its broadest sense: a group of individuals who share common values and traditions that may be based on racial or ethnic identity and country of origin, but may also be based on gender, sexual orientation, class, age, or other factors.) You can seek out training opportunities that will increase your sensitivity to issues of culture and diversity.

More than this, you can begin to broaden your sense of citizenship to include more than nationality. Begin to think of yourself as a citizen of the world, or even as living on the planet with your big extended family, with your fellow world citizens as brothers and sisters. In this view there are simply a lot of brothers and sisters you haven't met yet. Travel to other countries. Travel to other states. Walk around neighborhoods where people are visibly different. Go to places where you are an obvious member of a racial minority. Consider living there to see what it feels like. Some of the most multiculturally aware people I know have served in organizations like the Peace Corps, where immersion in another culture not only awakens one to notions of difference but also to amazing similarities. When you travel—not as a tourist but as a traveler—your attitudes about "difference" take on whole new meanings, as do your attitudes about global politics and international relations.

You can choose to do simple things to push your cultural comfort zones. You can eat foods from different countries or learn another language. You can expend effort to expand your cultural awareness. See it as a professional obligation. Travel, like taking time to read great poetry and literature, should be viewed as a professional development activity. Reading about culture is a great way to expand your awareness, and experiencing other cultures is even better. Lived experience is probably the best avenue to increasing cultural competency.

Concluding Thoughts: Beyond Difference

In a sense, all counseling is multicultural counseling (Patterson, 1996). While we may focus attention on learning about different cultures, about issues of diversity, and about socioeconomic class differences, we cannot forget that within each of those cultures are people who are uniquely different from each other. In other words, each of us is our own culture and should be seen absolutely uniquely.

This should not excuse us from trying to learn about those cultural issues and ways of perceiving the world that are shared by groups of people from different countries, races, or genders. We should not lose sight, however, of the essential obligation to seize the empathic opportunity to view the world through each individual client's eyes, regardless of the diversity issues that present themselves.

This can best be done by letting your client be your teacher. Let him tell you about his culture, about the issues that he thinks make him "different." Learn from him about the ways he may have been stigmatized, marginalized, or treated differently because of these issues. Use your listening and reflection skills to show your understanding. You can even let him tell you about the things you should read or learn about to help understand his cultural issues more completely.

Finally, do not be so caught up in looking for difference that similarity escapes you. In what ways are your client's experiences just like yours? In what ways are you alike? It is around the similarities, most likely in the inner layers of the "onion," that you are likely to find the common ground of understanding. It is around the similarities that you will be most able to identify with your client. In this identification lies the powerful possibility for building the therapeutic alliance so critical to the success of this counseling venture.

For Further Thought

1. Create a genogram (family map) of your family. For information on creating genograms, check the text on genograms by McGoldrick and Gerson (1985). Go back at least two generations with this mapping, if possible. How has your life been influenced by the cultural heritage of the generations that came before you? If you feel comfortable enough, share your genogram with colleagues who are of different cultural backgrounds. Ask them about the maps they have created of their families.

2. Interview school counselors in your area. Do they see changes in the cultural demographics of their schools? What are the prevalent ethnic/racial majority/minority characteristics of the student and faculty population, and how does that affect the cultural environment in the school?

3. Create your own cultural education "plan." Include in this plan all of those things you might want to do to increase your understanding of the differences discussed in this chapter. Share your plan with colleagues.

4. Talk with representatives on the ethics committee of the licensing board of your professional organization about their work on the committee. What kinds of complaints and ethical issues most regularly confront them, and what happens as a result of those complaints?

References

Adams, J., Jaques, J., & May, K. (2004). Counseling gay and lesbian families: Theoretical considerations. *Family Journal—Counseling and Therapy for Couples and Families, 12*(1), 40–42.

American Counseling Association. (2005). *ACA code of ethics*. Alexandria, VA: Author.

Arthur, N., & Stewart, J. (2001). Multicultural counseling in the new millennium: Introduction to the special theme issue. *Canadian Journal of Counseling, 35*(1), 3–14.

Basow, S.(1992). *Gender: Stereotypes and roles* (3rd ed.). Belmont, CA: Brooks/Cole.

tforest's run.

Berry, J., Poortinga, Y., & Segall, M. (1992). *Cross-cultural psychology: Research and applications*. Cambridge: Cambridge University Press.

Bingham, R. (2003). Fostering human strength through diversity and public policy: A counseling psychologist's perspective. In B. Walsh (Ed.), *Counseling psychology and optimal human functioning* (pp. 279–295). Mahwah, NJ: Erlbaum.

Daniel, J., Roysircar, G., Abeles, N., & Boyd, C. (2004). Individual and cultural-diversity competency: Focus on the therapist. *Journal of Clinical Psychology, 60*(7), 755–770.

Enns, C., & Hackett, G. (1993). A comparison of feminist and non-feminist women's and men's reactions to nonsexist and feminist counseling: A replication and extension. *Journal of Counseling and Development, 71,* 499–509.

Geraghty, R., & Warren, F. (2003). Ethnic diversity and equality of access to specialist therapeutic community treatment for severe personality disorder. *Psychiatric Bulletin, 27*(12), 453–456.

Gilligan, C. (1982). *In a different voice*. Cambridge, MA: Harvard University Press.

Gilligan, C. (2002). *The birth of pleasure*. New York: Knopf.

Gladding, S., & Hood, W. (1974). Five cents, please. *School Counselor, 21,* 40–43.

Gondolf, E., & Williams, O. (2001). Culturally focused batterer counseling for African American men. *Trauma Violence and Abuse, 2*(4), 283–295.

Hanna, F., Talley, W., & Guindon, M. (2000). The power of perception: Toward a model of cultural oppression and liberation. *Journal of Counseling and Development, 78*(4), 430–441.

Henderson, D. (2003). School counseling. In R. Cottone & M. Tarvydas (Eds.), *Ethical and professional issues in counseling* (2nd ed., pp. 236–259). Upper Saddle River, NJ: Prentice-Hall.

Herlihy, B. (1996). When a colleague is impaired: The individual counselor's response. *Journal of Humanistic Education and Development, 34,* 118–127.

Ho, M. (1990). *Intermarried couples in therapy*. Springfield, IL. Charles C. Thomas.

Ibrahim, F., & Arredondo, P. (1986). Ethical standards for cross-cultural counseling: Counselor preparation, practice, assessment, and research. *Journal of Counseling and Development, 64,* 349–352.

Jack, D. (1991). *Silencing the self: Women and depression*. Cambridge, MA: Harvard University Press.

Jackson, Y. (2003). Research in ethnic minority communities: Cultural diversity issues in clinical psychology (with vignette by Anne K. Jacobs). In M. Roberts & S. Ilardi (Eds.), *Handbook of research methods in clinical psychology* (pp. 376–395). Malden, MA: Blackwell.

James, S., & Prilleltensky, I. (2002). Cultural diversity and mental health: Towards integrative practice. *Clinical Psychology Review, 22*(8), 1133–1154.

Johnson, M., & Lashley, K. (1989). Influence of Native-Americans' cultural commitment on preferences for counselor ethnicity and expectations about counseling. *Journal of Multicultural Counseling and Development, 17,* 115–122.

Kelly, K., & Hall, A. (1994). Affirming the assumptions of the developmental model for counseling men. *Journal of Mental Health Counseling, 16*, 475–482.

Kim, Y. (2003). Understanding Asian American clients: Problems and possibilities for cross-cultural counseling with special reference to Korean Americans. *Journal of Ethnic and Cultural Diversity in Social Work, 12*(3), 91–114.

Kitchener, K. (1994, May). Doing good well: The wisdom behind ethical supervision. *Counseling and Human Development,* 1–8.

Lasser, J., & Gottlieb, M. (2004). Treating patients distressed regarding their sexual orientation: Clinical and ethical alternatives. *Professional Psychology: Research and Practice, 35*(2), 194–200.

Leslie, L., & Morton, G. (2001). Family therapy's response to family diversity: Looking back, looking forward. *Journal of Family Issues, 22*(7), 904–921.

Levitt, D., & Balkin, R. (2003). Religious diversity from a Jewish perspective. *Counseling and Values, 48*(1), 57–66.

Lewis-Fernandez, R., & Kleinman, A. (1994). Culture, personality, and psychopathology. *Journal of Abnormal Psychology, 103*, 67–71.

Looby, E. (2001). Valuing human diversity: Counseling multiracial and multiethnic children. In D. Sandhu (Ed.), *Elementary school counseling in the new millennium* (pp. 193–207). Alexandria, VA: American Counseling Association.

Marsella, A. (1993). Counseling and psychotherapy with Japanese-Americans: Cross-cultural considerations. *American Journal of Orthopsychiatry, 63*, 200–208.

McGoldrick, M., & Gerson, R. (1985). *Genograms in family assessment.* New York: Norton.

Meara, N., Schmidt, L., & Day, J. (1996). Principles and virtues: A foundation for ethical decisions, policies, and character. *The Counseling Psychologist, 24*, 4–77.

Miller, J., & Stiver, I. (1997). *The healing connection: How women form relationships in therapy and in life.* Northvale, NJ: Jason Aronson.

Mishne, J. (2002). *Multiculturalism and the therapeutic process.* New York: Guilford Press.

Mitchell, R. (2001). *Documentation in counseling records* (2nd ed.). Alexandria, VA: American Counseling Association.

Nassar-McMillan, S., & Hakim-Larson, J. (2003). Counseling considerations among Arab Americans. *Journal of Counseling and Development, 81*(2), 150–159.

Neukrug, E., Milliken, T., & Walden, S. (2001). Ethical complaints made against credentialed counselors: An updated survey of state licensing boards. *Counselor Education and Supervision, 41*(1), 57–70.

Pachankis, J., & Goldfried, M. (2004). Clinical issues in working with lesbian, gay, and bisexual clients. *Psychotherapy: Theory, Research, Practice, Training, 41*(3), 227–246.

Patterson, C. H. (1996). Multicultural counseling: From diversity to universality. *Journal of Counseling and Development, 74*, 227–231.

Pederson, P., Draguns, J., Lonner, W., & Trimble, J. (Eds). (2002). *Counseling across cultures.* Thousand Oaks, CA: Sage.

Real, T. (1997). *I don't want to talk about it.* New York: Fireside.

Real, T. (2002). The awful truth. *Psychotherapy Networker, 26,* 34–43.

Roach, F. (1999). Culture, counseling, and racial issues. In S. Palmer & P. Laungani (Eds.), *Counseling in a Multicultural Society* (pp. 71–89). London: Sage.

Robertson, P. (2004). The historical effects of depathologizing homosexuality on the practice of counseling. *Family Journal—Counseling and Therapy for Couples and Families, 12*(2), 163–169.

Sampson, J., Kolodinsky, R., & Greeno, B. (1997). Counseling on the information highway: Future possibilities and potential problems. *Journal of Counseling and Development, 75,* 203–212.

Schulte, D., Skinner, T., & Claiborn, C. (2002). Religious and spiritual issues in counseling psychology training. *Counseling Psychologist, 30*(1), 118–134.

Springer, C., & Lease, S. (2000). The impact of multiple AIDS-related bereavement in the gay male population. *Journal of Counseling and Development, 78,* 297–304.

St. Germaine, J. (1993). Dual relationships: What's wrong with them? *American Counselor, 2,* 25–30.

Stevens-Smith, P. (1995). Gender issues in counselor education: Current status and challenges. *Counselor Education and Supervision, 34,* 283–293.

Sue, D., Sue, D., & Sue, S. (2000). *Understanding abnormal behavior* (6th ed.). Boston, MA: Houghton Mifflin.

Sue, S., & Zane, N. (1987). The role of culture and cultural techniques in psychotherapy. *American Psychologist, 42,* 37–45.

Totton, N. (2005). *The politics of psychotherapy: New perspectives.* Maidenhead, Berkshire, UK: Open University Press/McGraw-Hill.

Welfel, E. (2002). *Ethics in counseling and psychotherapy: Standards, research, and emerging issues* (2nd ed.). Pacific Grove, CA: Brooks/Cole.

Zinnbauer, B., & Pargament, K. (2000). Working with the sacred: Four approaches to religious and spiritual issues in counseling. *Journal of Counseling and Development, 78,* 162–171.

Essential Action Skills: Working Toward Goals

> Twaddle, rubbish, and gossip is what people want, not action
> . . . The secret of life is to chatter freely about all one wishes
> to do and how one is always being prevented—and then do
> nothing.
> *(Søren Kierkegaard)*

Fritz Perls was fond of saying that no one coming into counseling is really interested in changing anything—clients really only want to be told that no matter how weirdly they're behaving everything is just fine. Perls is partly correct; people are reluctant to change. Change is often painful, and it requires giving up something that is known. Even if what is known is painful, there is a certain comfort in the familiarity.

Something drove your client into counseling, however, and it is that drive with which you want to ally yourself. A big part of your job will be to motivate your client to act on her own behalf, to pursue the goals that have been staked out as important. Perhaps you have become enamored with the dynamics of forming a relationship with a new client, of learning how to listen and respond empathically, and of how to help someone begin to be more disclosing with you. The relationship you develop with your client is not an end in itself, no matter how much joy you or your client receive from it. It is important to remember that these relationship development skills are always in service of helping your client get what she wants and needs.

A Call to Action

People seek you out, or are pushed into seeing you, because of a problem they want to resolve. The problem might be substance abuse, disputes with a partner or with other children, losing a job, or finding that one's career path has dead-ended. Whatever it is, it's been painful or provocative enough for them to decide to come into your office. You need to keep your eye on the goals. The contract your client made with you at the outset of your work is your real reason for being together. Remembering this helps to keep you focused and avoids making the process of counseling longer than it needs to be.

The relationship is a critical variable in successful movement toward goals, because without the relationship the goals and the articulated contract simply won't come together, at least not as effectively. The critical need for patience in building the relationship can be a difficult fact for new counselors to grasp, particularly those who are "fixers" by nature. It can be tempting to see a problem, decide what needs to be done, and then move toward that goal at full speed— unfortunately, leaving the client behind in the dust. The real challenge is to use the relationship with your client as the vehicle in which he might approach his goals more effectively in his own time.

The importance of a good counselor-client relationship has received increasing research attention in recent years (Horvath & Greenberg, 1994). It is the binding force that helps you to positively influence client behavior and outcomes. Regardless of theoretical orientation and the specific techniques used, the relationship itself seems to be a critical variable in the success of the counseling endeavor (Horvath & Luborsky, 1993).

This fact flies in the face of what many people, particularly insurance companies or others who reimburse us for services, seem to want from counseling. They want the counseling to be done expeditiously and quickly. They don't care about relationships; they care about results. It is your job to help convince the payers and your administrator of the fact that lasting change, the pursuit of goals that will really be effectively met, hinges on full client exploration and participation in the process. The development of a solid counseling relationship in this process is central. You can tell the administrators that there is considerable evidence effectively linking the development of a good counseling relationship to successful counseling outcomes (Luborsky, 1994; Saketopoulou, 1999).

Inevitably, counseling takes time. It needn't take twenty years of three times a week on the psychoanalytic couch, but it will typically take more than a couple of sessions of saying "snap out of it" to accomplish anything long-lasting. Experience will help you to move things along more quickly, but until you have done this work for a few years, you should not feel compelled to work for speedy solutions or quick fixes.

As a counseling colleague of mine says, "When you learn to fix a car, the first job is to learn to fix it well. After that, you can learn how to do the job more quickly. Why should it be any different for counselors?" Learning how to do it well should be your first priority, not speed. An eye toward goals, the contract for working together, and the developing relationship go hand in hand. One happens in service of the other, and the relationship all by itself may do much toward achieving the goals.

The Developmental Assessment and Movement Toward Goals

Much of what happens in your initial formulation of goals with a new client depends on the client's level of functioning. If a client is at Level 1, embroiled in crisis after crisis, the goals will most likely coalesce around trying to help him achieve some stability. With clients who are more generally stable, maintaining jobs and families, the goals we establish mutually with them will be more sophisticated, perhaps finding a better job or more satisfaction in relationships. First things should come first. If there are essential health, safety, or other basic needs, you must attend to them before you can deal with other things. If someone is suicidal, your first item of business is securing the client's safety. If a child in your office is hungry or has been abused, that takes obvious precedence over academic success or social skills development.

Your client may have lofty ambitions or unreachable desires. It is your job to honor the dreams while helping to inject some reality into the package. You both need to be convinced of the worth and viability of the journey you're on. The goals, the process, and the outcomes should be conceived with a high degree of mutuality. Counseling is a collaborative process.

From Crisis and Coercion to Engagement

At least some of your clients will not exactly be thrilled to be engaged in counseling with you. A client may have been court ordered or coerced, leveraged into counseling by someone in pain because of this person's behavior. It is your job to help this client acknowledge the personal things that she does that causes this pain among her friends, her family, or her community. It is your job to help her fully comprehend the personal responsibility she has for attending to the pain she has inflicted on others. It is your job, in other words, to help make others' pain more acutely felt by this person herself. You want the externalized pain to be felt more internally. This is the meaning of taking personal responsibility.

In fact, personal responsibility is our own universal unspoken goal for all of our clients. It is central to all of our work and is the most critical piece of what we do. We want people to acknowledge and assume more responsibility for who they are and what they do. Our clients will be seeking freedom in many guises and forms. We want to help them with that, but only when it is coupled with the search for accompanying responsibility. We want our clients to grow freely and to grow up. All of the goals we carefully articulate with them will reflect this desire. If we work with children, we want them to move incrementally in appropriate developmental directions. If we work with adolescents, we want to aid them in their efforts to move toward adulthood. If we work with adults, we want them to act as responsible adults, perhaps to heal wounds that have been inflicted along the way. In a sense, with all of our clients we act as some kind of surrogate parent, and in many cases we may actually be re-parenting.

For coerced clients, as well as for clients in crisis and those who are having trouble managing the basics of life (again, the Level 1 client), the largest initial steps toward action involve support, engagement, and creation of the therapeutic alliance. You will use engagement and fact-finding questions, your intelligent reflections of content and feeling, and gentle challenging skills to build this alliance. For most of the people with whom you'll work, this is the first order of business. No matter how articulate or lofty your goals and desires for your clients, there will be no action until they are fully on board with the process. If you are asking a new client to consider giving up drugs or to quit thinking about suicide, what do you have to offer in exchange? You offer the alliance. Through this alliance, you are telling him that there is hope for a healthier, more fulfilling life.

Moving from Engagement to Action

The first work in any counseling relationship is involved with engaging the client, in dealing with resistance, and in creating the alliance. Much of this work is designed to find out about this person, to assess her strengths and challenges, and to hear her story. Your next job is to mobilize action. This phase of the counseling process is about helping the client mobilize her inner resources in service of reaching the goals she has set for herself.

In this movement toward a more action-oriented phase, continue to pay close attention to the working alliance, making every effort to ensure that the client is consistently aware of your support and concern. You will often find in the alliance itself hints or suggestions of what is needed to move toward goals. In particular, you will come across clues about the ways in which your client subverts himself in the process of getting what he wants and needs. A client who yearns for a close relationship, for example, may consistently behave with you in ways that push you away, that are avoidant of intimacy and meaningful contact. A client who says that her goal is to be more assertive with people may have difficulty looking you in the eye when she speaks and consistently second-guess herself in everything she says.

In addition to the kinds of skills we have already discussed, some other skills and activities can be extremely effective in aiding your clients' efforts to become more active in pursuit of goals. These skills come from a variety of therapeutic traditions and theoretical orientations, and when used selectively, they can help your clients move forward. Knowing which skill to use and when to best employ it depends on counselor judgment and experience. Some theoretical orientations, such as the feminist approach, encourage the counselor to make the client a collaborator in selectively choosing some of these skills and means of working toward goals. Regardless of your chosen orientation, your selection of skills should relate directly to the perceived level of client functioning and the client's ability to grasp the meaning of what is happening.

In my experience supervising new counselors, I have many times encountered their frustration about this stage of counseling work. Counselors who have diligently learned how to engage clients and listen to their unfolding stories (sometimes referred to as "confessionals") are unclear about what to do next. "What now?" they ask. The skills that help to mobilize client energy and action comprise a toolbox of sorts, and each skill is a tool that can be used, sometimes in conjunction with other skills, to help a client move actively toward her chosen goals.

Skills for Action with Clients at Level 1 and Level 2

Here begins a discussion of those skills that might best be used with clients in the first two levels of our developmental "house." These are skills derived from a number of theoretical traditions, including analytic, cognitive-behavioral, and phenomenological (e.g., person-centered and Gestalt) schools. In keeping with the philosophy of this book, you are encouraged to think broadly about skills and their application to particular client issues. Although each of us naturally gravitates to a school of theory that resonates personally, we should be able to use techniques and specific skills from any theoretical tradition in service of a particular client need. Again, the notion here is to use techniques that fit the person rather than making the person fit the technique. Select tools based on your judgment of what might work most effectively. This perception of client need is based on your assessment of his level of functioning in the world, maturity, and capacity to manage freedom and responsibility. In sum, the skill employed should be congruent with the capacity of the client to utilize it. For example, use of the analysis of action-consequence sequences skill is appropriate with someone trying to get her life together (Level 1). It would not be as appropriate with an intellectually and emotionally sophisticated client (Level 3), wherein insight-oriented strategies such as interpretation (discussed in Chapter 10) might be a better strategy.

There is nothing sacrosanct about matching skills and client characteristics. You should feel absolutely comfortable using action skills with Level 3 clients when it seems appropriate. A client, for example, may operate with a high level of functioning and responsibility in the world yet have some real difficulties with assertiveness. Some basic assertiveness training could be exactly the right thing to do with this client. Conversely, there will be times when you want to use advanced action skills with Level 2 clients, especially if they have been working with you for some time and appear to be ready to begin transitioning to Level 3. Interpretation, analyzing dreams, and community service could all be appropriately employed to serve some of those people. This model for matching client functional level to counseling skills is a rough guide. Your judgment and intuition, as well as your client's preference, are your best guides in choosing what strategy to use.

Examination of Action-Consequence Sequences

How we think and feel about ourselves has a lot to do with the ways in which we experience other people's reactions to us. And, of course, the way we behave influences how others react to us. We get positive affirmations for jobs well done and recrimination and negative feedback for things done that rub people the wrong way. Yet a common characteristic of Level 1 clients is an apparent lack of appreciation for how their behavior affects others. They tend to blame all kinds of extraneous factors—addiction or a bad upbringing, for example—for their social difficulties. Your incarcerated client might say, "How did I wind up in jail? It was those cops, man! Cops! They've just got it in for me." This client fails to mention, or even perhaps to recognize, that he first threw a brick through a window, which then invited the police into his life. Examining the consequences of behavior is a mechanism for stopping the blaming and for the beginning of taking real personal responsibility.

Examining how certain actions create predictable reactions and consequences provides us with a framework for helping our clients take more personal responsibility for the consequences of their actions and the means for helping them see the linkages between their behavior and people's reactions to them (Glasser, 1965, 1998). Examination of the action-consequence sequence helps clients see the ways they wind up feeling (both positive and negative) as end products of what they have done. In this examination, the counselor helps the client break down the sequencing of thoughts and events into discrete elements. It is a way of looking at how they get hung up and finding new ways to avoid getting so tangled. It is particularly useful for those clients of ours who always seem to be in trouble, moving from one difficult situation to another.

In a school setting, for example, a counselor might work with a child who has been getting into a lot of fights by helping her look at what, very specifically, leads up to a fight, how she gets triggered by those events, and how she then responds. Typically, a child caught up in this kind of fighting sequencing not only draws a lot of negative reactions from others but also winds up with negative feelings about herself. Over time, the child could learn new responding patterns to replace the maladaptive ones. The sequence of events leading up to the fighting behavior may even start before the child gets to school. She may leave home in the morning having been yelled at or having witnessed a fight between her parents. She arrives at school fuming and in a funk. Then, if someone looks at her or speaks to her in any way that might be interpreted as antagonistic, she strikes out.

In an adult example, the sequence of events leading to trouble and bad feelings can be even more tangential and seemingly unrelated. Consider the man who consistently finds himself involved in adulterous affairs. He says he doesn't like what he's been doing, that he is committed to his partner, but no matter how hard he tries to avoid it attractive new women just keep entering his life and seducing him. Upon examination, the man finds that the "seductions" usually begin days, or weeks, before actual physical contact and that he is an active participant in the process. It may involve flirtatious behavior or hanging around places where he knows contacts might be made or putting himself in situations (e.g., using alcohol) where his natural inhibitions will be diminished. He learns that if he truly wants to avoid these affairs, he must change these early decisions and behavioral patterns.

The action-consequence examination process is a cornerstone of reality therapy. Glasser (1998) suggests four specific means for changing destructive behavior patterns:

1. *Uncover the essential desires, or "wants," behind a specific set of behaviors.*

Find out what it is that the client really is after when he gets involved in difficult situations. Our adulterous client, for example, may find that he really loves his wife and wants to stay married to her but that he also wants some danger and excitement to spice up his otherwise routine life.

2. *Discuss the direction and outcomes of current behavior patterns.*

For example, our client can see that staying with his present course of behavior will inevitably lead to his wife's divorcing him.

3. *Consider the effects of current behavior patterns and their relative success in getting what is wanted.*

When the client can see that his behavior is not really getting him what he wants, he will be more likely to want to try something different. Our client may realize that his behavior is leading to divorce, which is not at all what he wants. He may also realize that having affairs is actually not the most effective way to get what he really wants, which is a more interesting and exciting life.

4. *Plan for action.*

Using specific times and circumstances, plan for how a new behavior set can replace an old, unproductive one. Our client may decide to look for excitement in his work life instead of in his sex life, or he may quit his boring job and start the business he and his brother have been talking about for years.

These actions have been enumerated in the helpful acronym, WDEP, which can help you remember the process. In this series of steps, you first help your client identify what is essentially wanted (W), then help discover the direction (D) of her life, evaluate (E) the effectiveness of behaviors in getting what is wanted, and plan (P) for constructive change (Wubbolding, 1988, 1991). This work demands an engaged, active counselor. It may require even more energy, as well as a capacity for dealing with challenging and resistant behavior, than other counseling skills (Wubbolding & Brickell, 1998). By adding more thought, sometimes more time, and a behavioral action plan to the understanding of the sequence of events, your client can gain more control over how those events unfold. For some clients this will be a time-consuming, even tedious process of time and again looking at how particular behaviors cause problems and negative feelings. For others, it will involve little other than pointing out how these repetitive patterns occur. For all of your clients, this provides a mechanism for them to become actors in the events of their lives rather than victims.

Once your client has seen how these sequences unfold, he can make informed choices about whether to respond differently, and it is in this choice making that he can now see himself as being responsible for much of what happens in his life. While your client cannot influence all of the events that affect his life, he can at least acknowledge that he always has total control over how he acts and responds.

Reorganizing Unhelpful Thought Patterns

You can also help your clients to recognize and reorganize destructive thought patterns, particularly those that are self-destructive. Self-destructive and illogical thinking can lead your clients to subvert their own movement toward more effective living (Beck, 1988; Ellis, 1988). By helping your clients to examine and reevaluate these patterns, you can help them move more productively and happily in the world.

Ellis (1990) says that people get into trouble when operating from erroneous beliefs, many of which can be reduced to a relatively fixed set of assumptions about the world. He says that these belief systems are irrational and that they exist in varying forms almost universally. Any of these can have a negative impact on a

CASE EXAMPLE 9.1 *Invitation to Examine the Action-Consequence Sequence*

This boy is a sixth grade elementary school student, and he's been sent to the school counselor because he has been getting into a lot of trouble with peers. The counselor has watched him during recesses on the playground and during lunchtimes in the cafeteria, and he's seen how this child's rough, demanding behavior can put others off.

STUDENT: So here I am again. What now?

COUNSELOR: Trouble at recess again. Some teachers complained to the principal that you were hassling some other students, so here you are. She thought I might be able to help you not get into so much trouble. Also, I was out on the ball field this afternoon, and I saw that thing you got into with Sue Ellen over the kickball. What happened?

The counselor explains directly about the reasons this student's was sent to see him. He immediately assumes the directive, active stance of a teaching role, helping the student to look at how his behavior creates trouble. He follows this with an engagement question.

STUDENT: Nothing happened. I went over and asked her for the kickball, and then she gave it to me.

A typical elementary school response, not acknowledging—or maybe not even seeing— personal responsibility for the difficulties that transpired.

COUNSELOR: Really. I wonder if there was some way you did that that made her angry?

Tossing out a hunch for the student, wondering aloud about the action and response. It's a bit of a gentle challenge as well.

STUDENT: She' a wimp. I didn't do anything to her.

COUNSELOR: Well, I couldn't hear what was said between you, but she looked pretty bent out of shape. I sure would like to work with you to see if we can figure a way for you to avoid getting into so much trouble.

The counselor is assuming a collaborative stance here. He wants to be an ally in the student's efforts in staying out of trouble.

STUDENT: Yeah, right. Like that would make any difference. These teachers are all out after me. They just see me coming and they say, "Hey, let's give this kid a detention."

This sounds like a typical student blaming attitude, familiar to any parent who's listened to a child explain away a bad grade with, "It's not my fault. He gave me an F because . . ."

COUNSELOR: Maybe that's right, maybe not. I don't know. What I do know is that I can help you with your side of things so that maybe you can fly a little lower under the

The counselor should never assume, however, that teachers are always blameless. Some teachers do seem to have it in for certain kids and, unfortunately, sometimes class and race

(continued)

(Case example 9.1, continued)

radar. Maybe not draw so much flak from people.

issues play a role in that. A counselor should always have one eye on the environment in which his client operates.

The counselor takes a directive, active, collaborative stance. He is talking a good deal here—hopefully not too much—in an attempt to set the stage for teaching the student some trouble-avoidance strategies.

STUDENT: Yeah? How?

The student takes the bait, and now the work of looking at how his behaviors can be examined—and possibly altered—can begin.

Case Discussion

This child's question, "How?" is the key to the work that will follow. He has become a co-conspirator on his own behalf. The counselor can now ask him if he'd like to participate in looking at the sequences of behavior that cause problems, and the counselor can suggest other behaviors that might result in better outcomes. The process will begin with finding out what the client is really after, whether it is just getting the ball, attention, or a desire to play with these other children. Based on these "wants," the counselor can then help to identify how the ways in which he currently goes after those wants are ineffective and begin the discussion and planning for new ways of interacting.

These suggestions might include using the word "please" when asking for the kickball or learning some negotiation skills ("Could you use the ball for the first half of recess and let me use it for the second half?). It might include some simple strategies for avoiding explosive outbursts of anger when frustrated with others (e.g., stepping back and counting to ten). If the child learns to do these small interactions successfully, he'll eventually feel better about himself and his

overall interactions with others will improve. He'll receive less negative attention from others and may even receive positive support for his behavioral shifts. The counselor is taking an active teaching stance with this boy. He has direct evidence of the boy's behavior, having seen him in action on the playground, and knows how provocative he can be. The counselor is deciding to focus on teaching new skills rather than dealing with whatever thoughts or feelings the boy might have about this situation. If this child can change some of his behaviors with peers and teachers, he will inevitably wind up feeling better. If, on the other hand, the counselor were to focus on the feelings (e.g., using only engagement and fact-finding questions or reflections of content and feeling), the danger is that there would be no movement toward more productive action and that the child would simply continue feeling bad.

Naturally, the counselor will be supportive and will occasionally be reflective of the boy's thoughts and feelings. The relationship with this student will continue to be the foundation from which the counselor can make constructive suggestions.

LAB PRACTICE 9.1   *Action-Consequence Examination*

In the usual group of three or four, role play a young person like the one described in Case Example 9.1 when it is your turn to be the Client. In this session, try to get into the mindset of a middle school boy or girl who gets into a fair amount of trouble and doesn't seem to grasp how that happens. In this role play, however, take it easy on your Counselor, and don't be too oppositional. Be talkative, and allow your Counselor to engage you in the process. Feel free to invent facts and the details of this child's life, including the child's essential feelings and notions of what he or she really wants. There may be issues at home that contribute to difficulties encountered at school. The Counselor should attempt to build a collaborative process and work toward identification of some specific behavioral problem and ways of changing it. Be specific, and focus on only one or two behaviors. Think about and build a model of the specifics of how this student's behavior creates problems, and then unfold a means whereby the child could learn to substitute new actions.

After the role play, allow time for Supervisor feedback and then discuss this as a group. Did this seem realistic? Could you envision doing this with students—or other people—in a way that would be effective? What alternative strategies could be employed? What rewards could be used to supplement the teaching and performance of new behaviors?

person's self-esteem and should be challenged by the counselor. Here, in abbreviated form, is Ellis's (1994/1962) list of irrational beliefs that hang people up:

- I must be loved by significant others for almost everything I do.
- I must be awful or wicked because I acted that way.
- I feel horrible because things are not the way I like them to be.
- I cannot stop being miserable because I cannot control other people and events.
- I ought to be able to handle dangerous situations and not be fearful.
- I ought to be able to face life's difficulties and responsibilities.
- I absolutely need something other or stronger or greater than myself on which to rely.
- I must be thoroughly competent, intelligent, and achieving in all possible respects.
- This event strongly affected my life and will continue to affect it forever.
- I must have certain and absolute control over things.

- I ought to be happy most of the time.

- I have absolutely no control over my emotions and cannot help feeling disturbed about things.

According to Ellis, your primary job is to challenge your client's irrational beliefs and help your client revise these beliefs so the client becomes more "unconditionally self-accepting." The process of doing this is much like that described earlier for examining action-consequence sequences, this time looking at the ways in which events trigger negative thinking patterns. You can help your client to examine these triggering events and resulting negative thought reactions and teach her to revise the thought reactions in ways that are less self-punitive and more self-accepting.

In a similar approach, Beck describes "core schemas," which are individually developed belief systems about the self in the world (Beck, 1988, 1991). In people who are depressed, for example, these core schemas lead to a negative trio of cognitive distortions: that the self is inadequate, that experience is always negative (even in the face of positive evidence), and that the future is bleak. Beck also asserts that self-destructive thought patterns ossify into automatic thoughts that take control of an individual's responses to experience. These negative thoughts arise quickly, as though by reflex, and are assumed by the person to be perfectly reasonable. A bank clerk is passed over for a promotion and thinks, "I'll never get anywhere in this world." A student thinks she knows the answer to the teacher's question but doesn't raise her hand because, "I'm probably wrong and I'll just make a fool of myself." Again, the process of working with a client who has these self-destructive beliefs is to first flush out what the beliefs are and then create dialogue around how to correct them in a way that is less self-harming.

Other views of this business of correcting negative thinking should be mentioned as well. Some Gestalt therapists, for example, acknowledge the existence of self-destructive thought patterns, but their therapeutic approach is to bring them into people's awareness without undue efforts to try to change them (Perls, Hefferline, & Goodman, 1951). People may intellectually understand their irrationality and the negative ways they treat themselves yet be trapped within these self-defeating thought patterns (Fagan, 1970). "Each day, in each and every way, I treat myself like s—t," one Gestalt counselor friend of mine is fond of quipping to his workshop participants. A tenet of Gestalt therapy is that with increased awareness, particularly of how we remain stuck in patterns of self-defeating behavior, comes the paradoxical possibility of change.

You will find that many of your clients are absolutely wedded to their negative ideas about the world, as well as to their negative assessments of themselves. Disavowing them of these ideas and substituting kinder and gentler views can be a difficult and tiresome process. You will find that those most critical and negative about others typically carry the most negative and destructive views of themselves.

People project all of their self-hatred outward, working out their personal dislike on the world and on the people around them. You can help to counteract this kind of negative self-thinking by promoting a positive working alliance (Constantino, Castonguay, & Schut, 2002) and maintaining your own positive sense of your client. You can also encourage your clients to spend time with people who support them in positive ways, those who encourage and promote their best interests. Being with people who are negative and nonsupporting only serves to reinforce the toxic thinking of clients.

You will work with people who look for love in all the wrong places and who absolutely expect that the world holds out only a dark and forbidding future for them. Many of these people expect that the world owes them love and haven't a clue about the relationship between giving love and then getting it back. It is absolutely true that many people carry negative beliefs about themselves, but you can help them reshape these beliefs. This reshaping may take more than your intellectual challenges to those belief systems. You can perhaps best help clients to cognitively reshape their self-destructive ideas by providing ample doses of your acceptance and by modeling unconditional self-acceptance yourself. Empathy and love do heal. Your respect, your positive regard, and your acceptance can be infectious, a healing balm. These ways in which you deal with your clients can be tremendous assets in helping your clients to respect themselves. They might even be the best curative agents in helping to correct negative self-thinking.

EMOTIONAL PAYOFFS

One thought pattern that can serve to keep clients stuck in counterproductive behavior has to do with the ways certain behaviors and thoughts yield emotional payoffs. Gestalt counselors maintain that everything we do is designed to affect our environment in a way that will yield some kind of satisfaction. Each impact has potential for positive benefits and negative consequences.

Whenever a client is distressed about some life event, seems stuck in some recurring negative behavioral pattern, or is unable to move out of some untenable situation, we can ask what it is she gets out of repeating the same destructive pattern of behavior or staying in a destructive situation. First, we can ask ourselves, and when the time seems right, we can ask her. Typically, your client will deny that there is any positive benefit. Scratching below the surface of this denial, however, will typically yield some kind of satisfaction gained from this behavior pattern.

Consider a client that is unemployed and shows no inclination to look for a job. She may not understand, initially, what you mean when you ask her about the benefits of unemployment. "How can you sit there and ask me," she says, "what it is I 'get' out of being out of work? Being broke and having no job prospects is no fun!" When you investigate further, perhaps with some hunches or speculations, you may find that there are some definite underground payoffs. At least when she is not working, there's no chance of doing a bad job. Perhaps

---

REFLECTION EXERCISE 9.1   *Looking at Your Own Self-Destructive Thoughts*

Our clients are not the only ones who do not always treat themselves with unconditional love and acceptance. We too harbor unhelpful thoughts about ourselves. Little negative nagging voices inside can eat away at our self-esteem and happiness.

Using Ellis's list of typical self-destructive thinking patterns, survey your own worst thought enemies. In what ways, if any, do you think poorly of yourself? How do you think negatively about your life experiences? What negative ideas do you have about the future? Are you aware that these are most likely irrational and ill founded? What have you done to deal with these questions and ideas in the past, and how might you confront them now and in the future? Are there people in your life who could help you with these issues, or are you surrounded by people who only serve to reinforce your negative ideas?

Write about this self-reflection. Write about the people in your life as they relate to these ideas about yourself. Some of the people around you may make you feel empowered and good about yourself. They might not always agree with you, but they accept and value who you are. Others have the opposite effect. Are there implications for your relationships with others as they relate to the ideas you hold about yourself? To the degree you feel comfortable, discuss this with those who you trust will make you feel good about what you say.

---

she's figured out a way to draw unemployment benefits while only pretending to look for work. Or maybe she's being badgered to get a job by an angry parent or partner and not finding work is an indirect way of standing up for herself.

Most situations like this are complicated and defy simple solutions, but it can be helpful to examine underlying motivations. Discovering these "payoffs" can be a helpful step in this process. There are also some serious deficits—financial and emotional—associated with this behavior. For example, not working also means not earning an income or deriving satisfaction from doing productive work. The counselor can reflect with the client on these as well.

REFRAMING

The skill of reframing is an Adlerian counseling tool (Adler, 1929), and it is also used by logotherapists under the title "attitude adjustment" (Frankl, 1984/1946; Guttman, 1966). Reframing is a primary crisis intervention strategy (see Chapter 10), but it is also helpful in other counseling work designed to mobilize client action. Reframing refers to the restructuring of a recurring, ingrained, self-defeating, negative idea in a way that helps the client think about it in a new, more positive way.

A client who sees himself negatively because he tends to be attracted to women who are dangerous might, for example, be encouraged to view himself in a more positive light as someone who is interested in people who are different, intriguing, and definitely not boring. Posed to the client as a series of hunches, this reframing could help him to speculate as to what other kinds of women might be unconventional and stimulating, but not actually dangerous, and to explore ways in which his energy could be redirected. All of this presupposes, of course, that he really wants to give up the dangerous women. He might, in fact, be looking for permission to continue his pursuit of them. But that's another story. Reframing is a wonderful tool for helping people to directly challenge some of their most self-defeating ideas about themselves. It can be used in all kinds of counseling situations, with clients at all levels of functioning, as long as they have the cognitive ability to understand you. Amundson (1996), for example, has articulated a number of specific ways reframing can aid in career counseling.

Sometimes reframing can affect large numbers of people. For example, in the early 1980s the growing awareness of issues related to addiction and to children and families of alcoholics spawned a number of new self-help books. As a result, the word *codependency* came into vogue, and it is now used extensively in the lingo of self-help circles. Codependency refers to the ways in which the significant others who are involved with an addict meet their own needs by caring for the chemically dependent person. Many people, partners of alcoholics in particular, came to see any good done for others in a negative light. All actions on behalf of someone else came to be called codependency. Counseling was helpful in assisting clients to reframe at least some behaviors they had been labeling as codependency as simple "kindness." They were helped to discriminate over-the-top "doing for others as a way of being" from everyday acts of helping.

To use another example involving addictions treatment awareness, innumerable people suffering from addiction have been helped to reframe the notion of addiction from a problem of will power to a more self-compassionate notion of illness. The debate still rages in the helping professions over whether addiction can legitimately be called a disease, but there is no doubt that many people have been helped by the reframing itself.

For someone whose life is an intolerable sequence of difficulty after difficulty, it can be helpful to cast that life in a heroic perspective. Some people just seem to have trouble as a defining characteristic of their lives, and yet they continue to plug away valiantly, simply doing what needs to be done. How wonderful it can be for someone to put a face of the heroic on what they do.

Picture yourself working as a counselor with a middle-aged man, someone who has periodically come back to you for counseling help because of recurring difficulties in his family life. He has special needs children, a wife who abuses alcohol, and he is now developing some serious physical problems. He has periodically considered moving far away and starting a whole new life. He has chosen

CASE EXAMPLE 9.2   Use of Reframing

In the following situation, the client has been talking for a number of weeks with his counselor about his abusive upbringing. Note how the counselor uses reframing in this session.

COUNSELOR: What you've been telling me sounds like pretty tough stuff. Being left alone a lot, taking care of younger brothers and sister, your mom drunk a lot. Really tough.

She's heard him talk over the past weeks about material that's quite difficult—stories reflecting a history of a combination of abuse and neglect. She wants him to know that she's heard this and that she feels for him, so she reflects the content and feeling of all those past stories from this and previous sessions.

CLIENT: Yeah. It really sucked. I lost my childhood. I had to grow up too fast. My dad worked all the time, so he wasn't around to help me much, to save me from her. I still can't believe the stuff she had me do.

COUNSELOR: Like what?

She's trying to promote some specificity.

CLIENT: Like household chores, for example. From the age of eight on I had to wash and iron all of my own clothes. I'd be inside doing all these chores, and I'd watch other kids out running around. I'd be doing all of these chores while they're playing. That was me, always doing the washer-boy routine.

COUNSELOR: Well, maybe in the midst of all that difficulty there was the fact that you learned to do some things. You learned how to wash and iron. Maybe you learned a little earlier than lots of people, but still that's not a bad set of life skills.

The reframe.

Case Discussion

The purpose of the counselor's reframe is to help the client see that in the midst of the difficulties his childhood encompassed there were also some gifts. This is not to deny that his childhood was problematic and difficult; rather, that perhaps he's taken away some strengths from those experiences. Reframing cannot be offered too early, because the client needed to tell his story and have it validated. The counselor wants him to know that his experience was important and that she feels the pain of it all with him. But there may be more to the story than what he's acknowledging, and she wants him to see this as well. What he has only seen as difficulties, in other words, can also be seen in another more positive light. This is what reframing can do.

CASE EXAMPLE 9.3 *Using Paradox*

Here's an example involving a client who's having difficulty with her boss. He is a domineering man, and he's generally unsupportive of her work. She is quite intimidated by him and has been getting sick to her stomach just thinking about work. She has started missing work time and is worried about getting fired.

CLIENT: My job is killing me. Every morning as I'm driving toward work I start to feel sick to my stomach. Sometimes I just can't make it, turn the care around, and go home. Actually, it's not really my job; it's my boss. He's a jerk. A macho creep. I've had demanding, overbearing bosses before, but this guy takes the cake. He's making my life miserable. He never thinks I do anything right.

The counselor is remembering how many times this client has complained about this boss in the past. She just doesn't seem able to stand up for herself with him. Moreover, this is symptomatic of most of her relationships with men, relationships where she feels like she has significantly less power than the man. A difference here, of course, is the fact that the boss does hold real power over her job.

COUNSELOR: This is definitely not great. This job that you've liked is turning into a really unhappy experience.

Reflection of content. The counselor is not sure if the boss is really overbearing, or if it is only the client's perception. Either way, the client's work life is not pleasant.

CLIENT: I hate the way he treats me, and I hate the way he makes me feel. He undercuts my decisions, acts like I've got no brains, and gives me crummy work assignments. I've done everything I can think of to find a way to stand up to him, but when he starts up on me, I get so terrified and confused, I can't think of anything to do except mumble, "OK sir, sorry sir."

COUNSELOR: Well, maybe if you've really tried everything, here's a suggestion: Every morning, as soon as you get to work, go into your boss's office and ask him how you should feel that day.

This is the use of paradox. The counselor tosses out an absurd suggestion, which is designed to highlight the ways the client gives power away to the boss.

CLIENT: What? What are you saying? Don't joke with me.

COUNSELOR: No, really, I think I understand how miserable this guy is making your life. I just would like you to see how much power you're giving him to control how you feel— beyond the actual power he has as your boss.

Care always has to be taken when using a strategy like this to not sound flippant or uncaring. A bit of explanation usually helps.

(continued)

(Case example 9.3, continued)

Case Discussion

This counselor's suggestion is a good example of the use of paradox. Obviously, the suggestion is absurd. The counselor would not expect the client to follow through with doing what is suggested—and the counselor will make sure that the client understands that. The paradoxical suggestion is made to point out, graphically, how much power this client has been giving this boss. To be cowed and intimidated by another person to the point of getting physically ill is wrong. While some work will need to be done, eventually, to help the client deal with her boss more effectively, the first step is to bring into awareness the power that has been given away to the other. Naturally, the boss also has some real power over this woman's job, and some counseling work will need to focus on the ways that real power can be separated from the additional emotional power the client gives him. The intention of this use of paradox is to highlight how the client has allowed herself to be controlled by her overblown notions of this other person's power. Given that we have total control of how we feel, if not the situation, this points to an opportunity for her to take back control of her own feelings. In short, paradox is a way of eliminating or shaping an unwanted behavior or attitude by temporarily exaggerating it.

---

to stay with his family, however, and to not abandon these substantial difficulties. He sees his staying as cowardice and lives with the belief that if he were truly brave he'd leave to forge a new life.

How helpful it could be for this man to see his staying in his family as a significant act of courage, an act as brave as any warrior's. His is not a spontaneous act of bravery, like jumping into the ocean to save someone who is drowning. Rather, his courage lies in the fact that he gets up every day and fights against enormous odds to protect and provide for his family. He has the bravery of a great warrior and the fortitude of a long-distance runner.

PARADOX (OR COUNTERSUGGESTION)

Another tool to shift thought patterns that may sometimes prove useful has also been borrowed from the Adlerian theoretical school (Adler, 1929). The use of paradox, paradoxical intention, or countersuggestion is the dramatizing of a certain client characteristic in a way that makes it seem redundant or absurd.

Paradox typically involves using the problem behaviors, or so-called symptoms, themselves in service of change. The suggestion, or actual acting out of the suggestion, is designed to have the opposite effect as the suggestion itself.

Teaching More Helpful Behavior Patterns

Regardless of their theoretical orientation, there are occasions when counselors may find techniques derived from behavioral theory very useful. Psychoeducational training packages provide specific skills building experiences that can be easily taught, or even handed over to a client. These trainings suggest that people can learn to be more effective in certain skill areas without having to necessarily examine why they are deficient in those areas (Skinner, 1974). We will examine three behavioral techniques here: assertiveness training, relaxation training, and role playing.

ASSERTIVENESS TRAINING

Assertiveness skills training teaches clients that they have a right to express themselves and to go after what they need (Alberti & Emmons, 1996). This kind of training is designed to help clients deal more effectively with others and to take action on their own behalf—in other words, to assert themselves (Smith, 1975). I've found that this kind of training is extremely helpful with clients who are enmeshed in relationships where they tend to interact with a partner either too passively or too aggressively. People who interact too passively can learn to stand up more effectively for themselves in those relationships, and people who are too aggressive can learn to temper their interactions with more gentle kindness. Even when a lack of appropriate assertiveness is not an obvious presenting problem, it can lie lurking as a problem within many ineffective social relationships.

An assertiveness training sequence might be outlined as follows:

- Identify the ways assertiveness is a problem and could be bolstered for this client.

- Discuss assertiveness and get the client's acknowledgment of the right to be assertive.

- Review different responding styles (passive, aggressive, assertive).

- Identify one specific, not particularly emotionally loaded situation that causes difficulty.

- Review all the specifics (who causes the difficulty, when does it happen, where does it happen, how is the client left feeling, and what is wanted) with a focus on behaviors, not judgments or assumptions.

- Clarify what is wanted, getting very behaviorally specific, including consequences for what happens if the other person refuses to comply.

- Put together an action plan.

- Rehearse the action plan in a role play in which the client initially plays the part of the person with whom there is difficulty, with you, the counselor, doing the assertiveness routine; then reverse roles. Help the client look at how body posture, voice tone, and physical proximity affect the effectiveness of the interchange.

- Use the action plan in real life. (Smith, 1975)

Note that this teaching sequence happens within the context of a supportive relationship with the counselor. The counselor's support is a crucial variable, and her judgment about the timing and readiness of her client to try out this plan in the world outside is key to a successful outcome.

In Case Example 9.3, the woman having difficulty with her boss could be taught some more effective ways to deal with him using assertiveness training techniques (although she might initially be taught the fundamentals of assertiveness utilizing some lower stakes situations). It is tricky because the boss does have real power over her in his job role, yet there should be some ways that she can increase her sense of personal power in the workplace by learning to deal more effectively with him. Part of the training sequence could involve a discussion of some of these reality factors that make this a loaded situation, with an examination of some of the positive and negative outcomes that might result from her becoming more assertive.

RELAXATION TRAINING

Relaxation and meditation (and perhaps prayer, depending on the setting) is another effective training regimen and educational activity that counselors sometimes employ to help clients deal with stress and anxiety. To reiterate, in my experience this kind of training is most effective when provided by a counselor who is immersed in the tradition from which the training comes. In addition, it is imperative that the client be apprised of any value system that is attached to it and that the client be given free choice as to whether to participate.

Here is one relaxation skills training routine that is promoted as part of a yoga routine. This is an adaptation of the routine recommended by the Sivananda Yoga Center, typically utilized within the Corpse Pose, the final pose of a yoga routine.

- Lie down on your back, feet spread about 18 inches apart, hands about six inches from your side, palms up. Let your thighs, knees, and toes lean outward. Close your eyes and breathe deeply. Feel your belly rise and fall with this deep breathing.

- In order to feel relaxation, you should first experience tension. Working up from the feet, first lift and tense each body part, and then release it, letting it drop (but don't place it) to the floor.

- Lift your right foot an inch off the floor. Tense the leg, hold, and then let it drop. Repeat this on the other side.

- Clench your buttocks tightly together, lift the hips a little way off the floor and hold. Relax and drop them down.

- Tense and lift up the back and chest, keeping head and hips on the floor. Relax and drop them down.

- Lift your shoulders and hunch them up tight around your neck. Let them drop. Pull each arm, in turn, down alongside the body, and then relax them.

- Tuck in your chin and roll the head gently from side to side. Find a comfortable position in the center for the head to lie, and then relax.

- Squeeze every muscle in your face up tight, bringing it to a point around your nose. Open the face wide, stretching your eyes open and sticking out your tongue as far as it will go. Then relax the face.

- Now, having completed this tightening and relaxing sequence, visualize your body in your mind's eye, and bring relaxation to any body part that is still tense. "I relax the calves, the calves are relaxed," is the kind of mental formula that can be used with any tight muscle group. Feel a wave of relaxation sweep across your body as you guide your awareness through each part. When you inhale, feel the wave of oxygen flowing down to your feet, and when you exhale, you can feel the tension flowing out of your body, leaving your mind like a deep, still lake, without a ripple.

- Finally, dive deep into the center of this lake, deep within yourself, and discover your own true nature. (Lidell, 1983, pp. 26–27)

This is one of many relaxation routines that can be taught to your client. It shouldn't be too difficult to see how this could be a helpful training adjunct to the assertiveness training that might done with the client in Case Example 9.3. This client, in addition to becoming more interpersonally effective with her boss, could also gain more control of her inner world and experience through relaxation training. This training can be particularly helpful for highly anxious clients, and it can be taught in the office or given as a routine to be worked on at home. When working with this kind of routine in the office, remember that for some clients this may be provocative and threatening. For abuse survivors, for example, the simple act of lying down with someone else present, or closing their eyes with you there, can be terrifying. For these people, use of an audio- or videotape can be a helpful alternative to office instruction.

ROLE PLAYING

Role playing can be a helpful training and educational adjunct in many counseling contexts. Essentially, the client tries out new behaviors with an accepting counselor in a form of behavioral rehearsal (Lazarus, 1985). It is easy, for example, to see how this strategy might be helpful for clients working on increasing their assertiveness skill level. The client can practice the assertive behavior with the counselor without the harmful consequences of doing it poorly.

Role plays can be used in many kinds of counseling situations to support learning. Children in school settings can practice anger management routines with the counselor or with peers. Clients can practice job interviewing skills safely in the counseling office before going out for actual interviews. A shy young man could practice asking someone to go out on a date. It is better, and certainly safer, to practice and make mistakes with a trusted confidant, the counselor, than in the world outside the counseling setting. It is also a fine opportunity to provide counselor-to-client feedback about client assertive behavior.

Brainstorming and Little Experiments

Giving advice is generally not a recommended best counseling practice, but assisting clients to see viable options is oftentimes a great help. You will experience clients who have difficulty making decisions, and you may see that some of the difficulty has to do with the limited options they see before them. Helping them to widen the arena of choices by brainstorming all possible alternatives can assist in breaking the gridlock. This is particularly true for clients who think concretely, in typically black and white fashion. Adding some shades of gray, alternatives to their "all or none" kind of thinking, can be helpful. Making a list of pros and cons with a client to help arrive at some decision may aid the process.

For example, you could help a client who sees only two options regarding the constraints of an unsatisfying marriage—either getting a divorce or simply putting up with it—to see other options. "Let's look a little more broadly at this. Maybe there are other options we could consider. Maybe you could spend more time with your friends. What about you and your wife taking separate vacations sometimes? How about opportunities to spend more time exploring things you've said you want to try on your own—painting, writing, creative things? Help me out here. What are other things that might help without the trauma of a divorce or just sucking it up and staying the course?"

Small experiments can aid this brainstorming or decision-making process. The Gestalt-originated two-chair technique, for example, where two sides of a client's thinking or internal conversation can be played out using both chairs, can be effective. Most typically, one chair represents what is truly wanted and the other what one thinks is expected (the "wants" versus the "shoulds"). By alternately sitting in either chair and talking with the voice that chair represents, the client can graphically see how the dialogue reflects the inner conflict. For the client who feels trapped in a dead-end job but is afraid to take the jump to something new, one chair could represent the decision to stay on the job, the other a decision to try something new. He could sit in each chair and be encouraged to talk in the first person about the perspective that chair represents. From chair number one he could speak as the job: "I'm safe and predictable. I pay a good salary. You can do me well." From chair number two he could speak as the new direction: "I'm exciting but scary. I'm new, and I don't know if you can do me. But I'm worth a try."

And so on. Little experiments like this may spontaneously occur to you that you can use to dramatize a dilemma or an internal conflict.

Homework

Many times the experiments and skills training that are done during a counseling session will be aided by the client continuing to work on this material at home. Homework typically grows out of work done during the session, and it is meant to tie counseling work to a client's real life. This homework might involve writing, as in keeping a journal or making focused reflections on specific topics. It might involve trying out certain things practiced in the office on people on the outside, as in a role-played job interview. A counselor might role play with the client, followed by another role play with a friendly person at home, extending the possibilities for practice and confidence building before the actual job interview transpires. The homework might involve any reasonable extension of counseling work. It should always be relevant and related to the client's goals, and it should be reasonable for the client to accomplish (Tompkins, 2004).

If you ask a client to do homework, you should be prepared for potential problems. The largest of these is that oftentimes it won't be done. Here's an example. Assume that you've been working with a high school junior for a month or two around career and academic planning issues. You want her to take some responsibility for seeking out some possible college choices, and you ask her to do some online searching for schools that fit the characteristics she's looking for. Your assignment, tied nicely to work you've done with her in your office and meant to give her more control over planning her own future, is ignored. She comes back into your office the next time you meet only to tell you that she "didn't have time" to do the search.

This leaves you in the position of being like a teacher or parent who has to deal with a noncompliant student or child. If you have been working hard to avoid that kind of authority relationship, this can make for an interesting situation, one that presents significant opportunity to work with her about her resistance. You can choose to react, however, not as an authority figure but as someone speculating with her about her lack of follow through with this homework. You can offer her some intelligent hunches and wonder aloud about some of these reasons she's avoided the assignment, keeping yourself in the role of ally. You might say, for example, "It sure is interesting that you didn't follow through with this. I wonder if maybe there's something going on between us. You think maybe you wanted to let me know that I couldn't tell you what to do?"

The key to the effective management of homework assignments, as in all other counseling activities, is to keep focused on the client and the potential for new learning attached to whatever happens in the context of the relationship. Not doing homework might be as helpful a piece of learning as simple compliance. It's all about how it's handled. We look for both the client's meaning and the meaning in the dynamic between us that exists in whatever happens. We cannot be so wedded to the homework and the client's follow through with doing what we suggest that we lose sight of what is truly important—what it all means for this client.

This is tricky, but sometimes exactly what is called for is being upset about the client's noncompliance. It might be that our being upset shows a caring that is absent in other quarters. The point is that this reaction is for the benefit of the client, not as a result of the counselor feeling resisted. It is our ability to see what is needed that is the key to effective management of homework assignments, not our attachment to the assignment itself.

Appealing (or Cheerleading)

Appealing is another skill championed by logotherapists (Frankl, 1969). This kind of activity is similarly supported, under the broader title of "coaching," by reality therapists (Wubbolding, 1998). Simply put, this means cheerleading your client onward. It is about your attempts to exhort your clients to do the best that they can do, to help them achieve something specific with some additional energy and support from you. When your client has decided on a course of action, you can cheer him on, giving an added boost to his effort. This appealing can be threatening to counselors who want to remain aloof and neutral, yet it can be an effective strategy when used judiciously.

So, for that client who is learning to be more assertive with her boss, you might say, "You've got the routine down, you know what to say, you're ready. You've got the tools, now all you have to do is use them. Go for it. I know you can handle this." You're serving as her sideline coach, her booster, and you're letting her know that you think she can put her newly learned skills into action. Much of your encouragement will be based on your recognition of her readiness, your assumption that her ability to put these skills into action will be successful.

Using the Relationship in Service of the Goals

It has been said, repeatedly, that attention to the counseling relationship is central to successful counseling. The relationship is, in fact, one of the most potent tools for learning in the counselor's toolbox. It is the most direct evidence a counselor has of how the client operates in the greater world, with great potential for modeling and immediate client learning about how relationships can work well. The modeling that we do with our clients, their experience of us and our being in the world, is a primary source of constructive learning. The ways in which you have embedded the messages of all the skills mentioned in this chapter—the assertiveness, the cognitive and behavioral self-support and management tools, all of it—in your sessions is your client's direct experience of the usefulness of those activities.

This potential for firsthand, immediate learning means that your ability to notice and work with the relationship makes it the most significant tool in your bag of counseling strategies. Your ability to attend to the immediacy of the relationship, how it develops and grows, and your effort to make timely remarks about it with your client has tremendous potential for promoting learning which is oftentimes directly related to the goals your client has said he wants to reach. This requires paying close attention to a number of variables. You will need to listen to both your client's spoken and unspoken issues. You will need to hone your ideas about his ability to deal with your feedback, and you will need to pay attention to your own reactions and feelings to what is happening. This implies being able to put your own needs aside and really focus on what your client needs (Wallace, 1986). This can be a lot to juggle.

Sometimes things will happen between the two of you that catch your attention. Some may be related to how he keeps up his end of the arrangement, or contract, between you. For instance, he might not show up or he might come late or in some other way subtly undercut your work together. These events, which sometimes mask underlying feelings, can be mentioned, either with hunches or interpretation (discussed in Chapter 11). For example, "It's interesting that you've come just a little late these last few times. Sometimes that can be an indication of a little anger or something else going on under the surface. I wonder if any of that could be true for you." This kind of attempt at helping the client become more forthcoming about his true thoughts and feelings might be exactly related to why he is seeking counseling. This attention to the way in which the relationship unfolds, the process variables in the relationship, is always designed to help make the communication between you and your client more immediate.

Note, as well, and this is important, that in this example the counselor's musings about the client's lateness are in no way confrontational. The counselor's comments invite speculation on the meaning attached to the lateness and suggest that the counselor and the client are partners in the search for understanding. Sometimes, and this can be an exciting moment, it is the client who makes the relationship more immediate. These kinds of client-generated interventions for immediacy make for great counseling opportunities. It requires nondefensiveness and an astute counselor reaction for it to be utilized effectively. Oftentimes these client interventions take the form of challenges or direct questions put squarely to us, and our reactions should support the client's acting with immediacy and directness. If you can learn to deal nondefensively with your clients' challenges to you, you can turn those challenges into wonderful teaching moments (Burns & Auerbach, 1996).

CASE EXAMPLE 9.4   *Responding to a Client's Demands for Immediacy*

This client is a young woman who came into counseling over concern that her partner is losing interest in her. She wants to know what it is that she does, or doesn't do, that contributes to this loss of interest, particularly in that this has happened repeatedly in her love relationships. She has lots of interests, is well read, and is intelligent. She seems, however, to be fearful and tentative and has oftentimes let other people's needs and wants take precedence over her own. The counselor has done some assertiveness training with her, but that hasn't seemed to take hold. The client thinks that if she reads more books or travels more she will become more interesting. We pick them up in this session when she is beginning to talk of one of her latest readings.

CLIENT: You know, Louise (her partner), isn't much of a reader, and I'm a political junkie, so I read every newspaper and magazine I can get my hands on. I read all these articles, and then synthesize them for her. Let me tell you about this article about our congressman I just finished. *[She then goes on to describe, in minute detail, the substance of this piece.]*

COUNSELOR: Hmm.

The counselor's comment is a minimal encourager. He's not particularly captivated by her narration and lets his mind wander to speculations about how he'll make it to his son's soccer game that afternoon.

CLIENT: *[Continues with her recounting of the article, and then stops abruptly.]* I don't think you're listening to me. You've got that glaze in your eyes that I see sometimes in my students. Like they're sleeping with their eyes open.

COUNSELOR: *[Doesn't respond for a minute.]* Well, yeah, I think you're right. I was spaced out, preoccupied with some stuff in my own life. That wasn't a great thing for me to be doing. But you brought me back. And that was a great thing to do.

He sure is awake and present now. The counselor feels like he's been caught napping. His first reaction is to deny what she's saying, but he takes a breath and catches himself. He finally responds with self-disclosure and confirms her observation.

CLIENT: Well, I didn't want to be talking to myself.

(continued)

(Case example 9.4, continued)

COUNSELOR: Exactly, and you might be angry if you thought I wasn't listening. I do appreciate your bringing me back.

He's reflecting his ideas about what she might be feeling but does it tentatively. He also reinforces her direct action with him.

CLIENT: *[A minute of silence.]* So what now?

COUNSELOR: Good question. How about we talk about what just happened? About you challenging me like that. What was that like?

Now is the time to try to make this a teaching moment. This real life adventure in assertiveness is reflective of what she's been trying to do in life. The counselor is trying, in the midst of his own error, to make the most of this direct experience. He finishes with an engagement question.

CLIENT: It was hard. This has happened to me before in here, where you've glazed over. You just drifted off somewhere. It doesn't happen too much, but I know when you're all here. I told myself a week ago that if it happened again I was going to tell you. It was really hard. I have so much respect for you. It really hurts when I think you're not paying attention. I tie myself up in knots. I'm afraid I'm going to push you away if I confront you, alienate you, but you drift off anyway.

This is undoubtedly hard for the counselor to hear. He doesn't like to think of himself as inattentive, but he knows that there is truth in what she's saying. The counselor can use the value the client places on their relationship—some of which is transference— as a model for other close relationships she has. Learning to be more direct with him, and seeing that he values that directness, can translate into such action in other close relationships.

COUNSELOR: So the thing you fear is what happens anyway.

Reflection of content and feeling.

CLIENT: Yeah. It's like a double bind. If I try to get your attention, I risk making you mad, and losing you. But if I don't, you get bored, and I lose you anyway.

COUNSELOR: It's really difficult to risk blowing a close relationship through some kind of direct action, like confronting me. Scary.

Reflection of content and feeling.

CLIENT: Yeah. *[Tears up.]*

COUNSELOR: So, usually you stay the course. Keep quiet. Don't rock the boat.

Reflection of content, and maybe a tentative interpretation.

CLIENT: Yep. Just like with Louise and every other close relationship I've had.

COUNSELOR: Well, I can tell you, I'm sure all here now, and feeling really valued. I want to thank you. I'm really grateful you took the risk.

Self-disclosure, with genuine feeling.

Case Discussion

In this interchange lies much of the dynamic that undoubtedly transpires for this client in her interpersonal life outside the office, perhaps particularly with her partner. The counseling relationship is the counselor's direct evidence of how the client operates in her greater world,

(continued)

(Case example 9.4, continued)

with the counseling office acting as a microcosm of that world. This client says that she has difficulties in being direct and honest with her partner. The hope here is that she might be able to transfer some of this learning from this interaction with her counselor toward helping to make that relationship more satisfying. If she can risk confrontation with the counselor, and have it work out positively, maybe she'll be able to take those risks with others. It is this kind of experimentation in the counseling relationship that is potentially so potent a source of learning. This is particularly true when a client takes risks that are met with support and encouragement.

The counselor has turned his professional blunder, allowing his attention to wander, into a helpful teaching moment by virtue of his willingness to not parry her direct challenge to him. All of us will make mistakes, and we can turn them to solid client advantage if we manage mistakes well. It is exactly in these moments when we might feel most vulnerable, having made some kind of error, that our clients might make these kinds of challenges, and there is tremendous potential for immediate learning if we do not feel overly threatened. If we are willing to risk imperfection, to have our clients see us as less than perfect, it may serve to level the playing field and have our clients deal with us with equal power. This client empowerment, their becoming more immediate and direct with us, is almost universally helpful.

Concluding Thoughts: Skills and Relationship, a Potent Combination

Much of this chapter has been about the answer to the new counselor's question: "Now that I've established a relationship with my client, and I've heard his story, what do I do?" The skills, strategies, and techniques described here are all about the "what now" and are designed to assist movement toward goals. They are action skills derived from a number of theoretical traditions. Each of them may have a particular applicability given a client's assessed level of development, readiness, and desire to participate.

A new counselor may have a tremendous yearning to have a theory, a set of techniques, and a game plan with which to work with people. The "game plan" can help to assuage the counselor's anxiety and help her feel like she's got a grip on something. Unfortunately, this yearning for a game plan may not always be best for our clients. The more we can fight off this impulse for security, the more we can approach each client as a fresh, new experience, without preconceived notions of what will work best for him, the better he'll be served. Too often our game plan, which most often takes the form of rigid adherence to some theoretical approach, makes us lose sight of the person across from us. It can even become a bulwark of defense against experiencing this client directly.

Here is a brief story to illustrate some of what I mean. I was mugged in Rome a few years ago. It was a Sunday night, and I had just gotten off the train from Siena. I wasn't hurt, but one of the crooks who jumped me got away with a backpack that held my passport, credit cards, cash, and travelers' checks. For a number of hours, until I discovered that I had actually put another credit card in my luggage (a bit of traveling common sense that usually eludes me), I was alone and penniless in a strange city.

I had no notion of where I'd sleep that night, where I'd eat, or how I'd get by. I couldn't even speak the language. I knew that the embassy was closed, and there were no other similar resources for me to use of which I was aware. This predicament was frightening. I wandered the streets for a few hours, contemplating what I would do to survive. In those hours before I discovered the emergency credit card, my lifeline to security, I was anxious but also highly charged. I felt extremely alive. Time stood still. Things even looked different, with a new sharpness, an enhanced clarity. Those hours are now the featured recollection of that trip. I'm not sure that I'd willfully re-create an experience like that, but I do value it highly. I've often wondered what the trip would've been like if I'd never found the credit card.

It would be terrific if we could approach each new client, each new student, with that kind of fresh clarity and new vision. Who knows what would happen, how we would encounter each other. Who knows what we would learn. We need to nurture our ability to deal with ambiguity and to value the spontaneity and energy that emerge from not being certain about what is around the next corner. This kind of perspective, of not always having a detailed road map, can be terrifying and liberating, all at the same time. It is truly scary to not know exactly what to do, but it is also freeing to not think of oneself as always having to have the right answer.

It is best, of course, to travel with the credit cards. In the counseling luggage, it is best to have the tools and skills described herein tucked away and available for when we need them. It is important to remember, however, that just because these skills are safe and predictable to use, they might not be as effective a means of assisting client progress as the direct experience of the relationship itself.

For Further Thought

1. Look at the literature and research related to any of the action strategies discussed in this chapter. How do these studies assist and support the work you'll do with your client population? How can you use these studies to improve your work?

2. Interview local counselors in your community—both in schools and in agencies—and ask about the strategies they use to help move clients toward their goals. How might these discussions, as well as your impressions of these counselors' work, affect your future work?

3. Imagine yourself as a new client going for counseling. You form a good relationship with your counselor, and then he begins to talk about using specific strategies to help you achieve your goals. Which strategies would you hope your counselor would suggest?

4. What self-destructive thoughts do you need to revamp?

5. Picture a situation in which you are a client and your counselor has just suggested a homework assignment that she thinks might be helpful. What is it? Will you do it?

References

Adler, A. (1929). *Problems of neurosis.* London: Kegan Paul.

Alberti, R., & Emmons, M. (1996). *Your perfect right: A guide to assertive behavior* (7th ed.). San Luis Obispo, CA: Impact.

Amundson, N. (1996). Supporting clients through a change in perspective. *Journal of Employment Counseling, 33,* 155–162.

Beck, A. (1988). *Love is never enough.* New York: Harper Perennial.

Beck, A. (1991). Cognitive therapy: A 30-year perspective. *American Psychologist, 46,* 368–375.

Burns, D., & Auerbach, A. (1996). Therapeutic empathy in cognitive-behavioral therapy: Does it really make a difference? In P. Salkovskis (Ed.), *Frontiers of cognitive therapy* (pp. 135–164). New York: Guilford Press.

Constantino, M., Castonguay, L., & Schut, A. (2002). The working alliance: A flagship for the "scientist-practitioner" model in psychotherapy. In G. Tryon (Ed.), *Counseling based on process research* (pp. 81–131). Boston: Allyn & Bacon.

Ellis, A. (1988). *How to stubbornly refuse to make yourself miserable about anything: Yes, anything!* Secaucus, NJ: Stuart.

Ellis, A. (1994). *Reason and emotion in psychotherapy.* New York: Carol. [Original work published in 1962]

Fagan, J. (1970). The task of the therapist. In J. Fagan & I. Shepherd (Eds.), *Gestalt therapy now* (pp. 88–106). Palo Alto, CA: Science and Behavior Books.

Frankl, V. (1969). *Psychotherapy and existentialism: Selected papers on logotherapy.* New York: Simon & Schuster.

Frankl, V. (1984). *Man's search for meaning.* Boston: Washington Square Press. [Original work published in 1946]

Glasser, W. (1965). *Reality therapy: A new approach to psychiatry.* New York: Harper & Row.

Glasser, W. (1998). *Choice theory.* New York: HarperCollins.

Guttman, D. (1966). *Logotherapy for the helping professional: Meaningful social work.* New York: Springer.

Horvath, A., & Greenberg, L. (1994). *The working alliance: Theory, research, and practice.* New York: Wiley.

Horvath, A., & Luborsky, L. (1993). The role of the therapeutic alliance in psychotherapy. *Journal of Consulting and Clinical Psychology, 61,* 561–573.

Lazarus, A. (1985). Behavior rehearsal. In A. Bellack & M. Hersen (Eds.), *Dictionary of behavior therapy techniques* (p. 22). New York: Pergamon.

Lidell, L. (1983). *The Sivananda companion to yoga.* New York: Simon & Schuster.

Luborsky, L. (1994). Therapeutic alliances as predictors of psychotherapy outcomes: Factors explaining the therapeutic success. In A. Horvath & L. Greenberg (Eds.), *The working alliance: Theory, research, and practice* (pp. 38–50). New York: Wiley.

Perls, F., Hefferline, R., & Goodman, P. (1951). *Gestalt therapy: Excitement and growth in the human personality.* New York: Julian Press.

Saketopoulou, A. (1999). The therapeutic alliance in psychodynamic psychotherapy: Theoretical conceptualizations and research findings. *Psychotherapy, 36,* 329–342.

Skinner, B. F. (1974). *About behaviorism.* New York: Vintage.

Smith, M. (1975). *When I say no, I feel guilty.* New York: Bantam Books.

Tompkins, M. (2004). *Using homework in psychotherapy.* New York: Guilford Press.

Wallace, W. (1986). *Theories of counseling and psychotherapy.* Boston: Allyn & Bacon.

Wubbolding, R. (1988). *Using reality therapy.* New York: HarperCollins.

Wubbolding, R. (1991). *Understanding reality therapy.* New York: HarperCollins.

Wubbolding, R. (1998). *Cycle of managing, supervising, counseling, and coaching using reality therapy.* Cincinatti: Center for Reality Therapy.

Wubbolding, R., & Brickell, J. (1998). Qualities of the reality therapist. *International Journal of Reality Therapy, 17*(2), 47–49.

Skills for Managing Crisis Situations

> How did I get so lucky to have my heart awakened to
> others and their suffering?
> *(Pema Chodron)*

Imagine that you've been called down to the waiting room of the community clinic in which you work because the secretary doesn't know what to do about one of the new clients sitting there. This woman refuses to talk with anyone. She is sitting slouched in her chair, looking down at her hands in her lap. Her eyes have a vacant, far-away look about them, and she's motionless. Her clothing is expensive, but her appearance is disheveled and unkempt. Her hair hasn't been brushed.

You sit down next to her and try to make eye contact. She doesn't engage. You introduce yourself and ask her if she'd like to come upstairs to talk. To your surprise, she gets up and walks to the stairs. When you arrive at your office, she moves to a chair, drops herself into it, and slumps forward, assuming the same pose she had in the waiting room. What do you do now?

Welcome to the counseling work called crisis intervention. This is the kind of dilemma all counselors face, at least occasionally. Some of us work in schools or community agency settings where clients are rarely in crisis; others work in settings where crisis is the general means of operation. Some of our clients seem to move from crisis to crisis, even to thrive on the drama of it all. Similarly, some counselors thrive on working with people in crisis, as if they, too, thrive on the excitement. In a sense, all of the work we do as counselors is initiated by some kind of crisis. People don't usually seek us out for the pleasure of our company. There is some life event, task, or issue to be confronted that drives them to us: a drug addict overdoses; an "A" student does poorly on the SATs; a single young woman discovers that she's pregnant; someone's mother dies; a father of four is laid off.

Each of these is an event that might precipitate a crisis, either for a person directly involved or for someone close to the situation. Each of these events also might not precipitate any crisis at all. It's all about the ability to manage of the person involved. Crisis intervention often has less to do with interpreting the facts of the actual event than it does with assessing the individual's ability to cope.

When the immediate crisis intervention is done well, it buys time for longer-term, more substantial structural change. Crisis intervention is like sandbagging the banks of the raging river to keep it from flooding the town. Longer-term crisis counseling, like building levees to channel the river, comes after the crisis has been averted.

Defining Crisis

Crisis has been defined as "a perception of an event or situation as an intolerable difficulty that exceeds the person's resources and coping mechanisms" (Gilliland & James, 1997, p. 3). The key to thinking about crisis is to focus on the idea of "perception"; one person's crisis is another person's routine. Each of us, with our own resources and coping mechanisms, responds differently to the events of the world around us, having varying degrees of stress and capacity for response.

Sometimes the crisis is the result of a major disaster, such as a flood or a terrorist attack. Sometimes the crisis is the result of one individual's horrific experience, such as being raped or brutally assaulted. These situational crises touch many lives, yet they provoke different responses from different individuals (Aguilera & Messick, 1978). Each of us has a tolerance threshold beyond which we begin to lose our ability to successfully cope. All of us face maturational or developmental issues throughout our lives, but for some individuals those issues precipitate crises (Collins & Collins, 2005). Hence the midlife crisis or the crises of adolescence and early adulthood.

While helping someone negotiate a way through this difficult, charged time, bear in mind that there is tremendous potential for change or growth as well (Leitner & Stecher, 1974). Even in the worst of situations, as with the death of a loved one, the challenge is to find within the disaster the possibility for transformation and growth. If a person can be helped to survive and work through the immediate nature of the crisis situation, this opportunity to find new meaning looms large.

We live in comfortable ignorance of life's larger questions and harsher realities until we are forced to confront them. We all know, for example, that at some point our bodies decay, give out, and we die. The fact of our mortality, however, is not something that most of us, until we become terribly sick, choose to think about much. The psychological mechanisms (denial, repression, rationalization) with which we manage the harsh realities of the world in ways that make them tolerable break down under the great stresses of crisis. When we get the bad news, the terrible diagnosis, we are forced to confront realities in new ways, without blinders or rose-colored glasses. This is at once terrible, terrifying, and filled with possibility. When the old defenses break down, even momentarily, glimpses of new ways of perceiving and negotiating the world appear.

It is your job to help people manage the terror of these recognitions long enough so that the little peeks at the new ways of thinking and doing can be brought into the larger light of day. You help people in crisis shore up their abilities to cope and manage the crisis while exploring with them the greater context in which they might look at this crisis and their lives.

Effective Crisis Counselors

Some of us are better at dealing with crisis than others. Just as at an automobile accident scene there are some people who seem to know what to do, take charge, and mobilize helpful action, so there are counselors who simply seem to gravitate to this kind of work and to be unusually good at it. All of the characteristics and hallmarks of effective counselors detailed elsewhere in this book—wholeness, self-awareness, and a shared sense of humanity—apply to crisis counselors as well. The effective crisis counselor is an effective counselor with the added ability to work well in difficult situations, with people under duress.

Further, the crisis counselor also possesses many of the same generic engagement and action skills used by other counselors. She is able to use the range of engagement and fact-finding questions, as well as reflection of content and feeling skills, to build an alliance with the person in crisis. She has the necessary assessment skills to explore and define strengths and problem areas and the action-oriented skills to help the client move toward mutually agreed-upon goals. The effective crisis counselor is, in other words, fundamentally an effective counselor.

However, this counselor may need to be even more empathic, possess the ability to engage and fact-find more quickly, make even quicker decisions, and be able to deal with more disappointments than counselors who deal with clients not in crisis (Murgatroyd, 1983).

This kind of counseling calls for more flexibility as well. Crisis intervention may not be managed well within the confines of typical school or agency counseling time frames. Although of relatively short duration, perhaps six to eight weeks maximum, crisis counseling may require more frequent, time-intensive sessions in the short term (Brown & Rainer, 2002). Counselors who are able to deal with this kind of ambiguity are well-suited for crisis work.

The Immediate Crisis Response: What Needs to Happen?

Experts in the area of crisis intervention are in general agreement about the central ingredients of the effective counselor's immediate response. The specifics of their models may differ, but they all agree fundamentally on the need to engage the client and provide emotional support, to explore the specifics of the crisis and assess client strengths, and to quickly develop a solid plan for longer-term crisis management (Aguilera & Messick, 1978; Collins & Collins, 2005; Gilliland & James, 1997).

Engagement and Support

When you are seeing a client in the midst of crisis, you need to communicate that you are there to provide help, both by listening and by providing concrete assistance in dealing with the difficulty. Use all of your best listening and engagement skills to communicate this support as well as to communicate your availability and capacity to assist. Communicate respect and regard for your client as well as your belief that things will get better. Be a purveyor of realistic hope. The first critical task of the counselor dealing with someone in crisis is to make an emotional connection. The communication of steadiness, caring, and support can make all the difference to someone who feels adrift in a swamp of bad feeling and distress.

Exploration and Assessment

Do what you can to find out about the specifics of the situation. What events have precipitated this current difficulty? How long has this been going on? Who are the people involved? What are the immediate dangers and risks accompanying this crisis? Use engagement and fact-finding questions to flesh out the dimensions of the problems, make a preliminary estimate of key client strengths and deficits, and assess what best should be done. This process is very much like the assessment you would do with any client, but it has an added sense of immediacy, drama, and, sometimes, risk.

In addition, external supports and resources should be identified as part of this assessment process. These are the people, the agencies, and the services that might be enlisted to help in the event that this client's own internal resources prove insufficient, for whatever reason.

Using our developmental assessment model as a guideline, we may assume that the person in crisis operating in an out-of-control, "I can't manage" way is functioning at Level 1 on the continuum. Even when this is someone who does quite well in the world under normal circumstances, some situational or developmental issue has driven him into a state of dysfunction. Thus, a mature adult who ordinarily functions at Level 2 or even Level 3 can be thrown into the maelstrom of Level 1 dysfunction by crisis. Recall that a Level 1 client requires direct, action-oriented counselor interventions. This is a time for the counselor to provide guidance and direction, which will be best understood and optimally effective when provided in a context of emotional support and understanding. It may even be a time for very directive, supportive advice giving.

Planning for Crisis Management

Every crisis response should culminate in a specified plan for what will happen after the immediate situation is brought under control. This plan and its implementation generally become part of a longer "crisis counseling" process that follows the immediate crisis intervention. These two components—the crisis intervention and the longer process of crisis counseling—combine for an effective crisis response (Collins & Collins, 2005). Just as a concrete plan should be articulated for any counseling relationship, so should it be integral to any crisis counseling process. Support and exploration set the stage for creation of the plan for longer-term counseling. This plan specifies who will do what. What will be the client's responsibility? What will be the counselor's? What other services, or people, will be involved and in what capacity? What is the time frame of the plan, and how frequently will it be reviewed? What are the contingency plans if someone, or some event, breaks the contract? Most critically, what are the immediate dangers and risks that need to be considered? Is the client capable of managing the response to those dangers, or should the plan call for mobilization of outside assistance?

At the conclusion of any brief crisis intervention process, the plan should be outlined in a written contract that is clearly understood by all parties involved. These contracted plans will not always work. Some clients, because of severe temporary or more chronic impairment, will not be able to manage what they said they would do. Some clients will actively or passively subvert their own contracts (addicted client behavior is a classic example of this). Sometimes external forces, such as physical illness or moving (an event over which your clients who are children have little control), will impinge on the agreed-upon course of action.

You can safely assume that even a contract written with full client support and complicity in the light-of-day sanctity of your office stands a great chance of falling apart in the wee hours of the morning far away from your workplace. This is the nature of crisis intervention, an enterprise fraught with difficulties and human frailty. Your client in crisis is under tremendous pressure, of both internal and external origins, and you need to recognize that your best brief intervention is at the least a tourniquet to stop the emotional bleeding and at its best the foundation for more long-lasting structural change.

Crisis Counseling: Implementing the Plan

Specific counselor skills are associated with effective crisis intervention. Certainly, the ability to listen and relate without judgment serves as a foundation for these other active interventions. The empathic framework provides the context in which these other skills and actions can be utilized by your client in crisis. Tuning in emotionally to this other person is critically important. The essential fact-finding and engagement questions, as well as your ability to use reflection of content and feeling statements intelligently and sensitively, are mainstays of effective crisis intervention, as they are for all other counseling activities. They will serve as the basis for supporting the client in crisis and for exploring specific client strength and problem areas.

Some strategies will prove useful in both immediate crisis intervention and longer-term crisis counseling. Any of the foundation action skills described in Chapter 9 are appropriate crisis intervention counseling tools when matched with specific presenting problems. Behavioral and cognitive interventions, in particular, can provide helpful assistance in specific crisis situations (Collins & Collins, 2005).

Using Behavioral Strategies in Crisis Counseling

People who you see in crisis may experience severe anxiety or even panic. This can render ineffective any inner resources they might otherwise be able to mobilize in service of helping themselves. You can teach them some ways to manage this anxiety. You can also encourage them to use anxiety-reduction techniques that have worked for them in the past. For some people physical exercise may be one of these techniques, for others reading or focusing on pleasant memories

REFLECTION EXERCISE 10.1   *Remembered Crisis*

Take a few minutes to sit by yourself. Think of a time when something in your life was causing you serious difficulty. Maybe there was a significant loss or other traumatic event, or maybe it was just a time in life when everything looked unmanageable and out of control. Whatever the reason, this particular life situation or transition caused you considerable difficulty and grief.

Consider this crisis in your own life from all angles. What were the specifics of the situation? Who were the other people involved—or underinvolved—in this? Maybe some of these people were part of the difficulty and others played supportive roles. How did these people help or not help? Thinking specifically and behaviorally. What was it that people, maybe someone in particular, did or said to assist you that was truly helpful? If no one played this kind of role, what would have been helpful had someone made herself available?

Write down some of your observations about this situation, about your feelings as you remember them, and about your notions of the helpful interventions that did or could have happened. To the extent it feels safe, share these observations with one or two classmates. Look for general themes or contrasts in this sharing.

Exercise Discussion

Nearly all of us, even the most unshakeable, have experienced some time in our life when an event has pushed us toward the outer limits of our ability to successfully cope. Your ability to remember these times, the vulnerability and desperation, whatever complexities the situation brought your way will provide the basis of your emotional responses to your clients in crisis. It might even be that your past ability to work through crises in your own life gives you an added experiential benefit in dealing with these clients.

Your ability to remember your own frailty is part of what makes it possible to provide the necessary emotional sustenance for another. If you can also recall what you did, how you used the people around you to help you through those difficult times, so much the better. It is your own ability to survive and work through your own particular difficulties that provides the road map for working with others in crisis.

seems to help reduce anxiety. You can teach clients new, simple ways to manage their emotional distress, which can be a tremendous asset in beginning to come to grips with the difficulties that cause the anxiety.

I remember one distinct time in my own life when I was emotionally overwhelmed and used some internal visual imagery to save myself. I was a graduate student, sitting in a statistics class, trying to absorb material that was obtuse (to me) and intellectually out of my reach. I had come to class directly from my job as a houseparent in a home for emotionally charged adolescents, where dinner had involved a number of blow-ups and arguments about rules. I had spent most of my day at my internship in the local community mental health clinic, dealing with particularly demanding and difficult clients. I was emotionally and physically strung out. I sat in that statistics class, psychically overloaded and ready to snap, and decided that I had to retreat to some safer place, so I checked out. I tuned out the class and began a process of taking myself on a Caribbean journey. In my mind's eye I visited different islands in a little boat, I sat on beaches, and I meditated on swaying palm trees. It was a lovely little trip, and it preserved my sanity that difficult night. This cognitive checkout strategy served an immediate crisis response function. Similarly, your clients in crisis may have mental tricks like this that they've used before, or perhaps you could teach them some new ones.

Relaxation strategies or meditation exercises can also be taught to people as anxiety-reduction techniques. As discussed in Chapter 9, standard training packages, some of them in audiotape or compact disc format, provide a set of muscular, breathing, or imagination exercises on which to focus as a way of reducing anxiety. There are many guides to these kinds of exercises that a crisis counselor might employ. For clients who are so inclined, a program of meditation or prayer might be helpful. My experience suggests that these strategies are typically useful only to the extent that you as a counselor have utilized them yourself for personal benefit. Your own experience enables you to pass on the rudiments of the discipline with conviction and a certain amount of authority.

Caution needs to be taken to be sure that the activity is congruent with the client's value system (or, in the case of a minor client, the parents' value system). If you and your client think it might be helpful, you might consider utilizing another resource, such as a priest, rabbi, or meditation teacher whose belief system is congruent with your client's, to assist in this teaching. Such a person might be in a better position than you to teach some of these strategies. It is always important to remember that the point of teaching clients these techniques is to help them manage anxiety, not to proselytize for a particular point of view.

Your client in crisis can also be encouraged to avoid activities and substances known to heighten anxiety. Alcohol is a great temporary anxiety alleviator, for example, but it increases anxiety after the initial euphoria has passed. Other drug use, including excessive caffeine, can be similarly discouraged (unless prescribed by a physician as part of the agreed-upon action plan). Certain anxiety-provoking people should also be avoided.

Using Cognitive Strategies in Crisis Counseling

Clients in crisis can be encouraged to look at specific thought patterns and how they might affect anxiety and their ability to cope. This is typically part of a longer-term crisis counseling effort. If you accept that how your clients thinking patterns affect how they feel (Beck, 1976; Ellis, 1990), it stands to reason that helping to change self-destructive thought patterns can help them feel better. If you can help your clients rethink their specific problems, it may affect how emotionally immersed they are in the feelings that accompany those situations.

Your crisis client can be encouraged, for example, to examine self-defeating thoughts and negative belief systems. To reiterate briefly the discussion in Chapter 9, most of us carry some beliefs about the world and our place in it that are simply irrational. These irrational beliefs impair our ability to live easily in the world (Ellis, 1990). Thinking, for example, that "Everyone should like me" or that "Life is supposed to be fair" can lead to real difficulties in life as the reality of what happens to us collides with these beliefs. No one is liked by everyone, although we all know people who spend most of their lives trying to make that happen. And life is rarely fair. Bad things often happen to good people. When bad things happen, particularly to someone who is deeply entrenched in believing that life should play by the rules, a serious crisis can result. Ellis identified an array of these typical belief patterns and suggested that counselors could best help their clients by helping them directly confront their particular irrational belief demons. This would naturally involve first identifying the irrational beliefs and then demonstrating how irrational they really are.

An example might be helpful. A few years ago I counseled a woman named Ann, a young wife and mother who was having such severe anxiety attacks she had to be hospitalized. The crisis situation seemed to revolve around her relationship with her mother-in-law. Even though Ann's mother was alive and well, her mother-in-law wanted Ann to call her Mom. Every interaction with Mom was causing severe bouts of anxiety for Ann, and the anxiety was becoming debilitating because of the frequency of contact (they lived next door to each other) and the excessiveness of Mom's demands (she called at least twice a day, asking for specific favors). The mother-in-law's demands for attention seemed insatiable and were breeding not only anxiety but resentment in her daughter-in-law.

My immediate job with Ann was to bring the anxiety attacks under control so that we could engage in a process of longer-term crisis management. Providing the opportunity for Ann to talk about her situation and creating the structure of a plan for dealing with this situation were sufficient to manage these attacks. By providing support and engaging her in the process of looking at the dynamics of this situation and the relationship with her mother-in-law, I was able to manage the most immediate manifestations of the crisis, the anxiety attacks. Knowing that she had an ally was extremely reassuring to Ann. Having someone listen to her and take her seriously confirmed for her that perhaps she wasn't simply crazy. Had these discussions proved insufficient in stemming the debilitating panic, I would have sought physician assistance in considering temporary help by way of medication.

When you have clients who are experiencing significant anxiety or panic, consider this kind of support.

Together we orchestrated a plan to look at some of the ways her thinking about her situation set the stage for these anxiety attacks. In just a few sessions, we were able to identify a couple of Ann's clearly irrational beliefs. One of these beliefs linked pleasing her mother-in-law with being loved and respected. "My job is to please my mother-in-law and satisfy her wants and needs, and if I do that well enough she'll eventually love and respect me." Another belief had to do with her ability to be assertive, and her own self-respect. "I don't have the right to say no or get angry, even when she asks me to do unreasonable things." We spent some time examining these beliefs and their history. Although Ann was able to grasp the irrationality intellectually, she couldn't allay the feeling that if she just tried a little harder she'd be able to satisfy her mother-in-law's demands.

We constructed a simple experiment to test that belief. For one week Ann would do absolutely everything that Mom asked her to do, without questioning. No matter how large or small the request, it was her job to try to fulfill it. Ann quickly found that she was unable to meet her mother-in-law's requests. There were simply too many of them, and some of them were absolutely contradictory. The reality of how impossible her mother-in-law's demands were had finally hit home.

Dealing with the immediate crisis, the debilitating anxiety attacks, sets the stage for introducing the idea of how to deal systematically with the problem of the mother-in-law. The intervention was all about holding things together long enough so that the longer process of counseling work could be engaged. It was the communication of hope and a belief in better times ahead. That is the nature of real support. Then the longer-term crisis counseling helped to create a foundation of self-support so that Ann could manage future anxiety-producing events effectively on her own.

Reframing is another wonderful cognitive-restructuring crisis intervention tool that deserves special attention. In this process the counselor takes an idea of the client's, typically negative, and tweaks it so that it can be looked at from an entirely new angle. A client can often be helped considerably by simply being given a new way of thinking about a troubling situation. Highlighting some positive aspect of the thought pattern that may not have been considered previously is one way to do this.

Consider the case of Sally, an extremely bright twelve-year-old middle school student. In elementary school, she had been a happy child with lots of friends, but all that changed when she entered middle school. In this new school bright students, especially girls, were marginalized by other students. Many of the bright girls intentionally hid their intelligence and purposely performed below their capabilities. Sally refused to do so and continued to get good grades. She paid the price for this rebellious behavior by being set adrift socially by other girls. There was never overt teasing or harassment. She was simply ignored by other girls, even by the group of girls who had previously been her friends. Sally's parents were becoming concerned about her isolation, but Sally insisted she was fine. Lately, however, Sally's behavior at home clearly showed her parents that she was not fine. At dinner she said little and picked at her food. She was going to bed earlier and earlier and having trouble getting up in the morning. Some mornings she claimed to be sick and didn't want to go to school. She cried hysterically when her parents suggested that they might intervene with her friends and their parents. Sally did agree, however, to see the school counselor.

The counselor talked at length with Sally about the social situation. She offered up some suggestions, some reframes. She suggested that Sally might view the dynamics between ordinary students and smarter students as a highly charged political situation, and that while Sally might not be able to do a lot to change the situation, she could become a student of it. Instead of being personally enmeshed in all that went on, Sally could choose to become a more objective and astute observer of it all. The counselor encouraged her to observe, contemplate, and write about her observations. She also helped Sally form a little support group with the few like-minded souls in her school. Although these strategies did not totally alleviate the situation for Sally, it did give her a new perspective and vantage point from which she could view her dilemma. She could now see herself as a sociological observer of the situation rather than as a helpless victim of social discrimination. This kind of reframing, which helps people to see their difficult situations as not only personal but also political, can be extremely helpful in dealing with feelings of helplessness and futility. Reframes can be an especially effective tool in school counseling settings (Edwards & Gfroerer, 2001). Parenthetically, it should be mentioned that this counselor also began to work simultaneously with the other girls to try to get them to change their behaviors.

Another way to use reframing with a client is to help her view her dilemma as a positive event, as a wonderful opportunity to look at life in a new way. In this approach, the counselor is reframing the nature of the crisis event itself. Thus, with the woman who is devastated about the breakup of a relationship, you can say, "Yeah, I do understand how you feel that the world has fallen apart with this loss, yet what a great opportunity to look at what you really want and need in a relationship." The reframe is not meant to minimize the trauma of an event and should be used with sensitivity, but it can serve to expand the view of the event itself.

Skills Training as a Crisis Counseling Strategy

Finally, as a part of a longer crisis counseling process, clients can be taught some other kinds of skills. A client might, for example, be taught specific social skills or taught to see how his actions affect certain consequences. Teaching these skills, you are serving a behavior-shaping function. You are an educator. The student who fails tests, for example, can be taught some simple study skills. Those skills can be reinforced with periodic rewards that the client can initiate himself. The student who studies for a fixed period of time, for example, might then reward himself with a pizza break. Better results on tests then serve to further reinforce the studying behavior.

Most adults and adolescents can handle considerable responsibility for setting up and maintaining their own behavior-shaping regimens. Children, and those assessed at the lower end of the developmental continuum, need more active counselor involvement and supervision with this planning. Similarly, many of your clients find themselves in crisis because of some major breech of social or interpersonal norms. They have violated, as a single offense or even repeatedly, social norms in a way that has drawn negative attention. This creates a crisis for both them and for the people around them. Many of these clients can be helped by being taught some social skills in addition to behavior management skills. Learning the essential rules in social interaction, particularly for your younger or more impaired clients, can help them immeasurably in negotiating the world.

Even mature clients may have specific skill deficits for which a simple training sequence can be extremely beneficial. Parents who have little skill or experience in child rearing and are in extreme stress over juggling low-paying jobs and expensive day care can benefit from both crisis counseling and parenting training. A middle manager who has worked for a company for nine years but has never asked for a raise may have been propelled into crisis counseling by a drunk driving incident, but he may benefit as well from some assertiveness training. Behavioral and social skills training are part of a longer-term counseling strategy that follows crisis management.

Utilizing Outside Resources

In times of crisis you may need outside help, active intervention and the involvement of others on the behalf of your client. These interventions will most likely be needed on behalf of your most vulnerable clients: young children, people with limited emotional or mental capacity, and lower functioning clients. This might mean immediate referral to someone who specializes in a service that is needed, such as a rape crisis center or to a physician who can dispense medication.

Many of your clients, for whom anxiety is overwhelming and intolerable, can greatly benefit from medications that relieve anxiety. However, when a client is experiencing strong emotions (e.g., an acute grief reaction), it might be better to forget the medication and let the emotions unfold expressively. Deciding whether to medicate for anxiety is best done in consultation with a supervisor and a physician.

In some cases, where there is a suspicion of physical or sexual abuse, or where there is a suspicion of potential physical harm, you will most likely be obliged by law (and by sound ethical practice) to report the abuse to appropriate authorities. This, too, is a referral of sorts and needs to be handled sensitively and according to state laws and agency or school guidelines. Referrals to other agencies and professionals are most efficient and effective when they are based on good relationships with people in those agencies. Good referrals hinge on good relationships. Bear in mind that you are not referring your client to a school or agency but to a person in a school or an agency. Solid, genuine relationships with people in those other settings (and this means all professionals, including secretaries and paraprofessionals) are the grease that makes the referral wheels turn easily.

Crisis Intervention and the Risk of Suicide

Suicide is the eighth leading cause of death in America. It is the third leading cause of death among fifteen- to twenty-four-year-olds (Aguilera & Messick, 1978), and it happens all too frequently with even younger children. The reality of suicide and other varieties of self-harm is a solid presence among us, and every counselor should be ready to respond to that threat when it arises. It can be difficult to fathom the desolation and lack of hope that such a desperate act suggests, but most of us have had at least passing moments when fantasies or even more concrete thoughts of no longer existing have visited us. Each of us has developed our own ways of dealing with these dark moments, ways to make it through the night. You need to be prepared to assist those who are visited by thoughts of suicide.

Suicide has been called a "permanent solution to a temporary problem," and it is the job of crisis counselors to help buy some time so that those problems, whatever they might be, can be approached via other avenues. Research tells us some specific things to watch for and suggests how to respond (or not) with clients who may be contemplating suicide. Experts in the area of suicide prevention state that the following danger indicators are important factors that suggest heightened suicide risk:

- A history of previous suicide attempts (Jobes, Berman, & Martin, 2005)

- Presence of a plan and active discussion of suicide (Berman & Jobes, 1991)

- Extreme hopelessness or major changes in emotion (Beck, Resnick, & Lettieri, 1986)

- Serious interpersonal problems with peers and the lack of a close friend (McHenry, Tishler, & Kelley, 1982)

- Significant early losses, including parent death or divorce of parents (Miller, Chiles, & Barnes, 1982)

Aguilera and Messick (1978, pp. 114–119) identify some additional warning signs:

- Themes of death or depression evident in conversation, written expressions, reading selections, or artwork

- Statements or suggestions that the speaker would not be missed if he were gone
- Presence of other self-destructive acts, such as reckless driving or self-mutilation
- Sudden changes in academic performance, chronic truancy or tardiness, or running away
- Physical symptoms such as eating disturbances, sleeplessness or excessive sleeping, or apathetic appearance
- Use or increased use of substances

The seriousness and specificity with which a client talks about the possibility of suicide is an overall indicator of the degree of risk. The level of anxiety and depression that accompany this talking are similar indicators. Any threat should be taken seriously.

As a counselor working with a client in suicidal crisis, you would employ the essential activities of the Support → Exploration → Plan sequence as an overall counseling strategy. Clients can be substantially supported through your validation of their feelings and experience and through your encouragement to talk about the specifics of the situation. Talking about suicide, not obsessively but realistically, will not increase the risk; rather, the converse. Clients contemplating suicide will appreciate your acknowledgment of the reality and seriousness of their desperation. Your respect for them and for the ideas they express are a major antidote to a possible suicide attempt.

It is true that some people manipulate others through talk about suicide. Adolescents are notorious for this behavior. Sometimes people will even perpetrate a phony suicide attempt as a way of getting attention. Take this talk, or any phony attempts, seriously. Too often the pretend suicide can become real, accidentally or otherwise, particularly when alcohol or drugs are involved. You can respond to the client's desperate plea for attention that lies thinly veiled under such talk and action by providing some of that yearned-for attention and helping the client learn to express the need for it more directly. Use all of your relationship development skills, your engagement and fact-finding questions, and your reflection of meaning responding skills to draw this client out and find out the details of this situation.

There are many helpful things a counselor can do, but there also are some cautions about things to avoid. Hipple's 1985 list of these "don'ts" may prove useful for you as you deal with someone who is potentially suicidal:

- Don't lecture, blame, or preach to clients.
- Don't criticize clients or their choices or behaviors.
- Don't debate the pros and cons of suicide.

- Don't be misled by the client telling you the crisis is past.
- Don't deny the client's suicidal ideas.
- Don't try to challenge for shock effects.
- Don't leave the client isolated, unobserved, and disconnected.
- Don't diagnose and analyze behavior or confront the client with interpretations during the acute phase.
- Don't be passive.
- Don't overreact. Keep calm.
- Don't keep the client's suicidal risk a secret (be trapped in the confidentiality issue).
- Don't get sidetracked on extraneous or external issues or persons.
- Don't glamorize, martyrize, glorify, or deify suicidal behaviors in others, past or present.
- Don't forget to follow up. (as quoted in Gilliland & James, 1997, p. 213)

Much of this list will be self-evident to the savvy counselor, but it reinforces the guiding axioms of a general response to crisis: Don't panic. Provide emotional support. Get the facts. Put together a plan. "Putting together a plan" is the capstone of the counselor's response to the threat of suicide. A foundation of physical safety is at the core of the plan. This plan and the accompanying contract activate the client's internal resources and call upon external supports as necessary.

The counselor's role in any crisis intervention, particularly one involving the potential risk of suicide or serious self-harm, is to provide the support and active intervention necessary until more help and other resources can be mobilized. This is truly an "emotional first aid" kind of intervention. The specifics of the risk are identified as quickly and in as supportive a context as possible, and the groundwork is laid for future work on the surrounding context in which this risk has emerged.

Counselors who work in schools or in close-knit communities are aware that one suicide event spawns the possibility of others (Gredler, 2003). A model "way out" has been set for others who may be experiencing serious difficulty. Clear school and agency policies and protocols (e.g., designation of a media contact person and the extent to which outside professionals will be utilized) that anticipate such reactions can do much to set an appropriate response tone. This "tone" includes provision of ample community-wide caring and support without glamorizing the suicide event.

Your role, then, includes more than direct service to people in crisis. It also involves supporting and influencing the institutions in which you work to ensure that appropriate and carefully thought out support systems are in place. Support your clients individually and also help to humanize the environment in which you work and live.

CASE EXAMPLE 10.1   *Responding to the Threat of Suicide*

A student has dropped into his high school counselor's office toward the end of the school day. The counselor is busy, and she has a sense that the student is probably supposed to be in class. But there also seems to be some urgency in the visit, so she makes time for him. She knows him fairly well and has talked with him about his complicated relationships with his girlfriend and his parents.

STUDENT: *[Looking down at the floor.]* You know those kids from Colorado, the ones at that high school who shot other kids and then themselves?

COUNSELOR: Yes, I remember. Tough to forget.   *Her "oh-oh" antennae have gone up.*

STUDENT: Yeah, well, I think about that sometimes. Not the killing other kids stuff, but about just checking out. Not having to deal with all this b.s.

COUNSELOR: Things are tough, huh? You've told me about some of the stuff going on with your girlfriend, how that's not going so well. Is there more than that?   *She figures she'll find out more about the specifics of the situation while she emotionally regroups and considers how to deal with this "just checking out" comment.*

STUDENT: Yeah, well she's pretty much history. She's done with me. I don't think there's much hope of anything there. I heard she's interested in this other guy. He's a real loser. I guess that's what she's attracted to. I've had it with her.

COUNSELOR: So that's over. I'm really sorry. I know how much you cared about her.   *Reflection of content and feeling. A little self-disclosure as well.*

STUDENT: And my parents. What a drag. The divorce is getting really ugly. Now they're fighting over custody of me and my brother. They don't care what I think much, but my brother's only five, and they both want him. Like he's a piece of meat or something.

COUNSELOR: What do you mean, they don't care what you think?   *Engagement, open-ended question.*

STUDENT: They think that because I'm fifteen I'm pretty much grown, ready to be on my own. They fight over who's going to pay for

(continued)

(Case example 10.1, continued)

stuff for me, but I don't hear much squabbling about where they want me to live. I think either one of them would just as soon I live with the other.

COUNSELOR: So you're feeling like you've been pretty much set adrift by them too. Your girlfriend and your parents as well.

More reflection of content and feeling.

STUDENT: It really sucks. It's not like I need them or anything. I can get along on my own, and they've got their hands full. Money problems. The business with my brother. And they've each got new people in their lives. I think my dad might be gay, and he's been hanging around with this guy who's a real creep.

COUNSELOR: Man, this is a lot. In the space of 5 minutes you've told me about a bust-up with your girlfriend, your parents' divorce, questions about how much they want to be involved with you, and the fact that your dad's got a gay lover. Sheesh, any one of these is huge. You led with the really big one, though, that you think about "checking out," permanently. That's what's got me most immediately concerned.

The counselor summarizes with reflections of content and feeling. Note that she does not try to minimize the real difficulty of all this. She supports, and then at the end slides in her concern about the "checking out" comment.

STUDENT: Yeah, well, it's not like I obsess about it or anything. It just seems like it would be easier to not have to deal with any of this. That it would be easier if it were just all over. Kaput.

COUNSELOR: You ever get specific in your thinking? Like how, when, where, you might do something to check out.

Fact-finding questions, in exploration mode, designed to get a sense of the seriousness of intent.

STUDENT: Nah. I don't have a plan or anything. You don't need to freak out. Sometimes I just think it'd be easier to not be around. Out of it. Permanently checked out.

COUNSELOR: OK, I won't freak out. But we do need to start to figure out how to deal with all of this. Maybe if we break it all down a little. The first thing is to deal with this checking out business . . . we really need to make sure that nothing ugly is going to happen.

She's sounding solid, in control of the situation. Getting more active. She's combining reflections of content with a directive plan of action. Most important, she is taking the "checking out" comment seriously despite his minimization.

(continued)

(case example 10.1, continued)

You know, and as that sign over there says, I've got to talk with one of your folks about this. Just to let them know they need to be concerned. That might even help with some of the other stuff . . . get their attention. Maybe they'll start to get a little more concerned about your welfare in this divorce business. I could tell them, or we could tell them together.

No beating around the bush here. She's telling him about her obligation to talk with his parents, about her interpretation of the severity of the situation. While she is threatening the confidentiality of their relationship (safety always takes precedence), she is inviting him to be a full participant in the disclosure to his parents. If she has done a good job of talking earlier about the limits of confidentiality, this need to report may come not only as not a surprise but also as a welcome relief. He may have set this up as an indirect invitation to bring in his parents.

STUDENT: Yeah, this is what I knew you'd say. I don't really want them involved in my business, but I guess I'd rather you be telling my mom. And I want to be there.

COUNSELOR: You should be. You can be the one doing the talking if you want, I can be the backup.

STUDENT: I'll think about it, but OK.

COUNSELOR: And then there's all the rest of it. This is a lot for one guy to have to deal with all at once. It doesn't seem fair, but this is the way it is. You don't have to deal with it all alone, however. I'd like to set up a time to begin to sort it out with you, maybe even if you'd like someone, a counselor out of the school, to share a lot of this with.

The counselor here is capitalizing on the opportunity to address the other issues this crisis has afforded. In this, there is an assumption conveyed to the student that he won't be checking out anywhere, that in fact, he will be more fully engaged.

STUDENT: I don't want to see any shrink. My mother's tried to get me to do that before . . . no way.

COUNSELOR: Well, let's talk about that when we meet again. Now, when can we get your mom in here? We should do this sooner rather than later.

This sets the stage for longer-range planning, with an assumption that that will begin in the next session.

Case Discussion

The most serious issues often present themselves to you when you have the least amount of time to deal with them. This is probably no coincidence. For example, this student knows

that the counselor's time is limited. He is perhaps doing a bit of testing, maybe to find out if this will be one more person who doesn't pay attention to him. It is a mixed appeal: a bit of

(continued)

(Case example 10.1, continued)

manipulation and a lot of seeking some attention. The counselor doesn't really know what his motivation is here, but she does immediately grasp the importance of the situation and decides to be late for that after-school staff meeting.

This does not mean that the counselor needs to engage in lengthy analysis of all the issues presented. In this brief crisis interaction, the main focus is on finding out some very basic facts, noting reporting requirements (particularly sensitive when dealing with children), and setting the stage for more work on the issues presented. Her primary concerns are to make sure that the student is safe for the near future (tonight) and that an active plan is in place to follow up from there.

Notice that the counselor is not afraid to ask directly about the degree of intent for self-harm, and she is careful not to appear to be "freaking out" about the topic. Her openness frees the student to talk directly. This counselor knows that talking about the potential for self-harm will not increase the chances of anything actually happening, rather the reverse. The specific fact-finding and engagement questions are conducted along with a mix of reflection of content statements. This mix of responses creates the critical support and exploration context in which the student can discuss this important material. The counselor is providing an emotionally steady, secure environment in which the student may talk of his concerns. The interview ends with a clear-cut plan of action.

REFLECTION EXERCISE 10.2   Talk about the Case

Sit down with two or three classmates and discuss the specifics of Case Example 10.1. Consider the following questions in this discussion:

- What do you think of the counselor's responses? What did you like about how she responded, and what would you do differently?

- Did this seem like a realistic interaction? How do you think it would be different in another setting? How would it be different if the client were older? What would the counselor do differently if the client were younger?

- Speculate about the issues presented by this student in addition to the potential for self-harm. What kinds of things would be compelling for you to explore as a counselor? Which of these things are related to his being in school and his school performance? To what degree would you want to work with this student yourself, and at what point would you consider referral to an outside professional colleague?

- Articulate the specific ingredients of an effective short and longer-range plan for this young man.

- How should the school's policies be set to anticipate this kind of situation? What role should the school counselor play in helping to set those policies?

Crisis Counseling and Acute Grief

It is not difficult to imagine the terrible grief and pain that is felt by someone who has been left behind after a successful suicide. The people left behind are the real victims of such a tragedy. So, too, are the people left behind after the loss of anyone who has been truly beloved. The death of a spouse or partner, of a friend, sometimes even a pet, can be supremely agonizing, challenging our ability to get through the days. Similarly, people may react to the loss of a love relationship in much the same ways as they experience the death of a loved one.

When I was seventeen years old, my younger brother died in a terrible drowning accident. It was an awful, horrific event. I felt that I had suffered the worst hand that life could deal. I felt bad for my parents, but to tell the truth, I felt a lot worse for myself. It was only later, when I had become a parent myself, that I was able to contemplate the worst hand of all: to lose a child. The pain for my parents must have been unbelievable. As an adult I grieved again, this time for my parents.

We see people in crisis who have experienced all kinds of losses, from those whose loved ones have succumbed to a long illness, to the survivors of accidents where others have died, to the children or partners of divorce and separation. For some, the loss is not the loss of a person but rather the loss of personal safety and security due to an act of sexual or physical violence—a woman who has been raped or abused suffers her own particular grief and loss.

Any of these losses can be devastating and can challenge an individual's ability to cope and function in the world. When a client's grief reaction is because of a death, other complicated reactions may be involved based on the relationship the client had with the deceased, or as in the example of my brother's death, the relationship with other family members. If the relationship had been difficult, abusive, or estranged, there may be deeply held feelings of anger, shame, guilt, or any combination of those. There may even be relief, mixed with guilt, about the fact that this person is now finally gone. All of this may combine to form a veritable stew of feeling, much of which is submerged under ideas of their inappropriateness. Rando (1993) calls this stew and our reaction to it *complicated mourning.*

Any significant loss may have complicated overtones, feelings that seem confusing, even contradictory. Rage can be mixed with sadness; guilt can be embedded in relief. A friend and colleague of mine, Virginia Fry, who has worked extensively in the field of bereavement and death counseling, particularly with children, suggests that the vast majority of people we see suffer primarily from issues related to loss. All kinds of destructive behaviors, she says, such as addiction, or eating disorders, or violence, are symptomatic of the degree to which people try to accommodate or deny their losses.

Such is the baggage of the people who arrive in our offices in crisis, sometimes with the acute nature of their grief so traumatizing and intense that they are rendered virtually helpless. They may be unable to function, to eat or to sleep, or they may be trying to drown their pain in alcohol or other forms of self-abuse. There is nothing but despair. In the throes of such grief, there is no future, no satisfaction in the present, nothing that makes any sense.

As I write this chapter, I am reminded of a scene in filmmaker Michael Moore's documentary *Fahrenheit 9/11*. The movie is controversial, for it is very political and unabashedly biased. Its antiwar stance does not sit well with some. What is not biased in the film, however, is the piece that portrays the grief of a mother who has lost her son in the Iraq war. It is absolutely painful to watch her grief, her rage, her pain. It is doubly painful because her pain is so complicated; her mourning for the death of her son is mixed with the rage she felt about the government that she thought had unjustifiably put him in harm's way. Her pain is so visible it is palpable. We can touch it and cannot but be touched by it. Her pain, our pain, is the universal pain of loss. This pain takes on a tangible presence in the film.

This is the pain of people who come to us in crisis. Some losses may have been anticipated, as with a terminally ill friend or relative; others are unanticipated and sudden, as with an accident, suicide, or murder. Each loss is uniquely complicated. Each pain has its own dynamic. Just as Kubler-Ross (1969) delineated some stages of accommodation to the reality of dying, so others have talked about stages of grieving. These, like Kubler-Ross's stages, must be seen as fluid and interwoven. Just as there is no linear pattern to how people die, there is also no linear pattern to how they grieve. We all do it differently. After my brother's death, my parents put pictures of him all around the house. I took them down. Was one way of grieving more "appropriate" than the other?

There are some general things that people who have studied grieving patterns say about the process by which we come to grips with loss. Bowlby (1961) and Rando (1988) each talk of a process that involves an initial attempt to grapple with the reality of the loss, followed by a state of disorganization and despair, which gives way, finally, to some kind of accommodation and integration of the loss. There is, experience suggests, no guarantee that one will emerge from despair. Some people never recover. Some suicides beget more suicides; some lost loves result in an incapacity to love again.

When caught in the web of despair that can ensnare us after a profound loss, each of us must find a way to somehow transform the loss by integrating it into some larger life mission or purpose (Frankl, 1962). This does not mean "getting over" the loss or pinning any fixed time to how long that transformation period should take. It simply means that each profoundly grieving person, if he is ever going to be able to move on, must eventually find a way of making some kind of meaning of his loss.

People reorganize their lives after important losses. I had a counseling student years ago who lost her child to cancer. Her response was to begin a new career that involved medical school and a lifelong pursuit of study of the disease that had taken her little boy. Other students in our program have come to study counseling specifically to deal with others' losses that are similar to those that they have endured. Mothers Against Drunk Drivers is an organization driven by loss. For some, spiritual faith and religious belief can help chart the way. We all must find a way to endure, to transform, and to move on. The alternative is more despair.

When you see someone in a state of acute crisis because of some major loss in her life, you have a great opportunity to help set the stage for a transformation in a direction that leads to some place other than despair. Your immediate response is essentially the same as for any other client in crisis. You provide support, explore the need for external support, and come up with a plan for action based on those perceived needs. You help to buy time, to aid the passage of the acute crisis phase, so that the longer-term transformative work can begin. You use all of the engagement skills and action skills at your disposal to help your client manage and hang on through this difficult time.

Some unique things you can do in grief counseling involve dropping your professional role a bit. This is a time to allow your own humanity and range of feeling to come to the fore. Being "clinically neutral" is not helpful. Some of the people with whom you'll work will be awash in feelings of loss, sadness, and grief. The tears will appear to have no end. Others will be stoic and "strong" or captured in a kind of "frozen" state (Yalom, 1989). Each person suffers in a personal fashion. Some of this is also shaped by cultural heritage, with some cultures being much more conversant and open about showing demonstrable grief.

Your job here is to help your clients express of all of their feelings, whether they flow freely or are bottled up inside. You are on the side of talking or of finding some other way of expressing the feelings of grief. You can ask the person to tell you about the person who's been lost or use other media for communicating what is felt. Clay or paints or music can be wonderfully expressive vehicles for people's grief, especially those who have difficulty with language. These means can also be extremely helpful tools in working with children.

A person in acute grief may also be looking for ways to staunch the outpouring of grief's feeling, at least when normal functioning is important as in going to work or school. You can help with anxiety-reducing skills training and the practice of some control strategies (e.g., meditation or physical activity). Although the expression of feeling, the cathartic release, associated with acute grief is almost universally helpful (Rando, 1993), people prefer to feel in control of when and how they let those feelings loose. Your job is to provide the time, space, and understanding for the expression of grief as well as the skills to put the cap back on when necessary.

Depending on your work situation and circumstances, you may need to attend to some of the outstanding immediate physical needs that sometimes accompany major losses. Certainly, if someone has been physically or sexually assaulted, maintaining physical safety and initiating the appropriate reporting responses are preeminent. There are other ways of responding to physical needs. I know of a local school counselor who helped organize her entire school to conduct a clothing and fund-raising drive for the family of one of her schoolchildren who lost their house in a fire. Much of the best of what we have to offer can translate into elegantly simple acts of responding to the most obvious needs.

In allowing yourself to draw people in grief out emotionally, or to attend to essential immediate needs, you may show somewhat more vulnerability than you might in other counseling situations. This is no time to be clinically aloof and professionally neutral. The best that you can offer is your acknowledgment that you, too, can feel this loss. In allowing yourself to be touched, to feel, you communicate your understanding.

Concluding Thoughts: Crisis Counseling and Counselor Self-Care

The need for all counselors to keep their emotional balance while doing this work, and the dangers of "burnout," are discussed in detail in Chapter 14. Crisis work with vulnerable and sometimes volatile clients can be especially taxing, however, and counselors who regularly work with people in crisis are particularly in need of systematic support and emotional replenishment.

Counselors who deal with crisis on a regular basis are taxed in a variety of ways, much of it depending on the kinds of clients they serve. For example, in their study of counselors who work with survivors of incest, Pearlman and Saakvitne (1995) found that crisis counselors are susceptible to a secondary traumatization simply hearing story after story of abuse. Rando (2000) found that counselors who work in hospice programs and are surrounded by death and grief every day sometimes feel abandoned by the people who die. Each kind of crisis may create specific difficulties and problems for the counselor who works with those clients.

In addition to the difficult nature of the work itself, other factors can contribute in creating a burnout situation. Some counselors have their own unfinished business, which adds to the difficulty. If a counselor has her own history of abuse and trauma, for example, she may be retraumatized with every story of abuse and trauma that she hears. She may be inclined to become overinvolved, without appropriate separation and management of the distinctions between herself and her clients that is critical for maintaining sanity in crisis work.

Further, the organizations we work for can sometimes exploit our desire and natural inclination to be helpful. Organizations that profess to serve the needs of

LAB PRACTICE 10.1   *Crisis Intervention*

This practice session is a bit different from those described in previous chapters. This time, in each quadrad or triad, the Client will be one of the persons in crisis described here. When you role play one of these Clients, embellish the character with facts and events that seem realistic, as well as with the feelings you would imagine might be those of someone in this position.

Client 1. This person has just found out that his (or her) long-time partner has recently gotten involved in an intimate, sexual relationship with someone else. This person has just confronted the partner with knowledge of the affair and was told that he (or she) is being left in favor of this new person. The Client is devastated by this news as well as by the knowledge of the affair.

Client 2. This person is found just before closing time sitting in the waiting room of a community mental health clinic. She (he) had been roughed up and robbed a few blocks away from the clinic and was wandering around in a stupor when a passerby, thinking that she (he) was mentally ill, brought her (him) to the clinic. She (he) has had a physical examination and has suffered no apparent significant physical damage. The event has obviously traumatized her (him), however.

Client 3. This is an 80-year-old person whose wife (husband) of 62 years died six months ago after a lengthy bout with cancer. The Client is in excellent health for an 80-year-old but has no desire to go on living. He (she) has tried to commit suicide, is very resentful that children, neighbors, police, and doctors keep interfering, and certainly doesn't want help from "some shrink."

Client 4. This is a teenager who has recently been told that his (her) parents are about to divorce and that he'll (she'll) be moving away from this town to live with his (her) mother. The news of the divorce and the imminent move to another town are equally traumatizing. He (she) is angry, anxious, and very sad about the impending changes.

Each Counselor will engage (support) the Client in crisis and begin to explore the dynamics of the situation, including his or her internal and external system of supports, and then begin to articulate a plan. When you have finished each role play, take time to process the experience. Did it seem realistic? Could you see yourself being in any of these roles in real life? What kinds of things that were expressed did the person in crisis find particularly helpful, which less so? What feelings were generated, for all who took part in this, about the exercise? What things that you saw used here could be generalized to other crisis work situations?

its clients in crisis can sometimes be remarkably blind to the needs of its own counseling staff, encouraging them to work more than is healthy. The dance that can unfold between the overcommitted counselor and the manipulative organization creates a serious health risk for the counselor, the organization, and the clients they serve. An organization that deals with clients in crisis should not be operating in crisis mode itself. It can best support its clients by ensuring that its counselors practice reasonable self-care and by not overloading its counselors and other staff with unmanageable numbers of clients in crisis. The client in crisis is best served by a grounded counselor who has a full, rounded life.

Crisis counseling is difficult, challenging work. It is filled with joys and frustrations. There can be great satisfaction in working with people in crisis who are often in the best position to contemplate significant and meaningful life changes. Some counselors thrive on the energy this work engenders and prefer it to other forms of counseling. All counselors need to face crises occasionally, and it behooves you to be both skilled enough and emotionally healthy enough to confront the challenges those crises present.

For Further Thought

1. Talk with counselors who do a lot of crisis work. Your community may have mental health services that include crisis response teams or crisis hot lines. These would be good people to talk with about the joys and frustrations associated with this kind of counseling work. What is it that attracts them to this work, how long have they been doing it, how long will they want to continue?

2. Talk with area school counselors about recent crisis events in their schools. What were the specifics of those, and how were they handled? Do these counselors think that the crisis response was adequate? How have school protocols helped in those situations or been altered in their aftermath?

3. Take an inventory of the crisis spots in your own life. Survey the ways you handled these events and the people who were involved. Which of those, if any, would you want involved again in the event of another crisis? Why? Look critically at how you respond to crisis, either your own or those of others?

4. What kinds of crises do you imagine you'll most regularly confront in your own counseling work? How emotionally well prepared are you to deal with those? If you imagine yourself frightened by the prospect of these crisis situations, how could you prepare yourself by way of getting more exposure to those situations before being called upon to be the person responsible for responding?

References

Aguilera, D., & Messick, J. (1978). *Crisis intervention: Theory and methodology.* St. Louis: Mosby.

Beck, A. (1976). *Cognitive therapy and the emotional disorders.* New York: International Universities Press.

Beck, A., Resnick, H., & Lettieri, D. (Eds.). (1986). *The prediction of suicide* (2nd ed.). Bowie, MD: Charles Press.

Berman, A., & Jobes, D. (1991). *Adolescent suicide: Assessment and intervention.* Washington, DC: American Psychological Association.

Bowlby, J. (1961). Processes of mourning. *International Journal of Psychoanalysis, 42,* 317–340.

Brown, F., & Rainer, J. (2002). A systemic approach to crisis intervention counseling. In L. VandeCreek (Ed.), *Innovations in clinical practice: A source-book* (Vol. 20, pp.151–156). Sarasota, FL: Professional Resource Press.

Collins, B., & Collins, T. (2005). *Crisis and trauma: Developmental-ecological intervention.* Boston: Houghton-Mifflin/Lahaska.

Edwards, D., & Gfroerer, K. (2001). Adlerian school-based interventions for children with attention deficit/hyperactivity disorder. *Journal of Individual Psychology, 57*(3), 210–223.

Ellis, A. (1990). *Rational emotive therapy and cognitive behavioral therapy.* New York: Springer.

Frankl, V. (1962). *Man's search for meaning: An introduction to logotherapy.* New York: Washington Square Press.

Gilliland, B., & James, R. (1997). *Theories and strategies in counseling and psychotherapy* (3rd ed.). Boston: Allyn & Bacon.

Gredler, G. (2003). *Handbook of crisis counseling, intervention, and prevention in the schools.* New York: Wiley.

Hipple, J. (1985). Suicide: The preventable tragedy (mimeographed monograph, 25 pp.). Denton, TX: North Texas State University.

Jobes, D., Berman, A., & Martin, C. (2005). Adolescent suicidality and crisis intervention. In A. Roberts (Ed.), *Crisis intervention handbook: Assessment, treatment, and research* (pp. 395–415). New York: Oxford University Press.

Kubler-Ross, E. (1969). *On death and dying.* New York: Macmillan.

McHenry, D., Tishler, C., & Kelley, C. (1982). Adolescent suicide: A comparison of attempters and non-attempters in an emergency room population. *Clinical Pediatrics, 21,* 266–270.

Miller, M., Chiles, J., & Barnes, V. (1982). Suicide attempters within a delinquent population. *Journal of Consulting and Clinical Psychology, 50,* 491–498.

Murgatroyd, S. (1983). Training for crisis counseling. *British Journal of Guidance and Counselling, 11*(2), 131–144.

Pearlman, L., & Saakvitne, K. (1995). *Trauma and the therapist: Counter transference and vicarious traumatization in psychotherapy with incest survivors.* New York: Norton.

Rando, T. (1988). *Grieving: How to go on living when someone you love dies.* Lexington, MA: Lexington Books.

Rando, T. (1993). *Treatment of complicated mourning.* Champaign, IL: Research Press.

Rando, T. (Ed.). (2000). *Clinical dimensions of anticipatory mourning: Theory and practice in working with the dying, their loved ones, and caregivers.* Champaign, IL: Research Press.

Wiger, D., & Harowski, K. (2003). *Essentials of crisis counseling and intervention.* New York: Wiley.

Yalom, I. (1989). *Love's executioner.* New York: Basic Books.

CHAPTER 11

Advanced Action Skills: Moving Beyond Stability

> In the adult there is a hidden child—an eternal child, something that is always becoming, is never completed, and that calls for unceasing care, attention, and fostering. This is the part of human personality that wants to develop and complete itself. But the human being of our time is as far from this completion as the heaven is from the earth.
> *(Jung, 1953, p. 278)*

Throughout this book I have used the metaphor of three levels of a house to classify client functioning into broad categories. For most clients functioning at Level 1, the goal of counseling is to significantly resolve some presenting problem. If the problem is addiction, for example, learning to live without drugs is a successful outcome. For the high school student who is entirely disenchanted with school, staying in and finishing is seen as success. For most clients functioning at Level 2, maintaining stability and steadiness in the world is what they seek from counseling. Learning to do a better job of managing work or school and family and avoiding trouble is satisfaction enough.

A few clients come to us already functioning at or close to Level 3; they have achieved resolution of ordinary life problems and yet questions about life and their place in the larger scheme of things remain. Most Level 3 clients are our own Level 2 graduates—clients with whom we have worked to achieve stability. They ask, "What now? I've done the work—to get straight, to get a job or to stay in school, or to learn how to deal more effectively with people—and yet something still does not feel right. Is this all there is?" These people want to explore the farther reaches of their lives and the nature of the human condition. They have the intellectual tools to conduct such a search, and they most likely have the economic wherewithal to take the time for this as well. They may want to better understand how their family histories have shaped their current life situation or how their unique talents and gifts might best serve the world. There may be some unresolved yearnings to create works of art or to write or to make music.

Oftentimes counseling is part of their lifelong search for meaning and balance, a personal adventure, perhaps even a spiritual quest. Counseling may be only one part of a search that includes forays into religion, study with teachers, travel, and immersion in world experience. These clients will benefit primarily from insight-oriented counseling activities and from complex interactions with counselors that are rarely straightforward or linear. Such counseling activities embrace and celebrate the mysteries of life. Counselors who work with these activities have embraced these mysteries themselves, both in their work and in their lives.

Included for discussion here are counseling activities and skills that are designed to promote insight. Although some of these activities have demonstrable utility in helping clients solve specific life problems (e.g., the use of expressive arts for victims of sexual abuse or the use of metaphor for chronic offenders), they are most often employed in the service of deepening our appreciation of life's complexity. They serve to nurture the inner child that Jung believed is present in us all.

Interpretation

Broadly speaking, *interpretation* refers to a counselor's ideas about a client's situation that the counselor shares with the client (Levy, 1984). Interpretation is typically used to draw connections between the events or patterns of behavior in a client's life that the counselor sees as being interwoven. This skill is the backbone of psychoanalytic, insight-oriented counseling and psychotherapy. In many psychoanalysts' tool kit, this is the only tool. For therapists and counselors trained in other orientations, it is one skill among many used to promote a client's self-awareness and understanding (Hill, Thompson, & Mahalik, 1989).

Restatement and paraphrasing are the simplest ways of responding to the content of a client's story; interpretation is the most complex. On the continuum from simple to complex, reflection of content, and reflection of content and feeling, fall somewhere between restatement and interpretation. Interpretation allows the counselor the freedom to reflect most elegantly and thoughtfully on the client's issues and to suggest connections between past and current happenings in the client's life.

Interpretation can be a useful asset in promoting introspective, insight learning. It can help free a person from the constrictions of the past through understanding the connections—and the hold on the present—that those associations still have. You might, for example, suggest such a past-to-present connection to a woman having trouble with relationships: "It's probably not a surprise that you're having intimacy issues with men, given your dad's unpredictability and your rocky relationship with him." Or you might suggest to a man easily bored with jobs and relationships: "Your family moved so much, it's like you grew up with wheels under you. Staying in one place now—or with one person—seems unnatural."

With clients enmeshed in difficulties and problems, it is generally best to first deal with those issues using direct interventions, the action skills discussed in Chapter 9. Someone who is drinking herself to death needs to stop drinking first, and only after a reasonable period of sobriety might she want to look at some of her family dynamics that may (or may not) have been involved with the drinking. More directive interventions, as opposed to interpretations, are appropriate for steering this client toward focused action.

I had a friend with extensive experience in addictions treatment who was infuriated by professionals who would ignore this rule of thumb. He wore a button that said, "Help stamp out the search for the underlying causes of addiction." What he meant, of course, was that we should stop the drug use first. Once stability is achieved, clients who are interested can then explore older issues such as family relationships or school problems that may have contributed to their beginning drug use.

Sometimes it can be extremely helpful to make tentative interpretations with Level 1 clients who are working actively to resolve current life problems. Such interpretations can provide a context for some of the day-to-day struggles people have. Oftentimes the interpretation can be stated as a hunch, making it less of an absolute truth that you are foisting on your client. This kind of interpretation can help some clients to see their struggles in a larger light, being rooted in some kind of long-standing habit, pattern, or tradition, perhaps of an intergenerational nature.

The use of interpretation grows out of the relationship that's been developed. The alliance you've built with your client is a critical determinant of how well this skill can be utilized. A basic level of trust must be developed before the client can effectively take in and use interpretive remarks, making the timing of interpretations

CASE EXAMPLE 11.1   *Use of Interpretation*

This client and counselor have been working together for some time. Originally, the client came into counseling in the midst of serious financial difficulties. He had just been fired from an automobile sales job, not because of a poor sales record but because of his inability to work well with his colleagues, particularly his supervising manager. His response to his manager's directives was anger, and after the last angry outburst he was fired. This behavior was also problematic in his family, where he had similar outbursts with his wife and children. This was his third job loss in two years, and all of the firings had been because of these kinds of interpersonal difficulties.

His counselor had worked with him for some months, building a relationship and helping him by way of some cognitive and behavioral skills training. The client had learned some anger management skills, and he had worked at examining how the sequence of his behaviors contributed to his job difficulties. He seemed to be maintaining control of his temper, things were going more smoothly at home, and he was generally happier. He was now successfully working at another sales job, this time selling large excavating equipment.

But the client was not satisfied; he wanted more. He particularly wanted to understand the meaning of his anger and his dislike for supervision. He wanted to know why he seemed so angry most of the time and why he was so provoked by people in positions of authority. His insurance company had told him they would no longer pay for counseling services because his original goals had been met, but he suggested continuing in a fee-for-service arrangement, and his counselor had agreed. As he so graciously put it in a "joking" fashion, "Why trade horses when this one's still got good teeth?"

This session follows one in which the beginnings of some significant examination of his family of origin had taken place, in particular the client's relationship with his father. Note that the

(continued)

(Case example 11.1, continued)

interpretative comments are stated simply and are not prefaced with "I think."

CLIENT: I've been thinking a lot about me and my old man. What we talked about last week. You know, we're nothing alike. Not like what you said. He was a little guy, no sense of humor, totally under my mother's thumb. She ruled the roost all right. He used to hide out in his study, and God knows what he did in there. I think he read a lot. He was really interested in history and tried to find out stuff about how our family came to this country. You know, roots, all that kind of stuff. He was pretty much a wimpy little guy.

The counselor is probably trying to recollect what the client said last week that has fostered this thinking. Clients will often work over things we say in a session during the week. This is wonderful, even if what we think was most brilliant about what we said is not what they choose to focus on. The counselor is also noting the strong feelings here, typical of people talking about parental relationships.

COUNSELOR: So this was your model of what it meant to be a man.

A reflection of content, perhaps with a bit of interpretation, the counselor's own thinking.

CLIENT: Some model. More like a model of what it's like to not be a man. I kept wishing he'd stand up to her. Just once. Tell her where to go. Sometimes I wanted to go up behind him and shake him into doing something. It really pissed me off. She was such a witch to him. I'd watch these times when she'd browbeat him, and I figured that deep down she wanted him to stand up to her, but he just wouldn't do it.

COUNSELOR: And you told yourself that you would never let that happen to you, never let people push you around.

A pretty safe interpretation—the counselor's assumption about how this mother's behavior would translate into her client's stance in life.

CLIENT: Yeah. I'm not sure I ever said it, exactly, but that's been the attitude.

COUNSELOR: So maybe the things you get into with your boss, the one at your last job, aren't really so much about dealing with your father, maybe more like dealing with your mother.

Interpretation. Ties together the attitudes taken from the relationship with parents and situations at work. Note that it is tentatively offered, a hypothesis that the client can work over and confirm or deny. This is a puzzle that both the counselor and the client are trying to work out.

CLIENT: You should meet her sometime. Might've known she'd outlive him. She just wore him down, and his heart gave out. Now there's some symbolism. Get that. He died of a broken heart. She just picked at him and picked at him, and when he died she went on like nothing happened. Joined the country

(continued)

(Case example 11.1, continued)

club, redid the house, got a new "boyfriend." Gross.

COUNSELOR: You're still angry with her about all this.

Reflection of feeling.

CLIENT: You bet. Wouldn't you be?

COUNSELOR: And you still really miss your dad.

Another reflection of feeling, this time to the less obvious grief over the loss of his father.

CLIENT: *[Tears up.]* He was such a good guy, but he just couldn't stand up for himself. He let himself get pushed around, belittled, and made fun of. I hated it.

COUNSELOR: You told yourself that no one would push you around. Not a wife, not a boss, not anybody. And every time somebody does start to come at you, boom, there's the image of your mother.

Interpretation.

CLIENT: Yup, exactly.

Case Discussion

The counselor's interpretations of the relationship between the client, his mother and his father, and the connection to the client's problems with anger in his current relationships with bosses and family are made on solid ground. They are based either on direct evidence of what the client has said or on obvious indirect evidence. Future work, aided by some cognitive restructuring, might help the client to uncouple the interactions with people in authority from his older, more emotionally loaded interactions with this mother. That work would also include further exploration of the client's thoughts and feelings about both of his parents, that strange and complex mix of rage, grief, and affection that accompanies most of our clients' (and our own) family recollections. There may be ways that he identifies with—and has taken in positive and negative attributes of—each of his parents, no matter how distasteful that may seem to him. Interpretations will be helpful in leading him to contemplate these connections.

When interpretations are mixed with other responses, particularly reflections of feeling, they can lead to considerable exploration and release of emotion. In this case, for example, it is fairly easy for the client to allow feelings of anger about his mother to rise to the surface. Those feelings seem to lie just below the surface. What may be deeper, and perhaps more powerful, are his feelings of grief and loss about his father. The counselor listens for cues to ways to access that grief. Some tentative interpretations and reflections of feeling might make it possible for the client to express his loss more directly. One senses that there might be a well of grief here, both for what was lost and for what he wishes had been present but was not. The expression of this feeling, the "corrective emotional experience," could be a great relief for this client. It could also eventually help him temper his angry feelings, particularly as he comes to understand the more complex meanings of his relationships with his parents.

(continued)

(Case example 11.1, continued)

There may also be opportunities for the counselor to interpret how this client's dealings with her as his counselor are also representative of this unfinished business from the past. We can assume that his earlier comment about "not changing horses" is loaded with symbolic meaning about his feelings about being in counseling and about her as a person, as well as the transference at play in the relationship. This inclusion of the counselor as a player, and the counselor's acknowledgment of that, in his ongoing thought process will add a dimension of immediacy to these interactions. The counselor could also discuss the symbolism behind the choice of his wording (i.e., "horses") here.

---

important (Gaston, Thompson, Gallagher, Cournoyer, & Gagnon, 1998). You need to build some history and have a clear view of the facts of a person's life before you can make effective interpretations. Offer interpretations tentatively, with respect for the client's ability to take or leave the suggestion. The client best knows, after all, the facts and meanings of his life. It would be presumptuous for a counselor to fire off an interpretation about the meaning of some facet of his client's life without some sense that the client would agree with that idea. Case Example 11.1 illustrates this technique.

Like paraphrasing and reflections of content and feeling, interpretation allows the counselor to consider the meaning of the material a client brings to counseling. Unlike paraphrasing and reflection, however, interpretation allows for the interjection of the counselor's ideas about this material. This makes the skill a potent, tricky, tool in the arsenal. It should be used judiciously and tentatively. Interpretation should always be used to promote learning and to facilitate client growth, not to demonstrate counselor brilliance. It is always preferable for the client to discover aspects of herself for herself, and the best interpretations simply set the stage for that discovery. With good supervision and experience you will learn to use this tool wisely.

For further reading on how to use interpretation in counseling, I recommend Book (1998), Greenson (1967), Hill, Thompson, and Mahalik (1989), Levy (1984), and Silberschatz, Fretter, and Curtis (1986).

Working with Dreams

The inner life of an individual unfolds through dreams, and whoever carefully observes his dreams may gain access to his nature that would otherwise remain impenetrable. (Singer, 1972, p. 267)

Interpretation of dreams is another mainstay of some analytic approaches to therapeutic work, perhaps most notably in Freudian and Jungian analysis. Freud called dreams the "royal road to the unconscious," and Jung suggested that the unexamined dream is like the unopened letter. They both had great respect for dreams and worked extensively with people to help them decipher the meaning of their dreams. Freud and Jung developed different ways of thinking about dreams and their meaning and different methods for interpreting their importance, but both valued the dream experience's capacity to tie conscious and unconscious aspects of the self more closely together.

Other counselors may approach dreams a little differently, less intellectually. For example, Gestalt therapists believe that the importance of the dream lies in how we project aspects of ourselves into different dream components (Perls, Hefferline, & Goodman, 1951/1994). Working in this framework, a counselor might assume that different dream characters represent different parts of the dreamer's personality, or of her "unfinished business." A harsh mother in the dream might be representative of the dreamer's self-criticism. For these counselors, the stress is primarily on the emotional experience of the dream. A client might be asked to act out the dream, playing different parts of the dream herself; in group counseling other group members might represent these aspects and characters.

The Jungian analyst June Singer (1972) believes counselors and psychotherapists should track a client's dreams as much as they track the ongoing events of the client's life. She believes that most human difficulty exists because of the split between an unexamined inner life and an overly active outer life, and she suggests that dreams have the greatest potential for healing that split. She is a strong advocate for helping clients to befriend their dream lives.

I find a dream to be particularly helpful when it is spontaneously brought up by a client who is grappling with its meaning, and where there is a lot of feeling attached to it. The work, for me, is less about my interpreting the dream components themselves than it is about the client's desire to understand, as well as the strong emotional reaction to it. We search together for ways in which the dream relates to the themes of his general work, what relevance it has for his waking life, and what the feelings stirred by the dream are all about. The dream work becomes even more compelling when this dream is one of a series of repeated dreams.

Rather than more formal dream work, you might prefer to explore the client's own personal take on the dream. "So what do you think it means?" could be your approach. If obvious symbolisms or meanings occur to you, you might carefully share and check the meaning of those with this client. Dreams are a rich, potent source of material for counseling discussion and work. They may shed light on hidden desires or on concerns that lurk slightly out of the light of day-to-day awareness. Dreams have layers of meaning, some parts of which are more obvious than others (Jones, 1979).

If dreams, or the subjects of dreams generally, are truly compelling for a particular client, you might encourage some outside reading. She can become a student of dreams, read what others have said, and teach you what she learns. Dream work can provide new and illuminating ways for clients to consider aspects of their lives.

REFLECTION EXERCISE 11.1   Recording Your Dreams

You will be more convincing in your use of dreams in counseling work if you have some personal experience with dreams yourself. This is an opportunity to increase that experience.

Begin sleeping with a journal and pen next to your bed. When you have a dream, try to force yourself to awaken long enough to take a few minutes to write the dream down before you go back to sleep. If you simply can't get yourself to wake up after the dream, then write it down as soon as you wake up in the morning. Take the time to embellish this dream description with all the detail you can remember. Note its important characters. Are you yourself in the dream or someone else? Are you your present age or older or younger? What is the setting and time frame of the dream? Describe your feelings that surround this dream experience. Write it all down, as best you can remember.

Track your dreams. Note repeating themes and the feelings that accompany them. Pay attention to thoughts and images that float through your mind between sleep and wakefulness, just before you fall asleep at night and just before you fully wake up in the morning. Another kind of altered consciousness is active in those moments that may yield productive imagery. Write down these observations as well.

Treat your dream life seriously, and take this exercise seriously. Be cautious regarding with whom you share these dreams. These are private recollections, and you will want to choose confidants wisely. By treating your dream life seriously, you will be rewarded with a feeling that your life has taken on more texture and richness.

To learn more about the use of dreams in counseling, I recommend Jung (1963), Fontana (1997), Perls, Hefferline, and Goodman (1951/1994), Singer (1972), Vedfelt (1999), and Wolman (1979).

Poetry, Metaphors, Stories, and Humor

The beauty of poetry lies in its ability to communicate deep feeling and meaning in ways that ordinary language cannot. Poetry, like music and other art forms, seems to connect directly with our inner being, bypassing our linear thought mechanisms. Poetry that truly speaks to us seems to move directly toward the heart. Similarly, metaphors and teaching stories communicate with us in ways that are a bit different from everyday language. They pull us more deeply into ourselves while simultaneously connecting us more expansively to the shared human condition.

Like dreams, stories, poems, and metaphors can typically be viewed on multiple levels. On the surface level they may be funny or may simply relate an event, but when given more thought, they often reveal subterranean messages and meanings. Consider the following story, for example, from Arthur Deikman's (1982) *The Observing Self,* a work in which he makes a strong case for the use of teaching stories in counseling.

VANITY

A Sufi sage once asked his disciples to tell him what their vanities had been before they began to study with him.
The first said, "I imagined that I was the most handsome man in the world."
The second said, "I believed that, since I was religious, I was of the elect."
The third said, "I believed that I could teach."
The fourth said, "My vanity was greater than all these, for I believed that I could learn."
The sage remarked, "And the fourth disciple's vanity remains the greatest, for his vanity is to show that he once had the greatest vanity."
(p. 162)

This story is at once a humorous poke at human frailty, and more significantly, an invitation to reflect very personally on our own vanity and the pride-filled ways in which we deceive ourselves. Herein lies much of its beauty, for it can be appreciated by different people for different reasons. Some will take the story at face value; some will appreciate the deeper meaning. When given to a client as a teaching tool, the story can be understood as a message that is less "preachy" and moralizing than direct discourse about vanity's traps.

Metaphors use graphic comparisons as teaching tools. "So," said the client who was having great difficulty functioning after her husband left her, "My husband was the captain of my ship." "Yes," replied the counselor, "but when the ship started sinking, he jumped overboard with the rest of the rats." Of course, metaphors can be more elaborate and lengthier. Metaphor engages our thought process in a way that involves more imagery than that which is absolutely literal (Romig & Gruenke, 1991), and some have argued that a metaphor may even promote a quickened cognitive processing by uniting our two brain hemispheres as its meaning is unraveled (Barker, 1985).

William Shakespeare said, "Brevity is the soul of wit." Combined with humor, a short, simple saying can convey a very large message as this one does, displayed on the wall of a retreat center where I hold some of my classes: "At some point, we all need to give up our hope for a better past." This little one-liner serves to shake up thinking. It helps us to look at the world, particularly our own inner world, in a new way. The best humor communicates a message simply and forcefully.

Whether short or long, the intent of a metaphor, poem, or story used in a counseling setting is to engage the receiver in thoughtful inner dialogue with its meaning and its personal applicability. These dialogues may be particularly useful in helping concrete, linear thinkers to see their lives as having a richer complexity than they had previously imagined (Hendrix, 1992). Passing one of these metaphors, stories, or poems on to a client requires judgment. I have typically told directly only the shortest of metaphors. I am not a particularly good storyteller, so I rely more on clients reading the material themselves and then discussing it with them. The fit between the issue being discussed and the timing of introducing a story or poem is important, and the decision should be based on the client's readiness and openness to the idea.

Like many other aspects of counseling, this use of metaphor, poetry, and stories in your counseling work hinges on the degree to which you utilize them in your own life. Counselors who are avid readers, particularly readers of poetry, mythology, and literature, will find ways to integrate what they read and digest from that reading into their counseling work. We communicate best that which has meant the most to us personally. If you love the language of poetry and the meaning of specific poems, you will imbue your counseling with that medium of expression somehow. Reading widely and becoming a consumer of fine works of literature and poetry is a legitimate part of your growth as a counselor. The time you spend lolling with a good book next to a meandering river or on a sun-drenched beach is not "goofing off"; it's "professional development." Not only will this time

---

REFLECTION EXERCISE 11.2   *Collecting Poems and Stories*

Spend some time remembering poetry or stories that have meant a lot to you. Maybe you've collected poems as you've grown, or perhaps stories or myths that you read as a child are still remembered. Begin to collect these poems and stories. Keep a scrapbook or a journal that is filled with them. Design a beautiful cover for the book that holds them, or construct some other kind of container in which these will be held. Pay close attention and give care to whatever it is that contains these poems and stories.

Begin to make a practice of reading them aloud to yourself and to carefully selected others. Listen to others, both professionals and your friends, read poetry and stories. Attempt to commit some of them to memory.

Contemplate the meaning of these poems and stories for you. Where were you when you first heard them? Has the meaning changed over time? Who are the significant people that these writings bring to mind? What are the themes that draw them together?

expand your repertoire of ideas and images from the reading itself, it will also enhance your appreciation of the importance of the quietly spent moment.

> There is a way between voice and presence
> Where information flows.
> In disciplined silence it opens
> With wandering talk it closes. (Rumi)

Poems and stories, like dreams, add immeasurable quality to your life. Savor them and consider your time with them as important as anything you do.

> This is not/the age of information.
> This is not/the age of information.
> Forget the news/and the radio/and the blurred screen.
> This is the time/of loaves/and fishes.
> People are hungry,/and one good word is bread/for a thousand. (David Whyte)

For additional readings on the use of metaphor, stories, and poetry in counseling, I recommend Barker (1985), Deikman (1982), and Whyte (1994).

The Use of Expressive Arts as Counseling Strategies

A variety of arts and art-related activities can be utilized in helping clients express themselves in ways that are often inaccessible by verbal means. Even poetry and teaching stories cannot reach some parts of the human heart. Some of the things people may be trying to evoke within themselves may be beyond words, or at least beyond the language they typically employ. Expressive arts activities are wonderful tools for use with clients who are verbally impaired, or for clients whose verbal adeptness may be used as a form of defense, a resistance against experiencing strong feeling. Thus expressive arts can be utilized effectively with any of your clients. They should be used creatively, with attention to the level of functioning of your client and in the service of specific therapeutic goals.

It is beyond the scope of this book to explore in great depth the varieties of expressive arts that can be used as counseling strategies, but I will mention some of them briefly here. You can learn more about these modalities through workshops, further reading, and specific training classes. When utilizing these strategies, it is important to bear in mind that the performance is less important than the expression itself. This kind of work should not be just one more arena in which clients have to prove themselves. To the contrary, these modes of expression provide a freeing experience where clients can safely explore the farther reaches of their inner selves. Your nonjudgmental attitude and your ability to create a safe environment for your client to experiment with these new ways of self-expression will be key to the success of their utilization.

Dance and Movement

Dance engages the body to access thoughts, feelings, and memories that may be difficult to explore with verbal techniques. Dance has been used to treat survivors of sexual abuse (Lewis, 1996), to help people work through developmental blocks (Loman, 1998), and to help people feel more authentically rooted in their own bodies (Adler, 2003). By helping people to connect more solidly and authentically with their own bodies and physical environment, dance and movement strategies promote wholeness.

The emphasis in this work is on discovery and spontaneity of movement, however, not on performance. You may be the teacher of these activities, assuming you have interest in and pursue training in this kind of work, or you may refer your client to a skilled teacher.

For additional readings on the use of dance and movement in counseling, I recommend Espanak (1981), Levy (1995), and Siegel (1984).

Music

Like movement and dance, music has been used for centuries as a means of helping people connect more effectively with themselves and their experience of the world. Music certainly touches us and stirs our deepest feelings and emotional states in ways that everyday language cannot. It is not by accident that we use music to celebrate and commemorate our major life events, and many of our most cherished memories are closely linked to the music that accompanied those events. It has been said that music that is loved communicates directly with the heart.

A variety of music experiences are available to the counselor in work with clients, using different strategies from composing, to playing, or to simply appreciating music to promote growth toward client goals (Bruscia, 1998). Music has served to facilitate specific goals for some of my clients. With people grieving a lost love, for example, I have sometimes recommended spending an evening alone with the music that most reminds them of the person lost. The music facilitates the process of grieving. In working with clients who are musically inclined, I have often encouraged them to commit time to practicing and, if they have done it before, to go back to performing. They have sometimes been slow to recognize the central importance and contribution their musical hobby or avocation can make toward their overall well-being. Music expands a part of the person that rarely can be touched by other forms of communication. In the use of music—both in appreciation and in performing—the overarching desire is to help the client integrate past experiences and goals for the future in a way that enables him to experience himself as a whole, integrated person.

For additional readings on the use of music in counseling, I recommend Bruscia (1998), Lee (1996), and Ruud (1980).

Visual Arts

You may consider using visual arts to help people access and communicate difficult experiences or aspects of themselves that they feel unable to talk of in words, or for any other reasons that seem to make solid therapeutic sense. Art therapy has certainly been shown to be effective in helping clients with a variety of emotional difficulties, as well as for helping people to simply more effectively express themselves (Malchiodi, 2003).

Some clients—many children, for example—may feel more comfortable drawing than talking, and others may be encouraged to stretch themselves out of their verbal comfort zone with the use of art as a way of exploring unknown aspects of themselves. You could make this a regular part of your counseling work or draw upon it spontaneously to assist a specific situation and client. Painting, drawing, sculpting, and photography can all help people express themselves in creative new ways. This artistic expression can provide for some clients the cathartic release that may be unavailable through verbal means alone.

The emphasis, again, is on the creative process, not the product. One counselor friend of mine who uses art therapeutically suggests using the term *making things* instead of *creating art* as a way of taking performance anxiety out of the picture. If your client feels she needs to create art, or something that measures up to some external standard, it can inhibit her and squash the very spontaneity and creative expression that this work attempts to foster.

For additional reading on the use of visual arts in counseling, I recommend Malchiodi (2003).

Sandplay

Originally devised by a British physician as a way of helping children describe their horrific experiences of World War I (Lowenfeld, 1979), the sandplay technique was further developed in the late 1940s for therapeutic use with children by Dora Kalff (1980), a Swiss Jungian analyst. This medium of expression has grown in popularity and use among counselors who want to provide their clients with a safe means of expressing themselves (Malchiodi, 2005).

The technique employs a sandtray, a low-sided rectangular box of sand in which the client places miniature toys (people, animals, buildings, and so forth).

The toys can be played with spontaneously or placed in reference to some question posed by the counselor. When a client is satisfied with the picture he has created in the sandtray, the therapist photographs it. Having a record of the pictures created by the client is an important part of the technique and allows the therapist to monitor the therapy.

Sandplay gives the client the opportunity to talk about the events of his life in a way that is safe because the stories are contained in the tray, outside of himself. This externalization makes it easier to talk about difficult events in a way that would not otherwise be possible. Sometimes called "a waking dream," sandplay is used primarily with children, but it is also effective with traumatized adults (Mitchell & Freidman, 1994).

For additional readings on the use of sandplay in counseling, I recommend Homeyer and Sweeney (1998), Kalff (1980), Malchiodi (2005), and Mitchell and Freidman (1994).

Philosophical Counseling

My father and my father-in-law were both men of considerable faith and intellectual curiosity. My father-in-law was a Congregational minister, and my dad a self-taught biblical scholar. Both read widely. During my professional training to become a counselor, I frequently had lengthy conversations with them about my course work and about the theories of counseling I was studying. I remember being infuriated with each of them when I would talk about some intriguing new theoretical line of thinking I'd been following, only to be met with comments like, "Well, you know that's not exactly new thinking . . . that idea's been around for more than a thousand years."

They were usually right, of course. When you scratch below the surface, much of what we utilize in our theories about counseling has roots in long traditions of philosophical thought. Some theorists argue for a distinct new profession of "philosophical counseling," claiming that it is a viable alternative to the medical model that

---

REFLECTION EXERCISE 11.3   The Expressive Arts

Reflect on the variety of expressive arts that can be used in counseling. You may know something about some of these arts, little about others. Without thinking too long about it—using your immediate intuition, in other words—which of them has the most appeal for you? Which could you see yourself gravitating toward as a client or using as a counselor? Which peaks your interest enough to move you to pursue further information or training? Write about your reflections, or share them with a classmate.

---

is the underpinning of most counseling and psychotherapy practice (Raabe, 2001; Schuster, 1999). Like Thomas Szasz (1978), who has long argued for the abolishment of terms like "psychotherapy" and "mental illness," they suggest that most problems in living are rooted in incorrect thinking, in a distinct lack of wisdom.

> Living without the correct understanding—or wisdom, if you will—can lead to a painful state of body and mind. If this is the case, why should we continue to interpret suffering as the symptom of an illness, complex, or infirmity? . . . Looking for wisdom and suitable understandings can eliminate pain or make it easier to bear. (Schuster, 1999, p. 21)

At the least, they would say, we should make room for the inclusion of more philosophical discussion in the counseling work that all of us do. This seems a logical suggestion. Many of us, particularly when we work within a cognitive-behavioral framework, already challenge clients' thought patterns and destructive ideas about themselves. The philosophical approach of working with a client to "find wisdom and suitable understandings" is an extension of the cognitive-behavioral approach and seems particularly well suited for clients who are intellectually gifted. The inclusion of existential approaches to counseling and psychotherapy in most counseling theory courses acknowledges the central role our beliefs and attitudes play in our being in the world. The need to create meaning, to deal with fears of death and our mortality, and the freedom associated with being alone in the universe are certainly compelling philosophical issues that you may engage with your client.

You can expand on these themes and philosophical ideas. Counselors are in a wonderful position to implement thought not only from the philosophy discussed in counseling theories but also from sociology, economics, history, and other fields. When taking a philosophical approach, you have the latitude to engage your clients in discussion about ideas and the pursuit of knowledge. You can bridge the personal and the intellectual by virtue of both your emotional and thought-filled connections with your clients. You can challenge their thinking that seems to be destructive and lead them to intellectual work that is instructive. Again, this is an appeal for you to think, read, and learn broadly and expansively, to not limit your study to the fields of psychology and counseling alone.

There is danger here, of course, in becoming too intellectual with your clients. You need to always consider the possibility that a client might use intellectualism as a defense against becoming more personal or more emotionally involved. Choose your moments for injecting philosophical discussions carefully. Like any other counseling activity, the timing and judicious use of this skill are critical.

For additional readings on the use of philosophical counseling, I recommend Raabe (2001), Schuster (1999), and Szasz (1978).

LAB PRACTICE 11.1   *Dealing with Big Questions*

Assemble a triad or a quadrad. This will be another role-play situation, with one of you the Counselor, one of you the Client, and one or two Supervisors.

The Client has been diagnosed with a serious illness. It may be terminal, but no one seems to know with any degree of certainty. This is a single person, without children or much in the way of extended family. This person has been successful in her (his) chosen career and is financially well off. As you role play this Client, add any other life details that you feel fit the situation. When taking your turn as the Client, you may choose to play a character who is not terminally ill, but try to stick to discussion of the larger issues of life and death that concern people at a major crossroads in their lives.

The Client seeks counseling because she (he) has a great desire to explore the big questions about life, death, and the meaning of it all. The Counselor is directly being asked to be a guide in this search for meaning. Conduct one interview with the Counselor and the Client talking about all of this, and think about how to begin to create some goals and plans of action.

When each of the interviews has been completed, discuss it as a group. In particular, consider how this interview is the same as or different from any other counseling exercise you have done. How much should the Counselor focus on the obvious request (for a discussion of ideas) and how much on what might be imagined to lie beneath (for example, fears, sadness, and anger)? Is a balance between a counseling approach that asks for an intellectual journey and talking more personally possible or appropriate?

If these interviews are substantially different from others you have done, what are the reasons for that? Should those other interviews be done with some of the same attitudes? I sometimes challenge my students to consider how they might approach a new client if they knew that this person only had a few days to live. Why not consider taking the same care with each client as if that were exactly the case? Who, after all, knows that it's not?

Community Service as a Counseling Strategy

Many of our colleagues in education have discovered the value of community service as a helpful adjunct to classroom instruction. There is something about putting material learned in the classroom toward actively serving one's community that makes the material more relevant for the student and also benefits the community.

Community service, and the personal learning that accompanies this activity, can be a valuable adjunct activity in counseling work. Unlike other skills discussed in this chapter, this is clearly something your client will engage in outside of your office. Perhaps community service, when recommended to a client, could be considered as a kind of homework. You may create the impetus for this service, but the client will have to take responsibility for implementing it. In this regard, its like any other homework and requires your skill and full attention to help your client muster the initiative and energy to initiate it. You can use the same guidelines for this service assignment as for any other homework.

Social action—whether it is serving meals at a homeless shelter, doing trail maintenance at the local park, or reading to children—particularly when coupled with counseling work that promotes self-awareness, benefits the community and also promotes valuable personal learning for your client. Appropriate community service, meaning service which is not paternalistic or built upon the client's "need to be needed," does much to tie your client to the greater world community and to promote a feeling of belonging.

This community service can also help to put a client's personal problems in perspective. I once heard a counselor speak at a small gathering of counselor educators of his work with recovering addicts, where he told of listening to the addicts' stories of pain and suffering. Although their stories were genuinely painful, a crucial part of the treatment process was to help these clients feel less victimized, less like each had his own personal "pity pot," and to help them engage more directly with the world. He then said that he had a routine homework assignment for each of these clients. That assignment was for the client to buy a bunch of balloons and then go to the oncology unit of the local children's hospital where he was to give away balloons. This was a simple homework assignment with profound implications. What interpersonal interaction could more put one's situation in perspective than spending an afternoon with children with cancer?

I learned some months ago of a new psychotherapeutic specialty being developed to help people deal with the guilt associated with coming into newfound wealth. Particularly targeted for this counseling work are people who made financial fortunes in the "dot-com" market. Typically, these are young adults who were part of some small startup company that did very well and then was sold to a larger company. These individuals made very large sums of money from these transactions, capitalizing on being in the right place at the right time.

What therapeutic interaction could be helpful with a young person who has come into such wealth? Certainly, this client could be helped to see that there is nothing wrong with making money, as long as it has been done honestly. Aside from dealing with feelings of guilt, putting the money to work in a way that is personally meaningful is the challenge. This is a wonderful opportunity to enlist the community service counseling option, finding ways for clients to put themselves and their money to work in aiding some community endeavor.

A case can also be made for the role of social action and community service in helping to ameliorate some psychological problems. Gloria Steinem, giving the closing talk at the 1995 Evolution of Psychotherapy conference in Las Vegas, relayed her experience of the young women with diagnosed eating disorders who came to work at Ms. magazine in the 1980s. She recalled how they would often forget their eating issues and simply get better in the midst of the political work being done by the magazine. The collegial interaction with other women coupled with intensely committed social activity drew their attention away from themselves and into the greater political world.

We counselors talk a great deal about the importance of empathy, about the ability to see the world as our client sees it, about walking in their shoes for a while. It is this possibility of expanding our clients' own capacity for empathy that we extend to them when we suggest community service. We offer them the opportunity to experience the world of others through direct experience and shared effort. We offer them the joy and satisfaction of finding that their effort and service will be absolutely fulfilling if approached with the right attitude.

Community service is not a panacea for personal problems, nor should it typically serve as an alternative to personal counseling. Service to the community and personal growth are parallel projects, each feeding the other. In my experience, clients who involve themselves in community work feel better about themselves as a result of their effort. They feel more connected to their community, and they are less attached to their own personal problems. Further, clients who are aware of their own issues attached to their giving to the community (e.g., codependency issues) and who have some knowledge of the cultural and social issues at play in that community can have a positive impact on the communities they serve. They can make truly significant, positive contributions.

For additional reading on community service as a counseling strategy, I recommend Coles (1993).

Concluding Thoughts: Appreciating Life's Mystery

These advanced action skills can enrich and deepen a client's appreciation of his inner life. A counselor who has used these skills for her own benefit, perhaps as a client herself, will be in the best position to know when they might be effective with a client.

All of these skills and activities promote action, but perhaps action that is not immediately visible to the outside observer. Most of the action generated by these activities is internal, and it may take time for their results to emerge into the outer world. These activities are designed to feed and heal those inner parts of our clients that strive for wholeness and integration. They give life and voice to those aspects of our clients' inner world that may be perceived and heard only faintly in the bustle of everyday life. These small voices within are often buried beneath the obligations of daily life and the demands of others. The beauty of these activities lies in their ability to liberate those voices and give them power. When used intelligently, these advanced action skills may help our clients to lead more authentic lives in which their day-to-day life is more congruent with their inner experience. Such increased authenticity is surely a positive counseling outcome.

Clients and counselors who work with these skills at this level are less concerned about finding distinct, straightforward answers to life's big questions than they are in discovering the subtle nuances that make life rich and complex. They have come to appreciate these subtleties and even to appreciate the absence of solutions to many of life's contradictions.

> Everybody is wondering about what and where they all came from,
> Everybody is worrying about where they'll go when the whole thing's done.
> But no one knows for certain,
> And so it's all the same to me,
> I think I'll just let the mystery be. (Iris Dement, 1992)

For Further Thought

1. Pick one of the advanced skills discussed in this chapter and begin to read about the theory and research conducted on this skill. Use the suggested readings as a place to start, but then widen your literature search. Note how much or how little outcome research has been done on this skill. How might that affect your consideration of using it in your own work?

2. Consider the variety and range of community service opportunities in your area. In this consideration include not only human service volunteer opportunities but also environmental, homebuilding, and other projects. Do any of these projects appeal to you? Do you see any ways that you might integrate service into your counseling work?

3. Have you read philosophical or spiritual works that you might consider utilizing in your counseling practice? How might your thinking and beliefs about these subtly influence your work, even if you don't choose to use them overtly? Do you see any ethical considerations in how you go about this?

References

Adler, J. (2003). American Dance Therapy Association 37th annual conference keynote address: From autism to the discipline of authentic movement. *American Journal of Dance Therapy, 25*(1), 5–16.

Barker, P. (1985). *Using metaphors in psychotherapy.* New York: Bruner/Mazel.

Book, H. (1998). *How to practice brief psychodynamic psychotherapy: The core conflictual relationship theme method.* Washington, DC: American Psychological Association.

Bruscia, K. (1998). *Defining music therapy.* Gilsum, NH: Barcelona.

Coles, R. (1993). *The call of service: A witness to idealism.* Boston: Houghton Mifflin.

Deikman, A. (1982). *The observing self.* Boston: Beacon Press.

Dement, I. (1992). *Let the mystery be.* New York: Forerunner/ASCAP.

Espanak, L. (1981). *Dance therapy: Theory and application.* Springfield, IL: Thomas.

Fontana, D. (1997). *Teach yourself to dream: A practical guide.* San Francisco: Chronicle Books.

Gaston, L., Thompson, L., Gallagher, D., Cournoyer, L.-G., & Gagnon R. (1998). Alliance, technique, and their interactions in predicting outcome of behavioral, cognitive, and brief dynamic therapy. *Psychotherapy Research, 8*(2), 190–209.

Greenson, R. (1967). *The technique and practice of psychoanalysis* (Vol. 1). New York: International Universities Press.

Hendrix, D. (1992). Metaphors as nudges towards understanding in mental health counseling. *Journal of Mental Health Counseling, 14,* 234–242.

Hill, C., Thompson, B., & Mahalik, J. (1989). Therapist interpretation. In C. Hill (Ed.), *Therapist techniques and client outcomes: Eight cases of brief psychotherapy* (pp. 284–310). Newbury Park, CA: Sage.

Homeyer, L., & Sweeney, D. (1998). *Sandtray: A practical manual.* Canyon Lake, TX: Lindan Press.

Jones, R. (1979). Freudian and post-Freudian theories of dreams. In B. Wolman (Ed.), *Handbook of dreams: Research, theories, and applications.* New York: Litton.

Jung, C. (1953). *Psychological reflections.* New York: Harper.

Jung, C. (1963). *Memories, dreams, and reflections.* New York: Pantheon Books.

Kalff, D. (1980). *Sandplay: A psychotherapeutic approach to the psyche.* Santa Monica, CA: Sigo Press.

Lee, C. (1996). *Music at the edge: Music therapy experiences of a musician with AIDS.* London & New York: Routledge.

Levy, F. (1995). *Dance and other expressive arts therapies: When words are not enough.* New York: Routledge.

Levy, S. (1984). *Principles of interpretation.* New York: Jason Aronson.

Lewis, P. (1996). Depth psychotherapy in dance/movement therapy. *American Journal of Dance Therapy, 18*(2), 95–114.

Loman, S. (1998). Employing a developmental model of movement patterns in dance/movement therapy with young children and their families. *American Journal of Dance Therapy, 20*(2), 101–115.

Lowenfeld, M. (1979). *The world technique.* London: Allen & Unwin.

Malchiodi, C. (2003). *Handbook of art therapy.* New York: Guilford Press.

Malchiodi, C. (Ed.). (2005). *Expressive therapies.* New York: Guilford Press.

Mitchell, R. R., & Freidman, H. S. (1994) *Sandplay: Past, present, and future.* New York: Routledge.

Perls, F., Hefferline, R., & Goodman, P. (1994). *Gestalt therapy: Excitement and growth in the human personality.* Highland, NY: Gestalt Journal Press. [Original work published in 1951]

Raabe, P. (2001). *Philosophical counseling.* Westport, CT: Praeger.

Romig, C., & Gruenke, C. (1991). The use of metaphor to overcome inmate resistance to mental health counseling. *Journal of Counseling and Development, 69,* 414–418.

Ruud, E. (1980). *Music therapy and its relationship to current treatment theories.* St. Louis, MO: MMB Music.

Schuster, S. (1999). *Philosophy practice: An alternative to counseling and psychotherapy.* Westport, CT: Praeger.

Siegel, E. (1984). *Dance-movement therapy: Mirror of our selves.* New York: Human Sciences Press.

Silberschatz, G., Fretter, P., & Curtis, J. (1986). How do interpretations influence the process of psychotherapy? *Journal of Consulting and Clinical Psychology, 54,* 646–652.

Singer, J. (1972). *Boundaries of the soul.* Garden City, NY: Doubleday.

Szasz, T. (1978). *The myth of psychotherapy.* New York: Doubleday Anchor.

Vedfelt, O. (1999). *The dimensions of dreams.* New York: Fromm International.

Whyte, D. (1994). *The heart aroused: Poetry and the preservation of the soul in corporate America.* New York: Doubleday.

Wolman, B. (Ed.), (1979). *Handbook of dreams: Research, theories, and application.* New York: Litton.

Exceptional Counseling Challenges

I tell you, the more I think, the more I feel that there is nothing
more truly artistic than to love people.
(Vincent van Gogh)

When I was a younger, greener counselor, I had aspirations of serving people who would be energetically interested in pursuing their greatest potentials for growth. I envisioned legions of seekers of self-actualization banging on my door in search of answers to life's big questions. Together we would pursue those answers, skipping merrily off together toward some counseling nirvana.

In fact, many of the clients with whom I've worked over the years have fairly accurately fit that early dream. But like most counselors I have also had my share of clients who were reluctant to be in counseling, coerced by someone else to be there, and who had zero interest in nurturing an inner life. Some of these clients sought me out as an alternative to going to jail. Some came to counseling as a last ditch effort to keep a marriage alive. Some came because they were about to be thrown out of school. Some came because they were in so much personal pain they were desperate for any kind of relief. Many were primarily interested in getting through the day.

Many of these exceptional clients had been born into extremely difficult situations, had experienced trauma and abuse, or suffered from addiction or mental illness. For these people, personal growth would have been a luxury. For them, counseling was a matter of personal survival. These are the people referred to in this book as functioning at Level 1. It's tough to have much of a focus on an inner life when outer life presents the challenges of poverty, mental illness, addiction, and abuse.

I was prepared for racial, ethnic, gender, and sexual orientation differences. I was prepared for clients whose backgrounds were different and whose interests or ages were different. Diversity is the spice of life, I thought. But I was not prepared for people whose everyday lives and the devastating problems that beset them were so very different from my life and my problems. I found that I needed to learn to relate in ways that stretched me out of my zone of comfort. Over time I have come to be extraordinarily grateful for these exceptional people. By being forced out of my comfort zone, I have come to appreciate the great similarities we all share in spite of more visible differences.

Challenging Adult Clients

The special needs of clients with multiple problems, resistant clients, depressed clients, addicted clients, and seriously, persistently mentally ill clients are presented here because you will most likely work with one or more of these types of clients at various points in your career. There are particular challenges and joys associated in working with any of these clients, and each calls for some special knowledge and language of approach. One of the greatest challenges is to refrain from stereotypically categorizing individuals who may belong in one of these populations. Thus, for example, one addicted client will invariably be very different from another client with drug and alcohol problems. Some general things can be said about a counseling approach for each of these groups of clients but it should never be forgotten that each client is unique. Be prepared to throw out any preconceived assumptions about what might work in the face of the reality of the person who is sitting opposite you.

Some counselors may have wrestled with issues similar to those of their clients. But the counselor who is herself a recovering alcoholic cannot, for example, assume that any other alcoholic person's experience will be in any way like hers. The counselor who has struggled with depression cannot assume that anyone else's depression is like his. Our personal experience of these difficulties may help to enlarge our capacity to understand and empathize with the difficulties of others, but each person's experience is unique. It is critically important to try to see these issues through the eyes of the client, not as recollections of our own experiences.

Looking Behind the Behavior

When dealing with exceptional clients, great care must be taken not to be tricked, swayed, or cajoled by the presenting behavior. What we see on the client's outside is often very different from what goes on inside. Behaviors are often designed to protect the more vulnerable inside reality and feelings. Your job is to see behind the behaviors, into the reality of the person hidden underneath. To believe only in the reality of the surface behavior is to view human nature simplistically.

The schoolyard bully can be the loneliest child in school. The hostile, aggressive client may harbor deep fear and sadness. The seductive and charming person is often deathly afraid of intimacy. And so on. The behavior on the outside may be the opposite of what transpires internally. The more you are able to keep an intuitive eye on the unfolding relationship, the better prepared you will be to note how behavior can be used defensively. Little clues will unfold as to what is lying within, and attention to the process and the dynamic between the two of you will sometimes uncannily link to the content of what is being examined.

Much of this observation can take place within the context of the agreed-upon ground rules and contract related to how you work together. Small violations of the ground rules can be seen as little bits of resistance. Noting, for example, that an unassertive, shy client is often late for appointments can be a tip-off to hidden aggressions and angers. This kind of observation, when used sensitively, can be a great asset in dealing more effectively and more directly with clients.

The Importance of Self-Awareness

The counselor's level of personal awareness is a critical variable in her ability to see clients' issues clearly. The unaware counselor, who carries the baggage of unresolved conflicts and resentments from the past, will unwittingly be swept away by clients' defensive behaviors. Clients' natural inclination to foist their own unfinished business (transference) onto the counselor will become a muddled mix if the counselor's reactions are unclear (countertransference). Getting "clear" about your own history, becoming comfortable with yourself, is a prerequisite for all counseling work, but it is particularly critical for your work with challenging clients.

Clients with Multiple Problems

There has been significantly more attention paid to the notion of *co-occurring disorders* in recent years, with calls for counselors to think much more complexly about the people with whom they work. You will see people with chronic emotional and mental disorders who also have substance abuse problems; often the issues of resistance, depression, and drug or alcohol abuse will be overlapping. People who have pursued training primarily to work with clients with mental health issues need to be conversant in substance abuse issues as well because there is often a complicated interplay of mental health and substance abuse problems (Shulman, 1995). Similarly, training related to emotional and mental disorders is important for substance abuse counselors. There will hopefully come a time when professional licensing organizations collaborate more effectively to ensure that counselors receive a broad base of training in both mental health and substance abuse disorders, recognizing that these disorders all too frequently overlap (van Wormer & Davis, 2003).

If you are training in a community counseling or family therapy program, be aware that you will see depressed children with all kinds of combinations of issues. If you are a school counselor in training, you will need to be prepared for it all. While you may primarily be concerned with delivering a results-based developmental school counseling program to a wide range of students, you must also be aware that significant mental health, drug-related, and other pressing issues will intimately affect your students.

Resistant Clients

All clients are resistant. Nobody likes change or embraces giving up old familiar patterns for new, unsure ones. Change, no matter how positive, is equivalent to some kind of loss, the old giving way to the new. Resistance is a fact of life for our work and can be thought of as a universal characteristic of the people with whom we work.

For some clients, however, resistance seems to be a *defining* characteristic. Their resistance is worn like a badge of honor, and it is the first thing to greet you in this new client encounter. Two of my own experiences with resistant client behavior have been mentioned in earlier chapters (the client who hated ties and the one with profanity tattooed on his knuckles). Legions of other obviously resistant clients have come into my office, and they have presented both great challenges and great joys in my work. Often these most resistant clients end up making the greatest positive changes in their lives.

You may sometimes work with truly tough characters, people who have been in jail or who are antisocial. These clients can make you nervous, uncomfortable, and leave you wondering what you can possibly offer them. To work with socio-pathic clients, you need to protect yourself and align your counseling activity with the prescribed treatment/education regimen used in the program that employs you.

Varieties of Resistance

There are many forms of resistance. There is certainly the obvious tough, violent kind, but there is also the seductive, conning kind. There is the silent, non-compliant kind, and the emotionally distraught kind (Otani, 1989). Whatever the variety of resistance, your job is to seek the person within and behind the resistant façade. Remember that the resistant behaviors you see now may be the result of years of experience in learning how to survive in difficult, unpredictable environments. When seen in this light, the behavior is logical and understandable.

Culture and cultural differences play a role in negotiating common ground in a new counseling relationship as well. There may be significant, logical reasons for someone to distrust a counselor who is seen as representing the interests of government, or a ruling majority, or some predominant cultural paradigm. A counselor who works for a public service agency or a school may be seen as representing the interests of the government that supports those institutions, and that may breed distrust. In fact, counselors do sometimes, wittingly or unwittingly, support the ruling paradigm (Parham, White, & Ajamu, 1999; Sue & Sue, 1999). Some people come from cultures where it is seen as inappropriate and a violation of norms to reveal personal or family information. In a variety of ways, if a counselor and a client are from different cultural backgrounds, cultural differences may be interpreted as resistance by the counselor.

Counselors need to be aware of the cultural differences and political realities that their clients bring to counseling. We need to sharpen our cultural and political sensitivities, learn what we can about cultural difference, and heighten our "cultural empathy" (Chung & Bernak, 2002). It is imperative that we recognize and not minimize these political and cultural issues and that we not overinterpret differences as simple resistance.

A new client may come to your office displaying his disdain for counseling, for you as a person, and for the need to be there. He may well be someone who has frequently been coerced into counseling by a judge, a parent or teacher, or a partner, and without that push he would not be seeking help. If the client seems hostile and aggressive in some out-of-control ways, and you find yourself wondering about his grasp of reality, you may need to call for an outside assessment. Some clients may have had years of experience with social service agencies and may be very savvy to the ways of counseling. So savvy, in fact, that their resistance is cleverly hidden beneath a veneer of niceness and compliance. Your client, in short, may be a con artist. This passive form of resistance may be even more recalcitrant in its sophistication.

CLIENT RESISTANCE AND COUNSELOR ANXIETY

There are some key things to remember in working with resistant clients—both the hostile and the manipulative types. First, you need to manage your own fearfulness. If you are afraid of this person, you will not be able to afford much help (Pinta & Davis, 1987). Your work setting needs to be a place that supports your being safe, and you need to work out whatever anxiety issues you have in supervision or in some other supportive context. Sometimes more contact, in a safe and appropriate noncounseling context, can help to toughen you up a bit. If you haven't had much experience with clients involved with the correctional system, for example, you could spend some time doing volunteer work in a correctional facility in a noncounseling role. This might prepare you for the counseling work you might eventually do with this population. Similarly, if aggressive teenagers frighten you, spend some time as a volunteer in a school for difficult adolescents to familiarize yourself with the challenges of adolescence.

CLIENT RESISTANCE AND POLITICAL REALITIES

You can also examine and discuss with new clients political or cultural issues that may be playing into the obvious resistance. It is best to acknowledge the differences. Ignoring them may suggest support for whatever political difficulties may be associated with these differing cultural perspectives. You can always invite a new client who is in some way culturally different from you to become your teacher and inform you of the realities of his perspective.

It is critical that you bear in mind that the defensive, resistant posturing you see before you is the result of years of attempting to survive in a hostile environment. People do not learn to be so resistant overnight. They learn how to survive difficult, often abusive and violent upbringings by adopting these behaviors. These behaviors are taken on as survival strategies and are not easily shaken even when the circumstances of their lives change. It is your job not to accept the noxious, resistant behavior but to accept the person behind it.

Creating the Alliance through Nondefensiveness

Try to make any new client an ally of yours, a participant in her own treatment (Davis & Boster, 1992). Find something this new client wants from you, and use this leverage in beginning to form a relationship. Something that has brought this person to you, and you have the ability to use that to access a connection with her. Finding and capitalizing on this "need," generating some hope for your client about your usefulness may be the key to a successful outcome (Hanna, 1996).

A woman who comes to see you because her husband is fed up with her lack of attention to him and the children certainly wants her husband appeased, at least if she wants to preserve the relationship. A child who has been sent to your office by the school principal is certainly interested in getting out of trouble, and the person who's just gotten out of jail certainly wants to keep his probation officer off his case. You can agree to be helpful with those presenting concerns while negotiating to look at other things you might deem important. What this person wants, what you can do for him, provides what may be your only leverage in maintaining the relationship.

Maintaining the ground rules of whatever contract for working together is struck is of critical importance. Times of meetings and number of meetings need to be held securely. If you say that you'll be reporting noncompliance to some third party (e.g., a principal or a probation officer), follow through. You can adequately display your support while maintaining the rules.

Try not to act defensively when confronted by obnoxious behavior. Think strategically, and ask yourself, "What is this person up to?" What is being avoided, discounted, or not dealt with in this attack or whatever else is being thrown your way? Try not to be "hooked" by the resistant behavior, whatever form it takes. The exercise on page 281 that may demonstrate what is meant by not being hooked.

Dealing with Insulting Behavior

When you did the reflection exercise, my guess is that the insults became less threatening over time. As you became more adept at responding, they lost their sting. Here are some general guidelines for responding to insults or obnoxious behavior:

- Always take the complaint seriously. That does not mean you have to change anything you do, but you want this person to know you've heard them.
- Force the person to be specific and behavioral in her insult to you. You do not need to agree with (or allow) general, nonspecific attacks on your character. For example, "You may not call me a jerk. That is not acceptable. But what is it that I do that you think is jerky?"

REFLECTION EXERCISE 12.1   *Responding to Insult*

Ask a few of your friends or classmates to help you with this exercise. When you have collected them about you, ask them to gently, playfully, insult you. Tell them it's all in the spirit of fun and experimentation. They don't need to be mean or really nasty, but criticizing anything about you is fair game. They might insult your dress, your mannerisms, or your quirky behaviors—anything real or imagined.

Your job, with each of these insults, is to respond nondefensively. To the insult, "You wear the ugliest dresses I've ever seen," you might respond, "Yeah, I'm sure no fashion model." Or to "You make the stupidest jokes," you might say, "Sometimes my trying to be funny falls really flat." You get the drift of this? The key to responding nondefensively is to agree with the other person's view of reality. If you find yourself caring very deeply about this observation, about your dress or jokes or whatever else, you are getting "hooked," and you are in danger of defensive overreaction.

Let people insult you for a couple of minutes, and play with responding without defense. Don't let the exercise go on for too long; certainly stop it if it starts to feel hurtful. Remember that these remarks are not necessarily a reflection of reality, only their perception of it.

This may seem like a risky exercise, and it can be. It will be risky to the extent that you are stung by others' impressions and are vulnerable to the thoughts and opinions of others. The reality is that our clients will, in fact, on occasion shoot for these vulnerabilities of ours. Some of our clients will be eerily adept at finding our vulnerabilities. Better that we practice our responding with friends and colleagues. Building a thicker skin while being able to remain sensitive to the needs of others is a helpful asset in this business. Also, it's certainly safer to begin to get used to this kind of behavior with trusted colleagues than with new clients.

Note the feelings and reactions you have to this, and when you've asked your colleagues to stop with the insults, talk about the process of the exercise with them. What did they notice about your responses? What observations can be made about responding to insults?

- You have a right not to be abused. A client who is using profanity or has crossed over your tolerance line with insults can be informed that you will refuse to talk with him until he treats you with civility.

- If you are in a group counseling setting and a member of the group is insulting or confronting you, you can always check with others to see if they share the complaint. If nothing else, this buys you some time to gather your wits about you.

- If the person is complaining about something you do and wants you to change something, try to look objectively at what is being said and decide whether this is a change you are prepared to make. You can always respond noncommittally if you need more time to consider the request. For example, "This is something I'll consider seriously, and I will let you know what I'll do in the next session." You have a right to hold to a "bottom line," a position beyond which you won't accommodate the client.

- Consider your response style as a means of engagement. It is a bit like a martial art. Instead of meeting resistance with resistance, try to let the words smoothly move around and by you. An insult is only an insult to the degree that you let it be one.

This skill can be thought of as an extension of the essential reflection of content counseling response skill. This couples nondefensive responding to insult or attack with a reflection of what this attack is about for your client. Here is an example of responding to insult or challenge with reflection of content:

CLIENT: That was one of the goofiest questions I've ever heard. How long have you been doing this work? Are you a rookie, or what?

COUNSELOR: I guess I sure missed on that one somehow. And you've got a concern that I won't be able to intelligently stay with you through the tough stuff you've got to talk about. Tell me about that.

By avoiding defensiveness, the counselor is keeping the focus where it belongs, on the client. This also opens the possibility of exploring the meaning behind the attack. The counselor will also want to look at the reality of whether his questions have had a true element of "goofiness."

Passive Resistance

Dealing with resistance can be even more difficult when the client resists change through passive behaviors. Passive resistance may take a variety of forms, from seeming compliance, to seduction, to smiling acquiescence. A client's resistant behavior might even be sticky sweet and obsequious, treating you like a knowing sage. A mask of compliance covering a resolute reluctance to do anything differently is a form of resistance that I have personally found much more difficult to deal with than active, overt resistance. With active resistance you know what you've got, repellent though it might be. With passive resistance, your challenge is to make it more active. Like flushing a bird out of a bush, you must work to get the real person behind that façade of niceness to reveal himself.

The rules of engagement for passive resistance are the same as for the active variety. Remain alert and ready to act when those small opportunities to check on the real feelings and thoughts behind the presenting behavior arise. Here, too, it is all about not getting hooked by presenting behavior, even when it consists of compliments or statements about how great everything is. Watch for the leakages around the edges of this compliance, the sarcasms and subtle digs, and speculate with your client about their meaning.

Resistance as a Survival Strategy

With all forms of resistance, remember that it is not about you. It is about what you represent. Foremost, you represent authority; you are a parent extension or perhaps even someone who has some real power over your client. Because many of your most resistant clients have experienced unpredictable, aggressive upbringings and live in hostile environments (Davis & Boster, 1992), they will be volatile and suspicious. You can personalize the comments and other resistant behavior as a means of accessing what is really important, but you don't have to take the subtle abuses personally. If you can remain nondefensively secure in who you are and in your role with this client, you'll ride through the resistance smoothly.

Search for common ground around something your client needs from you, and try to engage the person behind the behavioral façade. Remember that the anger and hostility is most likely a cover for fear (Rasmussen, 2002) and sadness. Do what you can, with whatever means you have, including all of your best engagement skills, to access your client's real feelings and help her learn skills for coping with her environment. Managing conflict, improving social skills, or learning how to act appropriately assertive with others are all best taught within the context of this common ground and the relationship between you. Only when your client is a real ally and participant in her own counseling will you pragmatically be able to move toward some commonly agreed-upon goals and a contract for working together.

Drug or Alcohol Abusing Clients

Drug and alcohol abuse is epidemic. Scratch below the surface with any of your clients, regardless of work setting, and you will inevitably find these problems lurking about. It may be a problem of personal use and abuse, or that of a loved one, or it may be a matter of family history, but virtually all of us have been affected somehow by drug or alcohol abuse.

You may not choose to work with people with drug and alcohol problems, but you will, nevertheless. Addiction and abuse problems are found as a correlate in almost every social, health, and mental health problem we have. The vast majority of people in jails, in the correctional system, or who are involved with

LAB PRACTICE 12.1   *Dealing with Resistance*

In this role-play experience, each of you in the triad or quadrad group will have an opportunity to be a Counselor for a resistant Client.

In each case, the Client has been coerced by someone (e.g., a partner, a judge, a boss) to see a Counselor. Each Counselor and Client pair should discuss the kind of role and kind of Counselor this would imply before the role-play session begins. The Client can feel free to embellish the role with whatever factual information, thoughts, and feelings seem fitting. The Counselor, however, should tell the Client the level of resistance with which she (he) feels comfortable dealing, ranging from 1 for "least resistant" to 3 for "highly resistant."

It is the Counselor's job to try to draw out and engage this Client in productive conversation. Try to find out as much about this person's situation as possible given the brief amount of time you have in which to interact. The Client should not be so resistant that no dialogue is possible. It is best in these role plays if the initial resistance gives way, eventually, to some kind of meaningful connection.

When each role play is completed, the Supervisors should provide supportive feedback about the kind of Counselor interventions that seemed to be most productive in engaging this Client. The Client and Counselor can each talk about their feelings about being in these roles. Take a little time to talk about your general reactions to this experience and about whether it is the kind of counseling work that appeals to you.

child protective services are victims of drug or alcohol addiction and abuse. The majority of domestic violence, homicides, suicides, and incidents of sexual and physical child abuse are related to drug and alcohol abuse. A tremendous array of health problems, including emergency room visits, are drug or alcohol related, and the loss of economic productivity in our business sector has been calculated in the billions of dollars (Doweiko, 1999). In any classroom, a third to half of the students may be dealing with alcoholism and addiction in their home. Whatever counseling work you do, you will encounter drug and alcohol abuse.

Stigma and Denial

Drug and alcohol abuse and addiction is a tremendous problem, but it is often hidden and not obvious. Problems associated with addiction are stigmatized. Unlike other social or health problems, drug and alcohol addiction are seen as "bad," and the public generally has negative ideas about people with these problems, despite the fact that people with these problems come from all walks of life. This is one of the reasons people may be reluctant to come in for help, particularly when they have internalized these negative ideas, viewing themselves that way as well.

Another reason people resist getting help is that most clients deny the extent or seriousness of their drug or alcohol problems. Denial is characteristic of addiction. We all use psychological denial to protect our views of ourselves from the harsh realities of everyday life, but denial takes on a greater role in addiction. While everyone around the addicted person sees the wreckage caused by drinking or drugging, the addicted person refuses to acknowledge the extent of the problem. This denial may be incredibly entrenched, and the affected person's perspective typically runs counter to the obvious destruction others are observing.

Stigma and denial are two hallmarks of addiction problems, which make these issues difficult to treat. The combination of negative social judgment and a personal lack of acknowledgment of the severity of the problem conspire to keep someone who needs help away from treatment. Unfortunately, many people in the best position to help don't know what to do. There seems to be an inverse relationship between the extent of the addiction problem and the amount of training most professionals in counseling, psychology, and medicine receive to identify and successfully intervene with these problems. This is particularly unfortunate, given the fact that treatment works (van Wormer & Davis, 2003) and that there are tremendously satisfying opportunities for professionals to watch people recover and get well in this treatment arena.

Counselors need to know how to look for problems of addiction. You need to be able to ask the questions, sensitively but directly, that begin to flesh out the extent of a problem. If you don't look, if you don't ask the questions, you are complicit with the denial. The problems will continue, affecting not only the addict but also untold others.

In a real sense, all addictions counseling is a kind of crisis intervention. Although it does sometimes happen, most alcohol or drug abusers do not wake up one morning and declare, "Gee, I think I'll run down to the drug clinic to get some help today." These clients usually arrive at your door under some kind of duress. They are usually truly resistant clients, and they are almost always surrounded by an aura of crisis. You may, for example, have seen such a client one or more times before in either an individual or family counseling situation. And you may have encouraged the people close to the addicted client to precipitate some kind of intervention to help crack the barrier of denial. This may have taken the form of a direct, honest conversation, or perhaps a more formally planned family meeting where people talk about how the person's addiction or alcoholism has affected them. A crisis may have been brought about by a drunk-driving conviction, an accident, or an arrest. A judge may mandate treatment in lieu of jail time, or an employer may suggest counseling instead of being fired. There are any number of ways that a person with an addiction problem may come to you, and most of the time it is not because he is the primary one who thinks there is a problem.

Guidelines for Working with Addicted Clients

The addicted person sitting in your office most likely does not want to be there. She is most likely feeling a mixture of anger, humiliation, shame, and anxiety—and all of this translates into resistance. Much of what you do will be the same as for any resistant client, but you should be aware of some additional specific concerns:

- Physical safety comes first. If someone has been using alcohol or drugs for a significant period of time, he may need a safe, monitored way to physically withdraw. This usually involves a stay in a detoxification facility.

- Do not attempt any counseling activity with someone who is currently impaired. Set another time for this, ensuring to the best of your ability that in the interim the person will be safe.

- A number of helpful assessment tools can assist your efforts to work with someone who is trying to determine how much of a problem drugs or alcohol are in his life. These questionnaires make it possible for you and your client to mutually look at the extent of an abuse problem. Examples include the Michigan Alcoholism Screening Test (MAST; Selzer, 1971) and the Alcohol Use Inventory (AUI).

- There may be people in the addicted person's life who are at risk. Do what you can to ensure these people's safety (e.g., from physical abuse or risky driving situations).

- Do what you can to get an alcoholic or addicted client involved with Alcoholics Anonymous or Narcotics Anonymous. Try to get his significant others involved with one of these self-help organizations. Increase your familiarity with the workings of these organizations; they can be a tremendous asset for the person in an addictive crisis. If you've never been to an AA or NA meeting, attend an open speaker meeting to see what it is like. Do what you can to get the client involved with a residential or outpatient (sometimes intensive) program. Become conversant with options in your community, and develop good relationships with people who work in those facilities so that you can make referrals smoothly and efficiently.

- Be prepared to field lots of reasons this client believes she cannot seek appropriate treatment. These defensive maneuverings will include child-care issues, work commitments, and insurance reimbursement issues. All of these can be very real concerns. Your job is to anticipate them and try to consider viable ways to manage them. This may include, for example, helping to find decent child care for the time that someone is in treatment and affordable treatment options.

- If someone tells you he acknowledges a problem but wants to simply stop using without outside help, negotiate some way of monitoring this commitment as part of your contracting process. This may include the use of breathalyzers or urinalysis. You can assure someone that this is not a matter of personal trust, simply acknowledgment of the insidiousness of addiction.

You are not in a position of having to decide the degree of problem someone has with drugs or alcohol. You need never even use the words *addict* or *alcoholic*. This really can be a mutual assessment process, using the tools just mentioned to help you and your client talk about this. You can, however, trust the fact that this person will invariably underreport his use (a general rule of thumb is to double what they tell you) and try to minimize the problem.

Creating the Alliance

The biggest challenge you will confront in working with a chemically dependent client is shifting the client's thinking away from a "me-against-him" mentality and toward a "me-and-him-against-the-abuse-problem" mentality. This is not easy. It is akin to working with two entities in your office: the person and the addiction. The trick is to gain the allegiance of the person, siding with that part of him that knows there is a problem, against the addiction.

The assessment of the extent of the problem with drugs or alcohol is directly related to the kinds of problems (health, relationships, legal troubles) associated with use. The number and severity of related problems are a tip-off to the extent of the alcohol or drug problem. There are other simple ways to find out if there is an abuse problem. You can, for example, suggest that the client not use at all for a couple of months, just to see if there is a problem. If this person considers that a ludicrous suggestion, you now have an idea that there's probably significant dependency. Even if the suggestion is accepted, much may subsequently be revealed by the client's efforts to follow through on it.

Stay current regarding the range and availability of local treatment options, and maintain solid working relationships with people in those facilities so you can get quick help for the addicted client. Treatment that is delayed, for whatever reason, often results in treatment that never happens (van Wormer & Davis, 2003).

Motivational Interviewing

If you work a lot with resistant, chemically dependent clients, you may find motivational interviewing (MI) strategies to be helpful. MI principles and essential tenets are congruent with what has been said about working with resistance

Case Example 12.1   *Counseling Work with a Resistant, Addicted Client*

This client has been referred to a drug clinic by his probation officer (PO). The officer believes that part of the reason this man was convicted of breaking and entering had to do with his needing money to buy drugs. The man can have his sentenced reduced by participating in this outpatient treatment. This is his first visit to the clinic.

CLIENT: *[Comes into the room, says nothing, sits down.]*

COUNSELOR: Hi, Tom. My name's Sally. Tell me a little bit about what brings you in here.

Simple prompt.

CLIENT: *[Looks down, around, avoids eye contact. Sits quietly for a minute or two.]* I guess you know why I'm here. My PO (probation officer) told me I had a choice. Come here or go to jail. Some choice.

While the counselor is prepared to be quite active in this session, here she waits for the client to respond to the initial prompt, avoiding the temptation to jump into the silence too quickly. If the silence had gone on much longer, the counselor would have acted, probably with some kind of reflection about the silence.

COUNSELOR: Well, the fact that this is a drug clinic suggests your PO thinks there might be some kind of drug problem mixed up in this.

CLIENT: Look. I just want to do my time. I can do it here, or I can do it in jail. It's shorter if I do it here, so that's the deal. I think this is stupid. I don't need counseling.

COUNSELOR: So, it seems logical that you'd choose this option. *[Sits silently for a minute.]* But now that you're here, I'm wondering what I can do for you, what we can do together.

She ignores the slam on counseling and reflects on the content of what the client has said. The next comment, this "wondering aloud," suggests mutuality in doing something together. This will be done with him, not to him.

CLIENT: What do you mean?

COUNSELOR: Well, the note I have says that you've got to come here for ten sessions or your probation gets violated. She wants a statement from me that you've filled that commitment. Is that right?

Simply states the basic ground rules as articulated by the probation officer.

CLIENT: Yeah, except she told me I had to come for twelve sessions.

(continued)

(Case example 12.1, continued)

COUNSELOR: OK. Twelve sessions. So, given that you do that, that we meet for an hour a week for the next twelve weeks, what're we going to do?

Here the counselor eases into the assumption that they will continue together for twelve weeks. Subtly directive.

CLIENT: You got me. Like I said, this wasn't my idea.

COUNSELOR: Well, sometimes I talk with people about personal issues, you know, like families or lovers or whatever. Or maybe about work— were you working before you got busted? Are you looking for work? I've got no idea about your situation. Or sometimes people just want to talk about what's gone on in their week.

If we're going to spend an hour a week together, it'd be nice to have some focus, some things to do together, and you should be the one to choose what that is.

The counselor is tossing out a smorgasbord of ideas, like a brainstorming of possibilities, hoping he'll latch onto one or more of these. She knows he's not comfortable here and wants to give him something concrete to hang onto. At the back of her mind, always, is the issue of drugs, the primary reason he's been sent to her, yet she knows if she leads too quickly with this, there may be an immediate defensive reaction.

CLIENT: I worked as a welder. I'm sure I'm fired now, but I haven't talked to my boss. Who knows what's up with that. I do want to get back to work. I've got to.

COUNSELOR: OK. So work is an item of concern. What else? How else can we spend our time here?

Reflection of content, followed by engagement questions.

CLIENT: Well, there's my wife. And my kid. I haven't seen them in a while. I guess maybe I'd like to see them again.

COUNSELOR: Work and your family. There could be a lot there. I'd like to hear more specifics about all of that, and that sounds like good stuff for us to do. To talk about that, I mean. Naturally, we'll also need to talk about how drugs fit into all this.

More reflection of content.

CLIENT: What do you mean, "fit into all of this?"

COUNSELOR: Your probation officer sent you to me, a drug counselor. She must've thought there is some kind of drug issue. I honestly don't know what's going on. Maybe drugs had something to do with you winding up in jail. If so, I can help you with that. I can also help you deal with her. I'll tell her that you're coming for

Now she slides in the idea about making discussion of drug use part of the package, assuming that he's already been hooked into coming back. Again, an assumption of mutuality. Even in the assessment of drug use, he is to be an equal partner in the discrimination of the extent of the problem.

(continued)

(Case example 12.1, continued)

appointments, and you can use the time in here to talk about your family, getting work, and whatever else seems important.

CLIENT: Yeah, that sounds OK.

COUNSELOR: And we will have to take a look, together, at whether you think you should do anything about drugs. That's got to be a part of the package.

CLIENT: I'm supposed to get a sign-off from you every time I come here.

COUNSELOR: So, we've got a deal? If so, let's get rolling.

CLIENT: Yeah, I guess so. But do you mind if we make it a half hour today? I've got an appointment downtown.

COUNSELOR: Terrific. I'll look forward to getting to know you. I'll be happy to do the signoffs. And no, a half hour won't cut it. We're agreeing to an hour a week, and it's my obligation that we stick to that. So, tell me how you wound up in jail.

Responds with support for his agreement to participate but holds firm to the basic time commitment. She knows that this client may try to push the limits of that commitment. Simple, directive prompt.

Case Discussion

A lot has happened in this brief beginning part of the session with this reluctant client. There is a sense that a basic engagement has transpired, that a deal has been struck to continue to work together. The counselor has provided enough information and structure about what can be done here to allay the client's anxiety about how to be a client, yet in a way that conveys the sense that he'll be in control of what gets talked about—as long as drug issues are a part of the package.

The focus here is concrete and reality-based on jobs and family, language that the client understands. The counselor will also explore what led up to getting arrested and the specifics of his legal involvement. Clients who become involved with the correctional system often have

a limited idea about how their own actions led to their being arrested. A victim mentality ("the cops busted me") can be gently confronted through careful examination of the actions-consequences sequence of events.

Some of the counselor's job, particularly initially, is to explain the process of counseling and to negotiate the specifics of working together, but there is also ample time here to be reflective, using a combination of engagement and fact-finding questions and reflection of content statements. There is in this a combination of education and active listening. The counselor tries to strike a balance by providing enough activity on her part to allay the anxiety of the unknown while providing the client with room for exploration.

in this chapter. While this set of counseling skills was originally articulated in the mid-1980s to work specifically with addicted, resistant clients, it has also been successfully utilized with other kinds of clients in a variety of settings (Bothelo & Novak, 1993; Easton, Swan, & Sinha, 2000; Hohman, 1998). Many agencies that work with reluctant clients now routinely require new staff to undergo MI training.

This set of counseling techniques focuses on resistance and the ambivalence to change self-destructive behaviors as the central reason for counseling. Its founder, William Miller, calls MI "a directive, client-centered counseling style for eliciting behavior change by helping clients to explore and resolve ambivalence" (Rollnick & Miller, 1995). A great deal of time and energy is spent helping clients to examine the nature of their ambivalence to change, and that examination relies heavily on the kinds of relationship-building skills talked about in this book (e.g., reflections of content and feeling, instillation of hope, and examination of emotional payoffs and debits). In particular, MI encourages an approach to resistance that is nondefensive and nonargumentative. A basic assumption of this approach is that unless the client's ambivalence to change destructive behaviors is successfully worked through, any immediate changes made by that client will be temporary.

Considerable time is spent in helping the client to see how he can move toward goals that are personally rewarding. The client is encouraged to examine past ambivalence to change and to look at how the development of personal goals can aid a process of behavioral change. An important tenet of MI is the belief that the motivation for change can only be mobilized by the client. External pressures are not seen as being effective. The counselor's central task is to help the client look at and resolve his ambivalence.

Miller maintains that much of the resistance encountered in chemically dependent clients is engendered by the counseling process itself. If we counselors can provide a truly empathic environment, where respect and regard prevail, then our clients will not feel the need to mobilize so much defensiveness. When clients feel respected, they will be able to let down their resistant guard. This, then, sets the stage for trying on new behaviors, including reduction in drug use. You are encouraged to check the MI website (www.motivationalinterview.org) for information about this intriguing counseling approach, as well as for information about related readings, research, and training.

Seriously, Persistently Mentally Ill Clients

Over the last three decades, most people who would have been committed to large psychiatric hospitals in the past have been moved to smaller community care facilities. They now live with their own families or in supervised group home settings or in some other private care setting. The discovery of drugs that are more sophisticated at controlling symptoms (e.g., auditory or visual hallucinations or anxiety) has made much of this possible. A complex system of community mental health services has grown up to meet the demand of caring for these people in their own communities. The large hospitals have closed or now house only the most dangerous (to self or others) mentally ill.

Similarly, public schools now mainstream many students who in years past would have been institutionalized. Legislative action, much of it brought about by parent advocates, has brought children with serious challenges into the everyday classroom. Again, more sophisticated (sometimes controversial) uses of medication and paraprofessional aides have made this possible.

All of this suggests that the counselor in an agency or school setting needs to be prepared to deal with people with serious mental health problems. These problems will not be resolved, or cured, with a few sessions of counseling, and notions of "successful" outcomes need to be tempered to reflect the realities of the seriousness of the challenges faced by these clients. Some of these clients have serious mental health challenges, as with schizophrenia or so-called borderline conditions. These conditions, according to the DSM-IV (American Psychiatric Association, 2000), are characterized by unstable and intense interpersonal relationships, self-damaging impulsivity, and recurring self-destructive behavior. Some of these clients may have developmental challenges and have only limited verbal skills, and others may have a complicated mix of physical and mental health problems.

Usually the focus here is on promotion of basic functioning, perhaps a restoration (rehabilitation) of the ability to work, to be minimally self-supporting, or to function in a classroom. This can be a real challenge, particularly in communities where there are few services or in rural areas where geography and travel present major obstacles to getting effective help. It can be an even greater challenge when working with clients who have multiple problems, such as substance abuse problems mixed with persistent mental illness (Drake & Noordsy, 1994).

As in any counseling, the goal is to help the client to become as personally effective and responsible as possible. The counselor who works with clients with such multiple challenges, either in a school or in an agency, is like the orchestra's conductor. He pulls together all of the services in a client's community in a way that gets the client the help that is needed.

Case Management as a Primary Counseling Strategy

In our discussion of crisis intervention, we talked about key ways counselors can coordinate and access services for clients. These same strategies apply for counselors searching out services for their chronic care caseload.

Much of the work that needs to happen with these clients is not typically referred to as counseling, and counselors do not typically receive a lot of training in the kinds of tasks that need to be handled. Much of the work done by counselors falls under what would most appropriately be called "case management," which refers to managing and coordinating all of those tasks and services that are necessary in making your client's life easier.

A counselor's essential task here is to create cost-effective ways of helping people to maintain stability in their everyday lives. Typically, this includes working as part of a team (Baier, 1987) to provide assistance in helping to create healthy interpersonal social support systems, monitoring medications (and other substance use), and arranging a supportive living environment (McClellan, 1998; Pratt, Gill, Barrett, & Roberts, 1999). You may have to help find housing or employment, or help to negotiate appointments with a variety of service providers who can help your clients with particular issues they confront. Much of the talent and skill of this work involves being able to juggle a number of complicated scheduling tasks simultaneously and nurturing relationships with professionals in other agencies and schools.

Case Management and Advocacy

Much of this teamwork in working with the chronically mentally ill client (and many other clients) also involves becoming an effective advocate for your client (Rose, 1991). More attention in our field is now being paid to this aspect of the work (Kiselica & Robinson, 2001). This may mean trying to promote a special service for this client (Jenkins & Einzig, 1996) or bringing a unique perspective to bear on a problem with which a treatment team is grappling. You may, for example, be the person in the group with specialized expertise in one area, such as eating disorders or developmental disabilities, putting you in the best position to talk about the needs of clients with those presenting concerns. As a counselor, you have an opportunity to act as a voice in support of the personal and social needs of your client (Linz, McAnally, & Wieck, 1989). Other people may be advocating for other things, including saving money. Your job is to access the best level of service for this person that is possible, given fixed or limited resources. Your clients deserve the best services you can negotiate for them.

Many times, advocacy takes the form of community education, some of which promotes the kind of work you do with your clients (Tysl, 1997) and some of which is designed to inform the community about the special needs of your clients. Many people are ill informed and afraid of people with chronic mental disorders. The medications that people take sometimes give them particular physical movements or symptoms that can be frightening to people who have had little exposure to these behaviors. Your job here is to educate the public about the realities of mental illness and the benefits of having people with these challenges in our communities and in our children's classrooms. We all benefit from the successful integration of these people among us. Not only do they help us to become more compassionate in our dealings with others, they also serve to remind us of how we would wish our own particular challenges would be received by others. Beyond the benefit they may provide us, however, our clients simply have a right to be among us. The effective counselor advocates for services for those clients who are unable to advocate effectively for themselves. Advocating for people who do not need your advocacy, or undercutting their ability to advocate for themselves, is a disempowering disservice.

The counselor who plays a truly effective advocacy role eventually sees that there are forces greater than those taking place in the immediate community that shape policy and resources. If you wish to influence the decision making that affects those policies, you'll take your advocacy to the next level of action and become politically involved to try to affect change (McClure & Russo, 1996). This may take the form of sitting on local committees or on boards and commissions that directly enact policy decisions. You may decide that the best recourse is to become involved in electoral politics, where advocacy for your clientele can take on legislative enactment proportions.

Whatever level of political advocacy engagement you choose, it does behoove you to become involved in the larger spectrum of events and decision making that affect your clients. While your clients, particularly those most vulnerable, certainly have personal and psychological challenges, they are also confronted by larger political realities that directly affect them. You can help make sure that those political decisions are made as humanely and fairly as possible.

Counseling Children and Adolescents

When my wife (a school counselor) and I first settled down in Vermont, nearly thirty years ago, we had the pleasure of doing some teaching together for the local community college. Our first course was Child Psychology, and despite the fact that we did not yet have children of our own, we thought we had enough experience with developmental and learning theory to make the course worthwhile. We had also spent some significant time working with troubled children and adolescents in residential settings. Our students in that class turned out to be a group of single mothers. It was a humbling, eye-opening experience. We had the book experience, but they had significantly more hands-on experience. We all learned from each other. As in this situation we encountered, your growing personal experience, coupled with your theoretical knowledge, will serve you well in your work with children.

Working as a counselor with children, including adolescents, presents some special challenges. Foremost among those challenges for many counselors is a lack of sufficient training (Hollis, 1997). Many counseling theories are not particularly applicable to work with children, at least in terms of recommended techniques, and younger children may not even have the language skills to do what we traditionally call counseling. Remember, these are the Level 1 clients for whom immaturity, dependency, inability to handle abstractions, and lack of responsibility are developmentally appropriate!

If you work with children, you will need to find creative ways of adapting your communication style to their needs. Certainly, many of the relationship-building skills (e.g., engagement questions and reflections of content and feeling) and action skills (e.g., examination of action-consequence sequences) will serve you well in your work with children and adolescents. Working with children, however, may demand more spontaneity and more transparency than working with adults. Because children are typically less guarded and less defended than adults (unless there has been significant abuse or trauma), they will respond to those times when you, too, act in a less guarded fashion. You will need to find a bridge between what is written about working with children and what practical experience teaches you. Learning alongside supervisors is a great source of this firsthand knowledge. Inevitably, you will have to try things on your own, make your own discoveries and mistakes.

Foremost, it helps a lot if you enjoy children. I know more than a few counselors (and teachers) who work with children, particularly those who work with adolescents, who really don't seem to like them much. They seem wary and suspicious or even afraid of their charges. Young people, particularly adolescents, have built-in radar that can detect such wariness and outright dislike (Hemingway called these intuitive capabilities "crap detectors"). One wonders if any good work can happen in the context of such feeling, and I can't help but wish that these people would find another line of work or at least find some way of adjusting their thinking. Working with children can be wonderfully rewarding. They are typically more spontaneous than their adult counterparts, and they can warm quickly to a supportive, interested adult.

Sometimes there has been abuse and neglect, however, and these youngsters can be particularly challenging. Children raised in violent, aggressive homes toughen up at an early age. A school counselor friend recounts meeting a five-year-old in her school, a boy of kindergarten age, who walked into her office, slammed the door shut, and proclaimed, "Why'd you get me in here? I'm going to kick you're a—." We can only imagine what difficulties this little guy had already encountered.

This kind of troubled child can make for disturbing work. One of our graduate students recently confided that she was having second thoughts about becoming an elementary school counselor because of the troubled lives of so many of the children in the school where she was interning. In her school one of the children had recently committed suicide, and the entire community was reeling in the aftermath. It was a deeply disturbing event, made no easier by virtue of the fact that so many people saw the possibility of this coming. "I thought I was going to be dealing with career investigation and interpersonal problems and family issues, but this is way more than I bargained for," she said.

"I don't know if I've got the stomach for it." It can be extremely difficult to acknowledge the pain and emotional darkness experienced by many of the children with whom we work. We like to think of childhood as an easy, carefree time, and we may live in comfortable denial of the pain that so many children experience (Klein, 1975).

Skills for Working with Children and Adolescents

The usual skills and techniques for counseling adults do not translate easily into work with children. The lack of developed language and cognitive skills may render many of the techniques typically associated with counseling ineffective, at least for some children. There have been significant efforts to adapt traditional counseling theory to work with children (Thompson & Rudolph, 1992), and counselors who want to be able to verbally relate to children, as well as to understand a child developmentally in the context of a particular theoretical approach, would be well served to study these adaptations (Landreth, 2002; Landreth, Baggerly, & Tyndall-Lind, 1999).

Throughout this book you have read about the importance of employing a developmental approach to working with adults. Thinking developmentally should be a paramount concern in working with all of your clients, including children (Ivey, 1992, 2000/1986; Ivey & Ivey, 1998; Myers, Shoffner & Briggs, 2002). Much of this developmental thinking in work with children is based on Piaget's (1963/1952) models of cognitive development. Quite simply it means that the ways we talk with young people and the things we do with them need to be matched to their ability to comprehend, and the counseling interventions we employ must be matched to the child's needs and level of functioning.

Instead of trying to make children into little adults—which is what those using adult counseling models attempt to do—effective counselors seeks unique, new ways of working with young clients (Landreth, 1983; Landreth, Baggerly, & Tyndall-Lind, 1999). One surefire way to skirt the language gap with children is to employ ways of working with them that are less verbal. Counselors who work with children under the age of seven or eight rely heavily on play and art as a means of helping boys and girls express themselves.

Many of the expressive arts approaches to counseling, such as those described in Chapter 11, are easily adaptable for work with children and adolescents. Play therapy engages a child in the counseling process by providing a means for children to express themselves creatively. Play allows children to use their natural energy in ways that trying to sit and talk with them would not. There is, for example, something that helps to engage one's head, even for older children and adults, if one's hands are doing something. I know a school counselor who, as a matter of course, passes out pieces of sculpi (synthetic clay) for children to manipulate in their hands as she starts any group discussion.

Play, or some kind of activity that does not directly involved talking, provides many avenues to access children's inner ideas, fantasies, and feelings. Playing alongside children can allow for conversation about the nature of the play and the meaning of what transpires. This kind of play, structured in a way that will allow for some interpretation of the actual events and thoughts of a child's life, can be extremely helpful in giving a child the means to express things that he has no language for. Sometimes this expression provides clues as to real difficulties in the child's home, such as abuse or drug addiction.

Play therapy has been used widely with children in all kinds of settings. It is used with "well" children and with children who have significant problems. Play therapy can be used with children in school settings (Ray, Muro, & Schumann; 2004) and with children who have experienced trauma and abuse (Lantz & Raiz, 2003). It has also been adapted for use with adolescents, particularly specialized play therapy techniques. Sandplay, for example, allows the child the freedom to create representations of his world using miniature figures in trays of sand, increasing the possibilities for expressing and sharing thoughts and feelings about his life (Draper, Ritter, & Willingham, 2003).

Helpful resources for counselors interested in pursuing more information about play therapy and other play-oriented ways of working with children include Axline (1947), Bettelheim (1987), Landreth (2002), Moustakas (1953), and Schaeffer (1985, 1993). Some approaches to play therapy reflect specific theoretical orientations (Jones, Casado, & Robinson, 2003; Kottman, 2003), thus allowing the counselor to use techniques that best fit his theoretical style.

Guidelines for Working with Children and Adolescents

As you work with children and adolescents, choose techniques that fit your personal style and that are appropriate for the children with whom you work. If you can choose activities that have been shown by research to be effective for certain children in specific situations, so much the better (Russ, 2004). The following guidelines may aid you in your work with these special populations:

- Keep it short and simple. The younger the child, the shorter the session: 20 minutes, tops, for younger children and an hour maximum for younger adolescents.

- The play or art that is used should be planned carefully for a specific purpose. The goal behind the play should be therapeutic, not play for its own sake. Care should be taken in working with at-risk children to ensure that play activities are appropriate and do not serve to retraumatize them (Jones, 2002; Jones, Casado, & Robinson, 2003).

- Groups are a wonderful way to work with children and adolescents. They will talk with each other about things, even with an adult present, that they will not share with an adult alone. Sitting in an office and trying to talk with a twelve-year-old boy can leave a counselor feeling like she's attempting communication with a rock. But put a few boys in there with him, and maybe add an activity, and the energy level—and talking—skyrockets.

- Be real. Remember those "crap detectors," and allow yourself to be even a bit more spontaneous than usual when counseling adolescents and children. They will know if you're honest with them.

- Have fun with the activities you plan. If it's fun for you, it'll probably be fun for the youngsters as well.

- Think of yourself as a mentor. Promote a little anxiety in your relationships with adolescents, especially the anxiety fostered by appropriately high expectations that creates positive energy in the relationship. Too much anxiety may cause adolescents to become defensive and shut down; too little and they may become bored.

- Find other mentors (coaches, teachers, community adults) for children who don't have healthy adults in their lives. Children become productive, happy adults by way of their engagement with compelling interests and solid connections with positive adult role models. Help make those connections happen.

- Try not to be put off by repugnant behavior. Somewhere within each child is a deep yearning for emotional engagement and a need to be heard.

Anyone who works with children is inextricably tied to working with their parents and guardians as well. You will always need their permission to work with their children (except in work with adolescents dealing with adult issues, such as drug abuse and pregnancy, where confidentiality guidelines apply), and you should typically view yourself as a parental ally in helping the child. Knowledge of agency and school parental permission-for-service policies is an essential aspect of this counseling work.

Sometimes you may want to engage parents directly, particularly if the child is acting out problems that are indicative of family problems. Treating the child alone misses the greater opportunity to work with the family system as a whole. This is not always easy, particularly with parents who may have significant problems of their own. I distinctly remember the frustrations of trying to get some parents to acknowledge and participate in the treatment of their drug-abusing children. The parents would drop the child off at the clinic door with the implicit message of "fix him." It wasn't easy, but part of my job was to try to slow them up, draw them inside, and help them see that their child couldn't be "fixed" without their help.

Working with children and adolescents requires a distinct set of skills and its own knowledge base. If you are pursuing a school counseling program, your training program likely offers the necessary course work. If you are in a community or mental health program and you plan to spend significant work time with children, it is incumbent on you to take as much child-specific course work as you can, both within the master's program and afterwards as part of your continuing professional education. Find the right supervisor. If you plan to work with children as well as adults, you may be best served by having two supervisors, one for each area. Finally, when you work with children, be creative. Experiment. Have fun. Remember your own childhood. With a little luck, this kind of work will help to keep you young.

REFLECTION EXERCISE 12.2   Working with Children

This is an opportunity to pause and reflect on your experience and feelings about working with children and adolescents. When you have a few minutes to yourself, consider the nature and kinds of exposure you have had to young children. Have these been primarily personal or professional? Have you generally enjoyed this contact, and do you typically enjoy being around children? What about adolescents? What strengths might you bring to work with children and adolescents?

If you've only had minimal contact with children and adolescents, consider finding a way to increase this exposure, particularly if work with this population is something you are considering. You may be planning on working with children in a mental health setting or as a school counselor and yet have had little working contact with children. Arrange some kind of sanctioned work, perhaps as a volunteer, in a school or social services agency to find out more about your reactions to children, consider becoming a mentor for a young person, or help to coach a youth sports team.

Reflect on your own childhood experiences with adults. Some of those were probably more nurturing and supportive than others. Which of those relationships with adults stand out in your memory as having had the most impact? What was it about those people and the ways they interacted with you that were so important? What kinds of roles did these adults have with you? Were any of these people counselors? Did you ever have the opportunity to work with a counselor, or would it have occurred to you to talk with an adult about personal concerns?

Write about your thoughts, feelings, and reactions to considering this kind of counseling work. If and when you feel comfortable, discuss this with a small group of colleagues. If you are open to suggestion, they may have constructive ideas about how you might continue this exploration.

Concluding Thoughts: Every Client Is a Challenge

All clients are challenging, and each person presents the counselor with particular difficulties. All clients, to varying degrees and in varying ways, resist counselor interventions that promote change. Some of our clients are flat-out difficult. They work at being difficult. Others are difficult because they can't help themselves. Sometimes our clients are resistant because of things we do, or do not do, because we are unable to be accepting or empathic with that client.

It is our job to field all of these challenges and to view each challenge as a potential vehicle for change and growth. This potential exists not only for our clients but for ourselves as well. The more we are able to view our clients' challenges and resistance as similar to our own, the better able we will be to help them and to grow ourselves. The more we are able to see their resistance as growing out of their fear of vulnerability and exposure, and the more we are able to separate their fears from our own, the better we will be able to respond.

Learning about specific client problems and disorders and appropriate intervention strategies is an ongoing process that includes both personal experience and keeping up with developing theory and research. The real struggle for the astute counselor, however, is to view each client as a fresh, new person, without bias and preconception. Avoid stereotyping your clients by virtue of their presenting problems, and do all you can to avoid stigmatizing them further by the sloppy use of diagnostic labels or other kinds of pigeonholing. Assessment and diagnostic strategies can be useful tools, but not if they serve to dehumanize.

It is an interesting juggling act: having a storehouse of knowledge about particular problems and pathologies and simultaneously having the willingness to suspend that knowledge in the face of the actual person sitting across from you. You want your knowledge to serve your understanding of your client's dilemma, but not at the expense of the particular wisdom you gather from your direct experience of the person. It is this combination of knowledge learned from books and course work and your direct intuitive experience of your clients that makes the experience of counseling both a science and an art.

For Further Thought

1. Interview counselors who work with specific populations (e.g., children, addicts) and ask them about the joys and frustrations of the work they do. Are there general ideas or tips they can pass on to you about working with these clients? What impressions are you left with as you contemplate their work?

2. Consider what kinds of special populations you might be drawn to in your counseling work. What is the appeal, and what do you anticipate you might learn—either in terms of skills or about yourself—from work with these people? What special skills or training will you need to consider doing this work?

3. Pick one of these special populations and begin to investigate the literature to see how these clients and treatment strategies for them are described. What are your impressions of these descriptions?

4. Part of your role as a counselor, some would maintain, is to become involved in the larger social policy issues that affect many of our clients' lives. What is the appropriate advocacy role of the counselor in these larger social issues? More personally, how do you envision your own role as an advocate? Consider interviewing some counselor advocates in your area about their perspective on this as well.

References

American Psychiatric Association. (2000). *Diagnostic and statistical manual of mental disorders* (4th. ed., text revision). Washington, DC: Author.

Axline, V. (1947). *Play therapy*. Boston: Houghton Mifflin.

Baier, M. (1987). Case management with the seriously mentally ill. *Journal of Psychosocial Nursing and Mental Health Services, 25*(6), 17–20.

Bettelheim, B. (1987). The importance of play. *The Atlantic Monthly, 259,* 35–46.

Botelho, R., & Novak, S. (1993). Dealing with substance misuse, abuse, and dependency. *Primary Care, 20*(1), 51–71.

Chung, R., & Bernak, F. (2002). The relationship of culture and empathy in cross-cultural counseling. *Journal of Counseling and Development, 80*(2), 154–159.

Davis, D., & Boster, L. (1992). Cognitive-behavioral-expressive interventions with aggressive and resistant youths. *Child Welfare, 71*(6), 557–573.

Doweiko, H. (1999). *Concepts of chemical dependency*. Pacific Grove, CA: Brooks/Cole.

Drake, R., & Noordsy, D. (1994). Case management for people with coexisting severe mental disorder and substance abuse disorder. *Psychiatric Annals, 24*(8), 427–431.

Draper, K., Ritter, K., & Willingham, E. (2003). Sand tray group counseling with adolescents. *Journal for Specialists in Group Work, 28*(3), 244–260.

Easton, C., Swan, S., & Sinha, R. (2000). Motivation to change substance use among offenders of domestic violence. *Journal of Substance Abuse Treatment, 19,* 1–5.

Hanna, F. (1996). Precursors of change: Pivotal points of involvement and resistance in psychotherapy. *Journal of Psychotherapy Integration, 6*(3), 227–264.

Hohman, M. (1998). Motivational interviewing: An intervention tool for child welfare case workers working with substance abusing parents. *Child Welfare, 127*(3), 275–289.

Hollis, J. (1997). *Counselor preparation* (9th ed.). Muncie, IN: Accelerated Development.

Ivey, A. (1992). Developmental strategies for helpers: Individual, family, and network interventions. North Amherst, MA: Microtraining Associates.

Ivey, A. (2000). *Developmental therapy*. San Francisco, CA: Jossey Bass. [Originally published in 1986]

Ivey, M. B., & Ivey, A. (1988). *Structuring an interview in elementary school counseling*. Amherst, MA: Microtraining Associates.

Jenkins, G., & Einzig, H. (1996). Counselling in primary care. In R. Bayne, I. Horton, & J. Bimrose (Eds.), *New directions in counseling* (pp. 97–108). London: Routledge.

Jones, K. (2002). Group play therapy with sexually abused preschool children: Group behaviors and interventions. *Journal for Specialists in Group Work, 27*(4), 377–389.

Jones, K., Casado, M., & Robinson, E. (2003). Structured play therapy: A model for choosing topics and activities. *International Journal of Play Therapy, 12*(1), 31–45.

Kiselica, M., & Robinson, M. (2001). Bringing advocacy counseling to life: The history, issues, and human dramas of social justice working in counseling. *Journal of Counseling and Development, 79,* 387–397.

Klein, C. (1975). *The myth of the happy child*. New York: Harper & Row.

Kottman, T. (2003). *Partners in play: An Adlerian approach to play therapy*. Alexandria, VA: American Counseling Association.

Landreth, G. (1983). Play therapy in elementary school settings. In C. E. Schaeffer & K. J. O'Connor (Eds.), *Handbook of play therapy* (200–212). New York: Wiley

Landreth, G. (2002). *Play therapy: The art of the relationship* (2nd ed.). New York: Brunner-Routledge.

Landreth, G., Baggerly, J., & Tyndall-Lind, A. (1999). Beyond adapting adult counseling skills for use with children: The paradigm shift to child-centered play therapy. *Journal of Individual Psychology, 55*(3), 272–287.

Lantz, J., & Raiz, L. (2003). Play and art in existential trauma therapy with children and their parents. *Contemporary Family Therapy: An International Journal, 25*(2), 165–177.

Linz, M., McAnally, P., & Wieck, C. (Ed.). (1989). *Case management: Historical, current, and future perspectives*. Cambridge, MA: Brookline Books.

McClellan, K. (1998). Managing care for the seriously and persistently mentally ill. *Employee Assistance Quarterly, 13*(4), 23–32.

McClure, B., & Russo, T. (1996). The politics of counseling: Looking back and looking forward. *Counseling and Values, 40,* 162–174.

Moustakas, C. (1953). *Children in play therapy*. New York: McGraw-Hill.

Myers, J., Shoffner, M., & Briggs, M. (2002). Developmental counseling and therapy: An effective approach to understanding and counseling. *Professional School Counseling, 5*(3), 194–203.

Otani, A. (1989). Client resistance in counseling: Its theoretical rationale and taxonomic classification. *Journal of Counseling and Development, 67,* 458–461.

Parham, T., White, J., & Ajamu, A. (1999). *The psychology of Blacks: An African centered perspective*. Upper Saddle River, NJ: Prentice-Hall.

Piaget, J. (1963). *The origins of intelligence in children.* New York: Norton. [Original work published in 1952]

Pinta, E., & Davis, D. (1987). *Interventions with violent patients.* Columbus: Department of Psychiatry, The Ohio State University.

Pratt, C., Gill, K., Barrett, N., & Roberts, M. (1999). *Psychiatric rehabilitation.* San Diego, CA: Academic Press.

Rasmussen, P. (2002). Resistance: The fear behind it and tactics for reducing it. *Journal of Individual Psychology, 58*(2), 148–159.

Ray, D., Muro, J., & Schumann, B. (2004). Implementing play therapy in the schools: Lessons learned. *International Journal of Play Therapy, 13*(1), 79–100.

Rollnick, S., & Miller, W. (1995). Motivational interviewing: Resources for clinicians, researchers, and trainers. Retrieved December 29, 2005, from http://www. motivationalinterview.org.

Rose, S. (1991). Strategies of mental health programming: A client-driven model of case management. In C. Hudson & A. Cox (Eds.), *Dimensions of state mental health policy* (pp. 138–154). New York: Praeger.

Russ, S. (2004). *Play in child development and psychotherapy: Toward empirically supported practice.* Mahwah, NJ: Erlbaum.

Schaeffer, C. (1985). Play therapy. *Early Child Development and Care, 19*(2), 95–108.

Schaeffer, C. (Ed.). (1993). *The therapeutic powers of play.* Northvale, NJ: Jason Aronson.

Selzer, M. (1971). The Michigan Alcoholism Screening Test: The quest for a new diagnostic instrument. *American Journal of Psychiatry, 127,* 1653–1658.

Shulman, G. (1995). Reorienting CD treatment for dual diagnosis. *Behavioral Health Management,* September/October, 30–33.

Sue, D. W., & Sue, D. (1999). *Counseling the culturally different: Theory and practice* (3rd ed.). New York: Wiley.

Thompson, C., & Rudolph, L. (1992). *Counseling children.* Pacific Grove, CA: Brooks/Cole.

Tysl, L. (1997, January). Counselors have a responsibility to promote the counseling profession. *Counseling Today,* 16.

van Wormer, K., & Davis, D. (2003). *Addiction treatment: A strengths perspective.* Pacific Grove, CA: Brooks/Cole.

Skills for Ending

Any real change implies the breakup of the world as one has
always known it, the loss of all that gave one an identity,
the end of safety.
(James Baldwin)

I have been a witness to at least twenty college graduations and to quite a few high school ones as well. Much of my attention at these events is focused on graduating master's degree students in our counseling program, but it's also been a genuine pleasure to watch students get their bachelor's degrees after four, five, or sometimes uncomfortably (at least for the parents) more years of work in our undergraduate psychology program. I've taken care to observe the new graduates participating in these events, and some of the same themes repeat themselves. Once the ceremony has concluded, the graduates gather on the lawn with their freshly minted degrees in hand to hug and congratulate each other. Occasionally old memories and stories are swapped, and relatives are introduced. Eventually, for all but the best of friends, there then comes the time to head out in separate directions. A few final hugs are given, best wishes are exchanged, and the commitment is made to "stay in touch." Then they drift off.

At this point I sometimes wonder what would happen if, instead of promising to remain in contact, which seems only a remote possibility, they wished each other wonderful lives, thanked each other for the memories, said goodbye, and walked away. This would probably be a more honest and realistic departure, but there seems to be a studied refusal to accept such finality. So they drift apart, offering up the noncommittal "Stay in touch" and other clichés related to saying goodbye, such as "Take care of yourself" and "Don't take any wooden nickels."

None of us likes saying goodbye. Generally, we don't like endings. Yet the realities of life fly in the face of our dislike. Every relationship is defined by a beginning and an ending. No matter how wonderful the time spent together has been, it nevertheless must at some point be finished. The most spectacularly successful marriages and friendships must sometime conclude. Eventually we all must say the last goodbye, to life itself.

Counseling relationships must end too. In the language of the counseling profession, these endings are often referred to as "terminations," but this is a word that can carry significant negative imagery. I prefer to call this part of the counseling process simply "ending." Counseling relationships are *designed* to end; indeed, they become problematic when they outlive their usefulness. The central question for counselors is how to orchestrate these endings in a way that is meaningful, primarily for our clients but also for ourselves (Ward, 1984). Our endings should be more reflective, more seriously considered, and more consciously handled than those at a graduation ceremony.

This chapter is about orchestrating the endings of counseling relationships and managing the logistics and feelings around unplanned counseling endings as well. This is a remarkably important time in the life of the counseling relationship, and it deserves to be considered deliberately and carefully (Kramer, 1990). Ending is about saying a goodbye of sorts, and it is also about reflecting—on all the work the counselor and client have done together, on the present, particularly in regard to the feelings that both client and counselor have about parting, and on the future.

About Endings

Just as the counseling relationship has served as a microcosm of the client's interpersonal life, the ending serves as a reflective microcosm of the history of the relationship. You need to approach this stage of the counseling process as carefully and deliberately as you have any other critical component of the relationship (Quintar, 2001).

The Meaning of Ending

There is great symbolism attached to endings. Some themes are common to all endings, yet each ending also has myriad individual meanings for each of us. For those who think symbolically and metaphorically about counseling relationships, there is a wealth of literature and philosophical thought related to this concept of ending (Maholick & Turner, 1979). Endings present some fairly obvious meanings even for the most literal and concrete thinkers among us.

On one level, the entire history of the counseling relationship is analogous to a human life span. There is a birth of the relationship, followed by its childhood and adolescence, then its productive, working adult phase, and finally its completion and demise. Each phase of the counseling relationship has its duties and privileges. Each phase requires the counselor's attentiveness and careful orchestration.

One of the primary concerns about the ending of counseling is the way in which it replicates all of the other endings, all of the losses in your client's life (Donoghue, 1994). All of your clients have experienced losses. Some have experienced separations and divorces, some of them the actual deaths of friends, loved ones. Some may have experienced the loss of freedom through incarceration, others the loss of safety because of physical or sexual abuse or neglect. In recent years, our whole culture's sense of safety has been compromised by acts of terrorism and natural disasters.

If you work with children, you may see how they, too, have been affected by loss through family difficulty or by geographical moves. Sometimes children are simply moved out of a school with no warning, no opportunity to say goodbye to their friends and teachers, no chance to finish with people. Not a few of the children in our schools live in communities where violence and street crime are daily events, and themes of loss are a constant in their lives.

Some kind of loss is often the primary reason clients come into your office in the first place. Helping clients deal with all of these factors, all of these cumulative losses, is what makes the business of ending your counseling relationship such an important counseling function.

Ending becomes even more difficult when the relationship between you and your client has been particularly close and intimate. Consider, for a moment, a client who came to see you because of intimacy issues. Let's call her Jean. Her story is typical. This is a woman who has had difficulty in relationships with people. She wants intimate relationships desperately yet fears them at the same time. She is not married but has been in an intimate partnership with someone for some years. This relationship was characterized by fighting and long periods of separation.

Contributing to this difficulty in her intimate relationship and to her anxieties with most people were some early experiences of abuse and abandonment, a childhood filled with unpredictability and instability. Consider further that your work with Jean has been successful: You have worked your way through her relentless testing and her ambivalence about personal sharing with you. Eventually, through your reliability, your steadiness, and acceptance, as well as your combination of effective listening and action skills, you won her confidence and trust. She has come to depend on you; perhaps she has even become somewhat dependent. She talks about how you are one of the few people who seems to truly understand her (a hallmark of transference) and begins to translate her work with you into building successful relationships with people in her life outside. Her relationship with her partner is becoming less tumultuous and more satisfying.

Her stated goals for counseling—to feel more comfortable meeting and being with people—have largely been realized. While there is still much that she can work on in that regard, you are both in agreement that your work together has come to its logical conclusion.

As wonderful as this all sounds, the work you've done together can fall apart if Jean experiences your departure from her life as just another abandonment. If the ending is not handled sensitively and in a fashion that is congruent with the history of the relationship, it may be experienced as rejection. Without adequate preparation and an opportunity to work through the thoughts and feelings about the ending of this relationship, this could become one of her worst losses, particularly because of the closeness of the relationship.

Ending this counseling relationship is going to be tricky, because for the client it really will be a separation, a loss. You are leaving each other. What is different, however, is that this is a leaving that has been contemplated, planned, and talked about in a way that has maintained eventual leave-taking as part of the client's conscious awareness. Taking the time to talk about the meaning of the work you've done together, what you have meant to each other, and what the future holds will make this separation different from the other losses of her life.

There is another important symbolic meaning related to ending a counseling relationship, and that has to do with its reminder of our own mortality. Looming behind all of the other losses of our lives is the constant awareness, no matter how much the fact is denied, that our own lives are finite. Our days are numbered. When we mourn the loss of a friend, part of the mourning is about the knowledge that we will follow, sooner or later. So, too, the end of the counseling relationship entails a mourning of sorts, both of the loss and of the reminder.

The knowledge that the counseling relationship is finite, that it has a beginning and an end, shapes it and gives it meaning. Some counselors and psychotherapists consciously put time limits on how long a counseling relationship can last and share those limits up front with their clients. They believe that the important work will happen only within a fixed time frame. They also suggest that the really important material often only emerges as the end draws near. Just as Jung maintained that the second half of life is when we all contemplate the most serious questions, so many counselors work under the assumption that people will get most serious about the work of counseling when they see that they are running out of time.

Even in a single session this can become evident. Clients will often save the most important issue for last, or for when there is a lack of ample time to talk about it and begin to work it through. This important issue may be prefaced, at the end of the session, with an "Oh, by the way . . . ," followed by the disclosure of some major piece of business. Sometimes these disclosures are truly block-busters. "Oh, by the way, I left my wife," or "Oh, by the way, I've decided I don't need counseling anymore, and I won't be coming back." Sometimes referred to as "doorknob issues," these last minute statements must, nevertheless, be appropriately addressed in the brief time that remains. Whether in a single session or over the history of the counseling relationship, it is the knowledge that time is limited that shapes the way the client—and the counselor—approach the work that needs to be done.

Many clients approaching the end of counseling have real concerns about the degree to which they will be remembered by the counselor. Because of transference, a client may have some hoped-for belief that he has maintained a special place in the counselor's heart. Even though, on some level, the client knows that the counselor is probably busy and has lots of other people in her life, he wants to believe that he has been special. There may be great concern that he hasn't been, and that he will soon be forgotten. The worst fear that anyone can have, at the end of life or even at the end of counseling, is that he will not be remembered.

Much of what goes on for your clients happens slightly out of awareness, off the radar screen. They may have given little thought to what this ending means. It is your job to anticipate, consider, and acknowledge these underlying concerns and to provide opportunities to give them voice. This material includes the way this ending is a replication of other previous losses, their personal fears about mortality, and concerns about how much you care. You don't want to manufacture or overplay their importance, but you can speculate as to their presence. Specifically, consider that the ending of your relationship has the potential for kicking all of this underground material into action.

Client and Counselor Feelings about Ending

In addition to the symbolic meanings, attendant feelings—for the client and, to a certain degree, for the counselor—accompany termination. There may be one predominant feeling, perhaps sadness, perhaps relief, or more commonly a mixture of conflicting emotions. It is the conscious exploration and discussion of both thoughts and feelings that makes the ending of a counseling relationship uniquely unlike other relationship endings.

Let's again consider your ending with "Jean." She has known for some time that you will be ending your work together, and she is upset. Much of her upset is about her sadness over losing you and the time she spends with you. You have valued her, have nurtured her hidden wishes and desires for a life more connected to people, and have accepted her fully even when she has shown aspects of herself that she finds unappealing. She is sad about losing your caring attention.

In addition, she has come to enjoy this special time in her week that she has spent talking about herself, without distractions. Few people in her life take the time to listen to her this way, and she has precious few moments when she luxuriates in spending time devoted to herself. Thus she is also sad about losing this time focused on her own needs.

She is also angry. Although she knows it isn't rational, she thinks that if you really cared for her you would extend the time boundaries of this relationship. She is also angry about the fact that she wanted to accomplish some things that she hasn't worked on yet, and she had held out hope that you'd be able to help fix these things. Again, she knows this is not completely rational, but she did hope that you would have been able to do a bit more magic than you did.

These angry feelings lead unavoidably to some guilt. She really likes you and cannot accept being angry with you. Caring about someone and being angry with him at the same time seem, to her, to be incompatible. This combination of sadness, anger, and guilt is confusing.

Finally, she is scared. You have been an anchor for her, someone who has served as a reality checker and supporter in her efforts to create some substantial changes in her life. She will not have you in this capacity any more. She wonders if she will have what it takes to go it alone.

All of these feelings—sadness, anger, anxiety, and guilt—will be present in varying degrees in all of the counseling endings you orchestrate. The nature and extent of these feelings will depend on characteristics of your client and on the intensity and quality of the relationship you and your client have maintained. Some of these feelings will be directly related to you, and some will be related more to the associations (transference) and old personal unfinished business that have been triggered by the relationship.

In addition to this tumult of feelings, clients usually feel a fair amount of relief that this work is coming to a close. No matter how rewarding it has been, it has also been a commitment of time, energy, and sometimes money. If the work has been hard, there may be considerable relief about not having to endure that painful hour every week. I remember the distinct relief a client relayed to me when he was about to finally end a process of couples counseling that he and his wife had undertaken. He had come to refer to this couples counseling as weekly "oral surgery." The process had been helpful and had served to solidify his relationship with his wife, and he was delighted when it finally ended.

Counselors, too, experience a range of feelings in reaction to ending (Boyer & Hoffman, 1993). You may have become quite fond of your client and feel sad at the prospect of not seeing her any more. Maybe she has kicked some of your own unfinished business into action (e.g., she reminds you of other people in your life or perhaps has brought into question your competency issues), and this countertransference has you confused about the origin and meaning of these feelings. This kind of countertransference reaction can certainly complicate the process of ending (Kramer, 1986). Perhaps she has refused to do some things differently that you see as critical, and you may be angry about this. You may be anxious about getting another client to replace the spot that she had in your counseling schedule, and this may have financial implications as well. And, of course, you too may experience some relief in the fact that this is ending.

Ending a counseling relationship can elicit a range of feelings for both you and your client. Some of these feelings can be quite strong and powerful, and they can be complexly interwoven. A major function of the well-orchestrated ending is to provide an opportunity for your client to articulate and work through these feelings and to provide you with an opportunity to share some of your feelings with your client as well.

This is not a time, however, for counselors to work through their own unfinished business, the countertransference that has been activated by working with a client. It is better to do that with a supervisor or with other colleagues. The feelings you choose to share with your clients at the end are shared for their benefit only, not for your own edification, and not to satisfy your own needs.

Ending the Counseling Relationship

If your client has been well-prepared for the final stage in the life of the counseling relationship, if you have talked throughout the relationship about that time when his goals have been met and it is time for ending, the client will make the transition to independence smoothly, with confidence that he can "make it" out there without you.

When to End

The counseling relationship should end when the formulated goals have been met or when progress toward those goals has stalled. Every counseling relationship should work toward a set of goals that have been mutually agreed upon, and a contract for working toward these goals should be established. The contract typ-

---

REFLECTION EXERCISE 13.1   *Surveying the Losses in Your Life*

Take a few minutes to sit alone with yourself and do a quick survey of the major losses in your life. Those may have been deaths, separations, or other kinds of loss. Some of these losses were undoubtedly more difficult than others, and some were probably handled better than others by you and by other people around you. Which of these seem to have been dealt with well, which less so? What were the differences about?

How will these losses in your own life affect your endings with your clients? Do you recognize the importance of coming to grips with your own losses and its relevance to your professional counseling work? What kinds of counseling work might be affected most by a counselor's personal experience of losses?

You are invited to reflect on all of this in your journal and then to share your observations with others. How are your ideas and reactions similar to those of others?

---

ically specifies the length of time the relationship will last and states that at the end of that period the time parameters can be honored or extended. The relationship should be extended only for logical reasons (e.g., continued work toward goals) and by mutual agreement of both counselor and client.

As a competent, ethical counselor, you want the relationship to last long enough to realize the client's goals but not any longer than necessary. It is unethical to extend that time for your own purposes, as for making more money or because you want to see a client through some upcoming event, such as a wedding or graduation. To extend the time frame without justifiable reason devalues your client's ability to pursue her life goals without your assistance.

Unfortunately, not all endings are based on completion of goals. Not all of your clients will have engaged fully in the process in a way that helped to move them toward their goals. This may have to do with their reluctance or resistance, their lack of capacity, or your own lack of skill in finding the right tools to assist them. When this occurs, you need to fully accept the fact of stalled progress, or of client noncompliance, and make the decision to end the relationship. When a client is no longer making satisfactory progress toward stated goals, it is your obligation to consider alternatives to your work together. You consider and explain the most reasonable alternatives available to this client and make appropriate referrals. There will be many times, including when you make a decision to end based on the perception of minimal movement, that other work will be necessary and appropriate, either with another counselor or in a group counseling setting. Sometimes that further work may be in a noncounseling setting, as in some kind of service-related project.

How to End

The primary task of ending a counseling relationship is to provide ample opportunity for the client to express all of the thoughts and feelings about what the process, and you, have meant to her. It is a time to review the progress that has been made in working toward the stated goals and to think about the work that needs to be done in the future. It is also a time to consider whether other supports will be helpful and what kind of contact the two of you will have after the counseling relationship ends. Here are some things to consider in ending the relationship:

- Provide time for the client to talk about the process of counseling, and for him to review the progress made toward realizing goals. This is a good time for you to slip into your role as educator, to help your client see the process in a positive light. Even the difficulties could be placed (reframed) in a positive learning light. He can be encouraged to think of himself as a "work in progress," with this bit of counseling as one set of steps on a lifelong journey. The journey may even include additional periods of counseling in the future (Cummings, 2001).

- Provide the framework and time for your client to talk about whatever personal feelings she might have about you, and share yours in return. Although you have an opportunity to share some of your impressions and feelings about your client directly with her, it is best to wait until she has first had her go at it. You do not want your impressions to overshadow or short-circuit the things she has to say. She may be reluctant, for example, to share criticisms of you after you have talked about how much you have enjoyed working with her. Place your own feelings about the client and the process in a positive context without being dishonest. Just as you helped her to reframe her negative perceptions of her learning in a positive way, so you can reframe your own more conflicted feelings about her.

- Take the time to talk about the fact of ending, including the feelings and thoughts that accompany this, and speculate with him about how this is related to other endings in his life.

- If plans have been made for further counseling-related work, such as referral to another counselor, a counseling or self-help group, or other follow-up activities, talk about them.

- Negotiate the parameters of any interactions you may have after this counseling relationship ends. Naturally, you will not be negotiating to have another kind of relationship—for example, the client may be a crackerjack stockbroker, but you should not now be arranging for her to become *your* stockbroker. However, you may want to negotiate an appointment one or two months out or make arrangements for contact by mail. These kinds of

What to Do about Gifts

Clients will sometimes offer gifts at the end of counseling. It can be difficult to determine how to manage these. Do not accept gifts that have significant monetary value or that may have loaded symbolic meaning (such as roses, which may suggest romantic overtones). You don't want your refusal of gifts to be construed as any kind of rejection, and you walk an ethical tightrope here. Acknowledge the gratitude that a gift embodies, but do not benefit financially or in any other way that violates the sanctity of the relationship.

It is appropriate to accept gifts that are personal, homemade, and inexpensive. A card is a nice gesture of thanks. If your office is in a school or clinic, gifts that are somewhat larger and more questionable can be shared with others. "Oh, thank you for these beautiful roses. Let's put them out here in the outer office so everyone can enjoy them." The gift is acknowledged without buying into any special, private meanings that might be attached to it. As a last resort, which is usually the least appealing avenue, you can always simply say that it is a "matter of policy" to not accept any gifts.

postcounseling contacts can serve as a lifeline to someone who has become quite dependent on your support. If you live or work in close proximity to one another, you will also want to talk about how you will handle seeing each other in other settings, such as social gatherings or even in the supermarket, outside and after counseling. You want to protect your client's confidence, and anticipating these chance encounters with some ground rules and guidelines can be helpful for both of you.

Resistance to Ending

A client may resist ending even though the goals you'd initially agreed to work toward together seem to have been met. She may feel comfortable—maybe too comfortable—within the relationship and deny that the work you agreed to do together is really done.

Some clients, particularly those who are unable to verbalize their anxiety about stopping counseling, will backslide or regress or act out in some way that is designed to send a message about their lack of readiness. The times I've worked in residential drug treatment have provided for me the most glaring examples of regression at ending time. Some of the roughest behavioral difficulties would surface just as clients were about to graduate from a program. Some young man who had been doing so well in the program would invariably pick the week before his program completion to commit a minor crime or to violate program rules. Some young woman, anxious about returning to the community where she knew opportunities to do drugs would abound, would spend the last few weeks challenging staff and acting obnoxiously.

Case Example 13.1 *Talking about Ending*

This high school counselor has known this student for all four years of his school experience. They have developed a good relationship, and when the student has come in to talk with her, they've talked about his friends, his girlfriend, college searching, and career aspirations. There have been no major problems outside the normal developmental and adjustment issues that confront most teenagers. She has helped him with some difficult teacher relationships, written references for his college applications, and now is saying goodbye as he is about to graduate. They have already spent some of the session reviewing the history of their four years together, looking at some of his difficulties and accomplishments.

STUDENT: I can't believe it's almost over. There were times when I thought it'd never end, but now that it's here, I can't believe it.

COUNSELOR: It's been quite a road. A few bumps along the way, but you negotiated those OK.

Reflection of content.

STUDENT: *[Silent for a few moments.]* I don't know if I could've made it over some of those bumps if you hadn't been there to help me out. Remember that business with Mr. Clarke? That was pretty ugly. I thought he was going to get me kicked out of school. You sure saved my butt on that one.

COUNSELOR: He was pretty mad. I still can't believe what you guys did to his car. He'll never get those racing stripes off completely.

STUDENT: We thought the tape would just peel off. How'd we know the paint would come with it? I could name a dozen other times you bailed me out too.

COUNSELOR: Live and learn. You're leaving here a lot wiser than when you came in.

A simple reflection on client learning.

STUDENT: And the college stuff. I never would've gotten into the university without your help. Those references were great.

(continued)

(case example 13.1, continued)

They made me sound like some kind of hero. Where'd you come up with all that stuff, any-how?

COUNSELOR: I just passed on what your teach-ers told me, and what I know to be true about you. It was easy. And, thanks.

The counselor acknowledges the student's apprecia-tion and reflects on his positive contributions to his own success.

STUDENT: Yeah, well, thank you too.

COUNSELOR: You know, I really appreciate the credit you're giving me for helping out with some of the scrapes you got into and for help-ing out with the college stuff.

Self-disclosure of appreciation.

STUDENT: Yep, and I have no idea about what I'll do next year without you backing me up.

COUNSELOR: We should talk about that. Let me tell you, again, how much I appreciate your thanks and appreciation. I also want you to know how capable, how great I think you are. How much I've enjoyed knowing you, working with you on all this.

This supportive reflection on their work together combines self-disclosure of the counselor's apprecia-tion with commentary on the client. The counselor wants this experience to be the client's.

STUDENT: You're pretty terrific too. Not sure about how great I am, but thanks.

COUNSELOR: I've enjoyed you so much because of who you are. You've been straight and direct with me, and you haven't been afraid to try new things. You take responsibility for yourself. And you've got great skills. You'll do fine, believe me.

More counselor self-disclosure, coupled with positive statements about client learning. This is a form of "cheerleading."

STUDENT: I've done fine because you've been there to back me up.

COUNSELOR: Hmm. There might've been some times when I helped out, like negotiating that business with Mr. Clarke, but it's you who led the way. You, for example, were the only guy who had the guts to stand up and own up to what had happened. Don't sell yourself short. I really appre-ciate your thanks, and want you to acknowledge how much you do yourself. And I do hear you being a little anxious about next year.

More cheerleading. The appreciation comment is more self-disclosure, and the last comment is reflec-tion of feeling. This serves to move the focus back to the client.

STUDENT: Yeah, OK, I guess I see your point. But I am nervous about next year. I sure wish I knew you'd be around there. You know, just for a pep talk once in a while, or something.

(continued)

(Case example 13.1, continued)

COUNSELOR: Sure, I understand. It'd be weird not to be nervous. This is a big change. But you've got the tools to handle it all fine. I know one of the professors there pretty well, and I'll help you make a connection with her. And you can always give me a call if you want to yak about something. I'd sure like it if you'd stop in to say hi when you're home on break.

STUDENT: That'd be great.

More cheerleading, with suggestions for future support after the relationship ends. These final comments also provide reassurance that there could be future contact and support after ending.

Case Disscussion

This counselor and student have clearly had a good relationship based on mutual affection and respect. It is wonderful that this student can be so articulate and straightforward in his thanks, as well as his expressed nervousness about the future.

Not all students, or other kinds of clients, will be as articulate, and not all relationships will have been so conflict free. Your job is to help your clients, particularly the ones who cannot articulate themselves well, give words to what you perceive as their underlying thoughts and feelings. While it can be personally gratifying to hear expressions of thanks and gratitude, it is important to make sure that your client also acknowledges his strengths and gains. It is particularly helpful when he can see how his learning in the counseling work that he's done will translate into his life in the outside world.

In the discussion about ending, you can see that the client is hesitant to own his strengths and wants to credit the counselor for all the work that's been done. It is more important for your clients to recognize their growth and strength than it is for them to see what a wonderful job you've done. It would be better for a client, when ending, to say "Look what I've done," as opposed to "Look what you've done for me." It is ideal when clients can express appreciation for both your help and for their own gains.

In school settings the end of a school year, especially for the class approaching graduation, marks the period of major acting out. Some of this may be end-of-year exuberance, but some of the behavior is undoubtedly linked to the anxiety of ending and separation. The parents of an eighteen-year-old who is about to go to college can undoubtedly give you ample examples of this kind of separation anxiety.

This resistance to ending, with its attendant acting out, is all about anxiety. "I am not ready to go it alone" is the message. "Don't make me go. I can't tell you directly that I'm scared, so I'll act it out in any way I can to let you know how scared I am." It is your job, once again, not to be caught up in the behavior to the extent that you cannot hear the message underneath. You want to deal with the behavior but also to honor and address the anxiety that spawns it. You want clients to talk about this anxiety, to try to be clear and direct about their fears. If the anxiety appears to be overwhelming, you need to reassess the client's readiness for ending.

As you reconsider the client's readiness, it is important to be aware of your own possible contribution to the resistance to ending. Unless this counselor resistance is addressed and worked through, typically with supervisory assistance, the process of ending can be undermined (Brady, Guy, Poelstra, & Brown, 1996).

The more you anticipate resistance to ending, and the more you adequately plan for ending, the better the likelihood that the transition will be smooth. Here are a number of things you can do to actively deal with resistance to ending:

- Avoid stopping abruptly. Talk about the ending time periodically throughout the relationship, more frequently toward the end. As the end approaches, stagger appointments so that you are meeting less frequently. If you've met weekly for some period of months, meet every other week, with perhaps the last two meetings a month apart, for example. This staggering of appointments is sometimes referred to as *fading*.

- Always provide time for talking about ending. If you detect resistance behavior, gently interpret the meaning of the behavior in a way that allows for more active thinking and talking about what is really going on behind the behavior.

- Consider planning follow-up meetings, perhaps at six months and at one year after the official ending. Particularly for that client who has seemed anxious about ending, and for whom you staggered (faded) meeting times as you were coming to a close in the relationship, a six month follow-up could be a useful way for him to end while knowing that there will still be an opportunity for some future contact with you.

- Actively speculate and work with your client to reflect on whether it really is time to end. If the resistance to ending is truly great, if the anxiety seems above a reasonable threshold, consideration should be given to extending the relationship.

Unplanned Endings

Things do not always work out the way we would like. Sometimes clients do not or cannot complete the commitment made to counseling and quit before the agreed-upon time. This may happen for any number of reasons (Cavanagh, 1990; Tryon & Kane, 1990). Personal client issues or certain real-life factors may impinge on a client's ability to continue. A client may move away, or a parent may discontinue a child's involvement in some school-sponsored counseling program (Frayn, 1992; Heilbrun, 1982). Clients may get sick, or may even die. These kinds of abrupt endings can leave a counselor with all kinds of unresolved feelings.

Sometimes a client will abruptly tell you that things are great, much better, and that she doesn't feel a need to continue. This so-called "flight into health" usually takes place just as the counseling work is getting really interesting and probably quite scary to her because of its closeness to some touchy issues.

Whenever possible, encourage your client to talk about the factors that are leading to a consideration to end counseling prematurely. Try to avoid being manipulated into extending a session's length to address a last-minute declaration of stopping, but do what you can to make provision for a next appointment to discuss the client's reasons for thinking about ending.

There may be occasions when the client has some legitimate complaints about things that you have or haven't done that need to be taken seriously and addressed. It might be, for example, that your client does not believe that you have the skills or training to be able to help (Cochran & Stamler, 1989). Sometimes cultural barriers or misunderstandings that you might be unable to resolve may lead to a premature ending (Bein, Torres, & Kurilla, 2000). If you can provide an opportunity for the client to address these issues before she simply drops out of counseling, and if you can hear the complaints nondefensively and change your behavior to meet reasonable demands, there is tremendous potential for learning and for rescuing the relationship.

When a client simply stops coming for counseling without warning, it is appropriate to make an attempt to contact him to determine the reasons for not following through on his commitment, as well as to invite him to come in again to talk about those reasons. These efforts should not be overly solicitous, however. You don't want to be in the position of pursuing a client. In the event that he refuses to come back, or to give reasons for noncontinuance, you have little recourse other than to discuss the matter with a supervisor or colleagues. This can be particularly helpful for you in separating counselor error from whatever the client's issues might be.

When a client drops out of counseling, you might experience it as a matter of both personal rejection and professional incompetence. This is particularly true for newer, less experienced counselors. The more supervisory and organizational support you have, the better opportunity you will have to work through the reasons for these unplanned dropouts, as well as the feelings that surround them. The greatest assistance a supervisor can provide is in helping you to discern the difference between real errors in judgment that may have led to the client leaving and your generalized feelings of incompetence or rejection. Much of this latter unspecified material is the stuff of counselor countertransference, and it is another reason it is wise to work in a setting that has a lot of supervisory and organizational support, particularly when you start out doing this work professionally.

Sometimes counseling is interrupted or stopped because of some reason having to do with the counselor. Illness, or relocation, or job shifts can account for some of these (Pearson, 1998). Other factors, such as lack of client motivation, limited involvement with the counseling process, or even financial issues, may also play a role in a counselor's decision to end the relationship prematurely (Matthews, 1989). Whenever possible, provide adequate time for discussion and planning for this interruption, or the work that has already been accomplished could be compromised (Levin, 1998).

Measuring Success

Many counselors balk at the idea of quantifiably measuring their work. There is resistance to trying to reduce the intricacies and nuances of the relationship to numerical data, to judge the efficacy of counseling work by traditional scientific methods. Some of this resistance may be well founded; accurately measuring success in counseling is a complex task, with significant potential for misinterpretation.

This resistance is also reflective of a major dichotomy of thought in the field, one side arguing for a more scientific approach to what we do, the other suggesting that counseling activities are always more about intuition and artful interpersonal communication. The "intuitive" group argues that elements of the relationship are beyond measurement, even out of our realm of understanding. To reduce the counseling encounter to quantifiable examination, they say, is to miss the beauty of what it holds. It would be like trying to measure love.

Every year I show our graduate counseling students an hour-long video of Ronald (R. D.) Laing interviewing a woman who has been diagnosed as paranoid schizophrenic. This was an interview held as a demonstration before an audience of hundreds of people at the 1985 Evolution of Psychotherapy Conference. The interview was videotaped as the two worked behind a screen on stage. After the interview Laing and the young woman "client" came out from behind the screen to talk as part of a panel with the audience.

The interview is an interesting piece of work. Laing seems to empathically enter this young woman's intrapsychic world. He engages her in meaningful dialogue about her family, her beliefs, and her living situation. When the interview is over, they both engage in spirited conversation with the audience. She is lucid and clear, exhibiting no symptoms of schizophrenia. One of the most interesting features of the video, however, is the interchange between Laing and the audience. Some members of the audience berate Laing for not discussing technique and for his refusal to explain more thoroughly what happened in the interview. Laing dismisses them cursorily and tells one man that the least he could do is not be so arrogant as to assume that because he doesn't "get it" that nothing happened in the interview. Some in the audience continue to demand an explanation of technique, and Laing becomes even more intractable in his dismissal of them. At one point, the well-known family therapy theorist Salvatore Minuchin stands and commends Laing for the loving interchange he's just orchestrated with the young woman.

The audience at this interview was clearly composed of two solid camps, neither giving ground. On one side were those who look at counseling and therapy through scientific eyes, seeking explanation and elucidation of the process. On the other side were those satisfied with the lack of explanation, reveling in the mystery of the interaction between Laing and this young woman. This video, particularly the audience reaction, is a graphic depiction of the dichotomy between science and art (or intuition) that characterizes much of the current thinking in our field.

The controversy about the degree to which we can measure the effectiveness of counseling can be confused by variables other than real theoretical difference. Some of the reluctance to measure, for example, might be due to simple intellectual or other kinds of laziness rather than to adherence to any theoretical beliefs. There may also be anxiety about the efficacy of our work and underlying fear of being shown to be ineffective. In addition to these attitudinal issues, there are also concrete impediments to more rigorous measurement of counseling effectiveness. Time spent doing research on outcomes is time not spent doing direct service. Many counselors operate under severe time constraints, are burdened by reporting requirements, and have barely enough time to do necessary direct counseling work. They argue that they do not have the time to design and implement solid research studies of their work. Similarly, many programs would love to more effectively evaluate their service delivery systems, but they operate under extreme time and fiscal restraints. Research on counseling outcomes, both for individual counselors and for the institutions that employ them, can come to be seen as a dispensable luxury.

On the other hand, services to clients suffer when counselors and programs cannot adequately demonstrate to funding agencies (e.g., insurance companies, legislators, or school boards) that what they do is effective (Burlingame, Lambert, Reisinger, Neff, & Mosier, 1995). As a single obvious example, residential addictions programs across the country have been devastated by a lack of quantifiable support for their programming. They have been forced to cut back on lengths of stay, and some entire programs have closed because they typically do not have data that support the efficacy of their treatment as opposed to cheaper outpatient counseling. Insurance companies will not pay for more expensive services that are not verifiably effective. It is difficult to find fault with their reluctance.

Individual counselors and counseling programs, regardless of the school or agency setting, need to be sensitive to the vulnerability of their programs and services to forces of the marketplace. If we want funding agents to support our work, we need to be able to show them that what we do is effective. Conducting good research on the outcomes of our work is the best way to do this.

Conducting Studies of Your Counseling Work

You are responsible for conducting research studies of your own counseling work. You can begin to develop ways to measure client movement toward goals by using standardized tests (Tingey, Lambert, Burlingame, & Hansen, 1996). With these instruments you can compare your clients' movement and growth against larger populations. Your course work in evaluation and measurement will help to prepare you for this kind of outcome research.

You can also monitor your clients' progress using the movement (or lack of it) toward established goals as measurable markers of growth. When actual indicators of movement toward goals are elusive, secondary indicators may provide evidence of movement. Tracking drug use for one of your clients might be difficult, for example, but you might be able to monitor his ability to stay out of trouble, which would provide some relative indication of his use of drugs.

It may seem premature to be thinking about doing outcome research on your counseling work when you are just starting to learn how to do the work itself. It's not! If you assume, even as you prepare to do this work, that this kind of research is an integral aspect of the counseling profession, it will become an automatic feature of your work with clients. Even if no one is expecting you to do it in an agency or school where you work, you will come to find this rigorous examination of your work with clients invaluable. Not only will you be able to track your progress and growth in work with clients over time, perhaps finding out which of the strategies you employ are most effective, but you will also be able to demonstrate the efficacy of this work to other people.

Becoming a Consumer of Research Literature

Aside from verifying your own work with data, you should become a skilled consumer of counseling outcome research and be able to intelligently read the research literature of our field. You need to be current about what the research suggests is *best practice* and make informed decisions about how to let such research guide your counseling practice (Paul, 1967; Sexton, 1996; Sexton, Whiston, Bluer, & Walz, 1997). As you begin to define an area of counseling in which you'll specialize, your examination of the research literature should focus on the kinds of problems and people that your specialization serves (Smyer & Intrieri, 1990).

Concluding Thoughts: After Ending

I received a phone call a couple of years ago from one of my first clients, a woman I had seen many years ago when I was doing a doctoral counseling internship. She

LAB PRACTICE 13.1   *The Last Session*

This is another triad or quadrad small group role-play situation. Each of you will, in turn, play the Counselor, Client, and Supervisor role. This is the final meeting of a close, productive counseling relationship that has come to a natural, mutually agreed-upon close. When it is your turn to role play the Client, discuss with the person playing the Counselor the type of Client you will play. Regardless of the type of Client you portray, the ending session should be positive and upbeat. For example, the Client may be a student. This Counselor and Client have met together, though not necessarily every week, for the past two years, and the Client is about to graduate. The person in the Client role should feel comfortable enlarging on the role with invented material about academics, relationships, future plans, or whatever other issues might seem relevant.

The Counselor's job is to provide an opportunity for the Client to talk about his (her) thoughts and feelings about ending, including things that have been accomplished (obviously, the Client will need to invent these) and things left for future work somewhere else. It is also an opportunity for the Counselor to share his (her) personal feeling (again, imagined) about ending. Both people should also reflect on the history of the relationship.

At the end of the interaction, the Supervisors will provide feedback to the Counselor about the interaction. How realistic did this seem, taking into account the short amount of time allotted for this experience?

How could the Counselor have set up some ways to measure this Client's movement toward specified goals? Certainly, the client's level of satisfaction is central, but beyond that, what could have been utilized to measure the success of the overall counseling experience?

wanted to know if we could get together to talk, just to say hi and to compare notes about what had happened in our work together those many years ago. Although I had some concerns about the potential reasons for the request, and about having been tracked down after so many years and miles of separation, in fact I was eager to sit down and talk with her. I was curious about how she was doing and interested to hear what she had to say about the counseling work.

It was a great meeting. She reported that she was doing very well and that she was happy in her work and personal life, but that it hadn't come easily. She said that she'd been through a lot since we'd parted company, but that much of the work that she'd done with me had sustained her through the bad times. This was all very gratifying to hear. But to my surprise, her recollections didn't match my own at all. There were things that I thought had been helpful to her that she didn't mention, and some of the things she described that had been most beneficial

I couldn't recall. There appeared to be no hidden agenda in her desire to meet and talk; she just wanted to check in.

Encouraging your clients to check in, to say hi, or to drop you a line occasionally is usually appropriate and reassuring. You don't want to promote dependence, or deny the fact of separation and ending, but you also do not need to suggest that once the ending happens you drop off the face of the planet. It is a lovely and important gesture to your clients to suggest that they occasionally update you as to their goings-on. When you tell them that you genuinely want to know of their whereabouts and life after working with you, it is usually a reassurance that they will not be forgotten. It will also be wonderful, for you, when they do take the time to let you know.

For Further Thought

1. Get together with one or two of your colleagues and discuss what you see as hallmarks of a successful counseling experience. Which of these has to do with your perceptions of what constitutes the successful development of the counseling relationship, which are related to successful counseling outcomes?

2. In your current work setting, or one you envision, how could you measure the success of outcomes in your work, either directly or indirectly? Be creative as you think about this. Again, you might want to consult with your colleagues and brainstorm ideas.

3. Visit one or two counseling agencies in your area and talk with clinicians about how they handle endings. What happens if a client doesn't show up for an appointment or drops out of counseling? What happens in the ideal "termination" process? How do they handle gifts? Try to get a sense of counselors' general feelings about ending these relationships.

References

Bein, A., Torres, S., & Kurilla, V. (2000). Service delivery issues in early termination of Latino clients. *Journal of Human Behavior in the Social Environment, 3*(2), 43–59.

Boyer, S., & Hoffman, M. (1993). Counselor affective reactions to termination: Impact of counselor loss history and perceived client sensitivity to loss. *Journal of Counseling Psychology, 40*(3), 271–277.

Brady, J., Guy, J., Poelstra, P., & Brown, C. (1996). Difficult good-byes: A national survey of therapists' hindrances to successful terminations. *Psychotherapy in Private Practice, 14*(4), 65–76.

Burlingame, G., Lambert, M., Reisinger, C., Neff, W., & Mosier, J. (1995). Pragmatics of tracking mental health outcomes in a managed care setting. *The Journal of Mental Health Administration, 22,* 226–236.

Cavanagh, M. (1990). *The counseling experience*. Prospect Heights, IL: Waveland.

Cochran, S., & Stamler, V. (1989). Differences between mutual and self-initiated nonmutual terminations in a university counseling center. *Journal of College Student Development, 30*(1), 58–61.

Cummings, N. (2001). Interruption, not termination: The model from focused, intermittent psychotherapy throughout the life cycle. *Journal of Psychotherapy in Independent Practice, 2*(3), 3–18.

Donoghue, K. (1994). The impact of the termination of brief psychotherapy, and its implications for counselling practice. *Counselling Psychology Review, 9*(3), 9–12.

Frayn, D. (1992). Assessment factors associated with premature psychotherapy terminations. *American Journal of Psychotherapy, 46*(2), 250–261.

Heilbrun, A. (1982). Cognitive factors in early counseling termination: Social insight and level of defensiveness. *Journal of Counseling Psychology, 29*(1), 29–38.

Kramer, S. (1986). The termination process in open-ended psychotherapy: Guidelines for clinical practice. *Psychotherapy: Research, Practice, Training, 23*(4), 526–531.

Kramer, S. (1990). *Positive endings in psychotherapy: Bringing meaningful closure to therapeutic relationships*. San Francisco: Jossey-Bass.

Levin, D. (1998). Unplanned termination: Pain and consequences. *Journal of Analytic Social Work, 5*(2), 35–46.

Maholick, L., & Turner, D. (1979). Termination: That difficult farewell. *American Journal of Psychotherapy, 33*(4), 583–592.

Mathews, B. (1989). Terminating therapy: Implications for the private practitioner. *Psychotherapy in Private Practice, 7*(3), 29–39.

Paul, G. (1967). Strategy of outcome research in psychotherapy. *Journal of Consulting Psychology, 31*(2), 109–118.

Pearson, Q. (1998). Terminating before counseling has ended: Counseling implications and strategies for counselor relocation. *Journal of Mental Health Counseling, 20*(1), 55–63.

Quintar, B. (2001). Termination phase. *Journal of Psychotherapy in Independent Practice, 2*(3), 43–60.

Sexton, T. (1996). The relevance of counseling outcome research: Current trends and practical implications. *Journal of Counseling and Development, 74*(6), 590–600.

Sexton, T., Whiston, S., Bluer, J., & Walz, G. (1997). *Integrating outcome research into counseling practice and training*. Alexandria, VA: American Counseling Association.

Smyer, M., & Intrieri, R. (1990). Evaluating counseling outcomes. *Generations: Journal of the American Society on Aging, 14*(1), 11–14.

Tingey, R., Lambert, M., Burlingame, G., & Hansen, N. (1996). Clinically significant change: Practical indicators for evaluating psychotherapy outcome. *Psychotherapy Research, 6*(2), 144–153.

Tryon, G., & Kane, A. (1990). The helping alliance and premature termination. *Counseling Psychology Quarterly, 3*(3), 233–238.

Ward, D. (1984). Termination of individual counseling. *Journal of Counseling and Development, 63*(1), 21–25.

CHAPTER 14

The Whole Counselor: Maintaining Health and Perspective

> To change one's life: Start immediately.
> Do it flamboyantly. No exceptions.
> *(William James)*

Each of us has an obligation to our clients to stay enthusiastic, passionate, and excited about the work we do. Part of that obligation involves enthusiastic commitment to a lifelong journey of self-exploration and a commitment to staying abreast of the professional literature regarding the kinds of practices that are best for our clients. It makes sense that a happy, healthy counselor will do the best work and that self-care is as important as client care. Our clients have a right to expect counselors to model the kind of "wholeness" to which we want them to aspire.

You have probably heard about counselor burnout, and you may even have talked with counselors who seem a bit "fried." This chapter is about remaining fresh and optimistic about your counseling work and avoiding the pessimism and negativity that can seep into the often challenging, sometimes truly difficult, work that we do. It is about retaining a sense of personal wholeness and acknowledging the need for periodic renewal in a field that can sap energy and test the limits of your ability to remain enthusiastic.

Maintaining a Sense of Aliveness and Personal Growth

The counseling program in which I teach expects that all students will embark on a minimum of fifty hours of personal growth work (not for credit, and not with any program faculty) while they are in the program. The hope is that this work will help them to open up to some unexamined aspects of themselves that may not be touched by classroom activity. We suggest to our students that this personal growth work, like their academic training, should be viewed as the beginning of a lifelong process. We encourage them to think broadly about how they can approach this work, and we give them the latitude to choose what seems to fit best at this given point in time. Some involve themselves in individual counseling, some opt for participation in a support group, some go to workshops and seminars. Most pursue these activities eagerly, and it is only a danger sign for faculty when a student says that he doesn't "need it."

There is more to this business of personal awareness than the elimination of obvious problems, particularly for us as counselors. You are, in your person, the single greatest tool you have for working with others. Your cumulative intelligence, experience, knowledge, and personal awareness are certainly the best you have to offer your clients. Of course, you need to continue to learn new best practices and skills and to stay current in the growing knowledge of the field. But you also need to keep yourself psychically tuned so that you live with a certain amount of balance in your life. It is this awareness of your own balance, your ability to maintain a dialogue with your inner selves, that provides you with an ongoing assessment of how you are personally holding up in this work.

The Counselor as a Whole Person

Wegscheider-Cruze's (1981) model of the whole client, which we used as the basis for client assessment in Chapter 5, can also serve as a model for assessing your own well-being. As you may recall, this model of the whole person assumes that different aspects of an individual's life can be reviewed separately, as separate selves. Are your own internal selves in balance? Let's look at each of these critical aspects as they may affect your whole self as a counselor, and take time to think about these "selves" of your own life.

Caring for Your Physical Self

Noontimes at the college where I work finds a group of us on the basketball court or on the tennis court or doing something collectively that is an active antidote to the intellectualized ways we've spent our mornings. We are a coed group of student life professionals, administrative assistants, maintenance workers, faculty, and administrators. There is a lot of laughter, trash talk, and sweating. The basketball is sometimes ugly, the tennis usually of less than Wimbledon quality, but the exertion and the camaraderie always make those days the better for the effort. There are days when that physical regimen is the best reason for being on campus, and I can't imagine what my work life would be like without that rigorous break in the middle of the day.

You live in your body, and it is the physical reality your clients will meet when they first encounter you. Some clients will make snap judgments about you and your skills based on these first impressions of your physical wellness (Vargas & Borkowski, 1983). Your body might not exactly be a castle, but you should still treat it well. How comfortable are you in your body? Do you care for it, not obsessively, but with attention? Do you take time for exercise and have regular checkups? Do you eat and drink with good sense? Is your weight healthy? This is not rocket science but a simple set of commonsense questions you need to ask yourself.

The culture in which we live is a strange mix of ideas about the body. Television stars are thin, yet many advertised products promote obesity. We live in a land of plenty, yet eating disorders are among our most insidious behavioral problems. Books on fitness and weight reduction abound and weight loss diets and self-help groups are more popular than ever, yet our collective weight gain continues to rise.

To what degree have you found your own way in the midst of these messages, pressures, and daily temptations to abuse your body? Have you allowed yourself to sink into inactivity, perhaps consumed by work and the other demands of life? Or, on the other end of the continuum, have you become obsessive about the way your body appears to others? What is your comfort level with your body, and do you live comfortably in it?

These questions are about more than the actual physical condition in which you find yourself; they are about your attitude about your physical self. How aware and accepting are you of this aspect of yourself? If you are physically challenged, for example, to what degree do you view the challenge as a handicap? What are the realistic limitations related to what you can do? If you are in recovery for some kind of addiction, to what degree do you define yourself by your addiction? Is it possible for you to be overweight (by what the charts say is optimal) and still be comfortable?

Some psychotherapy theories use the body as a primary focal point for work. Wilhelm Reich, a controversial (and often misunderstood) analyst who was originally part of Freud's trusted inner circle, eventually broke with Freud in part over assertions that by working directly with the body, not only talking about it, one could resolve emotional and psychic difficulties. Reich believed that we actually carry all of our personal emotional history, particularly the trauma we have experienced, in our bodies. Our bodies develop a particular muscular character depending on the kinds and degree of emotional turmoil we've endured. His student and protégé, Alexander Lowen, devised an entire method of therapy called *bioenergetics* to help people live more healthy emotional lives in tune with their bodies. From a more Eastern perspective, some Yoga systems have traditionally used the body as a means of accessing wellness and enlightenment.

Some counselors make physical health (e.g., nutrition, diet, and exercise) a routine part of their counseling work with people (Reyak-Schelar & Feldman, 1984), but rarely do courses in counseling theories deal with these body-oriented approaches. This does not mean that the practicing counselor cannot personally explore and gain access to their wisdom. It makes good common, intuitive sense that our physical selves have a tremendous impact on how we think and feel about ourselves, and how we interact with others.

Caring for Your Emotional Self

Caring for your emotional self is a critical aspect of counselor self-care (Wilson, 1994). Your facility at monitoring, managing, and fluidly moving among your feelings is key to your success in work as a counselor. Your ability to track your own feeling state, while simultaneously paying attention to the thoughts and feelings of your client, is a critical skill you will develop with practice. Part of this skill

---

REFLECTION EXERCISE 14.1   *Taking Inventory of Your Physical Self*

You live in your body, and you want to treat it well. You also have ideas about your body, and these may either hinder or aid your ability to care for yourself well. Spend a few minutes taking stock of your physical self. Reflect on your body, both on its physical shape and how you feel in it. Is this a satisfying reflection? How might your physical health affect your work with people? Are there things you are doing with your body that you want to continue, or are there things you'd like to stop doing? What physical activities would you like to start? To the degree that you feel comfortable, share your reflections with a colleague or two.

---

involves a studied ability to track your feelings and watch the wor
internal world. You can practice Reflection Exercise 14.2 regularly
self-tracking process.

REFLECTION EXERCISE 14.2   *Paying Attention to Your Inner World*

This exercise was suggested earlier in this book. It is worth repeating here as it is worth repeating in your life. Sit quietly. Close your eyes. Take note of the ideas and feelings passing through you. Pay particular attention to your feeling state, note it without judgment or without trying to attach it to any particular ideas or series of events. Open your eyes, bringing your awareness with you back into your current environment. You can periodically do this each day, perhaps five or ten times a day, in various situations. With practice this will become quite fluid, and you will become much more adept at monitoring your ongoing feeling state and eventually linking that to the events and circumstances around you. This will be an invaluable skill in doing counseling work.

There can be no doubt but that your feelings, the tides and currents of your ongoing emotional life, are a critical aspect of how you define yourself. Your life is a constant stream of feeling, of variations of sadness, gladness, anger, and anxiety. Feelings are not bad or good, they simply are. You might think of your feelings as a series of happenings, or ongoing emotional events, as opposed to a fixed state of emotional "happiness" (Perls, Hefferline, & Goodman, 1994/1951).

One end result of repeatedly submerging your feelings under a tide of self-criticism and sanction is depression. This distinct kind of depression is often the end result of a chain of events that begins with the inability to act between opposing choices. Typically, one of these choices represents freedom and the other represents a more socially appropriate and culturally congruent action. This can be a dramatically unhappy spot in which to find yourself. It is particularly disheartening to see the depression of counselors who feel obliged to stay in the profession because of the extrinsic salary and safety rewards that it affords, despite the fact that they no longer derive satisfaction from the work itself. This situation holds the makings of counselor burnout, which we'll discuss later in the chapter.

Caring for Your Social and Familial Self

The family that nurtured and raised you plays a remarkable role in your approach to your counseling work and to your life in general (Clemente-Crain, 1996; Dryden & Spurling, 1989; Softas-Nall, Baldo, & Williams, 2001). If, as a child, you received enough consistent love, support, and nurturance from your family, there is a reasonable chance that as an adult you approach the world without unreasonable demands for support and personal emotional repair—with minimal unfinished business, in other words. If, on the other hand, your early life was marred by trauma, abuse, and lack of support, there may be an inclination to look to relationships in adulthood to mend what was harmed in those early years—lots of unfinished business. To the degree that a counselor's early life has been characterized by trauma, abuse, and family dysfunction, he or she will have to take extra precautions to ensure that the personal mending that needs to be done is not pursued via relationships with clients.

Some authors have written persuasively of the phenomenon of the "wounded healer" (Hayes, 2002) and how such early childhood nonsupport has unconsciously led many of us to work in one of the helping professions. They argue that many of us who work as counselors, psychologists, nurses, and teachers were raised in homes where conditional approval was a subtle substitute for unconditional love, and that we learned to read the subtle signals at an early age.

It may be extraordinarily difficult for those of us whose young lives were spent in clear sailing to fully come to understand the lives of those born into more difficulty. It is a strange paradox that early childhood difficulty may, in fact, make for an easier time in learning to be a truly skilled counselor (Wilcoxen, Walker, & Hovestadt, 1989; Witmer, Sword, & Loesch, 1973). The intuitive skill honed as a youngster in attempting to survive difficulty provides a great potential capacity to sense the hidden pain of others.

This does not mean that extraordinary childhood difficulty is prerequisite for eventual proficiency as a counselor (Barta, 1999). We all have difficulties in life. We are all human. None of us grew up in homes that were totally nurturing and filled with unconditional loving. There is probably no such thing as the totally functional family. All families have a certain degree of dysfunction. Some families, however, experience serious problems, which can include poverty, abuse, violence, and neglect. Your job is to bring the particular joys and difficulties you experienced in your family into awareness. You want to be able to own these experiences and to draw on them appropriately. I hope you will be able to see the ways you have been strengthened by the particular difficulties you have endured. In counseling, as in life, it is around our difficulties and suffering, not our successes, that we form our closest connections with others.

Having relationships with people who are not our clients, our students, or our colleagues helps us stay aware of our strengths and weaknesses. Some of those will be with immediate and extended family members. Our husbands, wives, and partners consistently remind us not only of our greatest qualities but also of our frailties. They keep us honest regarding our shortcomings and imperfections. They can also serve to anchor and support us during turbulent times and in the midst of job stresses. They know us like no other. Similarly, our children also keep us humble, reminding us daily that we, too, put on our pants one leg at a time.

Caring for Your Spiritual Self

Otto Rank, a psychoanalyst of the 1930s and 1940s, maintained that we have a burning desire to make our lives mean something, to encompass more than the "dust to dust" time we actually spend on earth. He suggested that this "drive to immortality" is as basic as our need for food, sex, or sleep. Rank said that the psychotherapy of his day (analysis) was not up to the task of helping people in this domain, for as a "mechanistic, reductionistic" medium, it failed entirely to address this hunger.

The last two decades have seen a rekindling of interest among counseling theorists and writers in this aspect of our lives, and they have begun to talk more openly of "spirit" and "spirituality." Whereas before only some analysts—Rank and after him the existentialists, including Rollo May, Viktor Frankl, and Irvin Yalom, and self-help groups such as Alcoholics Anonymous—talked openly of meaning issues and higher powers, today many in the counseling and psychotherapy realm address these questions.

Most agree that some degree of spirituality—broadly defined as nurturing an inner life and having a relationship with nature and the natural world, whether by prayer, meditation, or simply regular walks in the woods—is important for people's psychological well-being. Some, and not only pastoral counselors, maintain that spirituality is the central aspect of ourselves as counselors that serves a healing function in the counseling relationship. Our ability to be fully present and centered with our clients, a skill that is best nurtured by way of some kind of spiritual practice, is key to successful relationship building. It is this spiritual side of us, this contemplation of our connection to the universe, that shapes our values and our belief system.

Our lives are increasingly affected by the burgeoning world of technology. Cell phones, television, and computers threaten to overwhelm us, demanding increasing amounts of attention and time. We are now on call to voice mail, e-mail, and pagers, and we need counterbalancing ways to manage the onslaught. Contemplating the order of things and our place within that order, as well as our relationship with nature, are wonderful ways to keep our sense of perspective and balance. This is the same balance we encourage our clients to seek.

Caring for Your Working Self

Our work serves a critical function in how we define ourselves. It provides a role for us in the world. When people introduce themselves to others, they will most often start by stating what they do for a living. For some of us, our work provides our living, for others our work is distinct from the job we do to get paid. In this sense, while a job is what pays for food and shelter, work is our true vocation, what we are meant to do in the world. I know many artists who have a job to pay the bills while trying to find time and space to do their true work, their artwork. As counselors, each of us has to determine to what degree our work is simply a job or is congruent with our own deeper life meanings. As you contemplate a career as a professional counselor, is this work your primary calling or simply a means to making a living? Will this career satisfy you on both of those levels?

The attitude and enthusiasm you bring to your work will affect the way you work with others. It is a little like the story of the three bricklayers in Rome. The first, when asked what he was doing, answered "laying bricks." The second replied, "helping to build a church." And the third said, "laying the groundwork for a beautiful new cathedral." It's all about attitude.

There are many questions attendant to the ways you define your working self. Will you work privately or for a public agency or school? How much money do you require from your work? What ethical principles guide the kind of counseling work you will do and the workplace in which you choose to do your work? What are your *real* reasons for doing this work?

Caring for Your Aesthetic Self

Books about counseling don't usually talk about counselors nurturing a sense of an appreciation for beauty. Why is this? Is there some rule stating that aesthetic appreciation is off limits for people who work with people? Why is this not seen as being as important an area for counselor development as, say, knowledge of the jargon of the field?

We are all artists in the broadest and best sense of the word. We make things, we enjoy the things that other people have made, and we draw sustenance from the beauty afforded by the natural world around us. We grow things, we tend to the flow-

---

REFLECTION EXERCISE 14.3   *Thinking about Your Working Self*

First, consider the following questions and note your reactions in your journal. Then discuss your ideas with a small group of classmates: How much money do you want or expect to earn as a counselor? Is counseling to be your vocation or avocation? Will you work for a public agency or in private practice? What do you imagine the benefits of public versus private practice might be? What does your choice mean about the kinds of clients you will serve? If you work in a private setting, how will you maintain contact with colleagues and make provisions for supervisory support?

For school counselors in training: Would you prefer to work in a public or a private school? With elementary, middle, or secondary school students? Why?

---

ers in our gardens, even if our garden is no more than a houseplant on a windowsill, and this "dirt digging" fills us with renewed energy and a connection with the earth.

This is all art, these acts of making things and helping things grow, and it is symbolically just like the growth we help to nurture in the people with whom we work. This desire to make things grow will affect our clients more than the brilliant things we say to them about what they should do with their lives. The famous and mysterious philosopher-teacher Gurdgieff admonished his students to learn to care for plants before they moved on to animals or people.

Many of our clients have either not yet found or have lost this connection. They have ceased to see themselves as "growers" or as people with creative capability. Perhaps they never saw themselves this way. A major part of our work might be to help them connect or reconnect with that creative spark lying dormant within, yet this can only happen if we are well connected with our own creativity.

The quirky film *Harold and Maude* illustrates this point. In the film, which features a relationship between eighty-year-old Maude and eighteen-year-old Harold, there is an important scene where this unlikely couple rescues a sickly tree from a downtown street and brings it back to its home, to the forest, where they replant it so that it might survive. It is a small, vital revolutionary act, a statement about the need to connect and support the life around us. What is important about this statement is not the simple act of placing the tree in the woods but Maude's passion for this act. Maude also eventually transplants Harold into a more constructive, life-affirming way of thinking about himself in the world. It is her faith in life, coupled with her faith in Harold, that makes for such potent life saving. For us as counselors, it is precisely this kind of personal commitment and connection with life that can have such a great impact on those with whom we work.

It helps our own life-saving ability immeasurably if we are able to speak the language of art, to think and relate artistically. Without this skill we will be speaking with clients without the depth and richness that this symbolic domain affords. Many of life's problems and joys cannot adequately be expressed in everyday language. Some of our deepest sorrows and delights can only be communicated symbolically, perhaps via poetry or music or visual art forms.

Caring for Your Intellectual Self

You need to acquire the basic knowledge of the profession. You will, assuming you are in a formal program of counseling study, take the course work that will lay the groundwork for building that knowledge base. All of the course work in counseling theory and skills, research and evaluation, human development, and other critical areas will serve as part of that base. Graduation from an approved program of study, perhaps coupled with passing licensure examinations, helps to ensure a basic level of counseling competency.

However, you need to go beyond these basic standards. You should also be a student of life. You have a professional obligation to be a thoughtful, well-informed person. You should know something of the world and continue to learn of the world through a wide range of experiences. You should want to meet people from diverse backgrounds. Your experience of multiculturalism should not be only academic. Read widely, not only in the counseling and psychology field but also in philosophy, the sciences, and the arts. Become a committed student as well as a teacher, a curious seeker of truth and beauty.

When I was in my twenties and thirties, I had burning questions to which I thought I could find the answers by finding the right books. I awoke at 4 a.m. and 5 a.m. and read insatiably in search of the answers to those questions. Big questions like these: What does it mean to truly live freely? What kind of order can there be in the universe when such very bad things happen to so many people? Can you really help anyone else do anything? Is there any such thing as true altruism, or does self-interest rule everything we do? I read the original works of the great thinkers in our field. I read philosophy and literature, an eclectic mix of things. I found some answers, as well as many more questions. I talked and listened to my graduate student colleagues, professors, and friends. I was a sponge for ideas and soaked up good ideas—and sometimes bad ones—any where I could find them. Certainly, I thought that some of this information would help my work as a counselor, but when I was honest about it, I realized that the information itself was almost incidental. It was the Socratic searching for truth that kindled my desire to find out about people and molded my ability to find things out by directing my questions more pointedly. The more you talk with people who share your work, the more you will find this curiosity to be a common counselor characteristic.

Over time, my frantic searching has toned down some, and my demands for answers have been replaced by an appreciation for the mystery that the questions imply, but I hope that the passion to soak up ideas and experience continues unabated. I have tried, as well, to broaden my search through travel and service involvements and through relationships with friends and family. Some of the best answers and solutions to your most fundamental questions, in fact, can only be approached indirectly through work and intimate involvements with others.

You will need to find your own way in this, your own books, your own experiences, and your own teachers. The search is an incredible adventure, exciting and challenging, and it is amazing how things will appear to help you along the way. Perhaps paradoxically some of the most personal aspects of your search will sometimes involve your clients. You may be reminded of your own searches in their struggles, or your personal reactions to them may sometimes push you in directions you hadn't thought of before. By approaching this work, and its puzzles, with an attitude of "What can I discover?" in addition to "How can I help?" the greatest help is often tendered. Self-interest and assisting others need not be contradictory. In most human interaction there is usually significant "getting" in the "giving."

REFLECTION EXERCISE 14.4   *Your Counseling Experience*

Have you ever been a counseling or psychotherapy client? Did you ever have a relationship with a school counselor? How were you affected by these relationships? What skills or personal characteristics of your counselor did you find most or least helpful?

After considering these questions yourself, talk about those experiences with one or two others. Share only those experiences that you feel safe in revealing.

Nurturing the Whole Counselor and Avoiding Burnout

As you periodically take stock of yourself—and the collection of your various selves—you will review those aspects of yourself that seem to be stable and working well, and you will look for changes or areas where you are paying too little attention. Good supervisors, colleagues, and friends will help you with these inspections. When you get to your working self, be sure to ask yourself the difficult questions about your level of satisfaction and optimism about your work. The more honestly you can answer these questions, the better prepared you will be to make changes, should those be necessary. Consider whether this is work you want to continue doing and whether it is providing enough in the way of personal satisfaction to make it sustainable.

Each of us should be able to assess if and when it's time to do something else, if only for a period of time. I have certainly had to grapple with my own limits in this work. I have had two stints of working as a counselor in residential treatment centers, each of which lasted about two years. I don't know if you'd call it burnout, but I do know that after each of those two-year periods I was ready to do something else for a while. I found the intensity of that kind of work highly rewarding, and also highly draining. In the midst of living and learning in those highly charged environments, I seemed to find little time for outside activities and opportunities to personally recharge and replenish. There was more outgo than input, and two years was enough. I loved the challenge and excitement of that work, but I also recognized when it was time to take a break from it. You, too, will need to assess when "enough is enough."

Burnout is about slipping job performance and a dispiriting sense of futility about one's work. The following passage captures this futility succinctly:

> Where once there was enthusiasm, conviction, and compassion for
> helping others, only frustration, apathy, and terrible loneliness remain.
> Paradoxically, the need to reach out and help is still there, but it is

mired in a personal sense of reduced motivation, low energy, and an overwhelming sense of futility and fraud. (Kesler, 1990, p. 303)

To prevent this "sense of futility and fraud" and to stay fresh and optimistic about your work, you need to nurture yourself. Make strategies for increasing your awareness of your own level of well-being a cornerstone of any burnout prevention program.

REFLECTION EXERCISE 14.5   *Do You Really Want to Be a Counselor?*

David Mactas, a colleague who helps direct federal drug treatment policy, is fond of saying, "It's tough to burn out if you never had a flame." We have been talking about what to do to keep from burning out, all the while assuming that you will have entered the profession with a burning desire to do this work. Now and for the duration of your counselor training, periodically take stock of your true desire to be a counselor. Ask yourself, "Do I really want to do this work?" It's a tough question—even tougher to deal with if the answer is "No." But if the answer is indeed "No," now's a good time to find out. If you think your answer is "Yes," but you are not sure, that's OK. Just keep asking the question, and if you feel comfortable, share the question and the ramifications of possible answers with a few of your closer classmates.

Throughout your counseling career, continue to track your enthusiasm for the work. Ask yourself about your connection to the profession and to your clients. Regularly ask some fundamental assessment questions: "Is this the kind of work I want to continue doing, at least right now? On most mornings when I first wake up, am I thinking about the day ahead with excitement and anticipation, or is there foreboding and dread?" Naturally, there will be days when you'd prefer not to go to work, but on balance, you should look forward to it. If you do not, it may be time to contemplate taking a break, or perhaps doing something else altogether.

Maher (1983) enumerates a number of common warning signs of burnout:

- Exhaustion and fatigue
- Insomnia
- Negative attitude about work
- Increased use of tobacco, alcohol, coffee, or drugs
- Negative self-concept
- Aggressive feelings
- Psychosomatic illness
- Negative attitude about clients

- Absenteeism or poor performance
- Loss of appetite or overeating
- Guilt
- Passive feelings

You need not have most or all of these warning signs to be concerned about burnout. Any of these, in extreme, is a danger signal.

The worst scenario for a counselor is to feel trapped by your work. Economics or the safety of job benefits may be compelling reasons to want to remain in a job, but those are more than offset by the potential for not doing optimal work or for doing harm to the client. There are possibilities, as well, even of doing harm to yourself when you are truly unhappy. Counselor disaffection and burnout can have dramatically harmful consequences, including heart attacks and ulcers, for seriously unhappy counselors.

It is most unacceptable, of course, when counselors blame their clients for the counselors' own personal problems. There are no bad clients. If a client is troublesome, it is up to you to figure out how causing trouble came to be part of this client's behavioral repertoire. It is your job to determine what you can reasonably expect in the way of success with difficult people, and you must find the necessary supports in your life to counteract the difficulties your clients cause you.

Concluding Thoughts: Staying Fresh

Beyond the fundamental decision to stay in the work, there are any number of ways to stay fresh and alive on the job. The literature points the way to some of these. Boy and Pine (1983) identify a number of strategies for avoiding burnout, and I include my own ideas about how these suggestions might be optimally helpful:

1. *Commit most of your working day to actually counseling clients.*
Too many other activities will distract you from your essential mission. Although I have encouraged you to be an advocate and to research the outcomes of your work, never forget the primary reasons you decided to become a counselor. That passion should remain your focus.

2. *Carefully select the organization where you will do your work.*
Some agencies or schools are run more efficiently and are more committed to counseling activities than are others. At some schools, counselors are mired in scheduling or organizational minutiae, and some poorly run agencies seem to take on the dysfunctional characteristics of the clients they serve. Some agencies and schools do not pay their counselors well. You deserve to make a living

wage. You also need to feel good about the mission, the goals, and the work ethic of the place that employs you.

Choose your agency or school well. When you go on job interviews, be as concerned with how employers present themselves as you are with how you present yourself. You might not be able to negotiate some aspects of a job situation, such as salary, but you might have some control over other items. For example, one of our recent elementary school counseling graduates asked that teachers not leave the classroom when she came in to do presentations. Her rationale, that the teacher is integral in the ongoing support of this instruction, was acknowledged by the school board and written into her contract. You, too, can be assertive about asking for the support you think you deserve, both for yourself and for your clients.

3. *Associate with committed, concerned colleagues.*
You may identify people with whom you work who are not engaged positively with the workplace or their clients. Avoid them. They will suck the optimism and energy out of you, and if there are too many of them, they will subvert the well-being of the organization. Choose to be with people who are upbeat and optimistic about what they do.

4. *Develop a sense of organizational involvement.*
Avoid overidentifying with an organization, but become involved to the extent that you think you have influence over its directions and policies.

5. *Retain an attitude of hope. Be one of those people you'd like to be with.*
Choose the option of seeing the glass as half full, and nurture your own optimism.

You are being drawn to this counseling work because of a sense that this is work you are meant to do. Trust your intuition regarding your motives for doing this work, and continually assess your involvement with it. Watch how the work affects you—your *whole person*—and never lose sight of the fact that you can take a break from it when you need to. Your ongoing honest assessment and recommitment to your work will ensure that you are a happy and involved counselor. If you are feeling good about who you are and what you do, it will translate into good work with clients.

For Further Thought

1. Take a quick inventory of your personal strategies for dealing with job stress. How do you cope with difficult, tense job situations? Do you do a good job of this, or is this an area that needs improvement?

2. Talk with administrators of local community mental health, school counseling, and other counseling programs about turnover in their agencies and schools. How many people leave and for what reasons? Do those places have creative plans in place to deal with counselor stress and morale issues?

3. Examine the counseling literature on burnout. What does the literature say about this phenomenon, and what recommendations are made to prevent burnout? How might this apply to your own counseling practice?

4. Talk with counselors in your area about the joys and frustrations with their work. How much is stress a part of the job they do, and what do they do to deal with that? How long have they been doing this work, and do they ever consider doing something else? Pay attention to your general reactions and to your feelings as you conduct these interviews.

References

Barta, M. (1999). The effects of family of origin and personal counseling on self-perceived and supervisor rated counseling skills. (Doctoral dissertation, University of Northern Colorado, 1999). *Dissertation Abstracts International, 60*(4-A), 1023.

Boy, A., & Pine, G. (1980). Avoiding counselor burnout through role renewal. *Personnel and Guidance Journal,* 161–163.

Boy, A., & Pine, G. (1983). Counseling: Fundamentals of theoretical renewal. *Counseling and Values, 27*(4), 248–255.

Clemente-Crain, V. (1996). Divorce and psychotherapy: The perceived impact of therapists' family of origin experience upon their practice of psychotherapy. (Doctoral dissertation, Boston University, 1996). *Dissertation Abstracts International, 56*(12-B), 7040.

Dryden, W., & Spurling, L. (1989). *On becoming a psychotherapist.* New York: Tavistock/Routledge.

Hayes, P. (2002). Playing with fire: Countertransference and clinical epistemology. *Journal of Contemporary Psychotherapy, 32*(1), 93–100.

Kesler, K. (1990). Burnout: A multimodal approach to assessment and resolution. *Elementary School Guidance and Counseling, 24*(4), 303–312.

Maher, E. (1983). Burnout and commitment: A theoretical alternative. *Personnel and Guidance Journal,* 390–393.

Perls, F., Hefferline, R., & Goodman, P. (1994). *Gestalt therapy.* Highland, NY: Gestalt Therapy Press. [Originally published in 1951]

Reyak-Schelar, R., & Feldman, R. (1984). Health behaviors of psychotherapists. *Journal of Clinical Psychology, 40*(3), 705–710.

Softas-Nall, B., Baldo, T., & Williams, S. (2001). Family of origin, personality characteristics, and counselor trainees effectiveness. *Psychological Reports, 88*(3), 854–856.

Vargas, A., & Borkowski, J. (1983). Physical attractiveness: Interactive effects of counselor and client on counseling processes. *Journal of Counseling Psychology, 30*(2), 146–157.

Wegscheider-Cruze, S. (1981). *Another chance: Hope and health for the alcoholic family.* Palo Alto: Science and Behavior Books.

Wilcoxen, S., Walker, M., & Hovestadt, A. (1989). Counselor effectiveness and family of origin experiences: A significant relationship? *Counseling and Values, 33,* 225–229.

Wilson, J. (1994). Is there a difference between professional and personal development for a practicing psychologist? *Educational and Child Psychology, 11*(3), 70–79.

Wittmer, J., Sword, R., & Loesch, L. (1973). Effectiveness of counselor trainees: A comparison of perceived parental behavior. *Journal of the Student Personnel Association for Teacher Education, 12,* 68–75.

Author Index

Subject Index